EMPLOYMENT POLICY AND THE REGULATION OF PART-TIME WORK IN THE EUROPEAN UNION

Part-time work has been the fastest-growing of all forms of 'non-standard' work. All Member States of the European Union have given increasing attention to its regulation over the past quarter century. This book examines the influence of European Community rules and procedures on the development by Member States of their policies towards part-time working. It originates from the research project 'New Discourses in Labour Law' hosted by the European University Institute, and presents a detailed analysis of part-time work regulation for seven European countries.

The book consists of an examination of the relevant European Community rules, a consideration of the national policies and the impact upon them of the European-level provisions, and a suggested framework for the identification of these influences. The impact of European employment policies is considered in parallel with the implementation of the Directive on Part-time Work, thus providing a complete overview of both soft and hard law mechanisms available to national policy-makers.

In this original work, the interaction between law and policy emerges as a dynamic and constantly changing process of exchange between national and supranational actors, through the use of concrete examples of law-making. Labour law is put forward as being central in the current evolution of European law, and this centrality is presented as a confirmation of innovation and continuity in regulatory techniques.

SILVANA SCIARRA, former Professor of European Labour and Social Law at the European University Institute, is now Professor of Labour Law at the University of Florence Law School. She specialises in comparative and European labour law. She is co-editor of the *Giornale di Diritto del lavoro e di relazioni industriali*.

PAUL DAVIES FBA is Cassel Professor of Commercial Law at the London School of Economics and Political Science and editor of the *Industrial Law Journal*. He is also a vice-president of the Industrial Law Society and a deputy chairman of the Central Arbitration Committee.

MARK FREEDLAND FBA is Professor of Employment Law at the University of Oxford and a Fellow of St John's College Oxford. He is the Director of the Oxford Institute of European and Comparative Law. He specialises in employment law and public law, and co-teaches, among other things, a course in European Employment and Equality Law with colleagues in the Oxford University Law Faculty.

EMPLOYMENT POLICY AND THE REGULATION OF PART-TIME WORK IN THE EUROPEAN UNION: A COMPARATIVE ANALYSIS

Edited by

SILVANA SCIARRA, PAUL DAVIES
AND MARK FREEDLAND

CAMBRIDGE
UNIVERSITY PRESS

PUBLISHED BY THE PRESS SYNDICATE OF THE UNIVERSITY OF CAMBRIDGE
The Pitt Building, Trumpington Street, Cambridge, United Kingdom

CAMBRIDGE UNIVERSITY PRESS
The Edinburgh Building, Cambridge, CB2 2RU, UK
40 West 20th Street, New York, NY 10011–4211, USA
477 Williamstown Road, Port Melbourne, VIC 3207, Australia
Ruiz de Alarcón 13, 28014 Madrid, Spain
Dock House, The Waterfront, Cape Town 8001, South Africa

http://www.cambridge.org

First published 2004

Printed in the United Kingdom at the University Press, Cambridge

Typeface Adobe Minion 10.75/12.75 pt.   *System* LATEX 2$_\varepsilon$ [TB]

A catalogue record for this book is available from the British Library

Library of Congress Cataloguing in Publication data
Employment policy and the regulation of part-time work in the European Union:
a comparative analysis / Silvana Sciarra, Paul Davies, Mark Freedland (eds.).
p.   cm.
Includes bibliographical references and index.
ISBN 0 521 84002 3
1. Part-time employment – European Union countries.   2. Labour policy – European Union
countries.   3. Part-time employment – Law and legislation – European Union countries.
I. Sciarra, Silvana.   II. Davis, P. L. (Paul Lyndon)   III. Freedland, M. R. (Mark Robert)
HD5110.2.E85E46   2004
331.25′727′094 – dc22   2003069694

ISBN 0 521 84002 3 hardback

CONTENTS

FIGURES AND TABLES

Figures

Tables

NOTES ON CONTRIBUTORS

DIAMOND ASHIAGBOR is currently a Postdoctoral Fellow / Career Development Fellow at the Institute of European and Comparative Law, Faculty of Law, University of Oxford, and a Junior Research Fellow at Worcester College, Oxford. She was previously a lecturer in law at the University of Hull, and completed a Ph.D. at the European University Institute in Florence in 2002. Her research interests are in the areas of EC constitutional law, EC labour law and employment policy, UK labour law, and law and economics.

RONALD M. BELTZER studied Dutch Law and the Free Doctoral Programme at the University of Amsterdam (1993, 1995). He received a Diploma in English Law from the University of Kent in 1995. In 2000, he defended his doctoral thesis on transfer of undertakings (University of Amsterdam). Since 2002 he has been Assistant Professor of Labour Law and Social Security Law at HSI-Hugo Sinzheimer Instituut, University of Amsterdam. Besides these subjects, his interest lies in the field of the relationship between labour law, company law and insolvency law.

PAUL DAVIES FBA is Cassel Professor of Commercial Law at the London School of Economics and Political Science and editor of the *Industrial Law Journal*. He is also a vice-president of the Industrial Law Society and a deputy chairman of the Central Arbitration Committee.

RONNIE EKLUND, Professor of Private Law, has specialised in labour law since 1994 at the University of Stockholm. His focus of interest is labour law in its broadest sense. He defended his doctoral thesis on 'Transfers of Undertakings and the Employment Relationship' in 1983. He published *The Hiving–Off of Divisions into Subsidiaries within Groups of Companies* in 1992. During the last few years he has specialised in sex equality law, temporary employment agencies, and labour and economics, see, e.g., 'Temporary Employment Agencies in the Nordic Countries' *Scandinavian*

Studies in Law 43 (2002), and 'The Equal Pay Principle – Promises and Pitfalls' *Juridisk Tidskrift* 5 (2000–2001).

MARK FREEDLAND FBA is Professor of Employment Law at the University of Oxford and a Fellow of St John's College Oxford. He is the Director of the Oxford Institute of European and Comparative Law. He specialises in employment law and public law, and co-teaches, amongst other subjects, a course in European Employment and Equality Law with colleagues in the Oxford University Law Faculty.

MAXIMILIAN FUCHS has been a Professor of Law (Chair of Civil Law, German and European Labour and Social Law) at the Katholische Universität Eichstaet, Germany, since 1993. He previously held chairs in law at the universities of Frankfurt (Professor Stagiaire) and Erlangen-Nürnberg and was a Senior Fellow at the Max-Planck-Institute for Foreign and International Social Law in Munich. In 2000 he was Visiting Professor at the University Tor Vergata, Rome, and presently he is Visiting Professor at the University of Trento. He is currently Co-director of a research project, financed by the German Ministry of Research, which has as its aim the presentation of the German labour and social security law in a multimedia form. He has written widely on civil law, labour law, social law and legal theory. His publications include textbooks on torts (*Delitetsrecht*, 4th edn Heidelberg/Berlin, 2003) and on European labour law (*Europaeisches Arbeitsrecht*, Vienna/New York, 2001, together with F. Marhold). He is editor and author of a commentary on Regulation No. 1408/71 (*Kommentar zum Europäischen Sozialrecht*, 3rd edn Baden-Baden, 2003). Recently he published a commentary on the labour law provisions in the German Civil Code and a book on collective bargaining in Germany (*Tarifvertragsrecht*, Baden-Baden, 2003).

CLAIRE KILPATRICK is University Lecturer in Law and a Fellow of Emmanuel College at Cambridge University. Her research interests include EU law, labour law and discrimination law. She holds a doctoral degree from the European University Institute in Florence and was a Jean Monnet Fellow there in the year 2000. Her recent publications include 'Turning Remedies Around? A Sectoral Analysis of the Court of Justice' in G. de Búrca and J. H. H. Weiler, *The European Court of Justice* (Oxford, 2001), and 'Has New Labour Reconfigured Employment Legislation?' (2003) 32 *Industrial Law Journal* 135. She edits the European Developments Section of the *Industrial Law Journal*.

SYLVAINE LAULOM is Lecturer in Law in the Faculty of Law, Saint-Etienne University, and member of the research centre, CERCRID (Centre de recherches critiques sur le droit). Her fields of interest are labour law and European social law and comparative law.

ANTONIO LO FARO (Ph.D. EUI Florence), formerly lecturer at the University of Siena, is currently Associate Professor of Labour Law in the University of Catania Law School. His research activity has been mainly devoted to the study of comparative and EU labour law. Within this perspective, specific attention has been given to issues related to occupational health and safety, European collective bargaining, the judicial dialogue between the ECJ and national jurisdictions, immigration law, part-time work and telework. He is a member of the teaching board of the Ph.D. Programme in European Labour Law run by the University of Catania and founding member of the Massimo D'Antona Research Centre for the Study of European Labour Law.

SILVANA SCIARRA, former Professor of European Labour and Social Law at the European University Institute (1994–2003), is now Professor of Labour Law at the University of Florence Law School. She worked and taught in several universities, notably UCLA, Harvard Law School (Harkness Fellow and Fulbright Fellow), Warwick University (UK) (Leverhulme Professor) and Columbia Law School (BNL Professor). She has been an active member in some Groups of Experts for European Commission projects looking at comparative and European labour law issues. She co-edits *Giornale di diritto del lavoro e di relazioni industriali* and is a member of the editorial board of *European Law Journal* and *Comparative Labor Law and Policy Journal.*

FERNANDO VALDÉS DAL-RÉ holds the Chair of Labour Law and Social Security at the Universidad Complutense de Madrid; he specialises in collective bargaining, employment, fundamental social rights, and European Labour Law.

ESTHER KOOT-VAN DER PUTTE studied Dutch Law at the University of Amsterdam (2000) and Labour Law at the Free University of Berlin (1999). She received a Diploma in the Minor programme on labour from the Amsterdam Institute for Labour Studies at the University of Amsterdam in 2000. Since 2001, she has been working on her doctoral thesis on 'Individual Freedom of Contract and Collective Labour Agreements' at the

HSI-Hugo Sinzheimer Instituut, University of Amsterdam. Her interest lies in the field of industrial relations.

JELLE VISSER holds the Chair of Sociology of Work and Organisation at the University of Amsterdam. He is Scientific Director of the Amsterdam Institute for Advanced Labour Studies (AIAS), an interdisciplinary research centre consisting of economists, sociologists, psychologists and lawyers. He is also responsible for the programme on Labour and Inequality at the Amsterdam (Graduate) School of Social Science Research. His research interests are policy learning and benchmarking in labour market reform in Europe; comparative industrial relations, collective bargaining and trade unions; part-time employment; gender, organisations, labour markets and welfare state development; transitional labour markets and social security reform.

TON WILTHAGEN is the Head of the General Policy Research programme of OSA-the Institute for Labour Market Studies, located at Tilburg University, the Netherlands. He also holds a Chair in Institutional and Legal Aspects of the Labour Market in National and International Perspective at the Faculty of Law of the same university (Department of Social Law and Social Policy). Areas of research and expertise include: transitional labour markets, flexibility–security policies, industrial relations and reflexive labour law. He is the Dutch correspondent for the SYSDEM-network of the European Employment Observatory and co-ordinator of a newly established international research programme on 'Flexicurity'.

PREFACE

This book originates in the research project 'New discourses in labour law', funded by the Research Council of the European University Institute and co-ordinated by Silvana Sciarra. This research project is concerned with the interaction between the employment law and policy of the European Union and the employment laws and policies of the Member States of the Union. (Limits upon resources and opportunities have required us to be somewhat selective between member states and to decide upon which ones to focus most profitably.) The project takes as its starting point the idea that formulations of law and policy amounting to new discourses in labour law might be emerging from this interaction between law and policy created at the federal level of the Community as a whole and the laws and policies of individual Member States.

These discourses might be new ones in two distinct though inter-related senses: a procedural sense and a substantive sense. They might be new in the procedural sense that they emerge from a novel institutional process, namely that of increasingly intense interaction between law- and policy-makers at the two levels, the trans-national and the national ones. They might also be new in the substantive sense that the particular normative approaches which emerge from that process of interaction might be significantly different in their content from those taken by Member States in the absence of EU intervention.

Of course, this assertion, that 'new discourses in labour law' might be emerging from a European normative process, postulates the existence of an earlier state of affairs, a previously accepted set of discourses in labour law, or perhaps an absence of such discourses, with which a significant contrast may be drawn. We did not, in formulating this project, have in mind any one date, treaty, or event in the history of the EU as a hinge upon which a door between the old discourses and the new discourses might swing. However, we did incline to see the development, at EU level in particular, of a special concern with employment policy during the 1990s as a centrally significant phenomenon; so the formulation of the EU Employment Guidelines and the procedural steps culminating in the introduction of the

Open Method of Co-ordination are critical events, from the point of view of this research project, in distinguishing between the old and the new.

Also critical in this respect is the gradual transition in labour law from the late 1980s or early 1990s onwards, not least at EU level, towards a central concern with the situation of the actual or potential member of the labour force who is marginalised within the labour market or excluded from it. It therefore seemed appropriate to choose, as the location in which to explore our hypothesis about new discourses in labour law, the area of law- and policy-making which has been created by and around what is probably the most significant EU intervention to date in the pursuit of that concern. This meant concentrating upon the Framework Agreement and Directive on Part-time Work of 1997, and placing its reception and implementation by member states in the larger context of inter-action about employment policy between the central Community and Member States.

The participants in the project have been:

Diamond Ashiagbor – European University Institute, Florence, and University of Oxford
Ronald Beltzer – HSI-Hugo Sinzheimer Instituut, University of Amsterdam
Paul Davies – London School of Economics and Political Science
Ronnie Eklund – University of Stockholm
Mark Freedland – University of Oxford
Maximilian Fuchs – Katholische Universität Eichstaett
Claire Kilpatrick – University of Cambridge
Sylvaine Laulom – University of Saint-Etienne
Antonio Lo Faro – University of Catania
Silvana Sciarra – European University Institute, Florence, and University of Florence
Fernando Valdés Dal-Ré – University of Madrid
Esther Koot-van der Putte – HIS-Hugo Sinzheimer Instituut, University of Amsterdam
Jelle Visser – AIAS-Amsterdam Institute for Advanced Labour Studies, University of Amsterdam
Ton Wilthagen – OSA-Institute for Labour Market Studies, Tilburg University.

All meetings of the group took place in Florence, with the exception of two. One of these was held in London, on the occasion of the launching of a previous project in which most participants in the current one were involved (S. Sciarra (ed.) *Labour Law in the Courts. National Judges and the ECJ*, Oxford, Hart, 2001). For the organisation of that meeting held at Queen Mary College in June 2001 the group is very grateful to Claire Kilpatrick. The second was held in November 2001 at the University of Catania Law School, where Bruno Caruso and Antonio Lo Faro provided equally warm and efficient surroundings for the work of the group. Early versions of the seven country reports were published in Italian in a special issue of the *Giornale di Diritto del lavoro e di relazioni industriali* (*La regolamentazione del part-time in Europa*, with an Introduction by Stefano Giubboni and Silvana Sciarra, issue no. 4/2000).

Translations and language revisions are due to the multi-linguistic skills of Rita Inston. To her we are indebted for useful comments on early drafts of the manuscripts and for rendering clear difficult concepts through her unique style of 'interpretative' translation.

In the early stage of the project Stefano Giubboni and Sabrina Regent worked as research assistants, providing the group with valuable academic support. Diamond Ashiagbor then continued this task with equal dedication and competence. Latterly, from her base in the Oxford Institute of European and Comparative Law where she is currently a Career Development Fellow, Diamond has had a crucial role, both scholarly and practical, in the completion of the editorial and production process of this work. To all of them we express gratitude for sharing with us the enthusiasm for comparative research and their own knowledge and experience as researchers at the EUI Law Department.

Efficient, competent and good-humoured help was provided throughout the project by Susan Garvin, Secretary in the Law Department of the EUI. Her responsibilities included the organisation of workshops and general co-ordination of the group, tasks which she undertook in an enthusiastic and intelligent manner.

This book is the result of joint and collegial work. Although each author took responsibility for his or her own chapter, the broad scheme to be followed was agreed in one of the initial workshops held in Florence. The intention was to gather similar and comparable information. We are satisfied with such a choice and at the same time we value very much the distinctive and characteristic style that each author maintains, thus enriching a comparative exercise with the many different flavours of national legal cultures.

Silvana Sciarra
Paul Davies
Mark Freedland
S. Domenico di Fiesole, London and Oxford
Spring 2003

ABBREVIATIONS

AB	General Conditions (collective agreement covering local government employment)
AD	Swedish Labour Court, or Labour Court judgment
AKU	Swedish Labour Force Survey
ALFA	General Agreement on Pay and Benefits (Swedish collective agreement covering central government employment)
ATW	*Arbeidstijdenwet* (Working Hours Act)
BAG	German Federal Labour Court
BAGE	Official Report of the German Federal Labour Court
BAT	National agreement for German public sector white-collar workers
BDA	Confederation of German Employers' Associations
BEPGs	Broad Economic Policy Guidelines
BeschFG	Promotion of Employment Act (Germany)
CA	Collective agreement
CBS	*Centraal Bureau voor de Statistiek* (Dutch Central Statistical Office)
CC.OO	*Confederación Sindical de Comisiones Obreras* (Spanish Trade Union Confederation of Workers' Commissions)
CDA	*Christen-Democratische Appèl* (Dutch Christian-Democratic Party)
CEEP	*Centre européen des entreprises à participation publique et des entreprises d'intérêt économique général* (European Centre of Enterprises with Public Participation and of Enterprises of General Economic Interest)
CEOE	*Confederación Española de Organizaciones Empresariales* (Spanish Confidation of Employers' Organisations)
CEPYME	*Confederación Española de Pequeñas y Medianas Empresas* (Spanish Confederation of Small and Medium-Sized Enterprises)

CPB	*Centraal Planbureau* (Netherlands Institute for Economic Forecasting and Research)
D'66	*Democraten '66* (Netherlands Social-Liberal Party)
DGB	German Federation of Trade Unions
Ds	Swedish Ministry Report Series
EC	European Community or European Community Treaty
ECJ	European Court of Justice
ECT	EC Treaty
EES	European Employment Strategy
EMU	Economic and Monetary Union
ESC	Economic and Social Committee
ET	*Estatuto de los Trabajadores* (Spanish Workers' Statute)
ETUC	European Trade Union Confederation
ETUI	European Trade Union Institute
EU	European Union
EUTI	European Trade Union Institute
FNV	*Federatie Nederlandse Vakbeweging* (Federation of Dutch Trade Unions)
FTE	Full-time Equivalent
GL	*Groenlinks* (Dutch Green Left Party)
IAB	Labour Market Research Institute of the German Federal Labour Office
ILO	International Labour Organisation
IRLR	*Industrial Relations Law Reports*
ISO	German Institute for Research into Social Equality
ITP	Supplementary pension plan for white-collar workers in Swedish private industry and commerce
JÄMO	Swedish Equal Opportunities Ombudsman
LO	Swedish Trade Union Confederation
MS	Member State
NAP	National Action Plan for Employment
OMC	open method of co-ordination
OSA	*Organisatie voor Strategisch Arbeidsmarktbeleid* (Dutch Institute for Labour Market Studies)
PA	Pension plan for Swedish central government employees
PA-KL	Collective agreement on pensions for Swedish local government employees
PFA	Collective agreement on pension and insurance agreements for Swedish local government employees
PvdA	*Partij van de Arbeid* (Dutch Labour Party)

RALS   Framework Agreement on pay, etc. for Swedish state employees

RCO   *Raad van Centrale Ondernemingsorganisaties* (Dutch Council of Central Employers' Federations)

SACO   Swedish Confederation of Professional Associations

SAF   Confederation of Swedish Employers (now *Svenskt Näringsliv*: Confederation of Swedish Enterprise)

SCB   Swedish National Bureau of Statistics

SCP   *Sociaal-Cultureel Planbureau* (Netherlands Institute for Social and Cultural Forecasting and Research)

SEK   Swedish kronor

SFS   *Swedish Official Gazette*

SOU   Swedish Government Official Reports

StAr   *Stichting van de Arbeid* (Dutch Labour Foundation)

SZW   *Ministerie van Sociale Zaken en Werkgelegenheid* (Dutch Ministry of Social Affairs and Employment)

TCO   Swedish Confederation of Professional Employees

TEU   Treaty on European Union

TGL-S   Swedish agreement on state employee collective insurance scheme

TzBfG   Part-time Work and Fixed-Term Contracts Act (Germany)

UGT   *Unión General de Trabajadores* (Spanish General Workers' Confederation)

UNICE   *Union des Confédérations de l'Industrie et des Employeurs d'Europe* (Union of Industrial and Employers' Federations of Europe)

VVD   *Volkspartij voor Vrijheid en Democratie* (Dutch Liberal Party)

WAA   *Wet Aanpassing Arbeidsduur* (Adjustment of Working Hours Act, Netherlands)

WAZ   *Wet Arbeid en Zorg* (Work and Care Framework Act, Netherlands)

WVOA   *Wet Verbod onderscheid arbeidsduur* (Prohibition of Discrimination by Working Hours Act, Netherlands)

PART I

New discourses in labour law: part-time work and the paradigm of flexibility

SILVANA SCIARRA

1 The centrality of comparative labour law in the open method of co-ordination

In deciding to undertake collective research on the regulation of part-time work, the authors of the present book agreed on a few methodological claims.

One had to do with the urgent need to revisit a long-lasting comparative tradition in European labour law and to do so from the new perspective of an ongoing process of integration in the European Union. Implicit in this choice was the equally strong urgency to confirm the centrality of a legal discipline – labour law – in the current debate on the European Employment Strategy (EES) and in the many concurring ways of implementing it.

The need to uncover a disciplinary point of view just at the time when EU institutions are developing a culture of co-ordination of all existing processes of integration – economic, structural and to some extent social – is due to the deeply rooted conviction that there is – and should continue to be – a specificity of legal analysis in this particular field.

In ascertaining the contribution of comparative law to labour law, Gerard Lyon-Caen wrote at the end of the 1960s that labour law 'was born comparative', because it aimed at providing answers to similar needs and aspirations inherent in the industrialised world. Solutions found in different legal systems were 'spontaneously analogous' at least as far as their purposes were concerned. Furthermore, in both civil law and common law systems, labour law endeavoured to gain autonomy from general

I am grateful to Sarah-Jane King, researcher in the Law Department of the EUI, for her efficient help in checking some bibliographical references. For those and for ideas expressed in this chapter I am solely responsible.

principles enshrined in other legal disciplines and did so irrespective of the different legal families to which it belonged.[1]

Over the years such a disciplinary pride strengthened its rational, as well as its passionate, grounds. Contemporary research dealing with countries of the European Union reveals the overall continuity of labour law institutions and their capacity to spread well across the boundaries of the discipline. This is so because labour law embraces in its legislative and academic tradition more than one field. It covers individual contracts of employment as well as collective labour law and links with the vast and fascinating territory of social security. In all these areas collective actors are present and capable of contributing both in the law-making process and in autonomous processes of norm-setting.[2]

While all these fields remain predominantly national, they are also closely intertwined with European law. It appeared very clearly to the authors of this book that a method which would blend national diversities into an indistinct process of Europeanisation could lead to weak results and – what is most to be avoided – to imperfect generalisations. We argue, on the contrary, that concrete choices made by national parliaments deserve to be fully evaluated and framed in a national historical context. The role of employers' associations and of trade unions must also be kept in the picture.

The proposition underlying this project is that the adoption of a comparative method facilitates the understanding of national labour law traditions in their entirety, namely a combination of individual and collective sources, a mixture of protective and supportive legislation, a system of norms more or less adaptable to external changes.

Legal comparison may also help to reveal the tension – if there is one – between national and supranational law-making. The inclusion in the spectrum of comparison of collective actors and national tripartite or bipartite institutions dealing with labour matters sets in place the controversial question of how to balance legal and voluntary sources in the regulation of part-time work.

---

[1] G. Lyon-Caen, 'Les apports du droit comparé au droit du travail', in a special book issued by the *Revue International de Droit Comparé: Un siècle de droit comparé en France (1869–1969)* (Paris: Revue International de Droit Comparé, 1969), pp. 315–16.

[2] This point, always at the heart of Lord Wedderburn's comparative analysis, is confirmed in Lord Wedderburn, 'Common Law, Labour Law, Global Law', in B. Hepple (ed.), *Social and Labour Rights in a Global Context* (Cambridge: Cambridge University Press, 2002), pp. 19 ff.

One further reason stands in favour of a comparative legal method, which would draw attention to labour law and to its centrality in current discussions on new regulatory approaches.

In the early 1990s, when Jacques Delors was still one of the main advocates of the enhancement of growth and the lowering of unemployment rates in Europe, labour market reforms – and among those the regulation of part-time work – became central to the co-ordination of macroeconomic policies and employment policies. In the Council held at Essen in 1994[3] a complex evolution of employment policies began and was further developed in subsequent Council meetings. The criteria agreed upon at Essen represent the precondition of what then developed into a more elaborate plan of action.

The launch at Lisbon of the EES and the subsequent emphasis placed on the Open Method of Co-ordination (OMC) as a way to implement employment policies[4] have activated a series of new regulatory techniques, useful to understanding changes that have occurred in labour markets and to fostering more advanced ones.

Structural indicators, the result of long and detailed research undertaken by the Commission in consultation with Eurostat and the Member States' statistical offices,[5] are meant to favour the measurement and the evaluation of both institutional and economic performances pursued by Member States through active employment policies or through structural and legislative reforms.

Attempts have been made to combine quantitative and qualitative analysis of all fifteen Member States' National Action Plans (NAPs) submitted within the Employment Strategy, on the understanding that such an

---

[3] This Council meeting, held on 9–10 December 1994, was the last one attended by J. Delors as President of the European Commission. It is interesting to observe the continuity between the Delors White Paper, *Growth, Competitiveness, Employment: The Challenges and Ways Forward into the 21st Century*, COM (93) 700 final, Brussels, of 5.12.1993, and the Essen criteria, aimed at facilitating reforms of the labour market and combating unemployment.

[4] Presidency Conclusions, Lisbon European Council, 23 and 24 March 2000.

[5] See, for instance, Communication from the Commission, *Realising the European Union's Potential: Consolidating and Extending the Lisbon Strategy*, COM (2001) 79 final, Brussels, 7.2.2001, Volumes I and II. This contribution to the Spring European Council held in Stockholm in March 2001 is a good example of the steps forward taken after Lisbon, in order to link employment growth to specific targets. Volume II collects general economic background indicators, data on employment presented with different breakdowns and data on innovation and research, as well as on economic reform and social cohesion. The early policy of the Commission can be read in its *Communication on Community Policies in Support of Employment*, COM (1999) 167 final, Brussels, 13.4.1999.

exercise could only capture the 'declared employment strategies' at that given moment in history and not reflect the overall national policies in their evolving patterns.[6] The results achieved by such sophisticated statistical approaches prove that there exists a variety of national responses and that it is artificial to constrain them within ideal–typical employment regimes.

In extending OMC to social inclusion,[7] objectives have been incorporated in social indicators. This has empowered the Commission to set the social agenda and to move it forward, with the technical support of a sub-group on social indicators established within the Social Protection Committee (set up according to Art.144 Nice Treaty). The outcome of this analysis now forms the basis of EU policy-making and is evaluated very positively in scholarly analyses, although comparisons between the first set of NAPs reveal great disparities.[8]

National policy-making remains a variable which cannot be entirely predicted. A stated aim of co-ordination is to support national actors, but it clearly does not operate to sanction reluctant or imprecise responses by the Member States, by virtue of the subsidiarity principle. Co-ordination also relies on comparable data, collected with similar techniques such as standardised questionnaires administered to representative samples in each country.[9]

Indicators have been linked to benchmarking, another technique of measurement and evaluation brought about by the OMC and then developed into a widespread practice for the enforcement of employment policies. They both reveal the necessity to 'compare the situation spatially,

---

[6] A 'cluster analysis' of the 1999 NAPs is proposed by P. K. Madsen and P. M. Munch-Madsen, 'European Employment Policy and National Policy Regimes', in D. Mayes, J. Berghman and R. Salais (eds.), *Social Exclusion and European Policy* (Cheltenham: Edward Elgar, 2001), pp. 255 ff. and in particular p. 261.

[7] Presidency Conclusions, Lisbon European Council, 23–24 March 2000, para. 32.

[8] This is reported by T. Atkinson, 'Social Inclusion and the European Union' (2002) 40 *Journal of Common Market Studies* p. 625 at 628–9. Social indicators proposed by the sub-group are: financial poverty, income inequality, regional variation in employment rates, long-term unemployment, joblessness, low educational qualifications, low life expectancy and poor health. See also T. Atkinson, B. Cantillon, E. Marlier and B. Nolan, *Social Indicators: the EU and Social Inclusion* (Oxford: Oxford University Press, 2002): research produced by successful collaboration between academics and policy-makers sponsored by the Belgian Presidency in 2001.

[9] Atkinson, 'Social Inclusion' at 631, refers to the work undertaken by the European Community Household Panel, which was replaced in 2003 by a new instrument for the preparation of statistics on income and social exclusion, the European Union Survey of Income and Living Conditions.

between Member States, and temporally, through time'.[10] Benchmarking, in particular, applies to situations in which national actors are eager to learn and, if necessary, compete in order to reach a common objective. They often choose to do so because a European frame of reference helps them to push forward national reforms, without having to find agreement on all detailed provisions.[11]

The principle of subsidiarity, which supports the overall structure of OMC, also applies inside each state, among different levels of government administration and among sub-national authorities, such as regions and municipalities. Each administration finds its own internal organisation to guarantee compliance, at times introducing indicators from higher to lower levels and therefore expanding the spectrum of comparison.[12]

There are no specific rules to manage this constantly spreading network of institutions and sub-institutions. National experience shows that ad hoc committees created for the enforcement of a specific NAP end up having a very limited impact on the state administration, if there is no stable structure to refer to. Even a high turnover of experts produces limited results in preparing the so-called 'Implementation Report' to be annexed to NAPs, whereas the setting up of a centralised 'Monitoring Group' has facilitated the collection of homogeneous data on employment policies at decentralised levels of the administration.[13]

The study on the UK reveals how different branches of the Government have been involved in the implementation of the Part-time Directive, while also ascertaining compliance with EU employment policies.[14] This

---

[10] C. de la Porte, 'Is the Open Method of Coordination Appropriate for Organising Activities at European Level in Sensitive Policy Areas?' (2002) 8 *European Law Journal* pp. 38, 41. The author distinguishes between different levels of indicators, some influenced by the European statistical database, some mixed, some purely national. She also describes the selected national experts as high-level civil servants, who prepare the ground for Council decisions. Final orientations are political and driven by bureaucratic elites.

[11] De la Porte, 'Is the Open Method of Coordination Appropriate?' p. 43.

[12] The Italian example of a 'Master Plan', elaborated in 2000 by the Labour Ministry in collaboration with ISFOL, a research institute for the development of training, shows how qualitative and quantitative indicators have been offered to local authorities as a basis on which to improve the reform of placement offices, following the negative evaluation of the Commission on Italian NAPs for 2000 and 2001. This is reported in M. Ferrera and E. Gualmini, 'La strategia europea sull'occupazione e la governance domestica del mercato del lavoro: verso nuovi assetti organizzativi e decisionali' – a paper prepared for ISFOL within the project 'Impact Evaluation of the European Employment Strategy' – edited by C. Dell'Aringa and published in the ISFOL papers (Rome, May 2002).

[13] Ibid., pp. 6 ff.

[14] See further the country study by C. Kilpatrick and M. Freedland in this volume.

example too seems to confirm the uneasiness of national administrations in dealing straightforwardly with European sources, either because of a lack of practice or, at times, due to an intentional manipulation of both hard and soft law measures, so that the national priorities may prevail.

The Commission itself admits that, despite the attempt to bring together national impact evaluation studies under a 'standardised structure, with a range of thematic questions covering policy reforms, performance and impact', it has proved difficult to constrain Member States' responses and to force them into a pre-defined scheme.[15] It is also true, as once more the Commission points out, that a positive evaluation of OMC cannot be proposed in a vacuum, nor can it be separated from an understanding of a broader economic context, wherein some economic improvement was achieved. A shift is proposed in focusing national policies 'away from managing unemployment, towards managing employment growth'.[16]

This observation highlights one further point: disparities in economic performances may not mechanically affect the evaluation of legal reforms. The latter must still be regarded as specific results of national legislative choices, albeit within the context of a Europe-wide co-ordinated economic policy.[17]

There are – as one can see – several reasons to write 'Lisbon' in capital letters in the history of European Council meetings. On that occasion the urgency to make all EU processes interact with one another and to foster their co-ordination was transformed from a platitude into an important innovation. The Portuguese proposal was, in fact, simple and pragmatic: refraining from adding a new process meant concentrating on the co-ordination of the existing ones.

The Commission now welcomes 'synchronisation' within the overall process of implementation of the Lisbon agenda, but also wishes that economic and employment objectives be considered autonomously. It is from this rather subtle perspective that we must interpret the Commission's recent commitment to simplify the Employment Guidelines and to focus more on implementation mechanisms.[18]

---

[15] Communication from the Commission to the Council, the European Parliament, the ESC and the Committee of the Regions, *Taking Stock of Five Years of the European Employment Strategy*, COM (2002) 416 final, Brussels 17.7.2002, p. 22.

[16] Ibid., p. 2.

[17] An analysis of Member States' willingness to implement the most important social policy Directives and yet to let the national priorities prevail is provided by O. Treib, *EU Governance, Misfit and the Partisan Logic of Domestic Adaptation*, at www.mpi-fg-koeln.mpg.de/socialeurope.

[18] *Taking Stock*, respectively at p. 21 and p. 19.

The impression we get from looking at the ways in which national administrations have internalised the proposals coming from European institutions and adapted them to the evaluation of their own domestic policies is that procedures are left intentionally undefined and that the choice is to proceed by trial and error.[19]

The still-experimental nature of both national and European procedures is giving rise to a new comparative method, extraneous to legal comparison. Documents and information exchanged while practising the OMC provide invaluable help in detecting phenomena which then become the object of legal regulation. Labour lawyers' uneasiness – almost too shameful to admit – has to do with an inborn fear that the language of statistics and economics may obscure the language of legal institutions.

Such a fear is not a new one. A solid methodology in comparative labour law was developed in order to explain the commitment of national lawyers to maintaining economic policy considerations as separate from legal ones and avoiding too contingent an analysis of legal institutions. 'Functional' comparison implies information on political and social institutions and appreciation of the role played by collective actors. A 'structuralist' approach – like the one suggested – gives priority to comparing the means and the goals, and concentrates on the functioning of a specific social policy.[20]

We argue, in drawing conclusions from this project, that comparative legal analysis can most usefully enrich the study and evaluation of economic and structural trends. We also maintain that the pressure to establish well-developed – and yet not too rigid – schemes of comparison is particularly healthy when dealing with labour market regulations and with welfare state responses to high unemployment.

Research carried out in neighbouring fields confirms that a variety of circumstances must be considered in order to establish a valid comparative framework. Part-time patterns are affected by different components, such as household structure, firms' behaviour and the state.[21] The state, in particular, attracts the attention of researchers dealing with 'societal

---

[19] Findings in the country studies on the UK and Italy seem to be going clearly in this direction.

[20] Lyon-Caen, 'Les Apports', pp. 316–17, with interesting references to French comparative studies not very often acknowledged in comparative literature.

[21] C. Fagan and J. O'Reilly, 'Conceptualising Part-time Work', in J. O'Reilly and C. Fagan, *Part-time Prospects. An International Comparison of Part-time Work in Europe, North America and the Pacific Rim* (London: Routledge, 1998), p. 13, show how theories on the segmentation of labour markets have gradually developed into more sophisticated approaches, taking into account cultural values and cross-national differences.

employment systems',[22] who must be attentive to the evaluation of social and cultural values when drawing up comparative schemes of analysis.

In a broader context of research on welfare regimes, states occupy a pivotal role in transferring income and in supporting family networks. These circumstances may change the nature of unemployment and consequently influence the selection of comparable data.[23] It is crucial that the family as an institution be considered central to the understanding of labour market reforms. Even the analysis of data on family instability reveals valuable comparative patterns and prompts policy recommendations as regards measures to be addressed towards unemployed people. A social policy leading to 'de-familialisation' or detachment from the family puts more weight on the state for the provision of services which are, otherwise, assigned to families.[24] The study of unemployed individuals in their household context, undertaken in comparative terms,[25] is relevant too for understanding the features of unemployment, so different across European countries and so central for the understanding of other labour market phenomena.

Indirectly, results of such studies are very important for labour lawyers dealing with measures to create new employment. Family support may very well channel the choice of unemployed people towards non-standard forms of work and make that choice a more permanent one, especially when earnings are very low or non-continuous.

On a methodological note, comparative research undertaken within disciplinary areas somehow related to labour law shows the emergence of diversities between countries and even within groups of countries held together by common geographic or historical traditions.[26] Different

---

[22] M. Maurice, 'Convergence and/or Societal Effect for the Europe of the Future', in P. Cressey and B. Jones (eds.), *Work and Employment in Europe* (London: Routledge, 1995), pp. 28 ff.

[23] See D. Gallie and S. Paugam (eds.), *Welfare Regimes and the Experience of Unemployment in Europe* (Oxford: Oxford University Press, 2000). This research project was centred mainly on 'the effort to achieve a high level of comparability of data', as we learn from the editors in the introductory chapter 'The Experience of Unemployment in Europe: the Debate' (p. 1). See also G. Esping-Andersen, 'Comments', in G. Bertola, T. Boeri and G. Nicoletti (eds.), *Welfare and Employment in a United Europe* (Cambridge, Mass: MIT Press, 2001), pp. 127 ff., criticising the approach taken by the editors of the book, which ignores the role of families in proposing European reforms for social inclusion.

[24] Gallie and Paugam, 'The Experience of Unemployment', at pp. 14 ff.

[25] I. Bison and G. Esping-Andersen, 'Unemployment, Welfare Regime, and Income Packaging', in Gallie and Paugam, *Welfare Regimes*, pp. 69 ff. and at pp. 84–5, where they deal with the issue of the young unemployed who receive family support, as opposed to the incurring of the costs of labour mobility.

[26] F. Maier, 'Institutional Regimes of Part-time Working', in G. Schmid (ed.), *Labor Market Institutions in Europe* (New York: M. E. Sharpe, 1994), pp. 151 ff.

'styles' of welfare state approaches facilitate the search for specific measures and help avoid deregulation of the labour market as the only remedy against unemployment.[27]

This explains the urgency, underlined in this book, of enriching legal comparison with a whole variety of institutional variables and of paying attention to all actors involved in the complex redefinition of national competence, when promoting domestic legislation and complying with European law.

When we look at the European institutional context, we notice that analysis pursued by European institutions in reviewing national employment plans (Art. 128 ECT) or in assessing national economic policies (Art. 99 ECT) appears inherently different from a comparative legal approach. Whereas the latter moves from the understanding of the ways in which legal and social institutions interact in a given system of norms, the former concentrates on objectives and results.

The rhetoric of the European institutions – monitoring, reviewing, evaluating, recommending – and the responses of Member States – drawing up programmes, showing compliance, proving efficiency and promising future improved accomplishment – enrich a political discourse which finds in the co-ordination of policies the ultimate goal. We want to ascertain, while drawing conclusions from this project, whether this net of soft rules hides a hierarchy of values and whether the apparent circularity of information conceals instead an asymmetric decision-making system, whereby priorities are often set at the top, rather than being jointly co-ordinated. To verify whether this element of the EES is not a negative outcome, but mirrors the search for a new arrangement of legal powers and competence within the EU social field, we need to explore further the potential of OMC.

The above-mentioned political discourse is inextricably linked to a soft regulatory technique, which is gaining ground and spreading to other fields: social inclusion, pensions.[28] Even policies on immigration seem

---

[27] Structural differences are highlighted by F. Scharpf, 'The European Social Model: Coping with the Challenges of Diversity' (2002) 40 *Journal of Common Market Studies* pp. 645, 651.

[28] On the application of OMC to social protection and social inclusion, see Presidency Conclusions, Lisbon European Council, 23 and 24 March 2000, para. 32, and Presidency Conclusions, Nice European Council, 7–9 December 2000, para. 20; on the application of OMC to pensions, see Presidency Conclusions, Nice European Council, 7–9 December 2000, para. 23, and Presidency Conclusions, Stockholm European Council, 23 and 24 March 2001, para. 32. See also C. de la Porte and P. Pochet, *Building Social Europe through the Open Method of Co-ordination* (Brussels: P. I. E. – Peter Lang, 2002), and Scharpf, 'The European Social Model', 655, interpreting the choice to expand OMC to pensions reforms

suitable for OMC and for the drawing up of NAPs;[29] these policies should be strengthened by the now envisaged possibility of extending to third-country nationals the right to export their social security rights from one Member State to another when moving within the EU.[30]

While OMC proves the willingness to go ahead in crucial matters, overcoming vetoes and inertia in decision-making, it may also lead to a new form of governance, ultimately transferring competence to the EU.[31] Notwithstanding possible future implications,[32] OMC constitutes at this stage of European integration a sign of vitality and of innovation not to be underestimated. If we look at the agenda of possible institutional developments in the social field, we find that the accent has been put on relevant pragmatic results to be accomplished through OMC: by setting common objectives, the abstract – and by now weakened – notion of the 'European social model' is nourished with new energy coming from a much larger group of stakeholders.[33]

---

as a spill-over from monetary union and an attempt to avoid imposition from the Council of Economic and Finance Ministers and the Economic Policy Committee.

[29] Commission of the European Communities, *Communication from the Commission to the Council and the European Parliament on an Open Method of Coordination for the Community Immigration Policy*, COM (2001) 387 final, Brussels, 11.7.2001. See also, for a 'fresh approach to immigration', *Choosing to Grow: Knowledge, Innovation and Jobs in a Cohesive Society. Report to the Spring European Council*, 21 March 2003, COM (2003) 5 of 14.1.2003.

[30] Under the Spanish Presidency in June 2002 a political agreement was reached to reform Regulation 1408/71, not only to revise its scope, but also to establish better co-ordination of the principles governing social security. See in general A. Numhauser-Henning, 'Freedom of Movement and Transfer of Social Security Rights' in *Labour Law Congress 2000, Reports*, VIIth European Regional Congress International Society of Labour Law and Social Security, Stockholm, September 2002, pp. 177 ff.

[31] See the arguments developed by D. Hodson and I. Maher, 'The Open Method as a New Mode of Governance: the Case of Soft Economic Policy Co-ordination' (2001) 39 *Journal of Common Market Studies* p. 719, and by H. Wallace, 'The Institutional Setting', in H. Wallace and W. Wallace (eds.), *Policy-making in the European Union* (4th edn, Oxford: Oxford University Press, 2000), pp. 3 ff.

[32] The Recommendation of Working Group V of the Convention (the working group on simplification) is that OMC should be considered 'as a soft instrument or method'. See CONV 375/1/02, REV 1, WGV 14, at p. 7. Another Recommendation of the same working group, at p. 10, is that 'an explicit text stating that all powers not conferred on the Union by the Treaty remain with the Member States should be inserted into a future Treaty'.

[33] F. Vandenbroucke, Belgian Minister of Social Affairs and Pensions, who combines academic expertise (as Professor of Comparative Social Policy at KU Leuven) with political determination, has been very active on these matters. See, in particular, *The EU and Social Protection: What Should the European Convention Propose?* – a paper presented at the Max Planck Institute for the Study of Societies, Cologne 17 June 2002, p. 9 of the typescript – and, in general, www.vandenbroucke.com. He has also been heard by Working Group XI 'Social Europe' of the European Convention, in the Expert Hearing of 21 January 2003.

The acknowledgment of diversities in welfare state regimes, reflecting 'legitimate differences of social philosophies and normative aspirations',[34] makes OMC the ultimate and only response for keeping at national level significant options on social policy reforms. On the other hand, legislative initiatives at national level may be constrained by financial limitations, be they the outcome of economic policy co-ordination at European level or the result of national budgetary laws. OMC – and employment policies in particular – may thus run the risk of being weakened in the implementation phase, because of the absence of supportive measures laid down at the centre, with the aim of binding national expenditure to certain policy options.

The Commission is, in fact, self-critically suggesting that consistency of employment strategies with other European processes should be better ensured. Furthermore, in simplifying the Employment Guidelines attention should also be paid to ways of involving national parliaments in the preparation of NAPs, so that financial provisions can be made.[35] 'Streamlining' is a new key word, indicating the Commission's intention to bring economic and employment 'cycles' as close as possible and to strengthen the medium-term implementation phases, rather than elaborate new guidelines.[36]

Within the framework of this rich and still uncovered institutional debate and pointing to the relevance of related labour law developments, this project locates one specific example – the regulation of part-time work – within OMC, drawing attention to the multidisciplinary environment in which acts arising from such a regulatory technique may encourage the spread of new legal discourses. The risk may be that, instead of following a coherent pattern of legal evolution, through reforms which build on previous and consolidated principles, legislatures are asked to adapt uncritically to supranational strategies and to do so via national legislation, ignoring national traditions and not acknowledging the role of domestic institutions.

Measures to enhance sound money and sound finance, as well as moderation in wage setting, have often been required – and still are

---

[34] Scharpf, 'The European Social Model', p. 663.
[35] Communication from the Commission to the Council, the European Parliament, the Economic and Social Committee and the Committee of the Regions, *The Future of the European Employment Strategy. A Strategy for Full Employment and Better Jobs for All*, COM (2003) 6 final, Brussels, 14.1.2003.
[36] Communication from the Commission on Streamlining the Annual Economic and Employment Policy Co-ordination Cycles, COM (2002) 487 final, 3.9.2002.

considered – as essential ingredients of national best performance. A combination of such measures, first a precondition for the adoption of a single currency, then a condition for enhancing stability within EMU, has been at the centre of legislative manoeuvres originated by governments of very different political orientations.[37] We claim that, by specifically taking into account national peculiarities and different styles of legal regulation, an abstract European social model may be filled with incisive content.

In circumstances of high unemployment, this soft invasion of national prerogatives, combined with the pressure to meet contingent deadlines, may create a situation of conflict with national values and an interference in setting domestic economic and social priorities. When active employment policies are required to meet the percentages of increases in employment rates, following the indications coming from Council conclusions, it remains to be specified at national level that new jobs should not be created under deregulatory regimes and should not infringe fundamental rights. Setting up indicators on work quality, as happened in the 2002 Employment Guidelines,[38] has different implications from binding Member States to respect legal standards which are not to be waived and are to be ranked at the top of a hierarchy of legal sources.[39]

We underline in our work the distinctive features of regulatory techniques which, in the current state of evolution of European and national labour law, frequently interact with one another. In our own analysis we envisage governance by guidelines as a technique which is not inconsistent with developing a labour law perspective fully respectful of national constitutional traditions. We also claim that the combination of both levels of legal intervention helps to reinforce the inclusion of a coherent system of rights in the new constitutional architecture of Europe.

This is the crucial intersection at which soft regulatory techniques meet a core of constitutional rights, some of which have been revisited and made even more visible through the Nice Charter of Fundamental Rights.[40] Through this wide angle of observation which has been kept throughout

---

[37] D. Cameron, 'Unemployment, Job Creation and Economic and Monetary Union', in N. Bermeo (ed.), *Unemployment in the New Europe* (Cambridge: Cambridge University Press, 2001), pp. 7 ff.

[38] Council Decision 2002/177/EC of 18 February 2002 on guidelines for Member States' employment policies for the year 2002, OJ 2002 No. L60, 1 March 2002, p. 60. The increase in the number of indicators is emphasised by C. de la Porte, 'Digest' (2002) 12 *Journal of European Social Policy* p. 159.

[39] See further the chapter by D. Ashiagbor in this volume.

[40] OJ C 364, 18.12.2000, p. 1. See M. Weiss, 'The Politics of the EU Charter of Fundamental Rights', in Hepple, *Social and Labour*, pp. 73 ff (n. 3 above).

the present project – namely the close consideration of soft guidelines within a system of constitutional rights – we wish to support the evidence that even in future scenarios of law-making such a combination may become the emblem of modern supranational labour law.

2 Innovation and continuity in labour law: why a comparative analysis of part-time work, and how to structure legal comparison

In the previous section we have argued in favour of adopting a comparative legal perspective when dealing with different regulatory techniques emerging from different European processes. In particular, a non-prejudiced observation of OMC from the angle of labour law and a clear understanding of its interconnections with macroeconomic policies are essential in reassessing national priorities, while pursuing supranational objectives.

With the intention of capturing the motivations behind national legislative choices and of understanding whether they were or were not conditioned by European law and policies, a series of country studies, rather than a horizontal analysis of part-time regulation, is offered in the following chapters.

The selection of countries included in this project is a function of the opportunity we had to organise national studies reflecting a deep and well-structured analysis of the legal systems concerned. However, we do suggest that a contingent choice developed into a particularly interesting gathering of diverse national approaches, each of them attentive to bringing forward peculiarities which also explain the options of the legislature.

An in-depth observation of national regulations on part-time work brings about a confirmation of the theoretical assumptions presented in the previous section. Comparative analysis confirms that convergent and divergent patterns of regulation are compatible with OMC and indeed add significant information to the overall assessment of regulatory techniques in the social field. After observing how complex and varied the gestation of legislation was in all the countries included in this study, we can argue that the recurring mention of part-time work in at least three pillars of the Employment Guidelines – with the exception of entrepreneurship – shows the attention OMC paid to existing models, rather than attempting to foster new ways of introducing flexibility.

For this reason part-time work is shown in the present project as an example of innovation and continuity in labour law. Innovation meant for most European legal systems coming to terms with the existence of new working time arrangements and new facets in contracts of employment. Continuity was pursued inasmuch as traditional labour law guarantees were adapted to new forms of work. Comparative research – we argue from the experience drawn from this study – facilitates the understanding of ongoing processes of transformation within labour markets and establishes a well-balanced point of view on future scenarios.

The chapter by Davies and Freedland provides a cross-country evaluation of national regulations and proposes interesting ways to interpret objectives, approaches and techniques, placing the comparative analysis at the crossroads of national and supranational legal initiatives. One of the suggestions is that, when looking at the historical evolution of the subject-matter in each national system, only a limited impact of EU regulation on part-time work comes into view.[41] This finding deserves to be fully acknowledged and explained.

Part-time work stands at the intersection of European soft and hard law measures. It is dealt with in a Council Directive[42] originated and – what is most interesting to observe for the purposes of this project – implemented in the climate generated by the European Employment Strategy. Whereas the Directive in itself may prove not to be the right legal instrument for forcing national actors to create new jobs, it nevertheless provides an incentive to do so, establishing the principle of non-discrimination as a solid marker.[43] As much as the inclusion of this fundamental principle in the Directive constitutes a significant step forward in the recent evolution of European social law, it may remain the only aftermath of a reduced and narrower activity in law-making.

Labour law reforms may have a very different influence on employment policies, according to a more or less accentuated predisposition of governments to bring about significant changes in the reduction of unemployment and/or in the creation of new employment. Some reforms may

---

[41] See further the chapter by Davies and Freedland, section 3. See also ETUI, *Survey on the Implementation of the Part-time Work Directive/Agreement*, Report 73 co-ordinated by S. Clauwaert, Brussels 2002, p. 12. The impact of the Directive is deemed 'minor', with the possible exception of candidate countries.

[42] Council Directive 97/81/EC of 15 December 1997 concerning the Framework Agreement on part-time work concluded by UNICE, CEEP and the ETUC, OJ 1998 No. L 14, 20.1.1998, p. 9.

[43] Clause 4: principle of non-discrimination – 'In respect of employment conditions, part-time workers shall not be treated in a less favourable manner than comparable full-time workers solely because they work part time unless different treatment is justified on objective grounds.'

prove easier to co-ordinate at a supranational level, some others less so, because of very resistant symbolic values counterbalancing the need to change and adapt to a new legal environment.

Comparative research on reforms affecting European labour markets shows how 'selective changes that do not completely overturn the existing social contract' have prevailed when, from the mid-seventies onwards, deregulation of the labour market has been presented as the answer to high unemployment.[44] Differences across countries of the EU had as a consequence the fragmentation of social policy interventions and highlighted co-ordination as the only technique pointing to a way forward.[45]

We largely confirm such assertions, adding to them an analysis focussed more on labour law, albeit on one single example of possible reforms. Over the years, part-time work has been perceived by most observers and policy-makers as an indispensable device in the hands of national legislatures, in order to create new jobs and to respond to companies' demands for increased flexibility. We start from this assumption, fully aware of the fact that it cannot be passively embraced.[46] It is by trying to link it with the evaluation of European employment policies and by assessing the impact they have on national choices that we isolate, whenever possible, a distinctive feature of part-time regulations among the many other labour market reforms.

Country studies reveal that in some cases part-time regulation has been driven by a spontaneous process, such as the return of married women to the labour market.[47] It is noteworthy that those who described the early emergence of the 'Dutch miracle' also underlined the increase of part-time work as a 'fortuitous' development, not planned by policy-makers, but

---

[44] M. Samek Lodovici, 'The Dynamics of Labour Market Reform in European Countries', in G. Esping-Andersen and M. Regini (eds.), *Why Deregulate Labour Markets?* (Oxford: Oxford University Press, 2000), pp. 52 ff.

[45] Ibid., p. 54; see also D. Ashiagbor, 'EMU and the Shift in the European Labour Law Agenda: from "Social Policy" to "Employment Policy"' (2001) 7 *European Law Journal* p. 311 at 314.

[46] A detailed survey on the expansion of part-time work in recent years in the EU is in M. Smith, C. Fagan and J. Rubery, 'Where and Why is Part-time Work Growing in Europe?' in J. O'Reilly and C. Fagan, *Part-time Prospects. An International Comparison of Part-time Work in Europe, North America and the Pacific Rim* (London: Routledge, 1998), pp. 35 ff.

[47] See further the Dutch country study in Chapter 7. This phenomenon was observed in almost all OECD countries in the eighties, as reported in ibid., pp. 35 ff. See the country study by R. Eklund in Chapter 9, underlining how in Sweden too the increase of part-time jobs runs parallel to the rising number of women entering the labour market. It is to be noted that part-time work is often the only choice for such new-entrants in active employment.

happening in real life.[48] In Germany the increase of income for working mothers evolves almost exclusively from an increase in part-time work; in Spain the proportion of female part-timers increased by almost 6 per cent in a decade; in the UK women constitute 81 per cent of part-timers in line with a long-lasting gendered public policy option.[49]

It is also challenging to look at the results of comparative research on social exclusion and find that in the Dutch case the emphasis put on employment creation and active labour market policies also gave rise to a wider gap between the rich and the poor and to the creation of a visible dichotomy between insiders and outsiders.[50] Furthermore, as the Dutch country study included in this volume indicates, a part-time economy is not a 'paradise', essentially because company culture shows resistance to profound changes.[51] All other country studies confirm that, even when there has not been a clear deregulatory mark in labour law reforms, part-timers are very often confined to jobs with lower pay and more limited career prospects.

This confirms that 'miraculous' solutions are often echoed by reformers who seek merely hypothetical alternatives, far away from what has been or can be achieved in a given legal system. Legal comparison can in such cases be easily 'misused', inasmuch as one single segment of an overall system of norms is extrapolated and offered as valid in itself, instead of being placed within a broader institutional context.[52]

The method followed in the country studies included in this project is predominantly legal. Figures on the expansion of part-time work are provided with no presumption to explain the complexity of statistical trends in this field, but simply to complement the evaluation of legal regulation and site it in a given social context. Neither do we attempt to address part-time work as 'a universal modification to the existing sexual

---

[48] J. Visser and A. Hemerijck, 'A Dutch Miracle'. Job Growth, Welfare Reform and Corporatism in the Netherlands (Amsterdam: Amsterdam University Press, 1997).

[49] See references in respective chapters.

[50] D. Mayes, 'Introduction' in D. Mayes, J. Berghman and R. Salais, Social Exclusion and European Policy (Cheltenham: Edward Elgar, 2001), p. 14. Smith, Fagan and Rubery, 'Where and Why' observe at p. 51 that 'the expansion of part-time work has not produced an even outcome across countries or sectors', although in most cases part-timers are concentrated in low-paid and low-status occupations.

[51] See further the Dutch country study, Chapter 7.

[52] This has frequently been the case in Italy, under the pressure of the centre-right government. See further the country study by A. Lo Faro, in Chapter 6, suggesting that only a 'negative' choice is offered to unemployed people, forcing them to accept part-time work, rather than making it compatible with other commitments.

division of labour',[53] although in most country studies we see the results of this well-known phenomenon.

The focal point of the present project must be found in the evolution of legislation in the 1990s. The indication, however, that country studies should refer back to the 1980s and include information on developments in those years is justified by the fact that at that time most European labour law systems had to come to terms with the non-legal notion of 'flexibility' and incorporated it in a legal discourse. Since all countries included in this project have a distinctive and very pertinent collective heritage, we tried to assess the role played by employers' associations and trade unions in collective bargaining or in negotiating legislation on part-time work.[54]

In putting an emphasis on trade unions and collective bargaining we point to the ambivalence that such institutions may have towards the introduction of more flexible forms of work. In doing so, once more we run parallel to comparative research on labour market deregulation.[55] Trade unions, like families, are capable of mitigating the impact of reforms which seem to impoverish labour conditions by showing that if there is a loss, it is temporary and will, in the long run, be transformed into a gain.[56]

Current discussion on the expansion of OMC to sensitive areas of social policy encourages the recourse to comparative research in order to reveal the further potential of the employment strategies, linked to labour market and welfare state reforms. We claim that, for the furthering of these perspectives, part-time work is a meaningful example of how to foster reforms in social security[57] and to approach and favour the reconciliation of family and working life.[58]

---

[53] C. Fagan and J. O' Reilly, 'Conceptualising Part-Time Work, The Value of an Integrated Comparative Perspective', in O'Reilly and Fagan, *Part-time Prospects*, p. 1. This comparative research convincingly shows differences between countries and over the life-cycle of women and men.

[54] The 'Alliance for Work' which started in Germany at the end of the nineties is an example of concerted action among trade unions, employers' associations and government. The dynamic role played by the social partners is underlined also in the Spanish and Italian country studies.

[55] G. Esping-Andersen and M. Regini (eds.), *Why Deregulate Labour Markets* (Oxford: Oxford University Press, 1999).

[56] G. Esping-Andersen and M. Regini, 'Introduction', in Esping-Andersen and Regini, *Why Deregulate?*, pp. 5–6.

[57] See in particular the country study on Germany, Chapter 5.

[58] France and Germany offer good examples of part-time regulations going in such a direction.

Most outcomes of the present study can be read and evaluated in conjunction with recent policy indications offered by the Commission, reflecting upon the first five years of the EES. The Commission states its intention to establish a new 'focus on priorities' in order to confirm a valid and updated role for the Employment Guidelines. It is indicative that flexibility, in terms of 'availability of different contractual or working time arrangements', while still appearing among the measures to be pursued, is now more strictly associated with 'transitions between different forms of work', as well as with access to training and to better health and safety conditions.[59]

These new policy indications open up a space for a wider interpretation of part-time regulation and of its role among other 'flexible' forms of work. Future Employment Guidelines seem to disentangle this important component of labour law reforms from the urgency to create new jobs. The emphasis is now – even more than before – on adaptability and on measures which can corroborate the individual employee's choice to seek specific support for his or her working life from a long-term perspective. The Commission seems aware of this trend and indicates health and safety as well as training among the elective fields of action in order to pursue a 'balance between flexibility and security'.[60]

Labour law would be at its best if future employment policies were to indicate stronger connections with such core areas of individual rights and if they were to find mechanisms to enforce such rights better. The intersection between soft and hard law measures could once more delineate a challenge to be met by national legal systems within a range of binding principles. Comparative labour law too would continue to be a useful resource, since it would draw attention to the evaluation of concrete results and to the role of national institutions in fostering convergence towards European targets.

In Chapter 3, Davies and Freedland suggest, within a comparative scheme of analysis, that 'reflexiveness' of national legislation on part-time work, into both the Part-Time Work Directive and the EU Employment Strategy, is one of the most interesting outcomes of our study. This metaphorical image confirms that there is a good degree of communication – as in a game of reflecting mirrors – between national and supranational systems of law and that decision-making shapes itself in a circular

---

[59] Commission Communication, *The Future of the European Employment Strategy* (quoted at n. 35 above), p. 14.
[60] Commission Communication, *Taking Stock* (quoted at n. 15 above), p. 14.

rather than vertical form. This is mainly due to the European 'soft law' context in which most exchanges take place, as will be further argued below.[61]

Reflexive exchanges of this kind lead us to a discovery which is also a confirmation of one of our working premises. The word 'atypical' – applied to non-standard forms of work and to part-time work among those – can safely be deleted from the dictionary of contemporary labour law. Such an expression also proves to be wrong when looked at through the lens of comparative labour law: the dominant current feature of part-time work is now to be found in its normality. This is not to say that research for enhancing better legal mechanisms to entitle non-standard workers to specific rights should stop. The analysis of the Part-time Work Directive indicates that existing European law could be further clarified in its scope, in line with the expanding role played by European anti-discrimination law and in connection with simplified – and therefore more focused – Employment Guidelines.

3 A brief history of the Directive on part-time work

The Directive on part-time work[62] has its own interesting – and at times revealing – background. To propose a short historical *excursus* of the various phases undergone by such a piece of legislation may serve a double purpose.

In the first place, the history of the Directive may better clarify the novelty of the most recent approach embraced by the Commission in dealing with employment relationships which differ from permanent contracts. Three contentious proposals were put forward in 1990, as part of the action programme following the 1989 Charter of Fundamental Social Rights.[63] When looked at from a distance, this ambitious and only partially

---

[61] See section 4.
[62] Council Directive 97/81/EC of 15 December 1997 concerning the Framework Agreement on part-time work concluded by UNICE, CEEP and the ETUC.
[63] COM (90) 228 final, OJ 1990 No. C224, 8.9.1990. Only the third proposal succeeded (in amended form: COM (90) 533 final, OJ 1990 No. C305, 5.12. 1990). See Council Directive 91/383/EEC of 25 June 1991 supplementing the measures to encourage improvements in the safety and health at work of workers with a fixed-duration employment relationship or a temporary employment relationship: OJ 1991 No. L206, 29.7.1991, p. 19. See R. Eklund, 'The Chewing-Gum Directive – Part-time Work in the European Community' in R. Eklund *et al.* (eds.), *Festskrift till Hans Stark* (Stockholm: Elander Gotab, 2001) for a useful discussion on the early debate in the eighties with regard to proposals for part-time directives and for a characteristic Swedish perspective.

successful attempt proves how complex it is to bring different categories of non-standard workers under a unitary set of legal measures.[64] The Part-time Work Directive marks a new start in dealing with only one category of such workers and, in doing so, by providing the guarantee of minimum standards.

In the second place, going through the various phases of negotiation preceding the adoption of the Directive, one can appreciate the links established with the contemporary and challenging debate on supranational and national employment policies. Whereas the latter are mainly dealt with through sophisticated soft law mechanisms, new emerging patterns of European social law are built around weighty fundamental rights. The principle of non-discrimination becomes the cornerstone of a new phase in European social policies.

The first phase of consultation launched by the Commission in 1995[65] could not hide some initial uncertainties as to the aims and purposes of the initiative. Commissioner Flynn ambiguously moved from the urgency to provide 'flexi-time and safety for workers' – particularly part-time and temporary workers – to the intention to 'do everything possible to encourage the creation of jobs'.[66] Whereas the former objective somehow reflected the limits of the legal basis in the regime prompted by the Single European Act – qualified majority voting limited to legislation related to workers' health and safety – the latter looks ahead towards new and broader objectives, attempting to find plausible solutions to increased unemployment.

In the attempt to set the Part-time Work Directive within a broader institutional framework, two subsequent important events must be recalled.

The European Council held at Essen[67] addressed the need to promote employment and equal opportunities, while increasing flexibility in the organisation of work. The Essen criteria were later recognised as a landmark in the history of European employment strategies, inasmuch as they offered a complete formula to enhance the effectiveness of labour market

---

[64] See M. Jeffery, 'Not Really Going to Work? Of the Directive on Part-time Work, "Atypical Work" and Attempts to Regulate it' (1998) 27 *Industrial Law Journal* p. 193, and 'The Commission's Proposals on "Atypical Work": Back to the Drawing Board' (1995) 24 *Industrial Law Journal* p. 296; and Council Directive 91/383/EEC (see n. 63).

[65] Consultation was conducted under Art. 3(2) of what was then the Agreement on social policy annexed to the Protocol on social policy.

[66] *Agence Europe*, 27.9.95.   [67] See above, n. 3.

policies, while taking into account the special needs of groups hard-hit by unemployment.

Furthermore, Title VIII on Employment was introduced by the Amsterdam Treaty. From then onwards the engine of the 'coordinated strategy' (Art. 125 ECT) started and slowly developed into what can now be described as a virtual circle. Council guidelines have, ever since, been issued each year to Member States; they have been followed by National Action Plans (NAPs), annually monitored in a joint report issued by the Council and the Commission (Arts. 126–8).[68] The objective of 'a high level of employment' (Art. 2 TEU and Art. 2 ECT) thus started to be formally pursued by European institutions and Member States.

One of the comparative outcomes we underline is that there is a sense of ambiguity in interpreting national responses to the Employment Guidelines as compliance with European soft law. The scene is further complicated by the fact that national law transposing the Part-time Work Directive may or may not be considered in compliance with the soft law mechanisms brought about by the OMC from the Lisbon Council onwards.

If we go back to the beginning of 1997, during a fourth session of negotiations between the Commission and the social partners, we discover that the latter still had divergent approaches to part-time work. Whereas UNICE seemed worried about signing a second Framework Agreement, so different from the one on parental leave,[69] because it captured 'the very logic of regulating the labour market', ETUC pushed for further improvement of social protection, in order to make part-time jobs more attractive.[70]

Only at the end of 1997, soon after an extraordinary summit on employment held in Luxembourg[71] in which agreement was reached on

---

[68] See the chapter by D. Ashiagbor for an analysis of the legal status of NAPs and the role of part-time legislation within the Employment Strategy.

[69] Council Directive 96/34/EC of 3 June 1996 on the framework agreement on parental leave concluded by UNICE, CEEP and the ETUC, OJ 1996 No. L145, 19.6.1996, p. 4. This was the first Directive incorporating a framework agreement, under the procedures set in the Protocol on social policy, annexed to the Maastricht Treaty.

[70] *Agence Europe*, 24.1.1997.

[71] Held on 20–21 November 1997. See Presidency Conclusions, Extraordinary European Council Meeting on Employment, Luxembourg, 20–21 November 1997, Bull. EU 11-1997, pp. 7–13, for the approval of a set of Employment Guidelines for 1998. Comments on the overall significance of decisions adopted in this Council meeting are in Cameron, 'Unemployment', especially at pp. 44–7.

the enforcement of the Essen criteria, did the prospect for the Directive become clearer. The extraordinary reasons for such a Council meeting were related to the urgency to adopt measures to combat unemployment and to do so even before the formal ratification of the Amsterdam Treaty. It is not hard to imagine that a lot of emphasis would be placed on part-time legislation, in accordance with a widely shared impulse to encourage flexibility in employment relationships.

Commissioner Flynn still had to insist, at the request of the President of the Council, that the principle of non-discrimination between part-time and full-time work be inserted in the agreement reached by the social partners in June 1997, so that it could be included with no modifications in the Directive. Having overcome this last and by no means secondary difficulty, the Directive saw the light of day in December 1997.[72] The time given to Member States to comply with its requirements – by January 2000 – also happened to be a most formative time for the consolidation of good practices in employment policies at national level. It was also the time in which the two different effects sought by the Directive, namely the enforcement of a 'minimum set of fundamental rights' and the introduction of flexible ways to organise work,[73] were meant to blend together in a new mixture of regulatory techniques.

The Framework Agreement signed by the social partners, then annexed to the Directive, captures this double necessity to 'contribute' to the European strategy on employment and to combat discrimination against part-time workers. The Agreement assimilates the idea that there is a positive connection between the increase of jobs and the introduction of non-standard forms of employment, so much so that the signatories to it announce that they will be dealing in the future 'with other forms of flexible work'. More specifically, the Directive refers to the Essen European Council and to the 'view to increase the employment-intensiveness of growth, in particular by a more flexible organization of work'.[74]

---

[72] Recital no. 23 of the Preamble to the Directive contains a reference to the Community Charter of fundamental social rights of workers and to the broad principle of non-discrimination based on sex, colour, race, opinion and creed. The Directive only deals with the principle of non-discrimination between part-time and full-time workers. See a critical remark on this missed opportunity in M. Bell, *Anti-discrimination Law and the European Union* (Oxford: Oxford University Press, 2002), p. 97.

[73] This is the language used by the Commission in its explanatory memorandum to the Part-time Work Directive, COM (1997) 392, Brussels, 23 July 1997.

[74] Recital no. 5 of the Preamble. More generally see S. Deakin and H. Reed, 'The Contested Meaning of Labour Market Flexibility: Economic Theory and the Discourse of European

These well-clarified objectives are the prelude to a body of norms characterised by a minimalist approach. The possibility of excluding casual workers from the scope of the Directive is left open to Member States, after consulting the social partners. The notion of a comparable full-time worker is introduced as a means to define the part-timer.[75] The principle of non-discrimination is laid down in its simplicity and yet in its very powerful implications, namely the ban on less favourable treatment, unless justified on objective grounds, and the recourse, whenever possible, to the principle of *pro rata temporis*.

The principle of non-discrimination becomes, in this way, a justiciable right, when read in conjunction with the notion of a comparable full-time worker within the same establishment or, where such a worker does not exist, with reference to collective agreements or other national legal sources. These are both traditional points of reference in national legislative traditions, when it comes to indicating the space within which individual rights are generated and protected. The presence of such criteria in the Directive is by no means to be under-estimated, because they aim at assimilating all forms of work under the same regulatory framework, thus intending to overcome the notion of atypical work.[76]

Other clauses of the Agreement, namely the progressive elimination of discriminatory requirements for access to particular conditions of employment and of other obstacles limiting opportunities for part-time work, are of more dubious interpretation, as far as the guarantee of individual rights is concerned.[77] Such clauses should put an obligation on

---

Integration', in J. Shaw (ed.), *Social Law and Policy in an Evolving European Union* (Oxford: Hart Publishing, 2000), pp. 74–5.

[75] Similar descriptions of a part-time worker and comparable full-time worker are in Art. 1 of the ILO Part-time Work Convention C175, adopted on 24 June 1994. To date, this Convention has been ratified by nine countries: Cyprus, Finland, Guyana, Italy, Luxembourg, Mauritius, the Netherlands, Slovenia and Sweden (source: www.ilo.org). See also ILO Part-time Work Recommendation R182, adopted on 24 June 1994, Art. 2.

[76] This is suggested throughout the Dutch country study.

[77] The 1994 ILO Convention (see n. 75) indicates in detail measures to be taken 'to ensure that part-time workers receive the same protection as that accorded to comparable full-time workers' (Art. 4 ff.). It is also specified in Art. 7 which 'equivalent' conditions must be guaranteed to part-timers, namely maternity protection, termination of employment, paid annual leave and paid public holidays, and sick leave. Criticism was raised by the European Parliament with the Commission, because the Directive incorporating the agreement did not include questions – such as social security – dealt with in the ILO Convention. See reference to this exchange of views in ETUI, *Survey on the Implementation of the Part-time Work Directive/Agreement in the EU Member States and Selected Applicant Countries*, Report 73, Brussels, 2002, p. 6.

Member States to act for the removal of discriminatory laws and practices, both on their own initiative, in order to comply with European law, and following individual complaints. However, there remains a grey area between the enforcement of non-discrimination principles and the right to have access to part-time jobs as ways of enforcing employment policies free of discriminatory practices.[78]

In order to ban these practices, clause 5(1) (a) and (b) indicates that Member States and the social partners, in their respective sphere of competence, should 'identify and review' obstacles which are likely to limit opportunities for part-timers. The non-binding nature of this command creates uncertainties as regards a clear definition of a right to access to employment free of discrimination.[79]

This is a clear example of the interesting but still unclear combination of regulatory techniques brought about by the Directive in question. Its hard law principles are inextricably encapsulated in the soft law environment of employment policies and of wider European policies surrounding them. It is on the latter that the next section will concentrate.

4   Labour market regulations in the European context: a soft law environment

In order to be even further aware of the potentialities intrinsic to the European employment strategy, it is useful to relate them to a series of recent documents which endeavour to create a soft law environment. It can be maintained that such an environment facilitates the spread of good practices and creates the preconditions for mutual monitoring across Member States and for reviewing mechanisms to be further improved from the centre to the periphery.

The theoretical assumption is that employment policies, as they have developed in recent years in the EU, are a successful example of 'integration through co-ordination'.[80] Increased flexibility of the labour market

---

[78] The same conclusions are drawn in ETUI, *Survey*, p. 13; country studies reveal that partial implementation of the Directive is due to the fact that Member States do not consider certain provisions legally binding.

[79] Criticism is expressed in the UK country study, both of the formulation of the Directive and of the 'soft' national response consisting in a 'Compliance guidance' for the implementation of the Directive. See, further, Chapter 10.

[80] This is what I argued, soon after the Lisbon Council, in S. Sciarra, 'Integration through Coordination: the Employment Title in the Amsterdam Treaty' (2000) 6 *Columbia Journal of European Law* p. 209.

is one of the expected outcomes of such a dynamic strategy, inasmuch as it fosters the creation of new jobs.

Co-ordination is facilitated by a subtle and yet resistant network of policies mostly coming from the Commission. All new processes of co-ordination in related fields, particularly the programme on social inclusion, should progressively interact with each other.

Such signals are important for most actors involved in law-making, both at national and supranational level. They are also meant to shape and in a way redefine the function of the social dialogue.

4.1 The White Paper on Governance

One of the leading ideas running through the White Paper on Governance[81] is the creation of a 'reinforced culture of consultation and dialogue', which should be addressed to the European institutions and should better include national parliaments. The suggestion is that, in order to avoid excessive rigidity in the adoption of policies and yet acquire objective and widespread opinions, a 'code of conduct that sets minimum standards' should be provided, with a view to improving the representativeness of civil society organisations.[82]

The Commission provides a follow-up to these early orientations in a Communication.[83] A point of interest for the present discussion is the more proactive role that should be assigned to the Economic and Social Committee and the Committee of the Regions. Protocols on co-operation with such bodies, signed in 2001 by the Commission, make them stronger intermediaries with civil society and the regional level.[84]

The image of a double network can be suggested, whereby the establishment of a more formalised link between institutions should lead to a capillary intersection with civil society. The local and regional ends of this network indicate that criteria of representativeness should include the geographical dislocation of organisations.

Another way to ascertain the spread of representation – and consequently of democratic deliberative structures – is the issuing of guidelines

---

[81] European Commission, *European Governance – A White Paper*, COM (2001) 428 final, Brussels, 25 July 2001, OJ 2001 C287, 12.10.2001, p. 1.

[82] COM (2001) 428 final, at pp. 16–17.

[83] Communication from the Commission, *Towards a Reinforced Culture of Consultation and Dialogue. Proposal for General Principles and Minimum Standards for Consultation of Interested Parties by the Commission*, COM (2002) 277 final, Brussels, 5.6.2002.

[84] COM (2002) 277 final, at pp. 6–7.

on the use of expertise.[85] This again may seem only remotely relevant for the present discussion, but it is not, if one thinks of the many issues that need to be clarified through scientific assessment in the field of employment, labour market reforms and the reform of welfare states. The discussion on social indicators, referred to earlier on,[86] clearly confirms that experts are already active in all relevant fields.

This is an example of exercising influence on policy-makers through consensual institutions and by recourse to dialogue, rather than by imposition and coercion.[87] In the delicate field of labour and social law, expertise should reflect different options and propose explicitly what the ultimate expected goal ought to be. It is, on the contrary, frequently the case that the economic model to be pursued remains 'implicit'.[88] Experts deal with it in a very abstract way, without attempting to elaborate comparative criteria around concrete examples.

In this search for legitimacy, traditional ways of establishing democratic representation are lost.[89] This should not necessarily be considered a negative outcome, if it gives impulse to the search for new modes of organising collective interests within trade unions or through other civil society organisations. The lack of criteria to ascertain that such collective actors are representative and democratic constitutes a challenge to both supranational and national labour law, to the point of questioning the centrality of this discipline. A most original process of supranational integration across different legal and economic systems is taking place day after day and innovative solutions slowly merge into a public sphere, where different actors at different times take the lead.

What we see emerging from the box of regulatory techniques is a mixture of hard and soft law measures, a combination of objectives to be reached and means to pursue them. The breaking up of hierarchies inside legal sources generates separate domains of norms, some of which may overlap, while some others may be complementary to each other and run parallel to a principal legal command.

---

[85] COM (2002) 277 final, at p. 10.   [86] See section 1.

[87] C. Radaelli, 'The "representation" of expertise in the European Union', in S. Saurugger (ed.), *Les modes de représentation dans l'Union Européenne* (Paris: L'Harmattan, 2003).

[88] Atkinson, 'Social Inclusion', pp. 633, 635.

[89] See the critique expressed by C. Scott, 'The Governance of the European Union: the Potential for Multi-Level Control' (2002) 8 *European Law Journal* p. 59, arguing in favour of alternative ways to exercise efficient governance. The Commission is encouraging 'parliamentary involvement' in the discussion on NAPs in the Communication quoted at *The Future of the European Employment Strategy*, p. 18 – see n. 35.

As a reaction to this earthquake, we witness the creation of both vertical and horizontal co-operation: European institutions instruct other actors with a top-down approach and expect that directions be horizontally implemented, at local and regional level and more generally within civil society.

4.2   The Laeken Declaration

In the Laeken Declaration on the Future of the European Union,[90] issues of openness, transparency and efficiency are put forward to the Convention responsible for institutional reforms. The mandate is very broad and yet very specific on certain points, some of which are relevant for the present analysis.

Among other priorities set for the Convention, it is indicated that in order to obtain 'concrete results in terms of more jobs it will be necessary to reform the existing system'. On the one hand the issue of competence is raised, having to do with better transparency in the distinction between exclusive, shared and Member States' competence. On the other hand, looking at the issue of simplification, it is suggested that existing instruments need to come under scrutiny, in order to achieve policy objectives better.

A reorganisation of competence in the specific field of labour law and labour market regulation, beyond the existing situation, brings about an overall reformist agenda that should soon be disclosed. If this occurs, a discussion on different options based on national preferences – and at times trapped in contingent ideologies – should not be avoided. This may originate comparisons between levels of legal standards, in order to establish whether existing national laws may be weakened as a consequence of the implementation of European measures, be they formal legal acts or guidelines.[91] It may also cause a discussion on financial resources to be used in order to reach the final objectives.[92]

It is not without meaning that employment policies dealing with labour market regulations have been recurrently associated with a non-legal

---

[90] Presidency Conclusions, Laeken European Council, 14–15 December 2001, Annex 1, in particular pp. 21–2.

[91] See, for example, Italy on *clausole*.

[92] S. Ball, 'The European Employment Strategy: The Will but not the Way?' (2001) 30 *Industrial Law Journal* 353; see also references to F. Vandenbroucke in n. 33.

notion such as flexibility.[93] The variety of deregulatory options available to reformers is very wide and implies a choice of means as well as of actors able to implement them. As pointed out above in discussing the role of expertise, the contours of a coherent economic model should be drawn, in order to understand fully which constraints are necessary and for what purpose.

Defenders of fundamental social rights have argued that the process of constitutionalisation should not be threatened by the implementation of legislation on flexibility.[94] The suggested distinction between employment law and employment policy and the specification that the latter should be considered outside social policies make the constitutional dimension even more important.[95] The fear that employment policy may follow a direction separate from the one indicated in broader institutional reforms is based on the observation of an existing disproportion between targets set by macroeconomic policies and by all related policies dealing with labour market reforms.

The language adopted in writing macroeconomic guidelines is indicative of certain options. To 'invigorate labour markets',[96] wage moderation and a greater recourse to temporary and part-time contracts are correct choices, in accordance with the goals set at Lisbon and Stockholm, in achieving a more employment-intensive growth. Unfortunately – the Commission points out – 'the pace of labour market reforms seems to have slowed down in 2001' and particular measures are forcefully indicated to Member States, among which reference is made to more flexible work organisation, in dialogue with the social partners.[97]

One may find the phrasing of the guidelines rhetorical and not too imaginative. The objective and thorough analysis reflected in this soft law instrument seems to leave aside the specificity of each national context,

[93] The centrality of labour market flexibility in designing the success of EMU has been underlined by commentators early on in the debate. See A. Scott, 'The Macro-economic Context of the Euro', in P. Beaumont and N. Walker (eds.), *Legal Framework of the Single European Currency* (Oxford: Hart Publishing, 1999), pp. 54 ff.

[94] An excellent discussion of this point, from a range of international and comparative perspectives, is presented in Hepple, *Social and Labour Rights* (n. 2 above), at note 1. See also U. Mückenberger (ed.), *Manifesto for a Social Europe* (Brussels: ETUI, 2001).

[95] M. Freedland, 'Employment Policy', in P. Davies, A. Lyon-Caen, S. Sciarra and S. Simitis (eds.), *European Community Labour Law: Principles and Perspectives, Liber Amicorum Lord Wedderburn* (Oxford: Oxford University Press, 1996).

[96] Commission Recommendation for the 2002 Broad Guidelines of the Economic Policies of the Member States and the Community, COM (2002) 191 final, Brussels, 24.4.2002, point 3.3 at p. 14.

[97] Ibid., at p. 14 and p. 16.

which only reappears in the country-specific economic policy guidelines, placed in the second part of the Recommendation and characterised by a more detailed set of indications.

Objectivity in guidelines is ascertained in view of the final expected goal, which is a common one. Art. 99 ECT sheds light on national economic policies as 'a matter of common concern', thus absorbing into the objective of 'open market economy with free competition' all the peculiarities of national choices and priorities. Abstraction in the delivery of expertise is also a sign of objectivity, although at times this exercise seems to depart from real life.

The fear that legal discourses may remain at the margins of such descriptive analysis and lose their normative contents must be put into perspective. The results of this research show, on the contrary, that legislation, even when urged by European targets, still maintains its internal coherence. Comparative legal analysis helps in understanding national differences and in making them a resource of European law, rather than a deficiency.

4.3   The High Level Group on Industrial Relations

The European system of industrial relations has been the object of in-depth analysis in a report drawn up by experts in the field.[98] The mandate to this group came from the Lisbon Council and in fact the spirit of the whole document reflects the main innovative points which emerged from the Portuguese Presidency in the Spring of 2000. References to this report help us to understand the climate in which what I have described as the paradigm of flexibility is expected to develop.

Furthermore, this report is thoroughly complementary to the other policy documents commented on above. It encourages the sort of outcomes sketched in the *White Paper on Governance*, by proving that national industrial relations systems are inhabited by consensus-building institutions. These play a positive role, to be reinforced even further, leaving aside forms of social protest which would shape emerging interests through conflict, as happened in the past in many national traditions.

The aim, when we move from domestic to supranational goals, is to increase the overall efficiency of the European system and to do so with a

---

[98] European Commission, Directorate-General for Employment and Social Affairs, *Report of the High Level Group on Industrial Relations and Change in the European Union* (Luxembourg: CEC, 2002).

'new instrument', the one which emerged at Lisbon from the co-ordination of the existing processes of Cologne, Cardiff and Luxembourg.

Social partners are encouraged by the experts to simulate the Lisbon strategy, building on 'their own experience of the open-method of co-ordination', in particular through the promotion of a network of national institutions that will follow-up best practices.[99] Even benchmarking the quality of industrial relations, by developing appropriate indicators, is suggested, with a view to the establishment of techniques very similar to the ones adopted in employment policies.

Messages of expertise are spread quickly across institutions. In the context of an overall evaluation of the first five years of employment policies, the Commission soon articulates its own suggestion to the social partners, encouraging an 'open method of co-ordination to develop relationships with their national counterparts', in view of 'improving governance and partnership'.[100]

In their policy documents, experts and institutions portray future scenarios which are vital and open to changes. They do not take into account the eventuality of social conflict, nor do they evaluate the problem of legitimacy in strict correlation with the interests to be protected. When moved to this supranational level of policy-making, collective interests – a crucial concept in the European labour law tradition – become so diffused and broad as to be almost non-definable and certainly difficult to interpret within a traditional scheme of representation. The mandate given to social actors is described as interacting with the objectives set at the centre, rather than being the result of a bottom-up process, leading to a new request to be represented.[101]

Trade unions, however, demonstrate their own capacity to follow autonomously agreed patterns of co-ordination, especially in dealing with matters, such as wages, which have traditionally been within the area of their competence. It is worth mentioning that the European Trade Union Confederation (ETUC) sets its own strategies in issuing recommendations on wage bargaining guidelines, in order to indicate optimal wage rises at national level. It is even more interesting to discover that in 2001

---

[99] Ibid., p. 37.

[100] Communication from the Commission, *Taking Stock* (n. 15 above), p. 20. See also Council Decision 2002/177/EC of 18 February 2002 (see note 38), which repeatedly mentions the need to develop further the role of the social partners in both the promotion and the implementation of reforms aimed at the creation of new jobs.

[101] The role of the social partners is analysed by C. Barnard, 'The Social Partners and the Governance Agenda' (2002) 8 *European Law Journal* 80.

national actors engaged in negotiations kept their demands very close to the guidelines, with no significant loss of purchasing power. Thus, meeting the intention of the guidelines through monitoring and advising, a result of convergence is reached.[102]

The message emerging from this report signals ways of correcting asymmetries among groups which are rather distant from most regulatory techniques adopted in national labour law regimes. We claim in this project that national social partners still play a significant role in enhancing labour market reforms and we also assign importance to the issue of democratic legitimacy, when setting the scene of collective representation for the protection of collective rights. In this regard, there is still a missing reference in European sources, namely the recognition of a positive right to form and join associations, partially counterbalanced by the mention of such a right in the Charter of Fundamental Rights of the European Union.

5   Conclusions

The regulation of part-time work offers an example of labour law reforms rooted in national legal systems and also linked to European objectives. It constitutes a solid ground on which to launch comparative labour law in a renovated and incisive fashion, taking into account many facets of the EES which still appear unexplored. We have argued in favour of establishing a labour law point of view, both to counterbalance an analysis based on economic and structural trends and to ensure that legal institutions be included in the spectrum of comparative research.

The net of soft rules arranged within the EES mirrors a wider European soft law context. Labour lawyers are very curious and vigilant commentators on such rules, in line with a tradition of pluralism in legal sources. Mutual learning processes set in motion by the EES seem to overturn a traditional hierarchy of sources in favour of a circular exchange of information. We argue that national priorities must continue to be visible in this new institutional order and that respect for fundamental social rights must inspire legal reforms enacted in compliance with employment policies.

---

[102] G. Fajertag (ed.), *Collective Bargaining in Europe* (Brussels: ETUI, 2002), pp. 27 ff. The so-called 'Doorn group' has been active since 1997 to avoid wage competition in unions active in Germany, Belgium, the Netherlands and Luxembourg, in order to increase employment and purchasing power. Its sixth conference was held on 11 October 2002 in Aardenburg, the Netherlands; a copy of the 2002 declaration is on file with the author. Reports of the activities of the Doorn group can be found at www.etuc.org/etui/CBeurope/euractiv.

The analysis of the Part-time Work Directive has also been central in this project. We have repeatedly underlined that the combination of hard and soft law mechanisms has created a double burden on Member States, very often leaving space for non-conventional solutions. Even so, part-time work does not in itself provide the answer to the still open question of how to create more and better jobs.

The Commission's recent attention towards 'synchronisation' of the different European processes and 'streamlining' of the same has been signalled as a policy orientation not irrelevant to the present analysis, particularly in the light of the subtle, if not contradictory, indication given by the Commission that the economic and the employment spheres should be left autonomous.

The task of comparative labour law is further enhanced by the present situation. The study of labour market institutions brings forward very clearly the fact that the autonomy of the economic sphere may lead to an imbalance within the range of policies to be pursued. Furthermore, autonomy of employment policies may mean very little, if no economic support is provided to decision-makers. A possible stronger emphasis on measures to favour adaptability, when pursuing employment policies, alerts once more the interest of labour lawyers in ascertaining that fundamental rights should be guaranteed in the various stages of an active working life and should favour mobility between jobs. The paradigm of flexibility could become more relevant for labour law and would represent not an aim in itself, but a frame of reference for the articulation of individual and collective rights.

2

The European Employment Strategy and the regulation of part-time work

DIAMOND ASHIAGBOR

1 Introduction

As will become evident from the subsequent national chapters, the opacity, vagueness and rhetorical style of the National Action Plans (NAPs) presents a challenge to analysis, and requires a different methodological approach from that involved in assessing the impact of, say, directives. This is, in part, due to the fact that Member States' responses to the Employment Guidelines generally take the form of administrative rather than legislative measures, which are likely to be less 'visible'.

A key question which will be addressed in this chapter is, therefore, how one can measure Member States' 'compliance' with the soft law requirements of the Employment Strategy. This will involve an assessment of the legal significance of the National Action Plans, how they have matured over time, and examples of Member States' responses to their obligations as evidenced in their NAPs published since 1998.

Furthermore, in the context of an investigation of the regulation of part-time work, it is also useful to explore the differing ways in which Member States have responded to the part-time work aspects of the Employment Strategy, a Strategy within which part-time work is promoted, to a great extent, as a means of increasing the level of employment and improving competitiveness and productivity.

2 The (legal) status of the Employment Guidelines and the National Action Plans

According to Art. 128(3) EC, each Member State must provide the Council and the Commission with an annual report on the principal measures taken to implement its employment policy in the light of the Employment Guidelines. The NAPs are thus the main documentary evidence of whether Member States are or are not complying with their obligations under the Employment Strategy. However, could one envisage the Commission initiating infringement proceedings, as provided for under Art. 226 EC, against a Member State which had failed to comply with policy recommendations under the Employment Guidelines? Would such failure be sufficient to amount to a failure to 'fulfil an obligation under this Treaty', as required by Article 226?[1]

To gain an insight into the possible legal status and influence of the NAPs, it is useful to compare the Employment Strategy and NAPs with traditional modes of EU governance, such as directives, and Member States' responses to them. Even existing soft law mechanisms, such as the social dialogue procedure, have a *core of hard law*, in that the social partners' agreements can lead to framework directives. The first two sets of Employment Guidelines for the years 1998 and 1999 were issued in the form of Council Resolutions;[2] since 2000, the Guidelines have taken the form of Council Decisions.[3] Although Art. 249 (formerly Art. 189) EC provides that 'a decision shall be binding in its entirety upon those to whom it is addressed', I do not, however, think that too much should be read into this change in form since the Guidelines would appear to be 'decisions' *sui generis*, i.e. without the legal significance of decisions envisaged by Article 249. Therefore, one can say that the Employment Strategy does not have recourse to the hard law machinery of, say, the social dialogue procedure, thus leaving a potentially wide range of legitimate responses to Member States' obligations under the Employment Strategy.[4]

A key aspect of the use of NAPs to evidence Member States' policies is the absence of sanctions for failure to comply with European guidelines. Co-ordination rather than harmonisation of employment policies means

---

[1] Article 226 (formerly Art. 169) EC provides that: 'If the Commission considers that a Member State has failed to fulfil an obligation under this Treaty, it shall deliver a reasoned opinion on the matter after giving the State concerned the opportunity to submit its observations. If the State concerned does not comply with the opinion within the period laid down by the Commission, the latter may bring the matter before the Court of Justice.'

[2] Council Resolution of 15 December 1997 on the 1998 Employment Guidelines, OJ C 30/98, 28.01.1998; Council Resolution of 22 February 1999 on the 1999 Employment Guidelines, OJ C 69, 12.03.1999.

[3] Council Decision of 13 March 2000 on guidelines for Member States' employment policies for the year 2000 (2000/228/EC), OJ L 72/15, 21.03.2000; Council Decision of 19 January 2001 on guidelines for Member States' employment policies for the year 2001 (2001/63/EC), OJ L 22/18, 24.1.2001; Council Decision of 18 February 2002 on guidelines for Member States' employment policies for the year 2002 (2002/177/EC), OJ L 60/60, 1.3.2002.

[4] I am grateful to Paul Davies for this observation.

that the Commission's role differs from its role under the 'classic' Community method: it can trigger the adoption of critical recommendations by the Council, rather than pursue infringement proceedings. This absence of real sanctions can be linked to the emphasis, in the open method of co-ordination, on *processes* and *methods*, rather than *outcomes* – the reverse of what is true in the case of directives.[5] Article 249 EC defines a directive as a measure which 'shall be binding, as to the result to be achieved, upon each Member State to which it is addressed, but shall leave to the national authorities the choice of form and methods'. Hodson and Maher suggest that the open method, with its focus on methods rather than outcomes, marks a maturation of the integration process, a key element in this new maturity being the acceptance of diversity in 'legal frameworks, ideational references and popular perceptions and reactions to either the European project generally or the specific policy being co-ordinated'.[6]

Thus, the OMC's openness to diversity of policy outcomes means that the legal status of National Action Plans (wherein Member States detail the outcomes of their policies) cannot be easily categorised. I would contend that – as in the case of the Council Decisions containing the Employment Guidelines – the legal nature of the NAPs is *sui generis*. This has the effect that there is scope for Member States to use the NAPs as a platform for existing national programmes and policies, devised independently of the Employment Strategy, so long as these national measures do not explicitly contradict the tenor of the Employment Guidelines. Such 'opportunism' by Member States will be considered further in section 2.2.

To return to the *sui generis* nature of the NAPs, initially, the production of NAPs can be seen as a re-affirmation of the 'shared commitment', made in the Employment Title, to make progress on employment. Thus the Commission considered it a 'major political achievement' that the first set of NAPs were prepared, adopted and delivered within such a short time frame.[7] Subsequently, it has become clear that the long time horizon of the Employment Strategy as a whole means that NAPs are not a 'once and for all' event, so that Member States do not have to 'get it

---

[5] See D. Hodson and I. Maher, 'The Open Method as a New Mode of Governance: the Case of Soft Economic Policy Co-ordination' (2001) 39: 4 *Journal of Common Market Studies* pp. 719–46 at 730–1.

[6] Ibid., p. 731.

[7] Commission of the European Communities (hereinafter CEC), *From Guidelines to Action: The National Action Plans for Employment*, including a Commission Communication, and a Background Report (Luxembourg: OOPEC, 1998); COM (98) 316 final, pp. 1–2 of the Communication.

right' first time. Process is more important than outcome, and the iterative nature of the Employment Strategy means that there is scope for a year on year improvement. With the exception of a few key targets, such as that for increasing employment rates, there is no final date by which a given measure *must* be transposed into a Member State's legal system, as there is in the case of directives.

To compensate for this, the Commission has engaged in very rigorous monitoring and assessment of the NAPs. In assessing the NAPs for 2000, the *Joint Employment Report 2000* gave a strong indication of the view taken by the Commission and the Council of what Member States should be doing in their NAPs:

> There is a clear learning process in the provision and presentation of the Member States' policy. The implementation reports are becoming more focused, while in some Member States, there is still an over-emphasis on individual initiatives, rather than a comprehensive, mutually supportive policy mix.
>
> The process of setting measurable objectives and targets should be strengthened. Under those guidelines that set common targets, policy progress is more visible, and an objective assessment of impact is made possible, on the basis of common indicators, underpinning further policy development.[8]

For those guidelines where there are no measurable targets, the role of the NAPs is, arguably, more important: the entire benchmarking and peer review process is dependent on what Member States choose to report in their annual NAPs. Thus the emphasis placed at Lisbon on establishing more quantitative and qualitative indicators[9] is essential to buttress the NAPs, by streamlining the management and presentation of policy, and thus increasing scope for comparisons of best practice. Lisbon also drew links between benchmarking, subsidiarity and 'partnership', all under the umbrella of the open method of co-ordination.[10] Such a multifaceted approach is also important in defining the role performed by the NAPs in this soft law regime: the 'fully decentralised approach' to the development of employment policy means that the regional and local levels, the social partners and civil society, are all to be actively involved by Member States.

---

[8] CEC, *Joint Employment Report 2000*, Brussels, p. 3.
[9] Presidency Conclusions, Lisbon European Council, 23 and 24 March 2000, Bull. EU 3-2000, 7–17, at para. 37.
[10] Ibid., at para. 38.

Indeed, the social partners are even given their own 'mini process'.[11] This suggests that the NAPs are better understood as tools of *management* than as tools of *regulation*. What is important is the process of putting the NAP together, the wide involvement of different parties and actors below the level of the nation state. For example, the *Joint Employment Report 2001* notes with approval the improving quality of the NAPs, and the involvement of an increasing number of partners in their preparation and follow-up.[12]

> The 2001 National Actions Plans for Employment (NAPs) provide a much clearer and more coherent presentation of Member States' employment policies than in previous years. This seems to reflect not only the continued commitment of Member States to the European co-ordination of national employment policies, but also the strengthening of the preparation process at national level. The elaboration of the NAPs involves an ever increasing number of actors at different levels – national, regional or local – and of different origins – different Ministries but also social partners – in a strong partnership approach. This trend is a positive factor for the better integration of employment policies with other related policies.[13]

Changes to the way in which policy developments referred to in the NAPs are presented can have an impact on the content of such policy. As Jacobsson argues, the Commission has a central role in managing knowledge and may function as an 'editor' of knowledge and ideas into standards, thereby exerting an indirect influence on policy content.[14] Thus, the legal significance of the NAPs lies not so much in the formal role attributed to them by the Title on Employment, as in the way Member States' interpretation of concepts such as employability and adaptability is managed by the Commission, and by the Council in its Recommendations. Knowledge

---

[11] '[T]he social partners are invited to develop, in accordance with their national traditions and practices, their own process of implementing the guidelines for which they have the key responsibility, identify the issues upon which they will negotiate and report regularly on progress, in the context of the National Action Plans if desired': Council Decision of 19 January 2001 on guidelines for Member States' employment policies for the year 2001 – n. 3 above.

[12] CEC, *Joint Employment Report 2001* (Luxembourg: OOPEC, 2002) (final version, 20.02.2002), p. 4.

[13] Ibid., p. 11.

[14] K. Jacobsson, 'Employment and Social Policy Coordination. A New System of EU Governance', paper for the Scancor workshop on Transnational Regulation and the Transformation of States, Stanford, 22–23 June 2001; manuscript on file with the author, p. 13.

is transformed into standards in the course of the benchmarking process, and in the tightening of the guidelines and the narrowing of the range of legitimate responses to unemployment.

2.1   The development of National Action Plans

In the view of the Commission, the purpose of the NAPs is to enable external scrutiny of what Member States have committed themselves to doing with regard to employment policies, so that it can be seen whether these commitments are in line with the contents and objectives of the Employment Guidelines.[15] NAPs are thus a key stage in the benchmarking process, and within the open method of co-ordination more generally, since they permit the Commission to assess the extent to which Member States have translated European guidelines into national and regional policies, by setting specific targets and adopting measures. In other words, NAPs (alongside the Commission's own system of performance indicators) provide an information resource from which Member States' employment performance can be monitored, evaluated and subjected to peer review.

This perspective on the function of NAPs for Employment is reinforced when one considers the proliferation of 'National Action Plans' – for social exclusion, for immigration policy, and for pensions reform, all areas which are now to be subject to the open method of co-ordination. A similar role is attributed to the NAPs in each of these divergent policy areas, which will follow the *modus operandi* of the Employment Strategy: a Joint Report, the establishment of common indicators, and then the submission of NAPs.

The Stockholm European Council had urged Member States to prioritise the implementation of National Action Plans for social inclusion, to achieve progress on the basis of the common objectives agreed in Nice, assessed by commonly agreed indicators.[16] In due course, the Laeken European Council in December 2001 was able to report how the first Joint Report on social inclusion and the establishment of a set of common indicators had furthered the policy defined at Lisbon for eradicating poverty and promoting social inclusion.[17] The first National Action Plans for social inclusion were submitted by Member States during June 2001, in response to the common objectives on poverty and social exclusion agreed in Nice. In these plans, each Member State presented its priorities

---

[15] CEC, *From Guidelines to Action: The National Action Plans for Employment*, n. 7 above, p. 1 of the Communication.
[16] Presidency Conclusions, Stockholm European Council, 23 and 24 March 2001, Bull. EU 3-2001, 1–40, at para. 28.
[17] Presidency Conclusions, Laeken European Council, 14 and 15 December 2001, at para. 28.

and efforts for the coming two years (July 2001 to June 2003) in promoting social inclusion and combating poverty and social exclusion. The second round of National Action Plans for social inclusion were published in July 2003.

In the case of immigration policy, the Commission also foresees the use of NAPs as a key element in realising a Community policy in this area:

> In order to implement each set of guidelines on immigration, Member States should prepare national action plans which will be reviewed and adapted on an annual basis. These would be in two parts so as to provide both an overview of results of the actions carried out in the previous year in relation to the European guidelines as well as proposals for the implementation of the migration guidelines in the year to come.[18]

Similarly, with regard to pensions reform, the Laeken European Council took note of the Joint Report on pensions drawn up by the Social Protection Committee and the Economic Policy Committee.[19] Although there is no specific reference to National Action Plans as such in the area of pensions reform, the Stockholm European Council does state that 'the potential of the open method of co-ordination should be used to the full' in the field of pensions, taking due account of the principle of subsidiarity,[20] with all that the OMC implies for resort to benchmarking, indicators and National Action Plans.

It is not surprising that, in those areas such as immigration and pensions reform where the competence of the Union to act is relatively new and still very much circumscribed, the perceived strength of the open method of co-ordination as a means of ensuring subsidiarity is brought to the foreground. This is particularly important in the context of immigration policy, which falls under the intergovernmental third pillar, on justice and home affairs.

To return to the NAPs for employment, it is clear that, as the open method of co-ordination has grown in sophistication, the NAPs too have evolved: in place of the rather perfunctory reports (such that the first set of NAPs were criticised for being too vague in some areas, or consisting of a mere list of initiatives)[21] we can now observe much more detailed

---

[18] CEC, *Communication from the Commission to the Council and the European Parliament on an Open Method Of Coordination for the Community Immigration Policy*, Brussels, 11.7.2001 COM (2001) 387 final, p. 12.

[19] Presidency Conclusions, Laeken European Council, n. 17 above, at para. 30.

[20] Presidency Conclusions, Stockholm European Council, n. 16 above, at para. 32.

[21] CEC, *From Guidelines to Action: The National Action Plans for Employment*, n. 7 above, p. 4 of the Communication.

accounts of policy implementation. This can be attributed to a number of factors: the intensification of the peer review process; the extension of benchmarking by reference to a greater number of performance indicators; the growing prescriptiveness of the Employment Guidelines and their greater resort to target-setting; and the annual adoption of Council Recommendations on Member States' employment policies – developments which have obliged Member States to use the NAPs to give a more revealing account of and insight into an otherwise opaque system of policy-making. Since most Member States' responses to the Employment Strategy are administrative rather than legislative in character, there is the danger that the elaboration of employment policy can take place at a purely inter-ministerial level, with little scope for public debate.[22] However, the obligation on Member States to ensure greater involvement of the social partners in policy-making over employment (which is unfailingly emphasised in every *Joint Employment Report*) and to document that this involvement is taking place,[23] serves to ensure more openness in the process of elaborating NAPs.

Commenting on the first set of NAPs for social inclusion, the Commission and Council reported that:

> most Member States have focused their efforts on improving co-ordination, refining and combining existing policies and measures and promoting partnership, rather than launching important new or innovative policy approaches . . . Thus, while most 2001 NAPs/incl are an important starting point in the process, in order to make a decisive impact on poverty and social exclusion further policy efforts will be needed in the coming years.[24]

---

[22] See, for example, the French NAP for 2001: 'The National Action Plan for Employment adopted by France for 2001 benefited from extensive interministerial preparations, involving the Ministry for Employment and Solidarity, the Ministry of the Economy, Finance and Industry, the Ministry for Education and the Ministry for Women's Rights and Vocational Training' – *France: National Action Plan for Employment 2001* (Luxembourg: OOPEC, 2001), p. 2; published by the Commission and available from the Commission's website at: http://europa.eu.int/comm/employment_social/news/2001/may/naps2001_en.html.

[23] The Dutch NAP for 2001, for example, details how, although the NAP is the full responsibility of the government, nevertheless the social partners were closely involved in drawing it up, with the use of tripartite consultation over the policy targets and measures in the NAP: *Netherlands: National Action Plan for Employment 2001* (Luxembourg: OOPEC, 2001), p. 3.

[24] CEC, *Draft Joint Report on Social Inclusion*, Brussels 12 December 2001, 15223/01, p. 9. This Joint Inclusion Report (JIR) was adopted by the Employment and Social Affairs Council on 3 December 2001 and submitted to the Laeken European Council on 14 December 2001.

The same could be said in the case of the NAPs for employment, which gradually moved away from describing measures already in train, formulated independently of the Employment Strategy.[25] As the Luxembourg process has over the years become more expertly managed by the Commission, so the NAPs for employment have developed in the way the Commission envisages the NAPs for social inclusion will develop: less a showcase for Member States' existing policies, and more a response to European-level guidelines and targets.[26]

2.2   What does compliance mean? Member States' compliance with the European Employment Strategy

What restrictions, if any, does the Employment Strategy place on the range of policy options open to Member States? Arguably, the issue of compliance with the Employment Strategy is much less troublesome than that of compliance with legislation, in particular with legislation enacted on the basis of qualified majority voting, which a given Member State may have opposed. Member States are being asked, through their NAPs, to show compliance with Guidelines which (a) they themselves have in large measure specified; and (b) cover such a wide range of labour market policies as to make it much harder for the Commission to measure 'compliance'. One should not overstate the distinction between the Community and the Member States: this distinction is less valid in the case of the Employment Strategy, which is much more intergovernmental than the supranationalist legislative procedures subject to Arts. 251 or 252 (the co-decision and co-operation procedures). Such intergovernmentalism is increasingly the case after the Lisbon summit re-affirmed the European Council's strategic responsibility for agenda setting, so that the heads of

---

[25] The first UK NAP, in 1998, is an excellent example of this: it was little more than a showcase for the employment policies of the New Labour government, which had been in office for one year, and dealt with New Labour policies which, for the most part, had the fortune to coincide with the objectives of the European Employment Strategy: (a) macroeconomic stability – stable public finances and low inflation; (b) increasing investment in education, training and human resources; (c) active labour market policies, in particular the 'New Deal', a programme designed to provide intensive support to the unemployed, especially the young and long-term unemployed, lone parents, people with disabilities and ex-offenders; (d) labour market flexibility – UK: Employment Action Plan 1998, Luxembourg: OOPEC, 1998, pp. 3–6.

[26] For example, '[t]he National Action Plan for Employment (NAP) 2001 outlines the progress made by the Netherlands in implementing the targets in the guidelines for 2001' – Netherlands: National Action Plan for Employment 2001 (n. 23 above), p. 3.

State and government are now responsible for 'taking on a pre-eminent guiding and coordinating role to ensure overall coherence and the effective monitoring of progress towards the new strategic goal'.[27]

One significant example of policy divergence which *does* appear to be permitted within the framework of the Employment Strategy relates to the French policy which is endeavouring to increase employment by means of reducing working time. The two 'Aubry' laws, of 13 June 1998 and 19 January 2000,[28] imposed an annual ceiling on working hours, to be implemented through collective agreements, which for most workers has been translated into a maximum 35-hour week. The explicit aim of the legislation was to create employment by distributing work, with the requirement that the 35-hour week not be accompanied by a comparable wage cut. According to the French Government, as at 16 August 2001, 364,000 jobs had been created or preserved since the adoption of the first Aubry law.[29]

However, economic orthodoxy is extremely dismissive of the idea that an economy supports a fixed level of employment, and that this lump of labour can be apportioned among a greater number of workers, with output remaining constant.[30] In the view of the OECD, for example, 'state funded early-retirement programmes and across-the-board work-sharing initiatives, such as legislated reductions in the work week that are not accompanied by adjustment of remuneration to productivity changes, are not viable long-term solutions to the unemployment problem'.[31] The European Employment Strategy clearly endorses the first part of this sentiment: one of the key elements in the objective of increasing the

---

[27] Presidency Conclusions, Lisbon European Council (n. 9 above), at para. 36.

[28] For a more detailed analysis, see Sylvaine Laulom in this volume.

[29] Laulom, this volume, quoting from the website of the French Labour Ministry on the application of the Aubry laws: www.35h.travail.gouv.fr.

[30] It is difficult to overstate just how dismissive most (orthodox) economists are of the notion that this lump of employment can be apportioned so that, whether there are fewer workers working more hours or more workers working fewer hours, output remains constant. This 'lump of labour' fallacy is one of *The Economist*'s favourite *bêtes noires*, rebutted by the argument that (a) technology creates new demand, either by increasing productivity and hence real incomes, or by creating new goods, and (b) the demand for labour depends upon labour costs and productivity, which are affected by the hours each employee works. See: 'Short Measure' *The Economist*, 31 January 1998, 346: 8053, p. 79; 'One Lump or Two?' *The Economist*, 25 October 1997, 345: 8040, p. 17. See also Charlotte Thorne, 'Another Country: France versus the Anglo-Saxon Economists', *FastFutures*, Industrial Society on-line essays, available at: www.indsoc.co.uk/futures/FastFuturesAnother.htm.

[31] OECD, *OECD Jobs Study: Implementing the Strategy* (Paris: OECD, 1995), p. 24.

employment rate is the targeted increase in the average employment rate among older workers (55 to 64) to 50 per cent by 2010,[32] thus reversing previous national policies which had encouraged early retirement.

What of the OECD's critique of legislated reductions in working time? The EU approach to employment creation rests essentially on supply-side principles – improving individuals' skills and employability, flexibilising work organisation and 'activating' welfare states to increase labour market participation rates. This approach by no means endorses the 'lump of labour fallacy' but neither does it appear to rule out the French approach to employment creation through reductions in working time. Indeed, the French NAPs repeatedly make reference to the Aubry laws as a response to many of the Employment Guidelines: for example, the objectives of the legislation happily coincide with the aims of the Adaptability pillar, and can also be promoted as a means of furthering the reconciliation of work and family life, as required by the Equal Opportunities pillar.

As far as the European response to the French approach is concerned, it would seem that the jury is out on the question of whether the improvements in the employment situation in France are truly attributable to the 35-hour week: the *Joint Employment Report 2000* goes so far as to say that the first Aubry law 'does not appear to be having an adverse effect on the competitiveness of enterprises';[33] whilst the Council Recommendations for 2001 and 2002 both advise that the French Government should 'closely monitor the net effects of the implementation of the 35-hour working week legislation'.[34] Thus, the French emphasis on the 35-hour week is acceptable within the context of the European Employment Strategy, *provided that* due emphasis is also placed on preventative measures and on increasing labour market participation, especially among older people, where the activity rate is among the lowest in the EU.

In essence, the French NAPs are a particularly striking example of what occurs to some extent in all the National Action Plans: national policies are being translated into the language of the EU guidelines, such that the NAPs become a platform for what the Member State would be doing

---

[32] Presidency Conclusions, Stockholm European Council (n. 16 above), at para. 9.

[33] CEC, *Joint Employment Report 2000* (n. 8 above), p. 123.

[34] Council Recommendation of 19 January 2001 on the implementation of Member States' employment policies (2001/64/EC), OJ L 22/27, 24.1.2001; Council Recommendation of 18 February 2002 on the implementation of Member States' employment policies (2002/178/EC), OJ L 60/70, 1.3.2002.

anyway.[35] However, it seems to me that the success of the French economy in creating jobs has helped to ameliorate any criticism that might
have been forthcoming of the economic thinking underlying the French
approach to employment creation: the *Joint Employment Report 2001*
observed that the French economy had witnessed a growth in employment of 2 per cent and a reduction in unemployment of −1.7 per cent.[36]
What is also important is that the French policy *as a whole*, as evidenced in
the NAPs, has adopted a growth-orientated macroeconomic philosophy
in line with that envisaged by the Employment Strategy,[37] with emphasis
on active labour market policies and development of human resources,
and in particular has made a concerted effort to address the Council's
Recommendations to the French Government.[38]

What, though, of policy which *does not* appear to be permitted within
the context of the Employment Strategy? One example is that of state-
sanctioned early retirement, encouraging workers to exit from the labour
market voluntarily, in the attempt to reduce unemployment by reducing
labour supply. Such a policy was certainly widespread across all Member
States up to the mid-1990s, although those with 'Continental' welfare
state regimes relied most heavily on this labour-shedding strategy.[39] The
interaction of a number of factors encouraged employers, trade unions
and governments to resort to early retirement strategies as a means to
combat mass unemployment: for example, the desire to ease industry
restructuring by offering 'soft landings' to workers with seniority; the
traditionally high normal retirement age (especially for men), combined
with a lower age at which workers could receive disability or incapacity benefits; the introduction of pre-retirement schemes (e.g. in Sweden,

---

[35] The French NAP for 2001 mentions the 35-hour week measure in the context of Guidelines 4 and 5 (education and training), 6 (recruitment and job-matching), 13 and 14
(adaptability) and 15 (lifelong learning) *France: National Action Plan for Employment
2001* – n. 22 above.

[36] CEC, *Joint Employment Report 2001* (n. 12 above), p. 54.

[37] 'Since the first National Action Plan for Employment was drafted in 1998, France's macroeconomic and structural policies, together with its proactive employment policy, have
resulted in a high rate of growth; it has continued with its efforts to raise its growth
potential. Growth has been maintained at more than 3 per cent': *France: National Action
Plan for Employment 2001* (n. 22 above), p. 6.

[38] 'This dialogue [between four government ministries] resulted in an organised synthesis
of the French employment strategy and, for the second year in a row, ensured compliance
with the European Council's recommendations for France': ibid., p. 2.

[39] Bernhard Ebbinghaus, 'When Labour and Capital Collude: The Varieties of Welfare Capi-
talism and Early Retirement in Europe, Japan and the USA', Working Paper No. 4, Center
for European Studies, Harvard University, 2000, p. 5.

Germany and France) to bridge the gap between early retirement and the normal pension age; and the relatively high replacement rate of public pensions.[40]

The European Round Table of Industrialists (ERT) adopted, as could be expected, a very critical perspective towards the culture of early retirement and early exit from the labour force:

> the Netherlands and the UK have implemented generous policies, not directly related to pensions, which give significant amounts of money to those who are leaving work because of disability or supposed disability. In countries like France and Italy early retirement schemes have been quite specifically used to ease people out of the labour market. All these disincentives, built into the social security systems throughout Europe, create an implicit tax on work: workers tend to leave the labour force through any existing loophole when the implicit tax on work is high.[41]

However, demographic changes throughout the EU – an aging population, increased longevity, plus significant reductions in labour force participation rates since the 1960s – have increased the dependency ratio, so that there are fewer working age employees to support the aging population. Such changes led many Member States, from the 1990s onwards, to adopt more market-orientated pension and retirement policies. Some Member States, notably Italy, are experimenting with the transition from a 'pay as you go' pension scheme, based on solidarity, with the working population paying for the retired population, to privatised or individually funded schemes, where workers invest in stock markets in order to fund their future pensions.

Member States are also responding to this demographic challenge at the European level, in the context of the Employment Strategy: the Stockholm European Council drew a clear link between, on the one hand, raising employment rates and, on the other, reducing public debt and reforming systems of social protection and pensions, so that these systems are sustainable.[42] However, what remains a very real question, when considering the issue of compliance with the Employment Strategy, is whether a Member State is free to 'solve' the demographic challenge by means other than those recommended by the Employment Strategy, for example, solutions which do not involve major reductions in welfare expenditure?

---

[40] Ibid.
[41] ERT, *European Pensions: An Appeal for Reform. Pension Schemes that Europe can Really Afford* (Brussels: ERT, 1999), p. 22; available at www.ert.be.
[42] Presidency Conclusions, Stockholm European Council (n. 16 above), at paras. 7 and 32.

Public opinion would appear to be resistant to any major departures from solidarity-based systems of pensions provision. For example, whilst arguing for a more radical reform of pensions systems, the ERT urged that governments must educate their publics to accept greater reforms of welfare states: 'The current size of the welfare state is supported by public opinion at large, not just by a powerful minority. In all four countries included in this survey [France, Germany, Italy and Spain] there is a majority against cutting it back.'[43] In the view of the ERT, early retirement is not yet effectively discouraged in some Member States.[44] The reality of such discouragement would be to reduce pension payments, limit eligibility or otherwise weaken early retirement and ill-health retirement schemes.

Although pensions policy is the prerogative of Member States, there is also a shared recognition that a rising EU pensions burden has major implications for the sustainability of public finances.[45] Thus, the Stability and Growth Pact and the Broad Economic Policy Guidelines, to which the Employment Strategy must conform, may well dictate the increased privatisation of pensions provision as a means of reducing public expenditure. Does this imply that Member States will be required to adopt a pattern of provision similar to that of the UK? 'In the UK, where private schemes make a relatively large contribution to pensioner incomes, the proportion of GDP needed to fund public pension provision should remain stable. In Spain and Greece, by contrast, unchanged policy suggests increases of 8 per cent and over 12 per cent of GDP respectively.'[46] The Barcelona European Council recommended that reform of pension systems be accelerated, to ensure that they are both financially sustainable and meet their social objectives.[47] In particular, the detrimental effect of early retirement on labour market participation had to be tackled. In the context

---

[43] ERT, *Pensions Reform: Europe Must Seize the Limited Opportunity* (Brussels: ERT, 2002); available at www.ert.be. A study by Boeri, Börsch-Supan and Tabellini found that a clear majority of voters support the overall size of the welfare state, opposing cuts to social security and welfare spending, but also opposing further increases in taxes and expenditure: T. Boeri, A. Börsch-Supan and G. Tabellini, 'Would You Like to Shrink the Welfare State? A Survey of European Citizens' (2001) *Economic Policy* pp. 8–50.

[44] ERT, High Level Meeting on Pension Reforms in Europe, Brussels, 31 October 2001, Summary of the Discussion, available at www.ert.be.

[45] HM Treasury White Paper, *Realising Europe's Potential: Economic Reform in Europe* (London: HMSO, 2002), Cm 5318, p. 23.

[46] Ibid.

[47] Presidency Conclusions, Barcelona European Council, 15 and 16 March 2002, Bull. EU 3-2002, 1–56, at para. 25.

of reinforcing the Lisbon strategy, the Barcelona European Council stated bluntly that: 'early retirement incentives for individuals and the introduction of early retirement schemes by companies should be reduced. Efforts should be stepped up to increase opportunities for older workers to remain in the labour market, for instance, through flexible and gradual retirement formulas and guaranteeing a real access to lifelong learning.'[48] Thus, it is likely that a Member State which was unwilling to contemplate disincentives to early retirement *and* was disinclined to reform its pensions provisions radically (for example, to move from a public pension system to a combination of privatised and occupational schemes) would find itself at odds with the requirements of the Employment Strategy, particularly with regard to the restrictive fiscal policy underlying the Strategy and the emphasis on increased labour market participation of older workers. To take one example: Belgium has the lowest participation rate among older workers and some of the highest taxes on labour in the EU.[49] In order to comply with the Employment Strategy, Belgium would need to implement a range of labour market reforms which, it could be argued, would undermine the social content of the welfare state.[50] In the context of the Broad Economic Policy Guidelines and the Employment Guidelines, Belgium is advised to: introduce further measures aimed at preventing the early withdrawal of workers; create adequate 'incentives' for older people to continue to work or re-enter the labour market; reduce taxes on labour; reduce social security contributions and reform benefit systems; and revise the special arrangements exempting older unemployed people (aged over 50) from active job search.[51] Fortunately for the sake of compliance with the Employment Strategy,

---

[48] Ibid., at para. 32.

[49] The employment rate for older workers is 26.3 per cent, 11.4 points below the Community average: Council Recommendation of 18 February 2002 on the implementation of Member States' employment policies (n. 34 above).

[50] 'A reduction in social security contributions by enterprises may appear to make the cost of labour cheaper and to encourage inward foreign direct investment. But this overlooks the question of who bears the cost of such contributions and what the costs of alternative provision would be. There are clear dangers that such competition will lead to an all round deterioration of public services and welfare state provision': European Economists for an Alternative Economic Policy in Europe, *Economic Policy against Recession and Polarisation in Europe: Proposals to Overcome Ideological Sterility and Policy Blockades* (Bremen: University of Bremen, 2001), p. 5; available at www.barkhof.uni-bremen.de/kua/memo/europe/euromemo/indexmem.htm.

[51] Council Recommendation, n. 34 above; and Council Recommendation of 15 June 2001 on the broad guidelines of the economic policies of the Member States and the Community (2001/483/EC), OJ L 179/1, 2.7.2001, at 19.

the political consensus in Belgium, as evidenced by the National Action Plans, appears to be in favour of such radical reforms. The NAP for 2001 describes the initiatives being introduced by the Federal Government – in collaboration with the social partners – to prolong working life, by means of a Fiscal Reform Plan, training programmes for older workers, reductions in working time, reductions in social security contributions for workers over fifty-eight, and other measures granting financial support to employers who retain or hire older workers.[52] Such measures are entirely in keeping with the Council Recommendations for Belgium and the BEPGs, and illustrate the convergence of policy responses to the demographic and employment challenges facing EU Member States.

The fact that there is such a convergence of opinion between the Belgian NAP and the Employment Strategy over both the *necessity for* and the *nature of* reform of the labour market and welfare state, is enormously instructive. It illustrates how the policy choices of individual Member States – even those which had, until recently, been following diametrically opposed policies or tolerating low rates of labour market participation – are constrained by the *collective consensus* at EU level with regard to fiscal restraint and high participation rates: in this context, early retirement is seen as imposing an unsustainable burden on increasingly fragile social security systems, as well as reducing the tax base. If this consensus extends to the adoption of the ERT's recommendations, it will result in the imposition of drastic reductions in the provision of public pensions, to make pensions less attractive and thus discourage early retirement.

It would seem, therefore, that the wide-ranging process of co-ordinating their employment policies has led to – or speeded up – a process of convergence in Member States' labour market reforms, to the extent that the differences identified by the OECD as recently as 1997 are no longer as valid. For example, the OECD noted that:

> The central issue dividing the more comprehensive reformers from the less comprehensive is differences in judgement about potential conflicts between better labour market performance and concerns for equity and social cohesion.
>
> A key reason for slow and sporadic implementation of the OECD Jobs Strategy is the perception that undertaking reform involves conflict with policy objectives concerning equity and social cohesion. In particular, concern has been expressed in some quarters that the Jobs Strategy

---

[52] *Belgium: National Action Plan for Employment 2001*, Luxembourg: OOPEC, p. 10.

recommendations to enhance wage flexibility and to reform social transfer systems would be at odds with the policy objectives of ensuring some degree of equity across members of the labour force or the population at large.[53]

In contrast to English-speaking countries, Continental European countries were identified as the ones most likely to be resistant to the reform measures recommended by the OECD's Jobs Strategy,[54] seeing equity as a more fundamental goal than low unemployment.[55] However, as illustrated by their NAPs, these same countries are now endorsing an EU Employment Strategy which advocates very similar reforms to social security systems, in particular with regard to social transfer systems, to those recommended by the OECD's *Jobs Study*.

Ultimately, one could argue that compliance with the Employment Strategy, and the Guidelines in particular, is best measured not simply by failure or success in meeting a centrally determined 'target' (though that, too, is important) but by assessing the extent to which Member States' understandings of what is a legitimate policy response to unemployment have been conditioned by the process of co-ordination. I would contend that the range of permissible policies has been narrowed, as Member States develop collective understandings of concepts such as 'full employment', 'employability' and 'active labour market policies'. The consistency with which the supply-side policies of the Employment Strategy are adopted by Member States makes it almost unthinkable for a Member State to contemplate encouraging early retirement, adopting passive labour market measures, or accepting low labour market participation. What remains to be seen is whether policies which leave 'rigid' labour market regulations unreformed still fall within the range of what is permissible or acceptable within the context of the Employment Strategy.

The soft law nature of the Guidelines, the lack of sanctions for failure to meet targets, and the openness to approaches such as the French 35-hour week, mask the fact that Member States face peer pressure to act in accordance with the main thrust of the Employment Strategy, and its 'policy mix' of four pillars. They further mask the fact that the policy 'experimentation' which is the hallmark of the open method of co-ordination

---

[53] OECD, *Implementing the OECD Jobs Strategy: Lessons from Member Countries' Experience* (Paris: OECD, 1997), p. 13.
[54] OECD, *The OECD Jobs Study: Evidence and Explanations* and *Facts, Analysis, Strategies* (Paris: OECD, 1994), p. 44.
[55] OECD (n. 53 above), p. 14.

in fact permits experimentation only within a framework firmly wedded to sound public finances, comprehensive economic reform and restructuring of welfare states and the labour market, thus limiting the extent to which Member States can depart from the Employment Strategy without also breaching the Broad Economic Policy Guidelines and the Stability and Growth Pact. By this reckoning, therefore, Member State compliance with the Employment Strategy is extremely high.

3   The Employment Strategy and the regulation of part-time work

The role of part-time work in the Employment Strategy is an ambiguous one. The preamble to the Framework Agreement on part-time work[56] describes the agreement as 'a contribution to the overall European strategy on employment'. This is in line with the Employment Guidelines for 2002 which make reference to part-time work as one of several types of flexible working arrangement which are essential to encourage 'active aging',[57] to help reconcile work and family life,[58] and to promote modernisation of work organisation more generally.[59] Further, the Broad Economic Policy Guidelines (BEPGs), with which the Employment Guidelines must comply,[60] stress the role of part-time work in enhancing labour market efficiency and promoting employment: '[l]abour markets have also tended to become more flexible, as indicated by the large contribution of the development of part-time and temporary employment to overall job creation'.[61]

By way of contrast, the objectives of the Part-Time Workers' Directive are stated as, *first* and foremost, to provide for the removal of discrimination against part-time workers and to improve the quality of part-time work; *secondly*, to facilitate the development of part-time work on a voluntary basis; and only *thirdly* to contribute to the flexible organisation of working time in a manner which takes into account the needs of employers and workers.[62]

---

[56] Council Directive 97/81/EC of 15 December 1997 concerning the Framework Agreement on part-time working concluded by UNICE, CEEP and the ETUC, amended by Council Directive 98/23/EC of 7 April 1998, OJ L 14, 20.01.98 and OJ L 131, 05.05.98.

[57] Council Decision of 18 February 2002 on guidelines for Member States' employment policies for the year 2002 (n. 3 above), Guideline 3.

[58] Ibid., Guideline 17.   [59] Ibid., Guideline 13.   [60] As provided by Art. 128(2) EC.

[61] Council Recommendation of 21 June 2002 on the broad guidelines of the economic policies of the Member States and the Community, OJ L 182, 11.07.2002, p. 6.

[62] Ibid., cl. 1: Purpose.

In an attempt to understand the interaction between the Directive and the Employment Strategy, and the differing objectives underpinning the regulation of part-time work (as outlined in the chapter by Paul Davies and Mark Freedland), the focus will be on two concepts, flexibility and 'quality in work', which figure so prominently in the discourse underlying the Employment Strategy, and, to a lesser extent, the Directive. The use of such *internally contested* notions as flexibility and quality illustrates the subtly divergent uses to which the regulation of part-time work is being put within the Directive, and within the Employment Strategy as a whole.

3.1   Flexibility and part-time work

The meaning of flexibility in the EU discourse is by no means clear or precise, but a significant component of this discourse is a tension between the emphasis on demand-side flexibility, focusing on the improvement of employment and competitiveness through a better (i.e. more flexible) organisation of work at the workplace,[63] and a perspective which sees flexibility as an issue of labour supply.[64] In the latter case, 'flexibility' would involve promoting 'atypical' forms of work, e.g. part-time work, temporary work, tele-working, to suit the priorities and lifestyle choices of workers, especially those with family commitments, in stark contrast to 'demand-side flexibility' which would 'grant employers greater autonomy to shape personnel practices to changing market conditions'.[65]

The two notions of flexibility often exist in parallel within the Employment Strategy. The Commission describes the Equal Opportunities pillar as recognising 'both the social need to counter discrimination and inequalities between women and men, and the economic loss resulting from not making full and effective use of the productive capacities of all sections of the population',[66] suggesting the use of non-standard work as a means of boosting the human capital of those formerly excluded from the labour market. This is particularly important in view of low

---

[63] See CEC, *Green Paper: Partnership for a New Organisation of Work*, Luxembourg: OOPEC, COM (97) 128 final.

[64] S. Deakin and H. Reed, 'The Contested Meaning of Labour Market Flexibility: Economic Theory and the Discourse of European Integration', in J. Shaw (ed.) *Social Law and Policy in an Evolving European Union* (Oxford: Hart Publishing, 2000), p. 74.

[65] Ibid., pp. 74–5.

[66] The Commission's summaries of the four pillars are taken from the website of the Directorate General for Employment and Social Affairs on the European Employment Strategy, at: http://europa.eu.int/comm/employment_social/empl&esf/ pilar_en.htm.

employment rates across the EU,[67] and, in particular, the gender gap in labour market participation: in 1997, the proportion of women employed in the EU was still only around 51 per cent of women of working age, some 20 percentage points below the rate for men,[68] a gap which only narrowed to 18 percentage points by 2001.[69]

An important feature of the fourth pillar is that, following the 1999 Guidelines, gender equality is to be mainstreamed throughout the entire Employment Strategy. However, this serves to highlight the difficulty of pursuing a job creation agenda whilst also attempting to realise fundamental rights – in this case, the right to gender equality. Similarly, under the Adaptability pillar, Member States are urged to revise their systems of employment legislation in order to permit more adaptable forms of labour, whilst at the same time to ensure that those working under such contracts should enjoy adequate security and higher occupational status, *compatible with the needs of business.*[70] However, if the tortuous history behind the adoption of the Part-Time Workers' Directive[71] and the case law of the European Court of Justice (ECJ) on part-time workers' rights[72] shows us anything, it is the fact that 'atypical' work, in its many forms, is precisely the sort of area where many Member States are most resistant

---

[67] The total employment rate for the EU 15 was 63.9% in 2001, ranging from 76.2% in Denmark to 54.8% in Italy: CEC, Communication from the Commission to the Council, *Draft Joint Employment Report 2002*, Brussels, 13.11.2002, COM (2002) 621 final, p. 111.

[68] CEC, *Green Paper: Partnership for a New Organisation of Work* (n. 63 above), p. 74.

[69] CEC (n. 67 above).

[70] Originally Guideline 13, now Guideline 14; emphasis added. The 2001 Employment Guidelines, the first revision following the Lisbon European Council, however, added that such security and higher occupational status also had to be compatible with 'the aspirations of workers': Council Decision of 19 January 2001 on guidelines for Member States' employment policies for the year 2001 (2001/63/EC), OJ L 22/18, 24.1.2001.

[71] See M. Jeffery, 'The Commission Proposals on "Atypical Work": Back to the Drawing-Board . . . Again' (1995) 24: 3 *Industrial Law Journal* pp. 296–9, and 'Not Really Going to Work? Of the Directive on Part-time Work, "Atypical Work" and Attempts to Regulate It' (1998) 27: 3 *Industrial Law Journal* pp. 193–213.

[72] Since 1986 (Case 170/84 *Bilka-Kaufhaus* [1986] ECR 1607) atypical workers have benefited from European Community sex discrimination law, on the grounds that in some circumstances it may be indirectly discriminatory to exclude part-time workers from employment protection provisions, since this group is predominantly female. However, the ECJ's jurisprudence on the circumstances under which such less favourable treatment of part-time workers can be objectively justified is far from predictable. For example, in Case C-317/93 *Nolte* [1995] ECR I-4625, and Case C-444/93 *Megner and Scheffel* [1995] ECR I-4741, the ECJ took an approach which was much more tolerant of state-level exemptions of part-time work from protective legislation.

to extending the full protection and benefits afforded to 'typical' workers. The Guidelines promote the use of atypical forms of work because these are considered to have advantages over traditional forms of work: encouraging the use of part-time work is seen as a means of increasing the level of employment[73] as well as improving competitiveness and productivity.[74] However, these advantages exist principally because atypical workers have traditionally been excluded from high levels of employment protection; often, the very *purpose* of atypical work was to provide a way of circumventing legislative and collective regulations, and their associated costs.[75] As Sandra Fredman shows, in recent years there has been a 'remarkable convergence' between arguments based on market efficiency and fundamental rights rationales; however, particularly in the case of the Part-Time Workers' Directive and the Fixed-Term Work Directive,[76] the result has been a 'significant dilution of standards'.[77]

It is submitted that a better way to understand the role of part-time work in the context of the Employment Strategy is as an aid to job creation through the improvement of labour supply – partly by promoting integration into the labour market of previously excluded or under-represented groups, partly by removing 'disincentives' to participation from tax and benefit systems. The BEPGs for 2002, for example, recommend that Member States should:

> adapt tax and benefit systems to make work pay and encourage the search for jobs. Reduce high marginal effective tax rates, in particular for low wage earners, and reduce unemployment traps. Address incentive effects of benefit schemes, such as conditionality of benefits, eligibility, duration, the replacement rate, as well as availability of in-work benefits and the use of tax credits, in order to make the systems more employment friendly; in addition, review administrative systems and management rigour. Reduce incentives for early retirement. Step up efforts to increase opportunities for

---

[73] CEC, *From Guidelines to Action: The National Action Plans for Employment*, including a Commission Communication, and a Background Report (Luxembourg: OOPEC, 1998); COM (98) 316 final, p. 18.

[74] CEC, *Green Paper: Partnership for a New Organisation of Work* (n. 63 above), 'Introduction'.

[75] See Jeffery, 'Not Really Going to Work?' (n. 71 above), p. 210; see also S. Deakin and G. Morris, *Labour Law* (London: Butterworths, 1998), chapter 3.

[76] Council Directive 99/70/EC of 28 June 1999 concerning the Framework Agreement on fixed-term work concluded by UNICE, CEEP and the ETUC, OJ L 175, 10.07.1999.

[77] S. Fredman, 'Discrimination Law in the EU: Labour Market Regulation or Fundamental Rights?' in H. Collins, P. Davies and R. Rideout (eds.), *Legal Regulation of the Employment Relation* (W. G. Hart Legal Workshop Series, London / The Hague: Kluwer, 2000), p. 191.

older workers to remain in the labour market, in order to increase by about five years the effective average retirement age in the EU by 2010, thereby increasing their labour market participation.[78]

In setting the goal of 'full employment',[79] the Lisbon European Council signalled a strategic shift in emphasis within the Employment Strategy, towards a focus on 'modernising' welfare states. The Lisbon strategy talked of 'modernising the European social model by investing in people and building an active welfare state', to which the Barcelona European Council added that '[a]n active welfare state should encourage people to work, as employment is the best guarantee against social exclusion'.[80] Ultimately, this discourse on 'modernising' welfare states in order to achieve full employment necessitates a shift from extensive employment protection and social benefits, towards investment in human capital, with the aim of improving 'employability' and self-sufficiency of individuals. Thus, social inclusion is to be achieved by equalising the marketability and employability of individuals, rather than protecting them from the market.

Such an emphasis on investment in human capital can be seen in the Employment Guidelines which urge the adoption of positive measures to maintain working capacity and skills of older workers and the introduction of flexible working arrangements such as part-time work, in order to enhance the capacity of, and incentives for, older workers to stay longer at work.[81] Similarly, an equal sharing of family responsibilities is considered crucial in order to support 'the entry of women and men into, and their continued participation in, the labour market',[82] thus necessitating '[p]olicies on career breaks, parental leave and part-time work, as well as flexible working arrangements which serve the interests of both employers and employees' and the speedy implementation of the various directives and social-partner agreements in this area.

---

[78] Council Recommendation of 21 June 2002 on the broad guidelines of the economic policies of the Member States and the Community (n. 61 above), p. 14.

[79] Whilst there is no explicit definition of full employment, an indication is given in the targets set for Member States – raising the overall employment rate to as close as possible to 70% by 2010, and the female employment rate to more than 60%: Presidency Conclusions, Lisbon European Council, 23 and 24 March 2000, Bull. EU 3-2000, pp. 7–17, at para. 30.

[80] Presidency Conclusions, Barcelona European Council, Bull. EU 3-2002, pp. 1–59, at para. 22.

[81] Employment Guidelines for 2002 (n. 57 above), Guideline 3.

[82] Ibid., Pillar 4.

That this discourse on flexibility as a tool of employment creation also permeated the Part-time Workers' Directive can be seen in the text of the Framework Agreement on Part-time Work. The preamble to the Agreement refers to the 'need for similar agreements relating to other forms of flexible work', the assumption presumably being that there would soon follow framework agreements covering fixed-term work, home-working and agency work. Furthermore, the fourth paragraph under the heading 'General Considerations' draws on the conclusions of the Essen European Council, which emphasised the need for measures aimed at 'increasing the employment intensiveness of growth, in particular by more flexible organization of work in a way which fulfils both the wishes of employees and the requirements of competition'.[83]

Member States' response to the need to 'flexibilise' their labour markets has resulted, as the *Joint Employment Report for 2001* noted, in 'a general trend towards new and flexible forms of work, facilitating the introduction and use of fixed-term contracts, temporary work and part-time work . . . through collective agreements'.[84] These measures, however, have tended to adopt a narrow approach to work organisation with little focus on the quality of work,[85] and there is, ultimately, little evidence of the wholesale modernisation of Member States' regulatory regimes envisaged by the Employment Strategy. For example, in relation to the annual Country-Specific Economic Policy Guidelines contained in the BEPGs, the 2002 implementation report noted that better and more consistent progress had been made by Member States in implementing the capital market and product market recommendations, than with regard to their implementation of the labour market recommendations.[86] In particular: '[s]everal Member States (Germany, Spain, France, Italy, Portugal) need to go further in reforming the existing regulatory framework with a view to combining greater flexibility with security in order to reduce structural unemployment and labour market segmentation.'[87] Tellingly, the Council of Ministers for Economic and Financial Affairs recommended,

---

[83] Presidency Conclusions, Essen European Council, 9 and 10 December 1994, Bull. EU 12-1994.
[84] CEC, *Joint Employment Report 2001* (Luxembourg: OOPEC, 2002) (final version, 20.02.2002), p. 32.
[85] Ibid., p. 33.
[86] CEC, *Report on the Implementation of the 2001 Broad Economic Policy Guidelines*, Brussels, 21.02.2002, ECFIN/16/02-EN, pp. 37–48.
[87] Ibid., p. 24.

in its proposals for the Barcelona European Council, that '[p]olicy action should focus on modernising the labour market in order to support the process of employment creation'.[88] This would necessitate not only continuing efforts towards active labour market policies and reducing the tax burden on labour, but also (i) reform of wage formation systems to allow greater differentiation of wages according to productivity developments and skills differentials; (ii) improvement in labour market efficiency through supply-side measures such as increased mobility, and education and training; and (iii) a review of labour legislation, to assess the costs attached to the formulation and termination of employment contracts, with a view to striking a proper balance between flexibility and social protection.[89]

Part-time work is one of the most prominent forms of atypical work which Member States are promoting, in the effort to encourage employment creation and modernise work organisation, in line with the Adaptability pillar. With regard to striking a proper balance, however, it is by no means clear that Member States are matching the liberalisation of labour market regulation so as to encourage atypical work, with the requisite assurances that those working under such flexible contracts 'enjoy adequate security and higher occupational status, compatible with the needs of business *and the aspirations of workers*'.[90]

Member States are at different stages of development, so it is inevitable that, with regard to flexibility of capital, labour and product markets, 'the precise nature of such flexibility is likely to differ from one national factor market to another'.[91] However, in the absence of 'social benchmarking'[92] or a sufficiently strong normative framework to balance the 'hard co-ordination' mechanisms of EMU and the Stability and Growth Pact, there is the danger that such balancing will inevitably favour the dominant criterion by which progress in employment policy and labour market reform is currently evaluated, namely, an economic criterion

---

[88] Economic and Financial Affairs Council, 'Key Issues Paper on the 2002 Broad Economic Policy Guidelines', paper annexed to the Presidency Conclusions, Barcelona European Council (n. 47 above), at para. 37.

[89] Ibid., at para. 39.

[90] Guideline 14, Council Decision of 19 January 2001 on guidelines for Member States' employment policies for the year 2001 (n. 70 above); emphasis added.

[91] Hodson and Maher, 'The Open Method' (n. 5 above), p. 735.

[92] The Lisbon European Council raised the possibility of extending the benchmarking procedure to social protection, and the combating of poverty and social exclusion. See also C. de la Porte, P. Pochet and G. Room, 'Social Benchmarking, Policy Making and New Governance in the EU' (2001) 11: 4 *Journal of European Social Policy* 291–307 p. 295.

which emphasises the requirements of competitiveness and labour market efficiency.

3.2   Quality in work

Despite the call at Lisbon for not just *more*, but also *better* jobs, it remains to be seen whether the discourse on full employment can prevent the pursuit of higher labour market participation rates leading to low-quality jobs. In particular, the 'disincentive discourse' is still prevalent in the BEPGs, which present extensive work protection and social benefits as a disincentive to take up work and therefore as an obstacle to more jobs.[93]

However, the EU institutions – at the Nice and Stockholm European Councils, in the Commission Communication on Quality – have made efforts to incorporate a discourse on 'quality' into the discourse on 'quantity'. In particular, the Stockholm European Council, whilst setting intermediate targets for achieving full employment,[94] also gave a much fuller definition of what 'quality' would involve,[95] which was further developed in the Commission Communication:

> increasing quality in work by increasing skills and/or by increasing job satisfaction may increase productivity. Increasing quality by providing a better work–life balance, and by increasing the attractiveness of work, may contribute to increasing the overall employment rate and the employment rate of women and older workers. Increasing quality may contribute to increasing employability and adaptability, it may facilitate organisational change and increase access. In this way, increasing quality in work can form

---

[93] Council recommendation of 19 June 2000 on the broad guidelines of the economic policies of the Member States and the Community, OJ L 210, 21.08.2000, 1–40, at para. 2.1; see also Council Recommendation of 21 June 2002 on the broad guidelines of the economic policies of the Member States and the Community (n. 61 above), at 182/6.

[94] The new target is now employment rates of 67% overall and 57% for women, by January 2005, as well as a new target of 50% employment for older workers (aged 55 to 64) by 2010: Presidency Conclusions, Stockholm European Council, 23 and 24 March 2001, Bull. EU 3-2001, 1–40, at para. 9.

[95] 'Regaining full employment not only involves focusing on more jobs, but also on better jobs. Increased efforts should be made to promote a good working environment for all including equal opportunities for the disabled, gender equality, good and flexible work organisation permitting better reconciliation of working and personal life, lifelong learning, health and safety at work, employee involvement and diversity in working life': ibid., at para. 26.

part of a virtuous circle of increasing productivity, rising living standards and sustainable economic growth.[96]

Whilst generally dismissing fears that increasing employment in the service sector would lead to a proliferation of dead-end jobs of low quality,[97] this upbeat assessment of the harmonious interaction between social and economic policy does acknowledge that new and flexible employment patterns may conflict with some of the main dimensions of job quality, especially in jobs which combine low or no skills with temporary or precarious status and lack of career development opportunities.

Indeed, the Commission's own report on recent trends in employment found some evidence that changing forms of employment and ever-tighter rhythms of work have prevented working conditions from improving.[98] Although part-time workers report similar rates of job satisfaction to full-time workers, the quality of their jobs – in terms of earnings, job protection and career prospects – is mixed. More worryingly, over a third of temporary contractual relationships can generally be described as involuntary: 'Involuntary temporary contracts seem particularly pronounced in Spain, Greece, Belgium, Portugal, Sweden, and Finland, with more than half of all employed in temporary contracts declaring themselves to be so [involuntarily]'.[99] Therefore, an increase in the employment rate brought about by an increase in the use of temporary contracts or involuntary part-time work can be problematic, given the aim of ensuring quality in employment, since both these forms of atypical work are generally related to strong degrees of workers' dissatisfaction with their jobs.[100]

As mentioned above, the purpose of the Framework Agreement on Part-time Work is stated primarily to be the removal of discrimination against part-time workers and the improvement in the quality of part-time work. This is to be achieved by means of equal treatment of part-time workers and comparable full-time workers. However, the principle of equal treatment is no guarantee that there will be job security, access

---

[96] CEC, *Communication from the Commission to the Council, the European Parliament, the Economic and Social Committee and the Committee of the Regions. Employment and Social Policies: A Framework for Investing in Quality*, COM (2001) 313 final, Brussels, 20.6.2001, p. 8.

[97] Ibid., p. 9.

[98] CEC, *Employment in Europe 2001: Recent Trends and Prospects* (Luxembourg: OOPEC, 2001), p. 66.

[99] Ibid., p. 69. In 2000, 14.5% of women and 12.5% of men in employment were in temporary contracts: ibid., p. 17.

[100] Ibid., p. 71; see also CEC, *Employment in Europe 2002: Recent Trends and Prospects* (Luxembourg: OOPEC, 2002), p. 82.

to training or career development opportunities for part-time workers, particularly in view of the fact that the majority of part-time workers are located in workplaces which are highly segregated along gender lines,[101] making comparison with high-quality full-time jobs extremely difficult. The extent to which the Agreement and Directive can improve the quality of part-time jobs is particularly important when one considers that, although such jobs of low quality may ease the access of unemployed people into the labour market, they face a higher risk of subsequent unemployment and inactivity.[102] Further, on the question of quality of part-time work, studies show that job quality (as measured on a scale measuring good jobs; jobs of reasonable quality; low-paid, low-productivity jobs; and finally, dead-end jobs) is on average lower for part-time workers, with almost half of them in dead-end or low-paid, low-productivity jobs.[103] However, the Directive and Framework Agreement do not provide for compulsion: Clause 5 on Opportunities for Part-time Work merely urges that 'as far as possible, employers should give consideration to' requests to transfer between full- and part-time work, and measures to facilitate access to part-time work at all levels of the enterprise. As Jeffery notes,[104] the Directive does not impose any legal obligations on employers to ensure, where there are no comparable full-time workers, that part-time work must be of good or reasonable quality.

4 Conclusions

It has been argued that Member State compliance with the Employment Strategy is in fact extremely high in spite of the absence of 'hard law' sanctions, due in part to the self-policing aspect of the Strategy, the Commission's intensive scrutiny of Member States' policies in the context of the open method of co-ordination, and the growing consensus between Member States as to the range of 'acceptable' responses to the problem of unemployment. The process of co-ordination of employment and economic policies has led to a process of convergence around a growth-orientated macroeconomic philosophy, supply-side agendas, active labour market policies (committed to the reduction of benefit dependency and the strengthening of labour market attachment), the

---

[101] See CEC, *Employment in Europe 2002* (n. 100 above), pp. 36–43; and A. McColgan, 'Missing the Point? The Part-time Workers (Prevention of Less Favourable Treatment) Regulations 2000 (SI 2000, No. 1551)' (2000) 29: 3 *Industrial Law Journal* pp. 260–7.

[102] See CEC, *Employment in Europe 2002* (n. 100 above), pp. 10 and 87.

[103] Ibid., p. 82.   [104] See Jeffery, 'Not Really Going to Work?' (n. 71 above), p. 197.

promotion of labour market participation, wage restraint, and flexible work organisation. Thus, an Employment Strategy consisting almost entirely of soft law mechanisms has nevertheless been able to Europeanise national policy.

With regard to the goals of 'flexibility' and 'adaptability', such soft law co-ordination of national policies is supplemented by a number of hard law measures such as the Part-time Workers' Directive. Whilst the objectives of this Directive overlap to a great extent with those of the Employment Strategy there are, however, important differences in emphasis. Whereas the Employment Strategy and guidelines view the use of part-time work essentially as a tool of job creation, the Directive places greater weight on the removal of discrimination against part-time workers and the quality of such work. The attempt, since Lisbon, to integrate social policy with economic and employment policy discourse has yet to result in sufficiently strong institutional means by which social rights can be built into the Employment Strategy, especially since economic policy in the form of the BEPGs continues to emphasise a shift from extensive social protection, 'rigid' labour markets and disincentives to job creation. Thus, in respect of the wider question of the regulation of 'atypical' forms of work, it remains an open question whether the interaction between the overarching Employment Strategy and specific regulatory measures such as the Part-time Workers' Directive can successfully reconcile competing discourses on flexibility and security, quality and quantity in job creation.

3

The role of EU employment law and policy in the de-marginalisation of part-time work: a study in the interaction between EU regulation and Member State regulation

PAUL DAVIES AND MARK FREEDLAND

1 Introduction

In this chapter, we advance some suggestions towards a general assessment of the significance which EU law and policy have had and are having in the regulation of part-time work in the Member States whose experience is recounted and analysed in other chapters of this work. Our starting point is that, in those Members States, there has occurred, since the early 1980s, a process which we can identify as the de-marginalisation of part-time work. That is to say, part-time work has moved from the outer edges of employment policy and practice towards the central area of the labour market. Our inquiry is to understand what impact EU regulation has had and is having on that process.

We concentrate on EU measures or interventions specifically directed to part-time work, particularly the Part-time Work Directive of 1997, but also the part-time work element in the EU Employment Guidelines. However, those measures or interventions have to be seen in the context of a larger set of measures and interventions which bear upon or regulate part-time work, at both national and supranational levels. For example, specific measures or interventions cannot be seen in isolation from more general ones designed to stimulate employment and combat social exclusion, to regulate basic labour standards, or to control gender discrimination in employment. Nevertheless it is useful to single out measures and interventions which are specific to part-time work for a case-study of interaction between EU regulation and member state regulation.

It is important to identify from the outset what we have in mind when depicting this volume as a whole, and this chapter in particular, as a study in the *interaction* between the EU regulation of part-time work and its regulation in and by the Member States which are surveyed. Our primary concern, which is a conventional one, is with the impact of EU regulation upon the law, policy and practice of Member States with regard to part-time work. However, perhaps less conventionally, we are also concerned with the EU regulation of part-time work as itself, to a significant extent, the product or reflection of Member State regulation. Moreover, we suggest that the Member State regulation, which is thus reflected in the EU regulation of part-time work, displays a particularly subtle and interesting pattern of convergences and divergences between Member States since the early 1980s.

This chapter seeks to explain and pursue those concerns, and to show how this study might usefully be understood in terms of them. It is in this sense that we hope to be able to provide an analysis of the interaction between EU regulation and Member State regulation with regard to part-time work. That analysis will lead on to a further question, which it is important to approach with an open mind. If we can succeed in establishing a convincing or robust analysis of the interaction between EU regulation and Member State regulation in this particular area, there will be an inevitable temptation to see that analysis as a possible paradigm for the interaction between EU regulation and Member State regulation across a wider area of employment law and policy, perhaps for instance the whole area of regulation of 'atypical' or 'flexible' forms of employment. It is important to be open to that possibility, but no less important to be sceptical about it, and to question it rather than to assume it. So we shall engage in some concluding discussion of that possibility, but it will be decidedly tentative in its character. Meanwhile we proceed with the attempt to carry out our primary task, first by constructing a framework of analysis, and then by suggesting how the succeeding chapters of this volume might be seen as fitting into that framework.

2   Establishing a framework of analysis

Our framework of analysis takes the following form. Firstly, we identify the notion of an abstract and functional framework which is suitable for application to any given body of regulation of part-time work. We suggest how such a framework might be constructed by reference firstly to the objectives, secondly to the approaches, and thirdly to the techniques of regulation of part-time work. Secondly we seek to show how such a framework gives rise to a set of questions which may usefully be posed about the evolution and the actuality of regulation of part-time work in each particular member state, in terms of both its domestic policy agenda and the impact of Community law and policy. We seek to suggest how that Community impact might usefully be approached with reference not only to the Part-time Work Directive but also to the Employment Guidelines.

Firstly, then, as to the notion of an abstract and functional framework we suggest as follows. Here, we are seeking to identify a set of regulatory objectives, approaches and techniques, any or all of which might characterise a given regime for part-time work. This set of possible objectives, approaches and techniques is not derived from any one national regime, nor from the regime of Community law; indeed, it is important that the framework should be a free-standing one in that sense. In fact, we seek to derive it largely from our overall reading of the national studies which form the core of this book. The purpose of the framework is to display the commonalities and the differences between the regulatory structures which they describe.

2.1   Objectives

We suggest that there emerge from the national studies three possible sets of objectives which the regulation of part-time work may aim to achieve.

1. Improving or protecting workers' quality of life. Regulating part-time work, when it has this objective, may be seen as being part of a set of measures directed at improving the quality or security of people's working lives, or their work–life balance. This could be referred to as the worker protection rationale for the regulation of part-time work.
2. Increasing the employment rate in the economy (i.e. the percentage of those of working age who are in employment). From this perspective, the regulation of part-time work should aim to induce those who are unemployed to come on to the labour market, or persuade those who are already in employment to remain there, as part-time workers. Measures having this objective might form part of a programme directed at combating social exclusion.
3. Increasing the competitive efficiency of employing enterprises by facilitating the matching of the supply of labour to the demands of employers for workers. From this perspective, the regulation of part-time work might be part of a set of measures aimed at promoting the labour flexibility of productive enterprises.

2.2   Compatibility between objectives

Given that the main possible objectives which those engaged in the regulation of part-time work may be pursuing are those of inclusiveness, flexibility, and worker protection, the question arises whether, and if so how far, those objectives can be pursued in conjunction with each other. In other words, how far does the lawmaker have to choose *between* those objectives when constituting the regime for part-time work? In general terms, we are not putting these forward as mutually exclusive objectives. However, this is not to say that these objectives are mutually compatible in all conditions. The compatibility between these objectives is conditioned to an important extent by the particular conception which is held of each of them, and of the regulatory strategies which will best achieve each objective.

Thus, for example, in relation to the objectives of inclusion and flexibility, a rule-maker might have a strategy for part-time work which was so strongly de-regulatory as to impair the parallel pursuit of the third objective. On the other hand, with regard to the objective of worker protection, the rule-maker might have a conception of that objective which was so integrally associated with the model of full-time employment that it pointed overwhelmingly towards the restriction of part-time work, and hence rendered the pursuit of the other two objectives inadmissible so far as part-time work was concerned. Our framework thus contemplates a partial though not complete compatibility between these three objectives.

Within that zone of compatibility, the law-maker is free though not obliged to pursue more than one objective in its regulation of part-time work. Much of the current regulation of part-time work takes place within that zone, or at least is regarded or presented by its protagonists as doing so. For example, measures which equalise the conditions of part-time work with those of full-time work can be regarded and are frequently presented as serving the objectives not only of worker protection but also of employment stimulation and social inclusion (by making part-time work more attractive to those in the labour market or capable of being drawn into it).

2.3   Regulatory approaches

Our analytical framework envisages the law- and policy-makers who are concerned with the regulation of part-time work not only as having a set of choices between objectives, but also as having further sets of choices as to how to achieve them. One of those choices is between *regulatory approaches*. We distinguish between:

1. approaches which consist of *discouraging or restricting* part-time work; for example, the hiring of part-time workers might be made dependent on the collective consent of the corresponding set of full-time workers.
2. approaches which consist of *moderating* the relationship between the terms on which part-time work is performed and those on which full-time work is performed; for example, part-time workers might be accorded rights to pro rata treatment with the corresponding set of full-time workers.
3. approaches which consist of *encouraging* part-time work; for example, subsidies might be provided for employing workers on a part-time basis.

These approaches may be applied either to part-time work generally or to particular types of part-time work; thus, for example, the rule-maker might restrict part-time working involving a very small number of hours per week, within a general policy of encouraging part-time work above that threshold.

2.4   Regulatory techniques

We also envisage those who are concerned with the regulation of part-time work as making a further set of choices, namely between the regulatory *techniques* which they may deploy. Here we distinguish, broadly speaking, between two kinds of techniques, namely those of 'hard law' and 'soft law'. The distinction is, of course, itself a soft or 'fuzzy' one, but in this context at least it is useful to make such a distinction between, on the one hand, specific normative propositions, especially addressed to employing enterprises, as to the circumstances and conditions in which arrangements for part-time work may be made, and, on the other hand, less specifically directorial measures or policy pronouncements which create incentives or disincentives for part-time work, either generally or in particular circumstances and conditions.

2.5   Relationship between objectives, approaches and techniques

We envisage an essentially fluid and interactive relationship between these sets of objectives, approaches and techniques. There is nothing resembling a direct, static, or one-to-one relationship between them. The most likely relationship is that changing preferences between sets of approaches and techniques will reflect either changing choices of priorities between objectives, or changing ways of conceptualising particular objectives. For example, the introduction of a right, or entitlement, for a worker to move between full-time and part-time work might reflect a greater prioritisation of the second objective by encouraging older workers to opt for part-time work rather than retirement. It might, equally well, reflect a changed way of conceptualising the objective of worker protection, so that this objective was less closely tied to the full-time work model and more closely related to enabling a worker to strike an appropriate balance between work and non-work commitments. This shift of objectives might contribute towards a change in approach, from encouragement or discouragement of part-time work towards moderation of the conditions for part-time work. It might contribute to a shift of technique from soft law to hard law. Those shifts, however, would not follow directly or ineluctably from the shift in objectives. The relationship in the shifts between objectives, approaches and techniques would be one which was highly contingent upon the history and profile of regulation of part-time work in the particular national system concerned.

2.6   Applying this analysis to particular national systems

This brings us to the second part of our discussion of our suggested framework of analysis, in which we suggest how that analysis might usefully be applied to particular national systems. The central focus of this study is to identify and assess the interaction between European Community measures and policy on the regulation of part-time work and the measures and policies formulated within the national systems of Member States. For this purpose we shall firstly seek to identify a particular set of EC measures or policies whose impact we think it useful to consider in this context. This will place us in a position, secondly, to suggest a particular form in which the inquiry about their interaction with the national systems might usefully be pursued.

2.7   The relevance of the Employment Guidelines

We have always regarded it as obvious, so far as the impact of EC measures and policies is concerned, that the Part-time Work Directive should be accorded a central place. Less obvious, but nevertheless highly germane to our particular project, are the annually revised Employment Guidelines, which demonstrate a continuing Community interest in the regulation of part-time work. In addition to the specific references to the regulation of part-time work which are to be found throughout the Guidelines, these recommendations express a set of broad policy objectives whose furthering can be seen to suggest modification of national regimes for part-time work. It would seem useful to begin to assess whether such modification has occurred, for example, by identifying the treatment of part-time work in National Action Plans.

2.8 Pursuing the inquiry into the interaction between EU regulation and Member State regulation

Our purpose here is to suggest that the inquiry into the impact of this set of EU measures and/or policies upon the evolution of national systems should be conducted on the footing that our initial concern is to identify the particular evolution of measures and policies with regard to part-time work which is taking place within each national system, so that the impact, if any, of the EU set of measures and policies can be assessed in a fully contextual sense. So the first stage of our inquiry will accordingly be to consider what evolution of measures and policies, of regulatory objectives, approaches, and techniques was occurring, with regard to part-time work, within a particular national system during an appropriately identified period before the introduction of the Part-time Work Directive and the Employment Guidelines. The appropriate period varies from national system to national system, and we shall seek to identify and clarify the different starting points of Member States in relation to the regulation of part-time work. In many cases the appropriate period begins in the early 1980s, the point at which serious debate about the regulation of part-time work at Community level got under way.

That first stage leads on to the second stage, where the idea is explored that the Part-time Work Directive and the part-time work elements in the EU Employment Guidelines are themselves to a singular extent shaped by and reflexive of the national evolutions which were identified at the first stage. That is one part of a process of interaction between EU regulation and Member State regulation of part-time work. That discussion is complemented and completed by the third and final stage of the inquiry, where we consider what, if any, re-balancing or re-prioritisation of regulatory objectives or regulatory approaches the law- and policy-makers within particular national systems, including the social partners, have perceived as demanded of them by the Part-time Work Directive and/or the

Employment Guidelines. It is not an easy matter to disentangle those perceived demands and the responses to them from the continuing evolution of domestic policies with regard to the regulation of part-time work. For example, it may be that the Directive had an impact upon domestic policy formation even before it was adopted by the Community. Again, this kind of analysis is even more challenging with regard to the Employment Guidelines than with regard to the Directive, because of the continuing process of annual modification of the Guidelines. However, we hope that the prior identification of national policies will have facilitated this task.

3   The first stage of the analysis – the development of regulation of part-time work in the Member States

3.1   The typical pattern in the Member States in general

At some risk of over-generalisation, we can identify a fairly typical pattern of development in the regulation of part-time work in the Member States since the early 1980s. Two features stand out as typical ones. Firstly, each of the Member States surveyed in this study has experienced its own historical evolution in the regulation of part-time work which is largely independent of the influence of EU law in general, and is not primarily the result of EU regulation of part-time work in particular. Secondly, although there are very significant divergences in these national evolutions, there are nevertheless quite strong parallels, which can be identified by using the scheme of analysis which we have suggested above, and especially by deploying the distinction between objectives, approaches and techniques with regard to the regulation of part-time work.

The typical pattern across the Member States surveyed has been a movement from a narrow or simple pattern of objectives, approaches and techniques towards a broader more complex set of combinations of objectives, approaches and techniques. The starting points vary from state to state, and so do the combinations subsequently arrived at, but this diversification of objectives, approaches and techniques has been a common theme. Moreover, although there is considerable variation in the pattern between states, there is nevertheless a considerable clustering or convergence of patterns both at the starting point and at the end point. In the next paragraph we sketch out those fairly typical starting points and end points.

The typical starting point, let us say in the early 1970s, was for the employment and social legislation of the Member States, and their collective bargaining practice, so far as they specifically regulated part-time work, to be focussed upon the first objective, the first approach and the first technique. The special regulation of part-time work was not generally intensive. Such regulation tended to be concentrated on the objective of worker protection, the approach of restriction of part-time work, and the technique of hard law. The typical end point, let us say by the time that the Part-time Work Directive was enacted in 1997, was for Member States to have become rather more intensively involved (whether in the form of legislation or of collective bargaining) in the special regulation of part-time work, and for that regulation to have diversified towards pursuing (1) all three *objectives* of worker protection, employment promotion, and flexibilisation of work relations; (2) the second two *approaches*, those of encouragement of part-time work and moderation of its relation to full-time work; and (3) both sets of *techniques*, those of soft law as well as of hard law.

The establishing of this typical pattern would, if it can be convincingly carried out, be highly significant in throwing into sharp relief some hitherto not very clearly visible features of the context in which the EU interventions of the late 1990s into the regulation of part-time work took place. That is to say, it would indicate that those EU interventions during that period were, to an extent which has not been fully perceived, replicating or reflecting a pattern of regulation *which had already become fairly typical* in the Member States surveyed in this study. So it will be important to assess whether the experience of each of these Member States does sufficiently conform to this pattern to identify it as a typical or paradigmatic one. It is essential to conduct that inquiry with a critical and discriminating eye. The diversities in objectives, approaches and techniques which are canvassed here are subtle ones, and the combinations of them are complex. It is quite easy to coerce the evidence into various different shapes or configurations. With those caveats, we suggest that the following paragraphs will show that developments in the Member States surveyed, when considered state by state, do support our general theory quite strongly. The development will be considered down to 1997; the subsequent reaction to EU regulation will be separately discussed.

3.2   The development of regulation of part-time work in particular Member States down to 1997

The development in *France* fits rather neatly into the pattern which we have identified as typical. Down to the early seventies there was very little specific regulation of part-time work, save to the extent that French employment law, by being generally prescriptive as to the standard forms of work relationship or contract, implicitly discouraged part-time work. Sylvaine Laulom's chapter shows how there was a move into more specific regulation of part-time work in the 1970s, cautiously opening the door to more use of part-time working, and, in the Law of 27 December 1973, introducing a principle of equality between part-time and full-time workers. The Law of 28 January 1981 marks a shift into the positive encouragement of part-time work, and thereafter there seems to have been exactly the diversification of objectives, approaches and techniques which we have identified as a typical one; indeed, Laulom expressly confirms that analysis. The *lois Aubry* of 1998 and 2000 represent a further, and very Franco-specific complication of the situation with regard to part-time work, because they represented a shift of focus onto the thirty-five hour working week, which is a tangential movement so far as the regulation of part-time work is concerned; we revert to that point later when considering the post-1997 situation below.

The developments in *Germany* approximate to our typical pattern almost as closely as do those in France. Maximilian Fuchs' chapter shows there was little special regulation of part-time work before the mid-1970s, at least so far as employment law was concerned, though social insurance was already engaged in a kind of encouragement of part-time work in the sense that 'minor employment' was exempted from the statutory social insurance scheme. From this base, the first line of departure was the application by the courts of the principle of equal treatment between women and men to some of the inequalities between part-time work and full-time work. Fuchs goes on to show how that development was given legislative force in the Law on Promotion of Employment of 1985, in the context of a consciously invigorated pursuit of the objectives of employment promotion and the flexibilisation of work relations. Indeed, all three objectives were pursued simultaneously in the regulation of the form of part-time working, prominent in Germany, known as 'Kapovaz', which is essentially a system of annualised hours whereby the employing enterprise may vary the working hours within the year according to demand. Another very Germano-specific pattern of regulation of part-time work emerges in the shape of the Law on Old-Age Part-time Employment of 1996, which had the purpose of encouraging early partial retirement of older workers as an instrument of job creation for younger workers. Fuchs also displays how that legislation formed part of an initiative, the 'Alliance for Work' which interestingly combined hard law and soft law techniques.

The development in *Italy* is underlyingly a comparable one; but Antonio Lo Faro's chapter shows how it proceeded from its own rather special starting points, and according to its own distinctive timetable. He shows how part-time work remained, though not actually illegal, nevertheless seriously discouraged by the employment law regime until the enactment of Law No. 863 of 1984. In other words, a regime for part-time work committed to the objective of worker protection, the approach of discouragement of part-time work, and the technique of hard law persisted until that time. The new statute of 1984 represented the beginnings of the diversification of objectives, approaches and techniques which we have identified as typical; but Lo Faro has shown that the crucial episodes in this history of very contested and controversial diversification did not occur until *after* the enactment of the EU Part-time Work Directive. So we return to consider those episodes in a later section; suffice it to remark at this stage that Italy's regulation of part-time work, though it conforms to the typical pattern, did so from a base and at a velocity which led to a less speedy or extensive growth of part-time work than in many other of the Member States surveyed in this volume.

The development of regulation of part-time work in the *Netherlands* can also be related to our suggested typical pattern, though the chronological ordering of the developments seems to have been rather different from those in the Member States we have so far considered. Jelle Visser and his colleagues show how the very considerable growth of part-time work, from the 1980s and especially from the 1990s onwards, perhaps takes its origin from the diversification of the objectives, approaches and techniques of regulation, in which a turning point was the Wassenauer Agreement of 1982, a major initiative of the social partners for working time reduction and work sharing of various kinds including the expansion of part-time work. Visser *et al.* also show that a further significant episode in this diversificatory development consisted in the enactment of the Working Hours Act of 1996, which clearly has the objective of flexibilisation, and at almost the same time the Prohibition of Discrimination by Working Hours Act, coming into effect in November 1996, which sought to encourage part-time work by implementing a strong principle of equality of treatment between part-time and full-time workers. A third crucial episode occurred in the form of the enactment of the Adjustment of Working Hours Act which came into force in June 2000 and gave employees a right in certain circumstances to change from full-time to part-time work. We return later to consider the significance of this family-friendly measure of flexibilisation in the hands of employees. Visser *et al.*

leave us with a strong sense that diversification of regulatory objectives, approaches and techniques had an important part to play in identifying the labour economy of the Netherlands as one in which part-time work is a dominant feature.

The developments in *Spain* provide a particularly interesting variant upon the typical pattern. Superficially, they could be regarded as a very straightforward manifestation of this pattern. The view could be taken that a tightly worker-protective system of regulation, so far as part-time work was concerned, underwent the typical diversification of objectives, approaches and techniques, through a sequence of measures and interventions, in which the major episodes were, firstly, Law 32 of 1984; secondly, Decree 18 of 1993 and Law 11 of 1994; and thirdly, Decree 8 and Law 63 of 1997 and Decree 15 of 1998. However, Fernando Valdés Dal-Ré's chapter shows that, while the developments conform to this analysis of diversification in the policy discourse with which these measures are accompanied, they actually involve some more radical shifts of direction around the typical pattern. Thus he shows that the measure of 1984, while couched in a diversified rhetoric of worker protection and employment stimulation, actually amounted to an abrupt transition to flexibilisation for employing enterprises. That flexibilisation stimulated a greater use of part-time work, although it was primarily directed at liberating the use of the associated mechanism of temporary or fixed-term employment. The measures of 1993–4 seem to have intensified that flexibilisation and to have applied it more directly to part-time work. The measures of 1997–8 seem to have accomplished some re-balancing and more genuine diversification between the different objectives, approaches and techniques; but Valdés Dal-Ré shows how those measures should be regarded as being closely bound up with the contemporary EU interventions into the regulation of part-time work, so we shall revert to the consideration of them when we come to consider the impact of those EU interventions in the next part of this chapter.

The development of the regulation of part-time work in *Sweden* conforms least closely, of all the Member States surveyed, to the typical pattern, though perhaps that is more because the chronology of the evolution of part-time work and the profile of the labour market in Sweden have been rather singular ones because the underlying policy motivations have been very different from those of other Member States. Ronnie Eklund's chapter shows how government policy and measures sanctioned a radical growth in part-time work from the early 1970s, indeed from even earlier than that in the sense that the option of part-time work was conferred upon civil servants to assist in the discharge of parental responsibilities. Eklund particularly emphasises the importance of the legislation of 1966 which abolished the previous severe restrictions upon shop opening hours with effect from the end of 1971. Subsequent measures regulating part-time work are rather complex in their motivation and their impact; this is true, for example, of the provisions in the Working Hours Act 1982 which determined the conditions in which the employer could demand extra hours of a part-time worker. However, by 1996 we have the enactment of an amendment, s25a, to the Employment Protection Act 1982, which facilitated the increase of working time for part-time workers, and which Eklund regards as indicative of a general policy of encouraging full-time work and discouraging part-time work. It is as if Sweden is further advanced in a chronology according to which part-time work eventually becomes a victim of its own success in increasing the number or proportion of people in work, and comes to be regarded as a form of under-employment or sub-standard employment of the people concerned.

On a superficial or general view, the development of regulation of part-time work in the *United Kingdom* might appear to conform rather precisely to the pattern which we have depicted as the typical one; however, a more searching inquiry does reveal significant variations. One might take the view that UK employment law underwent, in the course of the 1980s and 1990s, precisely the kind of diversification of objectives, approaches, and techniques which we have depicted as the typical pattern, and one might assume that this pattern applied to the regulation of part-time work in particular. However, Claire Kilpatrick and Mark Freedland's chapter suggests that something slightly different was going on with regard to part-time work in particular. It is crucial to recall that until the mid-1960s the level or intensity of legal regulation of the employment relationship was lower in the UK than in many of the countries under consideration in this volume. Kilpatrick and Freedland remind us that, because of the strength of the 'male breadwinner' paradigm in British post-1945 employment and social policy, there was an 'almost mechanical' exclusion of largely female part-time workers from the raft of worker-protective measures introduced between 1963 and 1975. This exclusion persisted, and was abandoned only in the mid-1990s under direct pressure to comply with the requirements of EU law for equal treatment between men and women in employment. In that situation, the general rhetoric of employment stimulation and flexibilisation, as deployed by governments between 1979 and 1997, largely concealed a very straightforwardly *laissez-faire* approach to the part-time work relationship. It was only after 1997 that the rhetorical diversity of objectives started to be matched by real attempts to balance those objectives against each other, and by that stage there was, by comparison with our typical paradigm, something of a historical backlog with regard to the regulation of part-time work.

4 The second stage of the analysis – the interaction between EU regulation of part-time work and its regulation in the Member States

4.1 The reflexive character of the EU regulation of part-time work

In this section we draw upon the conclusions of the previous section to argue for a particular view of the interaction between EU regulation of part-time work and its regulation in the Member States surveyed in this volume. The particular view which we advance is somewhat different from the one which is conventionally taken of the relation between EU regulation and Member State regulation in the employment sphere, indeed in the particular sphere of non-standard employment relations. The conventional view tends, or at least has tended in the past, to characterise EU regulation in the employment sphere as pro-active in pursuit of the objective of worker protection. The debate has been whether EU regulation has been, according to the standpoint of the critic in question, either too pro-active, or insufficiently pro-active, in pursuit of that objective. For example, Mark Jeffery's very powerful critique of the Part-time Work Directive[1] argues that it fails to live up to an earlier set of aspirations, at EU level, for pro-active intervention to improve the quality of part-time work. That is, of course, a valid and important line of criticism of EU regulation in this area. The suggestion which we put forward is not inconsistent with that critique, but may be a further aid to the understanding of the interaction between EU regulation and Member State regulation. We suggest that it is appropriate to view EU regulation of part-time work as characterised, not so much by a simple failure of pro-activeness in the protection of workers, but rather by a particular kind of *reflexiveness* of the pattern of regulation which was becoming typical in the Member States. This is a subtle difference, but a very important one. In order to explain it, we need to take account of the significant relationship, amounting to an integral continuity, between the Part-time Work Directive on the one hand and

---

[1] M. Jeffery 'Not Really Going to Work? Of the Directive on Part-time Work, "Atypical Work" and Attempts to Regulate It' (1998) 27: 3 *Industrial Law Journal* pp. 193–213.

the elements in the EU Employment Strategy which have a bearing upon part-time work.

Our argument about the reflexiveness of EU regulation hinges, in the following way, upon the typical pattern of regulation in the Member States as we have identified it in the previous section. The essence of that typical pattern was that the regulation of part-time work in the Member States surveyed manifested, despite many particular variants, a common trend of diversification, within each Member State, of objectives, approaches and techniques. The common thread was a tendency to bring into the regulatory equation a new or enhanced emphasis upon the objectives of employment stimulation and flexibilisation, the approaches of encouragement of part-time work and the moderation of its relation to full-time work, and the techniques of soft law. The treatment of part-time work in the Member States which are surveyed in this work conforms better to a broad notion of *de-marginalisation* than to a narrower conception of regulation as worker protection. Our suggestion is, in essence, that EU regulation of part-time work underwent a parallel diversification, in both an ideological and a practical sense; it reflected quite directly the evolution of the pattern of regulation within the Member States.

One might say there is nothing remarkable in such an analysis; but it represents a somewhat different perspective from the one which is taken by those who expect, whether with approval or disapproval, that the EU will function as the avant-garde of worker protection, aligning itself with worker-protective policies in particular Member States. This parallelism or reflexiveness of EU regulation of part-time work, with regard to the developments in the Member States, is apparent within the Directive itself, and is even more evident when, as we suggest is fully appropriate, the Directive is considered as part of a regulatory package, the other part of which is the EU Employment Strategy (to be more precise, the elements in the Strategy which address part-time work). That conjunction between the Directive and the Strategy is explained and analysed especially in the chapter contributed by Diamond Ashiagbor, and in the introductory general perspective which is provided by Silvana Sciarra.

Thus within the compass of the Directive itself, a diversification of regulatory objectives, which mirrors the typical pattern in the Member States, is already apparent. The duality or mixity of objectives between the protection of part-time workers and the promotion of a flexible positive attitude towards part-time work permeates the Directive. On the one hand, the Directive contains an essentially cautious formulation of the Principle of Non-Discrimination in Clause 4 of the Framework Agreement, which hardly bites deeper than the existing regulation exerted by the EU law of gender discrimination and which expressly permits objective justification of direct discrimination against part-time workers. On the other hand, that rather limited intervention is complemented, one might almost say counter-balanced, by the relatively strong formulation of the notions of facilitation of part-time work and flexibility between full-time and part-time work in Clause 5. The prominence of those latter *objectives* is greatly heightened by the priority which the Strategy accords to them. The Strategy moreover enhances this commitment to an *approach* of encouragement of part-time work; and it represents, *par excellence*, the super-imposition of the *techniques* of soft law upon those of hard-law regulation.

When the Directive and the Strategy are considered as a composite body of new regulation of part-time work, it becomes clear that something more complex, and perhaps more holistic, is going on at EU level than a simple retreat of Member States with re-regulatory agendas in the face of rearguard action from Member States with de-regulatory ones (such as, prominently, the United Kingdom for most at least of the recent period of this evolution). It is rather that EU regulation is in the course of being re-cast and diversified in very much the same way as the regulation is typically (albeit with significant variations) being re-cast within the several Member States surveyed in this volume. There is always the temptation to analyse EU interventions in the employment sphere as the outcome of a contestation between Member States of a welfarist disposition and other Member States of a neo-liberal disposition. No doubt there is some value and importance in an analysis from that perspective; but from that perspective we may lose sight of the extent to which a diversified kind of EU regulation emerges, quite consensually, as a reflection of a typical pattern of evolution within the Member States. The recent EU regulation of part-time work provides a good illustration of that kind of generalised reflexiveness. That assertion provides a useful starting point for the analysis of the impact which that EU regulation seems so far to have had upon the situation in the individual Member States.

4.2   *The impact of the Directive and the Strategy upon the regulation of part-time work in the Member States*

We have argued above for an understanding of EU regulation of part-time work as being reflexive of quite a high degree of convergence and consensus of the Member States around a regulatory agenda which has become diversified as to its objectives, approaches and techniques. EU intervention has matched or replicated the action of the several Member States in creating a regulatory space within which multiple or divergent tendencies may co-exist quite easily, if not comfortably. It was predictable in view of this analysis that the impact of the Directive and the Strategy upon the regulation of part-time work in the Member States would not be a dramatic one. One could expect, firstly, that Member States would not on the whole need to make radical adjustments to their existing regimes for part-time work directly by reason of the new regulatory interventions at EU level. One could also expect, secondly, that Member States could continue on their individual policy trajectories without being greatly deflected by EU interventions; those interventions would leave a wide range of policy options or mixtures within which diverse national agendas could be accommodated. A brief survey follows of the experience in the individual Member States since the making of the Framework Agreement in 1997, experience which is recounted in detail in the subsequent chapters of this work. That survey seems quite strongly to bear out our predictions.[2]

Thus Sylvaine Laulom's chapter shows how in France, regulation since 1997 has been constructed around the introduction and modification of the thirty-five hour working week by the *lois Aubry* of 1998 to 2000. This highly complex agenda is tangential to that of the regulation of part-time work as such; Laulom argues that it has involved the abandonment of the direct use of part-time work as a tool of employment policy, and that the only specific and overt response to the Directive has consisted in the modification of the definition of part-time work. She argues that even where the second *loi Aubry* represented policy shifts corresponding to the Directive, there was no impulse to relate them to the Directive.

In Germany, there was a specific response to the Directive in the shape of the *Teilzeit und Befristungsgesetz* effective from 2001 which introduced a right for a large category of workers to apply to reduce working time, with the objective of facilitating part-time work not least among managerial staff. However, Maximilian Fuchs' chapter conveys a picture of a system which was decisively embarked upon its own particular programme of regulation of part-time work, with its own special pre-occupations, for instance with the facilitation of transfer into part-time work of older

---

[2] In preparing this section we have been assisted by the recently published *Survey on the Implementation of the Part-time Work Directive/Agreement in the EU Member States and Selected Applicant Countries* by Stefan Clauwaert (Brussels: European Trade Union Institute 2002).

workers, and whose really significant interaction with EU regulation was in relation to EU gender discrimination law rather than with interventions specially focussed upon part-time work.

Antonio Lo Faro's chapter suggests that the recent changes in Italy strongly bear out our theory about the nature and level of impact of recent EU part-time work regulation. A superficial view of that evolution might be that there was a strong direct impact in the shape of the implementation of the Directive by Decree 61/2000. Lo Faro leaves us in no doubt, however, that this Decree has to be understood in terms of an intense and intricate labour law debate within Italy. As that debate was pursued by means of the challenge to the Decree posed by the White Paper produced in 2001 by the succeeding, more rightward-leaning government, it is notable how the protagonists of rival positions in that debate have each been able to claim that they alone have understood and are following the true agenda of EU regulation of part-time work.

Jelle Visser and his colleagues in their chapter describe the evolution of part-time work regulation in the Netherlands in a way which also exemplifies our theory, though in a rather different sense. They show how the law and policy of that country, with regard to part-time work, fully anticipated, and presumably to some extent provided an example for, the developments at EU level. So much did the Dutch legislation of 1996 (the Prohibition of Discrimination by Working Hours Act) and 1999 (the Adjustment of Working Hours Act) amount to an implementation of the Directive *avant la lettre* that Visser *et al*'s chapter concludes that no further response to the Directive was perceived as required or took place.

As we mentioned earlier, Fernando Valdés Dal-Ré's chapter shows how the legislation enacted in Spain in 1997 and 1998 was closely bound up with the evolution of EU regulation of part-time work; and one could also see Decree 5/2001 and Law 12/2001 as part of a process of implementation of the Directive. However, Valdés Dal-Ré's account, properly understood, both contributes to our theory of the reflexiveness of the Directive, and confirms that the Directive did little to deflect Member States from their previously chosen and independently evolving policy paths. Thus there was a particular Spanish pre-occupation with the *voluntariness* of part-time work and of the conditions upon which it is carried out, which may have contributed to the evolution of EU policy as much as it was influenced by that evolution.

The story in Sweden is a different one, though no less corroborative of our theory about the rather limited impact of EU regulation of part-time work in particular Member States. Ronnie Eklund's chapter shows how Swedish governments have in recent years tended to take the view and stance that Sweden long since went through its processes of promotion of part-time work and creation of an appropriate legal regime for such work. Hence they no longer feel a need to engage in reform to implement the Directive, and are more than slightly resistant to pressure towards further encouragement of part-time work, which they have come to regard as something of a brake upon the maintenance of full employment, rather than as the engine of employment creation and the inclusion of women in the labour market which it was once envisaged to be.

The case of the United Kingdom is different again, though in its own way no less supportive of our theory about the reflexiveness of EU regulation and the corresponding slightness of its impact in the Member States. The chapter contributed by Claire Kilpatrick and Mark Freedland provides this support in various ways. It shows how the United Kingdom, while in formal terms engaging in compliance with the Directive as single-mindedly as any Member State (in accordance with its self-image as singularly and scrupulously law-abiding with regard to its EU obligations), nevertheless was in substance minimalist in its implementation of the non-discrimination principle, so much so that Kilpatrick and Freedland evoke the notion of 'vertical dissonance' between EU governance and that of the UK in the regulation of part-time work. It may be added that this vertical dissonance is such that the UK Government preferred to present the measures which it introduced for facilitation of transfer to part-time work, to aid with the discharge of parental responsibilities, as entirely a product of its own family-friendly policies, although it could have been presented as an implementation of the Directive.

We suggest that these possibilities for 'vertical dissonance' within an appearance of formal compliance with EU regulation illustrate the amplitude of the regulatory space which the EU has created in relation to part-time work, and the diversity of national policies which may be pursued within it. Moreover, the way in which UK governments have engaged with the EU Employment Strategy, both generally and with regard to part-time work in particular, as analysed by Kilpatrick and Freedland, very effectively illustrates the theory of EU regulation of part-time work as reflexive, non-exacting and having a rather limited practical impact. These observations lead on to a discussion of the final element in our analysis of the interaction between EU regulation and Member State regulation with regard to part-time work. That element consists of posing the question of whether there is a feed-back from national regulation into EU regulation such as to establish a reflexive paradigm for EU regulation with regard to non-standard forms of work in general.

4.3   Conclusion – a reflexive paradigm for future EU regulation?

The final question to be addressed, very briefly, in this chapter is whether and how far the interaction which is surveyed in this book between EU regulation and Member State regulation with regard to part-time work, is on the one hand a contingent and circumstantial one, or on the other hand represents or might come to represent a paradigm of reflexivity and light-touch intervention for future EU regulation in the employment sphere. The possibility is that a preference on the part of Member States for regulation of this kind might feed back into the process of EU governance so as to identify this as the normal form of EU intervention. It is, in short, early days for an assessment of this possibility. We might wish to see the rather similar subsequent history of the Fixed-term Work Directive as confirming such a trend. It may well, however, be no coincidence that both those measures attach legally binding force to a Framework Agreement between the social partners, who might be more likely to reflect the generally prevailing status quo than the Commission, Council or Parliament would be.

We could also observe that it would seem to suit many states and interest groups for the Employment Strategy to cover the more difficult issues of EU regulation of the employment relation in a cosy blanket of soft law. On the other hand, we might wish to see the recent episodes of EU regulation of part-time work as strongly contingent upon the fact that EU measures controlling gender discrimination had borne and were continuing to bear much of the regulatory burden. The question is difficult to answer, but is a crucially interesting one. At the time of writing, we could regard the current debate about regulation of temporary agency employment as an experimental laboratory in which some further theoretical and practical discoveries might be made. The significant transformation of the Commission's proposals at the hands of the European Parliament (which proposed a complex series of amendments, some of which strengthened the proposals while others relaxed them) may point towards new relationships between the institutional actors, with rather different outcomes from those of the Part-time Work and Fixed-term Work Directives, so far as the regulation of non-standard patterns of work are concerned.

PART II

4

France: part-time work – no longer an employment policy tool

SYLVAINE LAULOM

1 Introduction

1.1 Some facts and figures

From the end of the 1970s onwards the number of people in part-time work expanded rapidly in France, rising from 6 per cent of the working population to 17.2 per cent by January 1999[1] and placing the country in an average position among the EC Member States as regards its use.[2] This increase was not continuous: an initial surge in the number of part-time workers from the start of the 1980s until 1986, when the first general regulation of part-time work was established, was followed by a period of stabilisation between 1987 and 1991 and then a phase of renewed growth starting in 1992 in parallel with the introduction of specific measures to encourage part-time work.[3] Since 1999, marking a departure from that rising trend, there has been a slight decrease in the proportion of part-time workers, who represented 16.9 per cent of the working population in March 2000, 16.4 per cent in March 2001[4] and 16.2 per cent in March 2002.[5]

In this chapter, all translations from the original French are by Rita Inston.

[1] M. Gaye and V. Le Corre, 'Les incitations en faveur du travail à temps partiel' (1999) 3–4 Dossiers de la DARES [Direction de l'Animation de la Recherche, des Etudes et des Statistiques], pp. 125–30.

[2] CEC, Employment in Europe 2002. Recent Trends and Prospects (Luxembourg: OOPEC, 2002), p. 22.

[3] L. Bloch and B. Galtier, 'Emplois et salariés à temps partiel en France', appendix to G. Cette (ed.), Le temps partiel en France (Les Rapports du Conseil d'analyse économique, La Documentation française, Paris, 1999), pp. 93–126.

[4] A.-T. Aerts and M.-A. Mercier, 'Enquête sur l'emploi de mars 2001' (June 2001) 785, Institut national de la Statistique et des études économiques (INSEE) Première.

[5] A.-T. Aerts and J.-F. Bigot, 'Enquête sur l'emploi de mars 2002' (July 2002) 857 INSEE Première, and 'Résultats de l'enquête trimestrielle sur l'activité et les conditions d'emploi de la main-d'œuvre au 3ème trimestre 2002' (2002) DARES, Premières informations No. 52.2.

The tertiary sector (more specifically education, health, social services, personal services and commerce) is still the main source of part-time jobs, with more than 87 per cent of all part-time workers concentrated within this sector. However, industry – and particularly the agri-foodstuffs industry – although lagging far behind, has witnessed a certain increase in the volume of part-time workers. The latter remain predominantly female (83 per cent); the increased use of part-time work involves few professional and managerial employees and mainly affects the lower-skilled occupations; and, lastly, the proportion of part-time workers is highest in the extreme age-groups, particularly among those aged under 25 (27.5 per cent of this age-group are employed part-time). As at March 2001 the average working time for part-time workers is 23.3 hours a week.[6] Following an increase from 1999 onwards, we are now witnessing a slight decrease in customary working hours for part-timers.[7]

Part-time work encompasses a wide variety of real-life circumstances, owing to its heterogeneous nature. It may be fixed-term or open-ended, combined with a programme of vocational training or undertaken for only a limited period before the resumption of full-time work. For instance, it features in certain employment and training contracts intended to assist the entry or reintegration into the labour market of young people with few or no qualifications or of the unemployed. In such cases it serves as a transitional period leading to a return to or access to a full-time job. It can also be designed as a transitional period easing the move towards complete withdrawal from working life[8] (although this form has not really been widely used). However, it also covers working part-time for health reasons, working 80 per cent of normal working hours as a means of reconciling working life and family life, or seasonal work within the framework of an intermittent employment contract. Although this diversity can sometimes involve the application of special rules, certain principles remain common to all part-time contracts, the most notable being the principle of equality between full-time and part-time employees.

1.2   Chronology of the legal environment

France is, unquestionably, the country in which Community influence on developments in national legislation and policies on part-time work is the least discernible. The direction followed by ECJ case-law on indirect

---

[6] Aerts and Bigot, 'Enquête sur l'emploi 2002' (n. 5 above).   [7] Ibid.
[8] This is the formula arranged under agreements on gradual early retirement, which can occur in redundancy situations.

discrimination, which primarily concerned part-time employees, has been ignored by the Cour de cassation (Appeal Court). Directive 97/81/EC on part-time work has not necessitated specific transposition, but at most a few adjustments which left the architecture of French legislation on the matter more or less intact. However – and perhaps this is where the real reason lies – part-time work has been the subject of continuous attention from the French legislature and government from the start of the 1980s onwards. The legislative developments that have accompanied the expansion of part-time work have taken place, particularly from the start of the 1990s, in the context of an employment-policy thrust.[9]

To start with, the use of part-time work developed outside any dedicated regulatory framework and was governed only by the provisions of individual contracts or specific collective agreements on the matter. Although the earliest legislative measures relating to part-time work date back to the 1970s they dealt only with particular aspects. For instance, an initial Law of 1970 authorised the use, in certain circumstances, of part-time work in the public service, and a Law of 1971 stipulated that collective agreements must contain a clause on part-time work. Most notably, the Law of 27 December 1973 on the improvement of employment conditions placed part-time employees on an equal footing with full-time employees as regards the rights deriving from length of service and therefore constituted the first example of applying the principle of equality between the two categories. It was not until the early 1980s that more extensive legislative measures ensued which created a generalised formal status for part-time work.

The Law of 28 January 1981 sought to foster the development of part-time work by abolishing certain rules that were a possible deterrent to its use from the employer's point of view. It became the target of criticisms which were to culminate in the Government Order of 26 March 1982, issued after the Socialists came into power in 1981. This Order set about laying down the main rules on part-time work and was intended to provide the regulatory framework for its use. It marked the establishment of the principle of equality between part-time and full-time employees as regards individual and collective rights.[10]

---

[9] M. Del Sol, 'Travail à temps partiel: le renforcement de la logique du temps choisi?' (2001) *Droit Social* p. 728.

[10] Even at that time, however, the government's primary objective was already to bring about a general reduction in working time: the statutory working week was reduced from 40 hours to 39 hours and a fifth week of paid annual leave was granted.

Following this, part-time work was the subject of a series of reforms[11] pursuing a variety of objectives and each focussing on one of the three main functions attributed to rules on the matter:[12] first, the use of part-time work can form part of a general employment policy directed at sharing out employment and reducing unemployment, on the assumption that more part-time work enables more job creation; second, from the company point of view it can be designed as a vehicle for more flexible operating conditions through the arrangement of working time it accommodates; and third, it can be used primarily as a way of improving employment conditions from the employee's point of view in that it makes it easier to reconcile private life and working life. These three main objectives, particularly that of employee protection and that of flexibility, naturally presented contradictions which the legislators resolved by choosing to give precedence to one or other aspect. Although since 1990 employment policy has, undeniably, been the key to an understanding of the provisions on part-time work, this objective has been accompanied by a shift in the treatment of the matter.

Starting from 1992, and for the next six years, the government's main objective was to promote the use of part-time work within the framework of an employment policy focussed on encouraging widespread individual reductions in working time in the interests of work sharing. To this end, major financial aid was introduced for companies making use of part-time work.

The advent of the so-called *Aubry* legislation (named after the Minister for Employment, Martine Aubry), in the form of the *loi Aubry I* of 13 June 1998 and *loi Aubry II* of 19 January 2000, which impose a general reduction in working time, marked a shift away from the previous thrust and a new approach to part-time work. The provisions on the latter now have to be interpreted in conjunction with the regulation of working time as it exists under the new legislation.

It was initially through collective bargaining that the government had sought to bring about a general reduction in working time.[13] Hence, in 1997 a national tripartite conference on pay and working time was

---

[11] Order of 11 August 1986, Law of 3 January 1991, Law of 31 December 1992, Law of 20 December 1993, *loi Aubry I* of 13 June 1998 and, lastly, *loi Aubry II* of 19 January 2000.

[12] F. Favennec-Héry, *Le travail à temps partiel* (Paris: Litec, 1997), p. 23.

[13] The *loi Robien* of 1996 had preceded the *lois Aubry* legislation but had relied purely on financial incentives, granting aid to companies that signed agreements on working time reduction accompanied by measures to promote employment (job creation or a freeze on redundancies).

organised in order to give fresh impetus to the social dialogue and arrive at an agreement on the 35-hour week. The breakdown of the negotiations led to the announcement, at the end of the conference, of legislative intervention. The first of the two new laws was passed on 13 June 1998, announcing the move to a 35-hour working week by January 2000[14] and encouraging companies to conclude agreements on working time reduction without waiting for the deadline. The second set the statutory working week at 35 hours and organised collective bargaining on the issue.[15] The shortening of the statutory working week does not, however, imply an automatic reduction in working time at workplace level: the 35-hour week merely represents a threshold above which the hours worked attract an enhanced rate of pay.[16] In order to encourage a generalised reduction in working time, priority was given to collective bargaining in its actual implementation,[17] and exemptions from social security contributions were granted to companies concluding agreements on working time reduction that create or preserve jobs.

Although the working time reduction and work sharing which the *lois Aubry* were designed to bring about were still at the heart of employment policies, the legislators had now set their sights on a general reduction in working time through the introduction of a statutory 35-hour working week. At the same time, all this carried implications for part-time work, which remained one of their concerns. The two *lois Aubry* therefore entailed a reform of the regulations on part-time work. However, the aim of these provisions was no longer, as it had been in 1992, to give priority to part-time work at all costs: this was because the individual working time cuts resulting from its use could limit the impact of the general reduction in working time intended by the government. Consequently, the financial subsidies attracted by part-time work were abolished.

In future, according to the government, the guiding principle as regards part-time work was to consist, in general, in 'making it easier to reconcile professional life and private life'.[18] The government therefore clearly intended to take control of the flexibility resulting from part-time work

---

[14] January 2002 for smaller firms with twenty or fewer employees.
[15] The *lois Aubry* were also the source of major upheavals in labour law. For instance, in order to allow collective bargaining on working time in all firms they challenged the union monopoly of negotiating and concluding collective agreements.
[16] J. Barthélémy, 'Droit de la durée du travail: la tendance à la contractualisation' (2003) *Droit Social* p. 25.
[17] Significantly, the title of the law introducing the 35-hour working week is 'Law relating to the negotiated reduction of working time'.
[18] M. Aubry, Preamble to the Law of 19 January 2000.

and to offer employees better guarantees, particularly as regards the voluntary nature of this form of work. Thus, the *lois Aubry* legislation undeniably signified a tightening of the regulation of part-time work and introduced a new balance between the twin objectives of flexibility and security. Consequently, implementation of the European Employment Strategy (EES) as initiated by the Luxembourg European Council prompts questions as to the compatibility of employment policy developments in France with the Employment Guidelines drawn up each year by the Council.

2   Part-time work and work sharing

2.1   Part-time work attracting financial aid

Starting from 1992, part-time work was the subject of a voluntarist policy pursued by the public authorities with a view to work sharing. It was therefore possible to assert that 'no other country offers companies such a systematic regime of financial assistance for part-time jobs as that now available in France'.[19] Although other measures with a variety of objectives had previously had an impact on the volume of part-time work, either directly or indirectly, none had been of such general scope. For example, the new provisions on parental leave allowed a switch to part-time work for employees with two or more children until the youngest child reached the age of three, and measures targeted at promoting the employment of young people and the unemployed[20] could also lead to the forming of part-time contracts.

The support granted to part-time work was part of a change of direction in employment policies.[21] Whereas, before 1992, priority had been given to special policies aimed at compensating for a particular disadvantage on the labour market, the emphasis was now placed on increasing the volume of jobs available or the sharing-out of this employment.

The method used to achieve those objectives was the establishment of a general system of exemptions from social security contributions with respect to employees recruited under part-time contracts or existing full-time employees who switched to part-time work. Although a number of adjustments were made to the details of its application, the principle of

---

[19] Cette, *Le temps partiel en France* (n. 3 above), p. 35.
[20] For instance, the formula known as the 'job creation contract' (*contrat emploi-solidarité*), primarily aimed at integrating young people into the labour market, was necessarily a part-time contract in order to allow parallel training schemes for them.
[21] C. Daniel, 'Les politiques d'emploi: une révolution silencieuse' (1998) *Droit Social* p. 3.

this mechanism remained unchanged: the hiring of part-time employees attracted a reduction in the social security contributions payable by
the employer, provided that certain particular conditions were fulfilled
to ensure that this financial aid did not encourage excessively precarious
forms of employment. Thus, in order to be eligible for the subsidy a part-
time contract had to be open-ended. Prior approval from the authorities
was also necessary if the employer had made redundancies during the six
months preceding the recruitment or switch to a part-time job. In addition, the part-time work week involved was defined so as to exclude both
contracts providing for very few working hours and contracts providing for working hours very close to the statutory or collectively agreed
full-time working week: to qualify for the subsidy, the working time
involved therefore had to be at least 16 hours excluding extra hours (*heures
complémentaires*) and not more than 32 hours including extra hours.[22]
The reduction in the employer's social security contributions varied from
30 to 50 per cent (it was 30 per cent when the subsidy was abolished).
This subsidy was not temporary – it was granted for the entire duration
of the contract concerned.

The subsidy was also granted in cases where an existing employee
switched from an open-ended full-time contract to an open-ended part-
time contract, subject to one special condition. The switch had to be
accompanied by the recruitment of one or more new employees to make
up the resultant shortfall in working time.

The policy of providing financial incentives for part-time work also
formed part of a statutory system which, while granting the part-time
employee a measure of protection, made this method of organising working time a fairly flexible form of work – something which certainly contributed to the expansion of part-time work sought by the government.

2.2 Part-time work regulations allowing flexibility

2.2.1 Establishment of a principle of equality independently of Community law

The protection of part-time employees was in fact the driving force behind
the adoption of a number of measures during the 1980s, and in particular the establishment of the principle of equality between part-time and
full-time employees. This signifies conferring on part-time employees a
status comparable to that of full-time employees. Essentially a principle

---

[22] These limits varied.

for employee protection, it nevertheless also tends to promote the use of part-time work by 'neutralising' its possible negative effects.

The principle of equality of rights between part-time employees and full-time employees was established in 1982.[23] Although the principle applied to collectively agreed rights as well as to statutory rights, the Labour Code conceded that, as regards the former, 'specific detailed provisions' could be laid down by collective agreement. Did this mean that a collective agreement could reserve the exercise of certain rights exclusively to full-time employees? After a few uncertain case-law decisions, the Cour de cassation[24] held that the possibility of departing from the principle of equality by general or specific collective agreement should be strictly regulated. A collective agreement can adjust a right to the special conditions of part-time work. It can define the content of or access to a right in proportion to an employee's working hours but cannot deprive part-time employees of a right solely because they work part-time.

The principle of equality affects both employees' individual rights and collective rights. It can be interpreted in two different ways, i.e. as implying either application of the principle of *pro rata temporis*, with employees' rights defined in proportion to the length of their working hours, or wholly identical rights. Except as regards the very broad issue of pay, France has opted for the identical rights approach. That approach can sometimes have positive consequences for the part-time employee in reducing the inherently precarious nature of this type of employment. In the case of vocational training, for example, a *pro rata* approach could make it far more difficult for a part-time employee to exercise this right effectively.

Thus, with respect to the calculation of rights linked to length of service the law places part-timers on an equal footing with full-time employees and the factor taken into account is the duration of the contractual relationship concerned, not the number of hours worked.[25] Similarly, application of the principle of equality does not entail any special provisions as regards annual holidays: the period of paid annual holiday entitlement and the rules on holiday pay are identical irrespective of the employee's working hours. Nor may the probationary period be longer for part-timers. This latter aspect was potentially open to criticism. Since the purpose

---

[23] Article L 212-4-2, Labour Code: 'Part-time employees shall enjoy the rights granted to full-time employees by law, general collective agreements and specific collective agreements concluded at company or plant level'.

[24] Cass. Ass. Plén., 29 November 1996, *RJS* 1997, No. 312. Cass. Soc. 15 January 2002, *Bull. Civ.* V, No. 17.

[25] See Cass. Soc. 29 January 2002, *Bull. Civ.* V, No. 40.

of a probationary period is to test the employee's professional abilities, there could be an argument for making the probationary period longer for part-time employees. However, the legislators opted for making the rules identical in order to avoid adding to the often precarious nature of the part-timer's situation. Employees' rights in the event of termination of the employment contract are also identical: the notice period must be similar and severance pay is calculated according to the same method. Lastly, this rule of identical rights also applies in relation to promotion and to vocational training. In the case of collective rights, part-time employees have the same status as full-time employees as regards the right to vote and to stand as a candidate in elections of workplace delegates and works council members. They can also be appointed as trade union delegates. The only eligibility criteria applicable are therefore ones relating to age and length of service, not to the number of hours they work. The one special feature, as laid down in Articles L 423-8 and L 433-5 of the Labour Code, is that 'employees holding part-time jobs simultaneously in more than one company shall be eligible in only one of those companies and shall choose in which one to offer themselves as a candidate'. They also have the same time-off rights as full-time employees for the purpose of performing such functions, provided the use of those rights does not reduce the monthly working time specified in their contract by more than one third.

Where the *pro rata temporis* rule does apply is in the method used to calculate the size of the company's workforce,[26] which does not affect the scope of the rights accorded to part-time employees as such. Also, the fact that it is permissible for collective agreements to adjust the principle of equality would appear to amount, in reality, to application of the *pro rata temporis* rule at the cost of recognition of equality of rights between part-time and full-time employees.[27] On this point it may be judged that the power granted to the social partners by the legislators to adjust the principle of equality is not actually contrary to the principle of equality within the meaning of Community law. It can, nevertheless, result in making it more difficult for part-time employees to exercise certain rights effectively.

---

[26] Part-time employees are counted towards the total workforce on the basis of whatever proportion of the statutory or collectively agreed working hours in the establishment concerned is represented by their contractual working hours.

[27] A collective agreement can make a promotion conditional on twice the length of service in the case of part-time employees, even though in this respect length of service as a part-timer is in principle treated in law as equivalent to length of service as a full-timer (Cass. Soc. 9 April 1996, *RJS* 1996, No. 550).

However, application of the *pro rata temporis* principle relates essentially to the amount of remuneration received by part-time employees. Under Article L 212-4-2 of the Labour Code, 'due regard being given to their working hours and their length of service in the company, their remuneration shall be proportional to that of an employee, possessing the same or similar qualifications or skills, who occupies a comparable job on a full-time basis in the same establishment or company'. This principle of proportionality is applied to all forms of remuneration, whether the payment in question constitutes basic pay or a bonus.[28] Although its applicability has been questioned in the case of bonuses or allowances which appear to have no direct link with working time (e.g. family allowances, travel allowances), the Cour de cassation takes the view that any payment having the nature of remuneration is payable to part-time employees in proportion to their working hours.[29]

The unambiguous recognition in the Labour Code of the principle of equality between part-time and full-time employees could well explain why the French courts do not appear to have been influenced by Community case-law on indirect discrimination. It is essentially in the field of part-time work that the ECJ has had occasion to develop its case-law on the subject of indirect discrimination, and in France the application of that concept might well have seemed superfluous in so far as the principle of equality between full-time and part-time employees had already been enshrined in the law.[30]

The fact that the Cour de cassation has taken no heed of the ECJ's case-law is not due to any lack of litigation on the issue of equality between part-time and full-time employees. Although analysis of the decisions delivered by the Cour de cassation on the subject of part-time work shows that the cases brought before it relate primarily to changes in the pattern of part-time work hours and the possible right of the employee to refuse to accept such changes,[31] application of the principle of

---

[28] Thus, a company practice cannot reserve the payment of a bonus or allowance exclusively to full-time employees (Cass. Soc. 13 April 1999, *Bull. Civ.* V, No. 177).

[29] This applies in the absence of any more favourable provision granting them 100 per cent entitlement to the benefit in question (Cass. Soc. 1 June 1999, *Bull. Civ.* V, No. 256).

[30] M.-T. Lanquetin, 'La preuve de la discrimination: l'apport du droit communautaire' (1995) *Droit Social* p. 435.

[31] In 1999, for instance, out of the forty decisions delivered by the Cour de cassation in connection with part-time work, twenty or so concerned this aspect (which is sometimes linked to the absence of a written contract, since in such circumstances the question arises of proof of contractual working hours and the pattern of their distribution). Such legal actions mostly arise in the context of dismissal when the employee refuses to accept the change. The figures on litigation in 2002 are basically the same.

equality makes up a significant proportion of the legal actions initiated in relation to part-time work. Most of the decisions delivered in connection with application of the principle of equality concern the amount of remuneration payable, with employees claiming full entitlement to certain bonuses or allowances. As mentioned above, the Cour de cassation maintains, save where some more favourable collectively agreed provision exists, that they should be paid in proportion to their working time.[32] This litigation is therefore dealt with by applying the national rules.

The lack of reference to Community case-law has not been without its consequences, however. One such consequence is that the courts have seldom, if ever, recognised the link between part-time work and female employment. The French system, and in particular the authority granted to the social partners to adjust the principle of equality, has not been tested against the principles of equality laid down by Community law, even though its conformity could be called into question.[33] Similarly, the implications of part-time work for women's employment in terms, in particular, of promotion or training have seldom been taken into consideration.

In addition, a number of partial exceptions to the principle of equality still exist as regards the social protection of part-time employees.[34] Eligibility for certain entitlements[35] remains subject to minimum conditions regarding working time or payment of contributions. Although the costs of administrating these schemes may offer some justification for such thresholds, they undeniably represent a very real infringement of the principle of equality. Consequently, in its report, the Conseil d'analyse économique proposed, in connection with the social protection of part-time employees, that all working time and pay criteria should be assessed on a *pro rata* basis to give part-time employees access to cash benefits or benefits in kind.[36]

---

[32] See, for example, Cass. Soc. 24 November 1999, Pourvoi No. 97-44.043, *Juridisque Lamy*, or Cass. Soc. 1 June 1999, Pourvoi No. 97-41.430, *Juridisque Lamy*.

[33] It should, nevertheless, be noted that the Cour de cassation judgments of the past few years have not given rise to any clauses in collective agreements that discriminate against part-time employees.

[34] Favennec-Héry, *Le travail à temps partiel* (n. 12 above), p. 171; M. Okba and J.-L. Pyronnet, 'La protection sociale des salariés à temps partiel', in Cette, *Le temps partiel en France* (n. 3 above), p. 143.

[35] This is the case with certain benefits payable under health, maternity and disability insurance.

[36] Cette, *Le temps partiel en France* (n. 3 above), p. 143.

2.2.2 Recognition of special rights

Alongside recognition of the principle of equality between part-time and full-time employees, a number of special rights have been defined. For instance, a part-time employee has a priority of access to any full-time jobs matching his or her skills which become available in the company.[37] Full-time employees likewise are entitled to an identical priority of access to part-time jobs when they work in a company where the employer has introduced part-time work. In situations where a full-time employment contract has been converted into a part-time contract, part-time employees can pay retirement pension contributions on a full-time employment basis. This mechanism was introduced in order to avoid penalising part-time employees as regards their retirement pension entitlement.[38]

In certain circumstances the employer is also required to offer a part-time job to an existing employee who requests one. For example, after the birth or adoption of a child an employee who fulfils the relevant length-of-service eligibility criterion can request, on the same basis as entitlement to parental childcare leave following on directly from either maternity leave or adoption leave (i.e. not restricted to women), a temporary conversion of her or his full-time contract into a part-time contract.[39] This entitlement, which is clearly intended to make it easier to reconcile professional life and family life, may be accompanied by a parental childcare allowance that assists the switch to part-time work for employees with at least two children including one under the age of three. When their child is seriously ill, employees with at least one year's length of service can also switch to part-time hours for a period of six months that can be re-granted every year.

As an atypical contract, the part-time employment contract has also been made subject to special rules as to its form, now reinforced by the second *loi Aubry*. Whereas a written contract is not a condition of validity

---

[37] The Cour de cassation's interpretation of this provision has led it to accept that the employee also has a priority of access to other part-time jobs which become available in the company provided the alternative job in question is compatible with the part-time job he or she currently occupies in terms of the scheduling, duration and distribution of working time (Cass. Soc. 26 October 1999, *Bull. Civ.* V, No. 414).

[38] The employer then becomes liable for a *pro rata* contribution. This measure, designed to compensate for certain disadvantages of part-time work, does of course present difficulties in its application as regards, in particular, the infringement of the principle of equality between full-time and part-time employees which it represents; see Cette, *Le temps partiel en France* (n. 3 above), p. 33.

[39] The minimum length-of-service qualification is one year, and the employee can reduce her or his working hours by at least one fifth but must work not less than sixteen hours a week.

in the case of open-ended full-time contracts, part-time contracts, like fixed-term contracts, must be in the form of a written document. In addition to the particulars common to all contracts of employment, such as the skill level or grade concerned and the various components of pay, a part-time contract must also include a number of clauses which the second *loi Aubry* has now made more extensive.

Failure to draw up the contract in writing or to include a particular clause incurs penalties of various kinds. In the majority of cases the penalty is that the contract is reclassified as a full-time contract of employment: in the absence of a written document, the presumption is that the contract is a full-time one. However, whereas in the case of fixed-term contracts that presumption is irrebuttable, in the case of part-time contracts it is a pure presumption: the employer can, despite the absence of a written document, establish that the contract of employment is a part-time contract. To do so, the employer must produce evidence showing the contractually agreed working hours and the distribution of those working hours over the week or month.[40] This difference between the regulation of part-time contracts and fixed-term contracts is due to the fact that the former, which in the circumstances envisaged are open-ended, are less precarious from the employee's point of view.[41] The absence of a written contract containing the particulars that are mandatory for part-time employees can also incur a penal sanction,[42] which is seldom imposed. If there is no written clause concerning changes to the pattern of working hours or the use of extra hours, the employer has no right to depart from the contractual terms and conditions without the employee's consent. Lastly, an employer who fails to observe the contractual terms and conditions could find the contract reclassified as a full-time employment contract owing to the permanent availability that is then demanded of the employee.[43]

---

[40] Cass. Soc. 23 November 1999, *Bull. Civ.* V, No. 451.

[41] This is because in the case of a fixed-term part-time contract the absence of a written document means that the contract is automatically reclassified as an open-ended contract.

[42] Article R 261-3-1 of the Labour Code, which stipulates a maximum fine of €1,500.

[43] Cass. Soc. 12 July 1999, *Bull. Civ.* V, No. 352. In this judgment the Cour de cassation observed that, despite the existence of a written contract, the scheduling of the employee's working hours varied from one month to the next in a manner that went beyond the provisions laid down in her contract of employment, which did not specify the distribution of working hours over the days of the week or weeks of the month. The employee concerned had thus been placed in a position where it was impossible for her to predict what the pattern of her working hours would be each month, obliging her to keep herself permanently at the employer's disposal. The contract of employment should therefore be reclassified as a full-time contract.

2.2.3   Flexibility offered by the use of part-time work

Nevertheless, the above regulation of part-time work by the legislators did not undermine the flexibility resulting from this type of work organisation. Part-time work allows an adjustment of working times that is impossible with full-time working and offers employers a fairly high degree of latitude in the organisation of work in their companies. In practical terms, the first aspect of that flexibility is the freedom of employers as regards using part-time work at all. Since they are free to run their companies as they wish, employers always have the choice of whether or not to introduce part-time work in the company. Their only obligation is to inform the employee representatives (the works council or, where none exists, the workforce delegates) of the intention to do so and to consult them on the matter.[44] This consultation merely signifies an opportunity for employee representatives to voice an opinion which the employer may then choose to take into account in arriving at a decision; their opinion must be forwarded to the Labour Inspector within fifteen days. In cases where there are no employee representatives the Labour Inspector must also be informed in advance of the introduction of part-time work, but in neither situation does the Labour Inspector have any authority in the matter beyond the right to be informed.

The flexibility inherent in part-time work also includes the considerable degree of latitude it allows in managing the working hours of part-time employees. The distribution of working time over the year, the possibility of varying the scheduled working hours of part-time employees and the use of extra hours (*heures complémentaires*), which, in contrast to overtime (*heures supplémentaires*), do not attract an enhanced rate of pay, are all factors that offer the company greater flexibility in the management of employees' working time. The Law of 20 December 1993 also sought to encourage intermittent work,[45] a form of annualised part-time work, by treating it as identical with part-time work in terms of the law.[46]

---

[44] The information and consultation of employee representatives must take place at the time when part-time work is first being introduced. Thereafter, the situation regarding part-time work within the company must then be the subject of annual consultation.

[45] Intermittent work, as established in accordance with the Government Order of 11 August 1986, characteristically involves an alternation of periods during which work is performed with periods during which no work is performed. It features in occupational sectors that are subject to major fluctuations in the volume of business activity over the course of the year under the effect, in particular, of the dates of the school year, tourism, the entertainment industry and the seasons of the year.

[46] Under the former Article L 212-4-2(4) of the Labour Code, 'the definition of part-time employees shall also include those whose employment is based on an alternation of periods

This meant that it could offer companies a fair degree of flexibility in that intermittent work could be introduced by straightforward individual agreement with employees and was not rigidly confined to occupations entailing periods of inactivity by their very nature, but could apply to any type of job.

Thus, up to 1998, part-time work was very clearly promoted by government employment policies, through the partial financing of this type of work in the form of an exemption from social security contributions with the publicly stated purpose of influencing the level of employment. Although the legislators were in fact concerned to protect and improve the situation of part-time employees, as demonstrated by the recognition of special rights for them, by the adoption of specific measures and by the definition of conditions of eligibility for the grant of exemption designed to avoid adding to the precarious nature of part-time work, it may be said that the government measure of exemption from social security contributions was also motivated by the advantages that companies could expect from making use of part-time work.

The effects of this financial incentive are not easy to assess. The growth in part-time work was indeed noticeable starting from 1992, but this development was no greater in France than in other countries where no government incentives had been introduced.[47] The change in the number of part-timers prompted by the measure was estimated at 25 per cent.[48] Every year, some 200,000 employees were the subject of the reduction in social security contributions[49] and in 1998 the number stood at 454,000. This meant that 35 per cent of part-time employees were the subject of the 30 per cent reduction, which seems a fairly modest proportion in view of the financial advantages it represented. On the other hand, although the measure may have contributed to the development of part-time work, it was also accompanied by a sharp rise in involuntary part-time work: from the start of the 1990s onwards, the proportion of involuntary part-time

---

during which work is performed with periods during which no work is performed whose annual working hours are at least one fifth less' than the statutory or collectively agreed working hours. This marked the disappearance of the concept of intermittent work until its subsequent reintroduction under the second *loi Aubry*.

[47] CEC, *Employment in Europe 2002* (n. 2 above), p. 20.

[48] DARES, *La politique de l'emploi* (Paris: Repères, coll. La Découverte, 1997), p. 56.

[49] A. Gubian and V. Le Corre, 'Les incitations publiques en France en faveur du temps partiel dans le secteur privé' (Appendix to Cette, *Le temps partiel en France* – n. 3 above), p. 169; Gaye and Le Corre, 'Les incitations en faveur' (n. 1 above).

work was one of the largest in Europe,[50] reaching a peak in 1997 with an under-employment rate of close on 40 per cent.[51]

The second *loi Aubry* of 19 January 2000 marked a turning-point in this policy, by abolishing the reduction of social security contributions that had been offered as an incentive for using part-time work. Although the state still supports the notion of work sharing, the opportunity to lighten the burden of social security contributions is now directed chiefly at companies that commit themselves to a negotiated reduction of working time. In other words, employment policies are now focussed on a generalised reduction in working time.

3 A loss of flexibility?

The two *lois Aubry* signify a more rigorous regulation of part-time work, which has been reformulated with the stated purpose of making this a voluntary form of employment. They also introduce a new definition of part-time work that complies with the EC Directive on the matter.

3.1 Community influence on the definition of part-time work

The Law of 28 January 1981, which constituted the first attempt to regulate part-time work, gave it a broad definition. Any situation involving working hours 'less than the normal working hours in the establishment concerned and than the statutory working week' was classed as part-time work. The next enactment, i.e. the Government Order of 26 March 1982 designed to give part-time employees a status comparable with that of full-time employees, defined part-time work more strictly without really explaining the reasons for the change. From 1982 until January 2000, employees were deemed to be part-timers if their working hours were less than four-fifths of the statutory working week or the collectively agreed working hours for the sector or company concerned.[52] The five-year Law

---

[50] Conseil Supérieur de L'emploi des Revenus et des Coûts (CSERC), *Durées du travail et emplois, les 35 heures, le temps partiel, l'aménagement du temps de travail* (Paris: La Documentation française, 1998), p. 82. Thus, in 1997, four out of every ten part-timers stated that they would prefer to work longer hours. Between 1990 and 1997 the number of part-time employees increased by 40% while the number of those wanting to work longer hours increased by 75%. Nowadays that proportion is tending to decline. As at March 2002 it stands at only 31.6%: Aerts and Bigot, 'Enquête sur l'emploi 2002' (n. 5 above).

[51] Aerts and Mercier, 'Enquête sur l'emploi 2001' (n. 4 above).

[52] According to the Report to the President of the Republic (quoted in E. Aubry, 'Définition du travail à temps partiel', in Cette, *Le temps partiel en France* (n. 3 above), p. 89), the

of 20 December 1993 modified that definition by introducing annualised part-time work, although without removing its inherent restriction. From then on the concept of part-time employees also included those whose employment incorporated an alternation of periods of activity with periods of inactivity in cases where their annual working time was at least one fifth less than the statutory or collectively agreed working time for the same period.

The latter definition therefore created an intermediate gap between full-time and part-time employees. The intention of the legislators in 1982 in establishing this 'grey' area between 32 and 39 hours was possibly to avoid any confusion between full-time and part-time employees and in so doing 'to make room for a reduction of general full-time working hours'.[53] Nevertheless, the definition was increasingly seen as unjustified and became the target of criticism from the majority of commentators, who emphasised the disadvantages of the system it introduced: employees falling within the grey area, i.e. working between 32 and 39 hours, had no entitlement to the guarantees accompanying part-time work[54] such as the priority of access for part-time employees to full-time jobs becoming available in the company concerned.

French law was also at variance on this point with Directive 97/81/EC of 15 December 1997 on part-time work, which was due to be transposed by 20 January 2000. The second *loi Aubry* of 19 January 2000 therefore modified the definition of part-time work with the stated purpose of bringing French law into conformity with Community requirements.[55] This is, in fact, the sole influence of Community law on French national law acknowledged by the legal drafters and commentators on the subject. For instance, the government made no attempt to rely on the EC Directive to justify the measures introduced by the new law to facilitate transfers from part-time to full-time working.

Under these new provisions, any employee whose working hours are less than the full-time working hours is classed as a part-time employee. The new definition therefore still includes the necessary reference to

protective purpose of the 1982 Order implied an 'exact definition of part-time work'. Yet the definition given was no more exact than the previous one, since it was necessarily formulated with reference to full-time working.

[53] Ibid.

[54] F. Favennec-Héry, 'Le travail à temps partiel: changement de cap' (1999) *Droit Social* p. 1005.

[55] Report by G. Gorce to the National Assembly (Report No. 1826) stating that the proposed new definition of part-time work would 'make the French definition consistent with the Community definition of part-time work'.

full-time working that makes part-time work an inevitably relative concept.[56] The reference value used for full-time working is the statutory working week of 35 hours or, if it is less, that fixed by collective agreement at sectoral or company level. The new definition also takes account of modifications to the calculation of full-time hours, which may be assessed on the traditional weekly basis but alternatively on a monthly or annual basis.

Although the definition no longer specifies any lower limit below which an employee ceases to be classed as a part-time employee, certain limits do exist in practice. Eligibility for certain social security benefits is still, for example, subject to qualifying conditions as to minimum length of service or minimum payment of contributions.[57] The observance of minimum part-time work hours may, however, have been encouraged by the public authorities when they made the financial aid granted to part-time work conditional on a minimum level of working time.

3.2   Growing emphasis on voluntary part-time work

In addition to the above new definition of part-time work, the two *lois Aubry* seek to regulate the flexibility inherent in this form of employment by offering the employee more opportunity to refuse to accept changes that the employer wishes to introduce and by attempting to make part-time work a voluntary and predictable system.[58]

First, the second of the new laws (*loi Aubry II* of 19 January 2000) has extended the opportunities for employees to transfer to part-time work if they so wish. Whereas the employer's freedom to introduce part-time work had formerly been fully recognised, this legislation has now enshrined an actual right to work part-time. That right should preferably

---

[56] Favennec-Héry, *Le travail à temps partiel* (n. 12 above), and 'Les 35 heures et le travail à temps partiel' (1998) *Droit Social* p. 382.

[57] The performance of a part-time occupation gives rise to mandatory membership of the social security system, whatever the length of service involved. On the other hand, under the general system, eligibility for benefits is still conditional on qualifications as to length of service or contributions paid in. In reality, and under the effect of other social security mechanisms (such as universal health cover), there is no longer any real discrimination as regards benefits in kind. In the case of cash benefits (daily sickness or maternity benefit and disability pension), some employment involving less than two-fifths of full-time working hours carries no such entitlement.

[58] D. Jourdan, 'Le temps partiel: une nouvelle conception' (19 January 2000) *Petites affiches* p. 65; special issue of *Liaisons Sociales* on the 35-hour week, May 2000, p. 69; F. Favennec-Héry, 'Le temps vraiment choisi' (2000) *Droit Social* p. 295.

be organised by collective agreement, but in the absence of any such agreement the Law prescribes a procedure that must be followed. The employee
concerned initiates the procedure by informing the employer in writing
of his or her wish to transfer to a part-time job, stating in that letter the
desired working hours and the date envisaged for their introduction.[59]
The employer is required to reply within three months, and above all can
refuse such a request on only two grounds: either because no comparable
job exists in the company, or because he or she can demonstrate that the
transfer requested will have harmful consequences for production and
the company's satisfactory operation. The effectiveness of this right to
work part-time, in the absence of any specific collective agreement on
the matter, will undoubtedly depend on the Cour de cassation's interpretation of the circumstances in which employers can lawfully refuse such
requests: the wording used by the legislators regarding the second ground
for refusal, in particular, leaves it very broad scope in making its appraisal.

Another innovation is that the *loi Aubry II* gives the employee the
opportunity to request the use of annualised part-time hours. On the
basis of their family commitments employees can request a reduction in
their working hours in the form of one or more weeks' leave of absence.
This offers employees with dependent children, for example, the opportunity to reduce their working time to fit in with the dates of the school
year. When an arrangement of this kind is made, a special clause has to
be added to the contract of employment specifying 'the period(s) not
worked': the purpose of this provision is to ensure that the days worked
and not worked are known in advance. Hence, the new Law offers the
possibility of organising annualised part-time hours on the employee's
own initiative, without a special collective agreement and merely via a
clause in the contract of employment. In regard to this situation the Law
states that employees 'can obtain' such a reduction in their working time,
but is silent on the possibility of a refusal from the employer. Is this an
automatic right for any employee who requests it or are there recognised
circumstances where companies can legitimately refuse it? In his Report
to the National Assembly at the Bill stage, Gaëtan Gorce stated 'it would
appear that the employer is not legally bound to accept this way of organising working time if it proves incompatible with the company's needs
or patterns of production'. That suggests that the circumstances in which
the employer can lawfully refuse a request to transfer to part-time work
at all would also apply to this particular situation. Those circumstances,

---

[59] The letter of request must be sent at least six months in advance.

however, also admit of varying degrees of restrictiveness in their interpretation. So what circumstances constitute 'family commitments' sufficient to justify a request for annualised part-time hours?

It will take time to see whether these innovatory provisions will be enough to enable employees to make use of the opportunities offered. In situations where there is no collective agreement on the matter it may perhaps be difficult for an employee to claim the right to work part-time. Added to this, application of the provision involves problems of interpretation.

Not only has the employer's former freedom to choose whether or not to make any use of part-time work at all been restricted, through either collective bargaining or the opportunity given to the individual employee to request a transfer to part-time work, but the latitude formerly available to the employer in arranging the scheduled working hours of part-time employees has been reduced in order to enable employees to know the scheduling and length of their working hours in advance.

For instance, the length of the working day for part-timers and the way in which it is split has been restricted since 1998: within any one working day their scheduled working hours can include only one interruption, of up to a maximum of two hours.[60] The use of extra hours (*heures complémentaires*) has also been brought under stricter regulation. Part-time work consists of basic working hours, as specified in the contract of employment, to which extra hours can be added. Previously, the employer was free to decide whether to make use of these extra working hours and the employee was able either to refuse or to demand to work them. The only restriction was the number of extra hours legally available to the employer: the number of extra hours worked by a given employee could not exceed one-tenth of his or her basic working hours or bring the hours worked up to the level of the statutory or collectively agreed full-time hours. Under the new provision, the number of extra working hours the employee can be required to work is fixed by the contract of employment and a refusal to work extra hours beyond those limits does not constitute misconduct or a ground for dismissal. Furthermore, although the employer can require the employee to work extra hours within the limits fixed by the contract the latter can refuse if the employer has not observed the three days' reasonable advance notification specified

---

[60] Derogations from this rule are permitted through *erga omnes* applicable collective agreements at sectoral level, subject to special forms of remuneration and allowing for the particular requirements of the work in question.

by the Law. Here too, a refusal by the employee is protected since in these circumstances it cannot be deemed to constitute misconduct and therefore cannot justify dismissal.

As originally proposed, the Bill also provided for an enhanced rate of pay for extra hours identical with that for overtime (*heures supplémentaires*),[61] in order to dissuade companies from making systematic use of extra hours. This requirement, an expensive one for companies which under the effect of the same Law were also being required to adopt the new statutory working week of 35 hours, was not included in the final version of the Law. Nevertheless, when a sectoral agreement that has been declared *erga omnes* applicable allows the use of extra hours beyond the limit fixed by the Law,[62] those extra hours attract a 25 per cent increase in the rate of pay. Lastly, the systematic use of extra hours can lead to a modification of the employee's contract of employment. In cases where extra hours are used regularly[63] and, as a result, the hours actually worked by the employee have exceeded the hours specified in the contract by at least two hours a week, the contractual hours are automatically modified to take account of the number of hours being required of the employee, subject of course to the employee's consent.

The flexibility inherent in the use of extra hours has thus been reduced in order to ensure some measure of predictability in the scheduling and duration of part-time employees' working hours. The new procedures that must now be followed in cases where the employer modifies the distribution of the employee's working hours have the same purpose. Even before the *loi Aubry II* came into force, the decisions of the Cour de cassation had been moving things in that direction. Given that the distribution of part-time hours constitutes one of the elements of the contract of employment, the Court made any change conditional on the employee's prior consent. Although it was certainly possible for the contract of employment to include provision for changes to the contractually agreed working hours, the Cour de cassation made the validity of any such clause subject to two conditions: first, the contract had to define the change that was possible, and second, the circumstances in which that alteration could occur had to be stated precisely.[64] The *loi Aubry II* takes its cue from that case-law and gives it more precise definition. Where there is no

---

[61] This means a 25% increase in the rate of pay.
[62] I.e. more than one-tenth of the working hours initially fixed by the contract of employment.
[63] I.e. over a period of 12 consecutive weeks or for 12 weeks during any period of 15 weeks.
[64] Cass. Soc. 7 July 1998, *Bull. Civ.* V, No. 373; Cass. Soc. 6 April 1999, *Bull. Civ.* V, No. 166; Cass. Soc. 7 December 1999, *Bull. Civ.* V, No. 479.

contractual clause providing for it, the employee can oppose a change to his or her working hours, whereas the inclusion of a clause in the contract entitles the employer to impose a change. Nevertheless, to be enforceable against the employee the clause must state the exact circumstances in which a change can be made[65] and the nature of the change. In addition, again in order to give the employee advance warning of any change, the employer must observe a period of at least seven days' advance notification.[66] Lastly, the legislators included a new provision that moderates the effect of such contractual clauses: even where a valid clause exists, in certain situations an employee's refusal to accept the change may be justified and therefore not constitute a ground for dismissal. Three such grounds for refusal are envisaged: pressing family commitments,[67] participation in a formal course of study or higher education or the performance of another job occupied by the employee.

The *loi Aubry II* thus seeks to limit the variability of working time that is inherent in part-time work and to enable employees to organise their time outside working hours without the latter being subject to really major or unforeseeable variations. For some years previously the majority of the Cour de cassation's decisions relating to part-time work had in fact concerned the issue of changes to the distribution of working hours and whether or not employees were entitled to oppose them, so the new legislation should help to clarify the employee's position. The focus has now been placed firmly on the contract, which is by definition an instrument of predictability. The *loi Aubry II* has increased the number of clauses that must be included in a part-time contract: the contract must define the duration of working time, its distribution over the days of the week or weeks of the month and, where applicable, the exact circumstances in which that distribution can be changed. The contract should also indicate the scheduled working hours for each day worked. Although it is not mandatory for those hours to be stated in the contract of employment, the latter must give details of the procedure whereby they are communicated

---

[65] Thus, a clause merely referring to 'operational requirements' or 'circumstances that justify a change' would certainly not be deemed enforceable against the employee because it gives the employer discretionary power; see Jourdan, 'Le temps partiel' (n. 58 above), p. 64.

[66] An *erga omnes* applicable sectoral agreement can stipulate a shorter period, subject to a lower limit of three days and some form of recompense for employees.

[67] According to the authorities, looking after an ill or dependent family member, or the need to provide childcare in the case of a single parent, can be deemed to constitute 'pressing family commitments'.

in writing. Details on the arrangements for the use of extra hours must also be set out in the contract of employment.

The contract of employment has therefore been used as a means of reducing the precarious nature of the part-time employee's situation.[68] Owing to the information that the contract must now contain, employees will be able to organise their private lives without having to fear unexpected changes to their scheduled working hours. In this respect, part-time work has given precedence to regulation by the individual contract of employment.

The wish on the part of the legislators to make part-time work something that is voluntary for employees and to regulate its use in a manner facilitating a better balance between professional and private life could have the effect of reducing the flexibility inherent in this organisation of working time. Without doubt, the abolition of the 30 per cent reduction in social security contributions and the new constraints now imposed on part-time work may well rob it of its attractions as a management tool for companies.[69] Do these developments not contradict the objective of promoting part-time work as an instrument of flexibility within the labour market? The fear that this would be so was certainly expressed by the Opposition during the parliamentary debates on the matter: 'strict regulation of the use of part-time working could hamper growth in employment in many sectors of the economy. Part-time working is still a significant element of employment in all developed countries and there is reason to entertain doubts as to the effects of certain provisions that will make the use of part-time working more expensive.' That view, however, overlooks the fact that the legal framework is subject to adaptation by way of the individual contract of employment and, in particular, collective bargaining.[70]

---

[68] This is despite the fact that elsewhere the *loi Aubry II*, by establishing that a straightforward reduction of working hours under a collective agreement on the subject is not, in itself, enough to constitute a change to the contract of employment in legal terms, weakens the latter's function as regards protecting employees' rights; see M.-A. Moreau, 'Le contrat de travail face à la loi relative à la réduction du temps de travail' (2000) *RJS* p. 247.

[69] Del Sol, 'Travail à temps partiel', 728.

[70] For instance, if the contract of employment does not make specific provision for cases where the distribution of working hours can be changed the employee can refuse to accept any such change, whereas a refusal will not be justified where the contract makes provision for that eventuality.

3.3 Flexibility restored through collective bargaining

Ever since 1980 there has been emphasis on the role of collective bargaining in the regulation of part-time work. According to the view expressed by Jacques Delors in 1980, for instance, the expansion of part-time work was to be governed by two basic principles: the first was 'to grant part-time employees the same guarantees as those offered to full-time employees' and the second was to involve 'the unions in the implementation of voluntary part-time hours'.[71]

For a long time, however, the place of collective bargaining in the regulation of part-time work remained a relatively minor one. Although it had caught the attention of the legislators, part-time work was given little notice in collective bargaining. With only a few exceptions, the subject was entirely ignored in bargaining at cross-industry or sectoral level[72] (admittedly, the freedom accorded to employers to introduce and organise part-time work without prior consultation was hardly conducive to negotiation on the matter).

The first sign of change occurred with the national cross-industry agreement on employment of 31 October 1995, which was intended as a guideline for bargaining at sectoral level.[73] That agreement was the outcome of negotiations on 'the conditions likely to give a fresh impetus to employment and the fight against unemployment', and bargaining on the organisation of working time and its annualisation was accorded a key position. It organised mandatory bargaining on working time at sectoral level[74] which was to include negotiations on part-time work. Some of the rights recognised by the agreement, such as the right to return to full-time working or equal treatment,[75] merely echo principles that had already been laid down by the legislators. It also established the necessity of reconciling working life with family and personal life and the right of employees to request an adjustment of their working time. This is the point on which the agreement was the most innovative, in recommending

---

[71] Quoted in Cette, *Le temps partiel en France* (n. 3 above), p. 11.

[72] J. Marimbert, *Situation et perspectives du travail à temps partiel*, Report to the Ministry of Social Affairs Labour and Solidarity (Paris: La Documentation Française, 1992).

[73] F. Favennec-Héry, 'L'organisation du temps de travail au service de l'emploi. Commentaire de l'accord national interprofessionel sur l'emploi du 31 octobre 1995' (1996) *Droit Social* p. 20.

[74] An obligation had been laid down by the legislators since 1982 to bargain at sectoral level on pay and job classifications, but not on working time.

[75] The affirmation of the principle of equality was nonetheless useful, since the law authorised the social partners to 'adjust to' that principle (see above).

the introduction of individual and collective procedures to allow transfers from part-time to full-time working. The record of negotiations on this issue following the 1995 agreement was an uneven one.[76]

From 1996 onwards the *loi Robien*, which created the first system of financial incentives to encourage the collectively agreed reduction of working time, brought collective bargaining into the picture as regards the adjustment of working time, where it has since been maintained by the *lois Aubry I* and *II*. Nevertheless, such negotiations have not ignored the issue of part-time work. The generalised reduction in working time on which they are focussed necessarily has implications for part-time employees, if only because of the new dividing line thereby created between full-time and part-time work. Furthermore, the thinking on the organisation of working time within companies and the annualisation of working time that is often the objective also prompt thinking on the organisation of part-time work, and in particular its accompanying annualisation. Lastly, the legislators have also made part-time work a bargaining issue that cannot be ignored. The *lois Aubry* legislation explicitly made part-time work a collective bargaining issue by making it an integral part of ongoing negotiations on the generalised reduction of working time.

Nowadays, collective bargaining (at sectoral or company level) is intended to be the primary mechanism for the introduction of part-time work within companies.[77] The absence of an agreement does not prohibit the employer from making use of part-time work (after consulting the employee representatives or, where none exist, informing the Labour Inspector), but the new legislation identifies collective bargaining as the predominant mechanism for its introduction.

Such collective bargaining is also encouraged in the case of derogations from the legal framework that it implements, making it the instrument of a flexibility which has been reduced by the legislators. Finding the balance between flexibility and protection has therefore been made the task of collective bargaining. For instance, the use of intermittent working can

---

[76] Favennec-Héry, *Le travail à temps partiel*, p. 60.

[77] A reference to collective bargaining for the organisation of voluntary part-time work was to be found in Art. L 212-4-5(2). The original Art. L 212-4-2, however, provided that 'part-time hours may be put into practice on the initiative of the head of the company or at the request of the employees' and the organisation of part-time work lay entirely within the scope of the company head's traditional managerial authority. The *loi Aubry II* rewrites that Article and underlines the central role given to collective bargaining in the arrangement of part-time hours: 'part-time hours may be put into practice on the basis of an erga omnes applicable general or specific collective agreement at sectoral level or a general or specific agreement at company or establishment level'.

now be introduced only by collective agreement at sectoral or company level.[78] The introduction of variable part-time work is also conditional on the conclusion of an *erga omnes* applicable sectoral agreement or an unopposed company agreement. Likewise, a specific or general collective agreement is needed in order to extend the permitted use of extra hours[79] or increase the length of the permitted daily break and the number of breaks within a given working day. The period of advance notice of any change to the distribution of working hours can also be reduced by general or specific collective agreement.[80] These latter derogations, which have been authorised since the *loi Aubry I*, can be introduced only by *erga omnes* applicable collective agreement at sectoral level and the agreements concerned must provide for forms of recompense for employees.[81]

The *loi Aubry II* gives an added impetus to collective bargaining on part-time work. Under this second enactment of the new legislation, the conclusion of specific collective agreements on the generalised reduction of working time which thereby create or preserve jobs can give rise to a reduction in social security contributions. In order to establish eligibility for such reductions, however, the agreements in question must contain certain mandatory clauses including, in particular, measures aimed at assisting transfers from a part-time to a full-time job and from a full-time to a part-time job. Hence, the agreement must provide for:

> details of the mechanism whereby full-time employees can obtain a part-time job and part-time employees can obtain a full-time job, the procedure that employees must follow in informing the employer of their request and the deadline by which the head of the company must give a reasoned response to that request. In particular, in the event of a refusal the latter must explain the objective reasons for not agreeing to the request.

Although the *loi Aubry II* therefore abolishes any direct financial incentive for the introduction of part-time work, it nonetheless makes entitlement to a reduction in employment-related costs conditional on the collectively agreed organisation of voluntary part-time work for employees. Collective bargaining therefore simultaneously not only allows the introduction

---

[78] In the case of a derogation agreement at company level, it must not have been opposed by the dominant trade union organisations.

[79] The number of extra hours can be increased from one-tenth to one-third of the contractual working hours.

[80] From seven days to three days.

[81] The agreement must include arrangements providing part-time employees with equality of access to promotion, career and training opportunities. The agreement must also set the minimum period of continuous service necessary to qualify for access to rights.

of greater flexibility in the management of part-time work through the derogations from certain rules that it implements, but also contributes to the better regulation of this type of employment.

It is still too early to assess the effects of the implementation of the *lois Aubry* legislation. It has, unquestionably, fostered a considerable degree of bargaining activity.[82] By the end of June 2000, 34,700 company agreements and 147 sectoral agreements on working time had been concluded. The overall number of agreements concluded remained at the same level in 2001. Although slightly fewer deal with working time, it is still a major bargaining issue.[83] The average weekly working hours dropped from 39.01 in September 1997 to 35.07 at the end of 2002. To begin with, the move to a 35-hour week brought about a decrease in part-time work,[84] as well as longer part-time working hours. Nevertheless, for the past year the customary working hours of part-timers have been decreasing slightly.

The effects on employment are more debatable, however. According to the government, as at 16 August 2001 some 364,000 jobs had been created or saved following the adoption of the *loi Aubry I*.[85] To confer entitlement to reductions in social security contributions, agreements that are concluded must state the number of jobs created or saved by reducing working time. In order to arrive at an accurate breakdown of the number of agreements signed and jobs created or saved, the agreements have been recorded and entered by the *département* Labour Directorates, which then transmit the data collected to the Ministry. This enables the government to publish figures regularly on jobs created or saved as a result of agreements on working time reduction. Although these figures seem reliable, however, they represent only commitments recorded in the agreements. There is certainly a time-lag, not quantified by the government, between those commitments and actual new recruitment. In the case of jobs 'saved', the question is also for how long they will really be saved. Lastly, the figures take no account of the windfall effect, i.e. recruitment that would have happened in any case, independently of any measure on working

---

[82] In 1999 the number of specific collective agreements doubled.

[83] Some 35,000 company agreements were concluded in 2001; see Ministry of Labour, *La négociation collective en 2001*, vol. I, (Paris: Coll. Bilans et Rapports, Editions législatives, 2002).

[84] This is because the shortening of the working week encouraged the transfer to full-time of former part-timers working 20–30 hours a week.

[85] See the Ministry of Employment website on the application of the 35-hour week legislation. www.35h.travail.gouv.fr.

time reduction.[86] The government figures therefore have to be revised downwards. Nevertheless, if a recent survey is to be believed, 'the effects on employment of the agreements on working time reduction (RTT) so far implemented seem largely positive and probably lasting'.[87] Although the present government has just adopted a Law undermining some of the provisions of the *lois Aubry* legislation, one of its latest published reports estimates the number of jobs created by the shortening of the working week and the attendant reduction in social security contributions at 300,000.[88]

As regards part-time work, the proliferation of specific collective agreements entailed by the *loi Aubry II* and the need for such agreements to include provisions on part-time work seem likely to develop a collectively agreed organisation of this form of work.

Some thirty sectoral agreements containing provisions on part-time work were, for example, concluded in connection with the *loi Aubry I* of 13 June 1998.[89] Most make use of the derogations that are permissible at sectoral level and specify forms of recompense.[90] A very large majority also spell out the consequences for part-timers of the generalised reduction of working hours in their companies (possibility of transfer to full-time working, maintenance of previous working hours, reduction of working hours accompanied by compensation in terms of pay). Negotiations on working time reduction also give rise to new opportunities for employees to choose their own working hours.

According to a 1999 study, however, of the 3,035 agreements on working time reduction signed between June 1998 and March 1999 only 1 in 6 includes clauses on part-time work.[91] Even though some contain provisions going beyond what is strictly required, it may be asked whether, in the majority of cases, the clauses on part-time work are a pure formality or

[86] P. Boisard, 'Premier bilan des accords 35 heures', in T. Grumbach and L. Pinna (eds.), *35 heures: négocier les conditions du travail* (Paris: Les éditions de l'Atelier, 2000), p. 32.

[87] A. Gubian, 'La réduction du temps de travail à mi-parcours: premier bilan des effets sur l'emploi' (2000) *Travail et Emploi* p. 9.

[88] See the Ministry of Employment web site on the application of the 35-hour week legislation: www.35h.travail.gouv.fr.

[89] Confédération française démocratique du travail (CFDT), *Pour bien négocier la RTT* (Paris: CFDT, 2000), p. 72.

[90] For instance, the collective agreement for the pharmaceuticals distribution sector provides for a possible split of more than 2 hours in the working day (subject to an upper limit of 4 hours) with two additional rest days (*jours de repos*) per calendar year in lieu. Does this represent a true recompense?

[91] Ministry of Labour (DARES), *La réduction du temps de travail, les enseignements des accords (été 1998 – été 1999)* (Paris: La Documentation française, 1999), p. 193.

really allow employees the right to work part-time granted them by law. In 2001, 52 per cent of the sectoral agreements concluded (i.e. 51) dealt with part-time work. Only 10 of these, though, as against 17 in 2000, mention the option to work part-time.[92] For the moment, therefore, the effectiveness of that right remains very uncertain. A recent study on agreements on working time reduction reached the following conclusion:

> the content of many agreements does no more than recite the wording of the legislation and tack it onto the real-life situation within the company, ignoring certain aspects of the new legal rules such as the forms of recompense for employees. Nor have many agreements made use of the opportunities or mechanisms proposed by the legislators for introducing innovations as regards voluntary working hours or reconciling professional life with family or private life.[93]

Nevertheless, even though part-time work may still be subject to imposed working hours the *lois Aubry I* and *II* should at least make the scheduling of employees' working hours more predictable.

4 Limited influence of the European Employment Strategy (EES) on French policy on part-time work

4.1 The high profile of part-time work in EES Employment Guidelines

Part-time work occupies an important place in the European Employment Strategy initiated by the Luxembourg process, featuring in three of the four pillars for Employment Guidelines. It is one of the methods envisaged for improving the adaptability of companies and their employees through the new patterns of work organisation that it accommodates.[94] The social partners are therefore invited to negotiate on this issue and Member States are required to 'examine the possibility of incorporating in national law more flexible types of contract'. The more widespread use

---

[92] Ministry of Labour, *La négociation collective en 2001* (n. 83 above), p. 67.

[93] I. Daugareilh, P. Iriart and V. Lacoste, 'Le contenu des accords collectifs d'entreprise sur les 35 heures (observations à partir d'une analyse de 300 accords signés en Aquitaine)' (July 2001) *Droit ouvrier* p. 277. See A. Gardin, 'La prise en compte de la vie familiale du salarié dans les normes légales et conventionnelles du travail' (September–October 2002) *Droit Social* p. 854.

[94] Council Decision of 19 January 2001 on Guidelines for Member States' employment policies for the year 2001 [2001] OJ L 22, p. 18, and Council Decision of 18 February 2002 on Guidelines for Member States' employment policies for the year 2002 [2002] OJ L 60, p. 60, Guideline No. 14.

of part-time work is intended to make it easier to reconcile professional and family life[95] and hence contribute to achieving equality of opportunities between women and men. Perhaps more incidentally, part-time work is also involved in the first pillar, as a means of enhancing the capacity of older employees to continue participating in the labour market.[96]

As in Directive 97/81/EC on part-time work, the use of part-time work is thus conceived as both an instrument of flexibility and an instrument of employee protection. No hint is given of any contradictions possibly inherent in the pursuit of these two objectives. On the contrary, the words 'flexibility' and 'security' are used together in what is presumed to be an automatically happy combination. The social partners are invited 'to negotiate and implement at all appropriate levels agreements to modernise the organisation of work, including flexible working arrangements, with the aim of making undertakings productive, competitive and adaptable to industrial change, achieving the required balance between flexibility and security, and increasing the quality of jobs'.[97] The Member States are also urged to 'examine the possibility of incorporating in national law more flexible types of contract, and ensure that those working under the new flexible contracts enjoy adequate security and higher occupational status, compatible with the needs of business and the aspirations of workers'.[98]

However, the Joint Employment Report compiled in 2000 reveals the ambiguities of that approach. It notes that 'employment growth spans all types of work but the proportion of part-time work and temporary jobs continues to rise'.[99] The use here of the word 'but' does suggest that a growth in typical jobs would be preferred, despite the professed support for part-time work. All the more so since the majority of part-time jobs created have been taken up by women, who still make up 80 per cent of part-time employees. Such a trend may certainly help to reduce the gap in the respective employment rates of men and women and enable women to achieve a better balance between their working hours and family life, but it can also signify a form of marginalisation of women in the labour market. Although part-time work may be seen as proving the existence of the flexibility being targeted, it has to be acknowledged that women are bearing the cost of that flexibility. However, the Report also deplores the fact that 'despite some new initiatives, progress on the incorporation of more adaptable forms of contract into Member States' labour law remains

---

[95] Ibid., Guideline No. 17. [96] Ibid., Guideline No. 3.
[97] Ibid., Guideline No. 13. [98] Ibid., Guideline No. 14.
[99] CEC, *Joint Employment Report 2001* (Luxembourg: OOPEC, 2002), p. 17.

limited, with the great majority of Member States adopting only piecemeal or incremental reforms'. It also notes that several Member States report progress in the field of part-time work and that Spain mentions a rise in the number of part-time contracts, which appears to be a positive development from the Commission's point of view. The positive aspect of part-time work features in the analysis of the fourth pillar on equal opportunities.

Nevertheless, there are signs of a change in the Community position and closer attention could well be paid to the security element of the pairing. For example, in its Communication to the Council, the Commission, after reviewing the developments observed in the use of more flexible forms of work organisation, notes that persistent disadvantages remain for the employees concerned and that the Employment Guidelines 'call for a balance between flexibility and security'.[100] Similarly, the most recent *Draft Joint Employment Report* concedes that 'the concept of a balance between both [flexibility and security] – which is essential to the adaptability pillar – needs to be better explored'.[101] Consequently the Employment Guidelines, which are to be redefined in 2003, should, while continuing to encourage flexibility, place emphasis on a more dynamic approach to security that would include training measures.[102] Whether this new approach allows real clarification of the concept (central as it is) of balance between the two poles of flexibility and security is, however, perhaps doubtful.

In any event, the example of France demonstrates that the Community approach to part-time work offers the Member States and social partners considerable freedom in choosing where the balance should lie between the two poles of security and flexibility.

4.2   The more marginal position of part-time work in France's NAPs

Responsibility for drawing up the National Action Plans for Employment (NAPs) lies essentially with the Government and in particular the Ministry of Social Affairs, Employment and Solidarity. Initially, the involvement

---

[100] Communication from the Commission to the Council, the European Parliament, the ESC and the Committee of the Regions, *Taking Stock of Five Years of the European Employment Strategy*, COM (2002) 416 final, Brussels, 17.7.2002, p. 14.

[101] CEC, Communication from the Commission to the Council, *Draft Joint Employment Report 2002*, Brussels, 13.11.2002, COM (2002) 621 final, p. 46.

[102] European Commission, *The Future of the European Employment Strategy (EES). A Strategy for Full Employment and Better Jobs for All*, COM (2003) 6, Brussels, 14.1.2003, p. 14.

of the social partners was limited. They were merely consulted before the first NAP was submitted to the Commission. Subsequently, participation by the social partners was organised by, for example, establishing working parties on specific issues and was made more in-depth. Nowadays, greater and more visible weight is being given in the NAPs to comments by the social partners and their specific contribution is displayed in framed boxes. The government nevertheless still plays the predominant part.

From the first NAP the French strategy on employment was centred round an 'increased growth providing more jobs and benefiting everyone'. The change to the stated objectives of the European Employment Strategy made by the Lisbon European Council did not entail any redefinition of the main strands of the French strategy, but France recast that strategy in the context of the new European objectives. Thus, its 2001 NAP includes new targets in terms of increasing its employment rates.[103] It also emphasises the quality of employment: 'a more stable, better paid job with a higher knowledge content, within the framework of better organisational and health and safety conditions'.

The abolition of the financial incentives granted to promote part-time work could have been interpreted as creating a divergence between the Employment Guidelines and French employment policy. Although part-time work is given a high profile in those Guidelines, France has not only withdrawn financial support for it but also subjected it to far more rigorous rules that correspondingly reduce the potential flexibility to be gained by companies using this form of work organisation. What is more, since 1999 the extent of part-time work within the working population has tended to stabilise and even decrease, in a reversal of the former upward trend. Surely that is contradictory to the objective of promoting part-time work in the capacity of an instrument of flexibility in the labour market as it is conceived in the Employment Guidelines?

There are good reasons not to think so. First, the general reduction of working time brought about by the *lois Aubry* legislation is expected to generate effects similar to those anticipated from an expansion of part-time work. The objective defined in the second pillar is therefore still one of those being pursued by French employment policies even if there has been a change in the instruments employed to achieve that objective.

---

[103] One of the special features of the French situation was that its employment rate for people aged over fifty-five was among the lowest in the EU. The Council's Recommendations stress that feature and urge France to intensify its efforts to increase the participation of older people in working life.

Second, the more rigorous regulation of part-time work introduced by the *lois Aubry* legislation is perfectly in keeping with the general pattern of the Guidelines' fourth pillar. Nor have the various Recommendations made to France by the Council hinted at any contradiction in this respect.

Thus, France's NAPs have essentially broached the issues of part-time work through measures on the generalised reduction of working time, with the *lois Aubry I* and *II* occupying a predominant position as regards both their adoption and the description of their effects. The stated objectives of these two statutes are entirely in keeping with the pillar regarding adaptability. According to the government, the first objective of the negotiated reduction in working time is employment, in the form of a growth that provides more jobs; second, it is also aimed at leading to improved company performance as a corollary of the modernisation of forms of employment; and third, it is intended as a means of improving the situation of employees by, in particular, opening up ways of arranging working hours that accommodate a better balance between professional and private or family life.[104] These replicate the benefits hoped for from a development of part-time work, despite the fact that here they are expected to ensue from a generalised reduction in working time.

Part-time work has also featured in France's NAPs primarily as a subject of negotiation between the social partners on the modernisation of work organisation. Under the 1999 NAP, application of the 1998 *loi Aubry I* was to be the occasion, through the development of collective bargaining, for 'finding a meeting-point between the interests of the company and those of its employees, through the stipulation of rules where necessary, in order properly to reconcile professional and family life through the promotion of more appropriate forms of work organization and the development of a system of voluntary part-time work that takes account of employees' family commitments'. The 2000 NAP takes stock of the negotiations prompted by the *lois Aubry* legislation and points out that 'in the case of part-time employees, new guarantees have been defined as regards, in particular, extra hours, breaks and the minimum duration of contracts such that, in the long run, the agreements concerned represent progress towards a form of part-time work that is closer to voluntary working hours than that achieved by some of our fellow Member States'. Nevertheless, certain other analyses of the content of those agreements seem less optimistic than the government view.[105]

---

[104] *France: National Action Plan for Employment 2000* (Luxembourg: OOPEC, 2000).
[105] Daugareilh, Iriart and Lacoste (2001), *Le contenu des accords* (n. 93 above), p. 277.

Analysis of the *loi Aubry II* is focussed more on the fourth pillar, since this second enactment has the effect of bringing the part-time regime under stricter regulation. According to the government, it 'has given due regard to making it easier to reconcile professional life and family life, whether it be in imposing limits on extra hours for part-timers, improving procedures for transferring to part-time work, . . . or stipulating a minimum period of advance warning for any changes to work schedules'. Involuntary part-time work, after having reached a peak in 1997, is certainly continuing to decrease: the proportion of people working part-time who would prefer to work longer hours fell from 39.4 per cent in March 1997 to 31.6 per cent in March 2002. The introduction of the 35-hour week and the adjustment of work patterns that it has generated in many cases could be the reason behind that decrease as well as an improving situation in the labour market.[106]

France's policy on working-time reduction has prompted only very vague Council Recommendations. After a policy on the adjustment and negotiated reduction of working time had been adjudged one of the best practices in 1998 from the various NAPs, France was urged to 'pursue efforts to modernize work organization with a view to better combining security with greater adaptability to facilitate access to employment; closely monitor the net effects of the implementation of the 35 hour working week legislation, especially on small businesses'.[107]

After having occupied a key position in France's early NAPs, the *lois Aubry* of 1998 and 2000 on working-time reduction have nowadays ceded that position to new measures. Hence, the 2002 NAP gave prominence to the Law on Social Modernisation that was adopted on 17 January 2002. This contains a number of provisions on fixed-term contracts designed to bring the use of precarious forms of employment under tighter regulation.[108] It also includes a major section on vocational training. In

---

[106] Aerts and Mercier, 'Enquête sur l'emploi 2001' (n. 4 above), J. Bué and D. Roux-Rossi, 'Salarié(e)s à temps partiel et réduction collective du temps de travail: la question du choix' (April 2002) *Travail et Emploi* p. 39.

[107] Council Recommendation 2002/178/EC of 18 February 2002 on the implementation of Member States' employment policies (OJ [2002] L 60, p. 70. See also Council Recommendation 2001/64/EC of 19 January 2001 on the implementation of Member States' employment policies (OJ [2001] L 22, p. 27), and Council Recommendation 2002/178/EC of 18 February 2002 on the implementation of Member States' employment policies (OJ [2002] L 60, p. 70).

[108] The innovations introduced by the legislators are, nevertheless, very limited. The Law makes it more difficult to use a direct succession of very short fixed-term contracts and brings the amount of the end-of-service payment due at the end of fixed-term contracts into line with that in the case of temporary agency contracts.

particular, it redefines the rules governing redundancies and expands the consultation process that must accompany any programme involving more than ten redundancies. It should, however, be noted that these measures on redundancy have since been suspended by a Law of 3 January 2003 adopted on the initiative of the new government that was elected in June 2002.[109]

It is difficult to measure the influence of the European Employment Strategy on France's employment policies. The adaptability pillar is certainly the one whose implementation leaves the Member States and social partners the most freedom and in which an assessment of actions is the most difficult, whereas in the case of the first pillar the existence of quantified targets makes it possible to measure the progress achieved. The *Joint Employment Report* itself notes that 'implementation of the four pillars is still uneven. Most of the progress achieved has been in the employability pillar.'

In the case of part-time work any such influence seems very limited. Its current regulation is inextricably linked to the 35-hour week legislation, and none of the participants in the lively debates occasioned by the two *lois Aubry* used arguments that could have been seen as drawn from the Community context. The only visible trace of Community influence lies in the new statutory definition of part-time employees, expressly intended to transpose the 1997 Directive. Although in drawing up its NAPs the Government has obviously had to express its policy in terms of the vocabulary and syntax used in the Guidelines, in the case of working time that has necessitated very little adjustment since the objectives of the French legislators were very closely akin to the objectives regarding employment defined by the Guidelines.

Neither the Guidelines nor the Recommendations seem to have caused any modification of the policy decisions made on the subject of working time. The Guidelines are capable, however, of accommodating the measures taken by the new government without any real difficulty, despite the fact that these measures represent a departure from the employment policy pursued by the previous socialist government. For instance, the Law on Social Modernisation, which in particular modified the rules on redundancies, appears in the 2002 NAP in response to one of the Council Recommendations to France to intensify efforts to modernise work organisation. The suspension of that Law by the new Law of

---

[109] Law No. 2003/6 of 3 January 2003 on the revival of collective bargaining over economic dismissals, OJ No. 3 of 4 January 2003, p. 255.

3 January 2003 is very likely to feature, in its turn, in the 2003 NAP as also moving in the direction of a modernisation of work organisation. The inclusion in the next NAP of the Law of 17 January 2003[110] reforming the *lois Aubry* can also be expected. Without going back on the definition of a 35-hour statutory working week, this new Law conclusively breaks away from the financial support granted to the shortening of working hours. The reductions in social security contributions that had been offered to employers who concluded specific agreements on the generalised reduction of working time are to be gradually abolished and replaced by a single system for reducing employment-related costs in respect of the lowest-paid employees, whatever their working hours. The rules on the use of overtime have also been relaxed. Although they contradict the *lois Aubry* legislation, these new measures will probably feature in the NAPs as responding to the same objectives. Thus, the French example demonstrates the extreme malleability of the Employment Guidelines in accommodating widely diverse employment policies.

[110] Law No. 2003/47 of 17 January 2003 on wages, working time and the development of employment, OJ No. 15 of 18 January 2003, p. 1080.

5

Germany: part-time work – a bone of contention

MAXIMILIAN FUCHS

1 Statistical data

1.1 The proportion of part-time to full-time employees

In 1973 the proportion of part-time employees among the total number
of employees was 10.1 per cent, which increased in 1983 to 12.6 per cent,
and to 18 per cent in 1998.[1] In 2001 there were 6.8 million part-time jobs
out of 36.6 million employees, or 18.4 per cent.[2]

1.2 Categorisation by occupation

The categorisation of part-time employees into different types of occupation differs substantially between men and women. In the case of women,
the largest proportion of part-time employment is in the area of services
with a share of around 24 per cent, while in that of men it is in professional activities (lawyers, tax advisers, accountants, etc.) with a share
of over 20 per cent. For women this is followed by office workers and

---

[1] For the statistical and empirical data set out in sections 1–4, I refer to the following sources:
Ulrich Walwei and Heinz Werner, 'Mehr Teilzeitarbeit als Mittel gegen die Arbeitslosigkeit?'
(1996) 3 *Wirtschaftsdienst* p. 131 at 136; Petra Beckmann, 'Beschäftigungspotentiale der
Ausweitung von Teilzeitarbeit' (1997) 9 *Wirtschafts- und Sozialwissenschaftliches Institut
Mitteilungen* p. 634 at 640; Gerhard Bosch, 'Das Ende von Arbeitszeitverkürzungen?'
(1998) 6 *Wirtschafts- und Sozialwissenschaftliches Institut Mitteilungen* p. 345 at 359;
Stephen Lehndorff, 'Von der "kollektiven" zur "individuellen" Arbeitszeitverkürzung?'
(1998) 9 *Wirtschafts- und Sozialwissenschaftliches Institut Mitteilungen* p. 569 at 579;
Statistisches Bundesamt, *Fachserie 1, Reihe 4.1.1* (1990–8); Bundesministerium für Familie (ed.), *Die Familie im Spiegel der amtlichen Statistik* (Berlin, 1999), p. 113; Colette
Fagan, Jacqueline O'Reilly and Jill Rubery, 'Teilzeitarbeit in den Niederlanden, Deutschland und dem Vereinigten Königreich: Eine Herausforderung für den Geschlechter-
vertrag?' (1999) 1 *Wirtschafts- und Sozialwissenschaftliches Institut Mitteilungen* p. 58
at 69.
[2] Statistisches Bundesamt, *Leben und Arbeiten in Deutschland, Ergebnisse des Mikrozensus
2001* (Wiesbaden, 2002).

technicians with a share of 20 per cent each, and for men by so-called 'unskilled labour' with a share of around 20 per cent and technicians with a share of around 14 per cent. Part-time work plays no role in agriculture. These figures are based on the year 1996.

1.3   Division of part-time work by gender

For a long time it has been the general rule in the Federal Republic of Germany that part-time work is women's work. A distinction must nevertheless be drawn in this regard between developments in the *Länder* of the former West Germany and in those of the ex-GDR. In the former, 29.6 per cent of the total number of women employees were engaged in part-time work in 1985. This figure rose from 33.8 per cent (1990) to 37.3 per cent (1995) to 40 per cent (1998). For men, the proportion in 1990 was 2.2 per cent, which rose in 1995 to 3.2 per cent, and in 1998 to 4.5 per cent.

In the new *Länder*, in 1991 17.6 per cent of women employees were engaged in part-time work compared with 1.7 per cent of men. This was only half of the corresponding figure in the *Länder* of the former West Germany. The reason for this is the different systems. In the former GDR part-time work barely existed. Women provided a large share of the family household income. Women would work full-time even when the household contained a number of children. This was made possible by a correspondingly high number of childcare facilities. That the situation in the new *Länder* gradually began to resemble that in the West is shown by the figures for 1995, when 20.8 per cent of women and 2.9 per cent of men employees were engaged in part-time work. The corresponding figures for 1998 were 21.6 per cent for women and 3.3 per cent for men.

1.4   The family and part-time employment

There is an apparent connection between employment in part-time work and the fulfilment of family obligations, in particular the raising of children. In Germany in 1996, 55 per cent of all women between the ages of 15 and 64 who had children were employed, more than half of these in part-time employment. Unmarried or separated mothers are more often engaged in employment than mothers who are married or live together with a partner and they also have longer working hours. The smaller the number of children and the older the youngest child, the more often mothers are employed and the higher is the number of those who are engaged in full-time employment. The increase in the amount of income earned by mothers derives almost exclusively from the growth in part-time employment. The situation is quite different in relation to fathers. Nine out of ten fathers are employed, and only 7 per cent are engaged in part-time work.

2 Part-time work – the German context

2.1 Objectives

In principle there is no question in the Federal Republic of Germany that part-time work must be regarded as beneficial to the economy and that it must, therefore, be expanded and promoted. However, there is difference of opinion as to the objectives linked to part-time work and consequently what form it should take. It is therefore necessary to clarify those objectives briefly in the following.

2.1.1 Views of employees and trade unions

It has become customary with respect to perceptions of part-time work on the part of part-time employees to distinguish between involuntary and voluntary part-time work. The latter type refers to situations in which the employee consciously chooses to undertake part-time work because the resulting income improves the household income of the family or of two partners living together. In this context, part-time work contributes in particular to the compatibility of family and work for women. However, part-time work is no longer chosen solely with a view to family requirements. It may often be seen as part of a set of measures directed at improving the work–life balance of employees as they increasingly wish either to reduce their workload or to stop working altogether for a certain period of time in order to give priority to other interests. These interests can be of a purely private nature (e.g. longer stays abroad for tourism reasons) or they may be motivated by professional reasons. An employee may wish to make use of this time for participation in training or further education courses.

For a long time part-time work was regarded sceptically by the German trade unions. In addition to the experience that part-time employees were often working in positions below their qualifications and were hardly ever offered chances of further education or promotion, the fear arose that part-time work would endanger full-time jobs.[3] It was further feared that the expansion of part-time work would counteract gender emancipation and that a combination of so-called 'permanent' and 'peripheral' staff would evolve.[4] In more recent times, however, the unions have given indisputably positive recognition to an expansion of part-time work while simultaneously demanding a guarantee of legal protection for this group of employees.[5] 'Involuntary part-time work' refers to situations in which an employee works part-time purely as a preferable alternative to unemployment. In these cases, it is associated particularly with the hope of gaining easier access to full-time employment.

2.1.2 Views of employers and employers' organisations

From the perspective of the employer, part-time work – in particular in the services sector – is seen as a solution to problems of limited labour capacities. Advantages are seen in the improved ratio of capacity to client or production requirements, a reduction in overtime (premium rates of pay for overtime are thereby eliminated) and the higher productivity of part-time workers compared with that of full-time workers. In the opinion of the employers and their organisations, the question as to whether part-time work should be used, or for how long it should be carried out, should largely depend upon the needs of the company. In this way the competitiveness of enterprises would be strengthened in the long term and jobs would be secured or rather created.[6]

Against this positive view, however, some employers also have reservations as to part-time work. Partly it is argued that certain jobs are not divisible. Mostly, however, reference is made to the high co-ordination and supervision costs associated with the division of work. It is argued that because of increases in organisational and administrative costs, total wage costs do not remain stable when it comes to growth in part-time work. Economists have therefore proposed limited-term subsidies for businesses seeking to implement a general reduction in normal working time. These subsidies would be financed by savings in unemployment benefits. This

---

[3] See P. Pulte and R. Westphal, *Teilzeitarbeit und betriebliche Mitbestimmung* (Neuwied, Kriftel, Berlin: Luchterhand, 1997), p. 2.

[4] G.-A. Lipke, 'Individualrechtliche Grundprobleme der Teilzeitarbeit' (1991) *Arbeit und Recht*, p. 76 at 78.

[5] See 'Dokumentation: DGB – Anforderungen an eine sozialverträgliche Teilzeitinitiative' (1995) *Soziale Sicherheit* p. 14 at 18; Statement of the Deutscher Gewerkschaftsbund of 8 September 2000, p. 218.

[6] W. Küttner, *Personalbuch 2001* (8th edn, Munich: Besle, 2001), p. 2047.

assumes that newly created positions can be filled by the unemployed, who would otherwise have to rely on such benefits.

2.1.3   Views of political parties and government

The commonly accepted views of employees and employers are reflected in the spectrum of the political parties and the government. For years they, too, have taken a positive stand towards part-time work and encouraged the social partners to press for part-time work in enterprises, and are trying to create a favourable legal framework for the implementation of part-time work by making use of legislative measures. The interests and objectives of the employees and employers affected, as described in the previous two sections, have been acknowledged. Understandably, however, the political parties and the government place greater importance on the political aspect of employment. Quoting studies[7] that indicate a high potential for employment inherent in part-time work, they see the expansion of part-time work in enterprises as a decisive instrument for the reduction of unemployment.[8]

2.2   Strategies

There are, of course, different possibilities available for the realisation of the objectives described in section 2.1. above, leading to the question of the correct strategy for their implementation. In principle three important cornerstones emerge when developments in the Federal Republic of Germany are considered.

2.2.1   Alliance for Work

Efforts had already been undertaken in January 1996 by the former Federal Government under Helmut Kohl to forge an 'Alliance for Work' (*Bündnis für Arbeit*) between the parties to collective agreements and the government. The new government, which was formed by the Social Democrats and the Greens, placed great importance in their coalition negotiations at the end of 1998 on a new constitution for the Alliance for Work. The coalition agreement between the two ruling parties stated on this point

---

[7] See, for example, the study by H. Düll and P. Ellguth published in (1999) 3 *Mitteilungen aus der Arbeitsmarkt- und Berufsforschung* p. 269 at 280.
[8] The President of the Federal Labour Office said in a press interview in September 2000, that 1 million new jobs could be created if the current desire for part-time work were realised: cf. (1999) 1 *Mitteilungen aus der Arbeitsmarkt- und Berufsforschung* p. 5.

that in the battle against unemployment an Alliance for Work was necessary, by which was to be understood an accord between State, trade unions
and businesses on concrete measures, with fair compromises between all
concerned.[9]

This was no new idea; rather it was the old idea of a tripartite social
pact. It is an expression of the hope that important targets can be set and
thereby improvements in the labour market achieved through a social
pact such as this, which unifies the most important forces in the State and
economy. The agreements of the Alliance for Work are not binding on the
participants in a legal sense. In fact, they represent merely a declaration of
intent as to future behaviour. Nonetheless, the agreements reached should
not be underestimated. No signatory party can easily afford unilaterally to
pull out of the arrangement. The participating social partners undertake
to exert influence on their respective organisations, sub-organisations and
members to ensure that the latter comply with the consensus that has been
established. This applies above all in connection with the conclusion of
collective agreements. The task of the government under this arrangement
is to implement the Alliance's resolutions in the form of legislation. The
government is also supposed to convince Parliament of the necessity of
the measures.

The Alliance for Work enjoys high political acceptance. It is also overwhelmingly supported by academics. Nevertheless, there are still a number of critics among economists.[10] It is said in particular that the parties
to the agreements concluded do not possess the necessary information
on the economic sector. The criticism of corporatism, with its supposi-
tion that the participants primarily pursue group interests, has also been
raised. Finally, some have pointed to constitutional problems in that an
economic constitution in a State subject to the rule of law tramples on
the constitutive separation between the legitimate exercise of State power
and the guarantee of private autonomous action.

Irrespective of how the existence of an Alliance for Work might be perceived on theoretical or political grounds, it has led to a range of visible
and concrete measures in the labour market. As regards our present theme
of part-time work, this applies in large measure to the development of

---

[9] For a discussion about the political and economic premises of the Alliance for Work and
the problems of legal doctrine, see V. Rieble, 'Bündnis für Arbeit – "Dritter Weg" oder
Sackgasse?' (1999) Recht der Arbeit p. 169 at 177.

[10] See, for example, U. Fehl, 'Bündnis für Arbeit', in Eckhard Knappe and Norbert Berthold
(eds.), Ökonomische Theorie der Sozialpolitik (Heidelberg: Physica-Verlag, 1998), p. 207.

the system of partial retirement. It is not overstating the case to say that, from its beginnings in 1996 up to the last amendments which entered into force on 1 January 2000, the regulatory scheme governing partial retirement was agreed exclusively and in detail in the context of the Alliance for Work and that the legislation was merely enacted by the legislature.

2.2.2   Collective agreements

Apart from commitments by the social partners (trade unions, employers' associations) in the field of partial retirement, where numerous collective agreements have been concluded (see below, 4.3.), there is still no clear strategy for the place of part-time work in the negotiation process between employers and employee representatives. This is partly due to the fact that neither trade unions nor employers' associations have so far developed a homogeneous position as far as part-time work is concerned. What kind of part-time work is desirable, and what rules are to be developed for it in the framework of collective agreements, are still issues open to discussion.[11]

Trade unions place great emphasis on collective agreements in which part-time work is used as a means to prevent dismissals, and also to create new jobs. To give an idea of what is meant by these efforts I refer as an example to the collective agreement reached some years ago between the metal workers' union, Hannover, and the association of metal employers of the *Land* Niedersachsen.[12] Firstly, this collective agreement permits the reduction of normal working time at shop level in order to avoid redundancies. What is still more important and completely new, however, are guidelines for the promotion of employment set down by the trade union and the employers' association concerned. In these guidelines employers and works councils are empowered to conclude agreements to reduce the working time of the whole or part of the business or of a single worker. In this case the workers concerned are paid a premium provided that in exchange for the reduction of working time an unemployed person is hired. The premium is paid by an organisation founded by the trade union and the employers' association. The funds for this organisation are financed by the employers' association and amount to €5.1 million.

[11] For a brief outline of the different aspects of problems to be solved see U. Zachert, 'Flexicurity im Arbeitsrecht, eine schwierige Balance' (2000) 5 *Wirtschafts- und Sozialwissenschaftliches Institut Mitteilungen* p. 283 at 290.

[12] On this collective agreement see H. Meine, 'Der Tarifvertrag zur Beschäftigungsförderung in der niedersächsischen Metallindustrie' (1998) *Arbeit und Recht* p. 356 at 359.

Whether this experiment will prove a success and be of a pivotal character for other sectors remains to be seen.

2.2.3   Legislative intervention

In comparison with other European countries, the Federal Republic of Germany began to establish legal regulations on part-time employment for the first time relatively early, in 1985. From the very outset, the view has existed that part-time employees have a fundamental right to claim the protection of labour law. So a strategic objective of the law-maker has always been the flanking of part-time employment by labour law.

3   Research framework

3.1   Objectives and techniques chosen by the law-maker

The main emphasis of the deliberations in the rest of this chapter is upon the legal regulation of part-time work. The analysis is governed by two fundamental questions:

– to what extent has the law-maker attempted to take the objectives described in 2.1 into account?
– what instruments and techniques has the law-maker used to realise those objectives?

Since experience has shown that individual objectives can be contradictory to each other, it is essential to show how the law-maker has resolved certain conflicts of interest and objective.

3.2   The influence of European law on the regulation of part-time work

Given the activities of the European Community in the area of part-time work, it goes without saying that the legislation of the Federal Republic of Germany cannot be regarded in isolation from the rulings of European law. Therefore, on the one hand, the role of the European Court's jurisprudence in connection with the development of national law must be looked at, and, on the other hand, it must be shown in what way the German law-maker has followed the proposals of the European Commission and Council with respect to part-time work and, in particular, Directive 97/81/EC on part-time work.

4 Development of part-time regulation

4.1 The beginnings of part-time regulation in employment law in 1985

For years questions of part-time work hardly concerned German courts. It was not until 1976 that the Federal Labour Court (*Bundesarbeitsgericht*), the highest German court in labour disputes, was for the first time required to consider a question relating to part-time work.[13] The subject-matter of the dispute was a provision of a collective agreement which expressly restricted to full-time employees entitlement to a so-called transitional benefit payable on the termination of employment. The Chamber of the Court hearing the case held that there had been no violation of the constitutional guarantee of equal treatment. The first change to this position was in a judgment of the same Court in 1982.[14] In this case, a female part-time employee challenged her exclusion from a benefits rule applicable to her employer's workplace which applied only to full-time employees. The Court considered that the provision under which she was excluded from these benefits was inconsistent with the principle of equal treatment. The difference in the amount of work performed was in itself not a sufficient objective reason for the difference in treatment between full-time and part-time employees. This decision of the Federal Labour Court was of decisive importance and – as we shall see – the drafters of the Promotion of Employment Act took this case as a starting-point.

4.1.1 Provisions of the Promotion of Employment Act regulating part-time employment

The legislature expressly described the Promotion of Employment Act (*Beschäftigungsförderungsgesetz*) of 1985[15] as part of a comprehensive political programme for improvement of the employment situation. Section 1 of the Act consequently made it easier to reach agreement on part-time employment contracts. The intention here was to provide employers with an incentive to take on more employees without the risk of having to employ workers fully in unfavourable commercial situations.

---

[13] See Bundesarbeitsgericht (BAG) AP Nr. 2 for section 62 BAT.
[14] Bundesarbeitsgericht AP Nr. 1 for section 1 BetrAVG.
[15] For a brief outline of the Act see M. Löwisch, 'Das Beschäftigungsförderungsgesetz 1985' (1985) *Der Betriebsberater* p. 1200 at 1207.

During the drafting of the Act, the then government explained its objectives in regulating part-time work as follows.[16] The number of part-time employees had for a number of years risen substantially not only in absolute terms but also in proportion to the total workforce. According to various estimates, the proportion of part-time workers in the total workforce was of an order of magnitude of between 8 and 15 per cent. There was at the same time a serious shortage of part-time jobs. In December 1983 there were 240,000 registered unemployed looking for part-time work. It was therefore necessary to promote the creation of further part-time jobs. This would also meet the needs of employers, as a proliferation of part-time jobs could increase the flexibility and efficiency of businesses. At the same time, it would correspond to the wishes of those employees who either did not want or were unable to enter into full-time work for, say, family reasons. At the time this mainly concerned women, who constituted over 90 per cent of the total number of part-time employees. One in every four unemployed women was looking for a part-time job.

The provisions governing part-time work are contained in the second Part of the Act, in sections 2–6. The legislature proceeded on the assumption that part-time work could be made attractive only if employment conditions could be better protected than had formerly been the case. Only in this way could it be expected that full-time employees interested in part-time work would actually make the transition to part-time work. This goal was to be achieved primarily through the establishment of a ban on discriminating against part-time compared with full-time workers. In addition, the Act aspired to a generally acceptable formulation for those types of part-time work that have gradually developed in practice, namely flexible working hours and job-sharing.

4.1.2   The statutory definition of part-time work

Section 2(2) of the Act provides that employees are considered to be part-time employees when their regular weekly working hours are shorter than the regular weekly working hours of comparable full-time employees in the same workplace. Where no agreement exists as to the number of regular working hours, the relevant standard is provided by the number of hours which are on average worked per week over a year. The standard for determining the existence of a situation of part-time employment is therefore established in terms of the regular working hours of comparable

---

[16] See Bundesrat, *Entwurf eines Beschäftigungsförderungsgesetzes 1985 (BeschFG 1985)* Bundesrats-Drucksache 393/84, p. 17 at 18.

employees in the same workplace. The period of a week was chosen as the reference period because the working week is used as the most common means of specifying working hours not only in collective agreements but also in individual employment contracts. At the same time, it was intended that new developments in relation to the further flexibility of working hours should also be reflected.

4.1.3   The ban on discriminating against part-time workers

Section 2(1) of the Act states: 'An employer may not treat a part-time employee differently from a full-time employee on the basis of the fact of working part-time unless there are objective grounds justifying such different treatment.'

As has already been mentioned, this provision took its cue from a 1982 decision of the Federal Labour Court. According to this line of jurisprudence different treatment is deemed to exist if the reason for the difference in treatment is the number of working hours. This will always be the case when an employee is excluded from the application of a particular rule solely because he works less than the number of hours required for the application of that rule.

4.1.4   Specially regulated forms of part-time work

4.1.4.1 Adaptation of working time to the availability of work (*Kapovaz*)   When the legislature undertook the task of regulating part-time work in 1985, it also needed to formulate a position on a particular form of part-time work which has become common within the Federal Republic, namely, 'capacity-oriented variable working time' (*Kapovaz*). Employment relationships of this type are based on agreements reached in advance as to the amount of time to be worked per month or per year, the employer then being entitled to call on the employee to work as and when demand dictates within that period until the total amount of agreed working time has been exhausted.[17]

In regulating this form of working time (in Article 4 of the Promotion of Employment Act) the legislature was pursuing two goals. On the one hand, the intention was to give statutory recognition to this form of part-time work and to avoid doubts as to its legality. On the other hand, it

---

[17] For further information see Marion Malzahn, 'Das Beschäftigungsförderungsgesetz und kapazitätsorientierte variable Arbeitszeiten' (1985) *Arbeit und Recht* p. 386 at 390; Peter Schüren, 'Abrufarbeit mit variabler Arbeitszeit' (1996) *Neue Zeitschrift für Arbeitsrecht* p. 1306 at 1307; Hans-Jürgen Meyer, *Kapazitätsorientierte variable Arbeitszeit* (Neuwied, Darmstadt: Luchterhand, 1989).

seemed important and necessary to afford protection to affected employees. The issue was that of a generally acceptable form of employment conditions. In this respect, it was inconceivable that the employer should have sole discretion to decide the amount of work. This would have been tantamount to the employer having the final say on the amount of remuneration. Such a one-sided arrangement to the advantage of the employer would have contradicted the presumption, enshrined in German law, that the mutual obligations of the employment relationship are to be determined by statute, or by collective or individual agreements.

Against this background and in the light of the legislature's declared goals, the Act now stipulates that an agreement under which the employee is to provide labour as and when work is available must at the same time also specify the duration of the time to be worked. Where there is no such agreement, the Act deems a weekly working time of ten hours to have been agreed.

Furthermore, the Act also provides that an employee is obliged to provide services only when the employer gives him at least four days' prior notice each time. This notice period is designed to give the employee sufficient time to organise his private life correspondingly. It is also relevant that the employee should have the opportunity to utilise the time for alternative employment when not required by the employer, which would usually not be possible in the absence of such a notice period. The four-day period between the notice given to the employee and the commencement of employment is designed to take appropriate account of both operational requirements and the needs of the employee. If the employer fails to comply with this notice period, the employee is entitled to refuse to perform the work. This sanction is intended to ensure the effectiveness of the Act. It does not, however, rule out the possibility that in individual cases the employee might also voluntarily agree to work even in the absence of a notice period.

Lastly, the Act provides that in the absence of an agreement between employer and employee as to the length of daily working hours, the employer is obliged to engage the employee for a minimum of three consecutive hours. Following the model of existing workplace regulations, this is designed to avoid situations in which the employee, against his expectations, is engaged in work for only short periods on each occasion, which would place inappropriate burdens on him such as, for example, a long journey to and from the workplace and difficulties in making use of the remaining time. If the employer fails to make the use of the employee's services that he is obliged to do, this does not affect the employee's claim to wages for the prescribed minimum working time. This rule does not exclude the possibility that the employee may reach an agreement with the employer in advance establishing a daily working time under which he undertakes to work for periods of less than three hours. This is because in such cases an employee should be able to organise his time in advance to take this into account.

4.1.4.2 Job-sharing   Job-sharing is regulated under section 5 of the Promotion of Employment Act. In this respect the Act recognises two types of job-sharing employment relationship. The first is the customary form of employment where two or more employees share the same job. The so-called '*Turnus*' relationship, however, is regulated in the same way. A '*Turnus*' relationship exists when groups of employees alternate between specified jobs in fixed time periods.

Job-sharing raises a number of legal questions.[18] The legislature did not aim to regulate all of them. Rather, it dealt only with a selection of problems. The main problem was perceived to be the extent to which an employee can be obliged to substitute for another employee in the event that the latter is unable to work. This core question has been fully resolved by the rule that, in principle, employees who share a job cannot automatically be obliged in advance to substitute for another employee who shares the same job in the event that the latter is unable to work. Rather, there must be a special agreement for each occasion of substitution. On the other hand, this principle should not be applied rigidly. A flexible solution was therefore chosen, providing that in cases of 'urgent operational need' it is possible to agree on substitution obligations. Such cases of 'urgent operational need' are defined as situations when work needs to be completed that is so urgent that a failure to complete it would cause substantial damage to the operation of the business or to the third-party relationships of the business and when it would not be possible for this work to be completed by other employees of the business. In the performance of such an agreement the employee is still only under an obligation to work to the extent that this is reasonable for him in each individual case.

---

[18] See H. T. Danne, *Das Job-Sharing, seine arbeits- und sozialversicherungsrechtliche Beurteilung nach In-Kraft-Treten des Beschäftigungsförderungsgesetzes* (Neuwied, Darmstadt: Luchterhand, 1986).

4.2   The treatment of part-time work in social security law

4.2.1   Social insurance law

4.2.1.1 Reduced financial benefits for part-time employees   In the area of social security (health insurance, accident insurance, pension insurance, unemployment insurance), under German law the fundamental principle applies that the amount of cash benefits depends on the amount of income earned from employment. The higher the income, the higher the benefits received on the realisation of a risk (sick pay, disability or old-age pensions, industrial injury pensions). Entitlements under social security law are therefore significantly weakened in the case of part-time work. It is only in those – in practice very few – cases where there is a high part-time income that social security benefits applying in the event of the realisation of a social risk are sufficient to support an appropriate standard of living. It is unquestionably the case that the dependence of social security benefits on earnings is a decisive impediment to the acceptance and growth of part-time work.

4.2.1.2 'Minor' employment   Employees engaged in 'minor' employment (regulated in section 8 part IV of the Social Security Code) have no insurance protection in respect of health insurance, pension insurance or unemployment insurance. The statutory definition of 'minor' (also called 'marginal') employment is when the job regularly consists of less than 15 hours per week and the average monthly wage does not exceed DM 630 (€325 from 1 January 2002). The original intention of the legislature in passing the Law, which specifically excludes social insurance, was to promote greater flexibility. The purpose was to take account of the interests of both employees and businesses. It was intended that a person who already had a permanent job or who wished to improve his financial situation through such a job on an occasional basis should not be burdened by social insurance contributions. At the same time, the intention was also to cater to the interests of business in having access to the use of such 'second jobbers' in addition to the traditional workforce (from a taxation point of view these employment conditions were attractive to businesses because they had only to pay a one-off tax of 20 per cent which they then frequently passed on to the employees).

What was originally conceived as a sensible exception increasingly developed into an important form of employment. According to a study carried out by the Federal Ministry of Labour and Social Affairs, in 1996 there were 5.6 million workers engaged in 'minor' employment[19] (other studies arrived at far higher figures). This meant that 17.4 per cent of the total of 32.18 million employees were engaged in 'minor' employment. The overwhelming majority of these jobs were and still are filled by women.

This was also the reason why German Social Courts (*Sozialgerichte*) called upon the ECJ by way of preliminary references to review the compatibility of these rules with ex-Art. 119 EC. The ECJ denied that there was any infringement of this Article.[20] The Court was of the opinion that the German Law was justified by objective factors which have nothing to do with discrimination on grounds of gender. Such objective measures not amounting to discrimination will always be present when the means chosen serve a legitimate objective of the social policy of the Member State whose legislation is in question and are designed for and necessary to the achievement of this objective. Against this background, the ECJ accepted as objective, non-discriminatory social and employment policy goals the submission of the German government that on the basis of the social demand for minor employment the abolition of the insurance scheme exclusion would lead to a proliferation of illegal forms of employment and to an increase in de facto circumventions (formally but not factually self-employment situations).

On 1 April 1999 the Act Newly Regulating the Conditions of Minor Employment entered into force.[21] The new Federal government wanted to resolve this long-debated issue by countering the erosion of the financial basis of the social insurance scheme, which is financed by contributions. It further sought to create disincentives in order to control the expansion of this type of employment relationship while simultaneously avoiding, as a reaction, defections from the scheme into forms of illicit work or a further splintering of employment conditions. Lastly, it was intended that women, who are the main workers under these conditions of employment, should be given the option of improving their old-age security.

In pursuing these goals, the basic exemption from the statutory insurance scheme for minor employment relationships was retained. But under the new Act employers are obliged to pay a flat 10 per cent of the wages

---

[19] See Bundestags-Drucksache 14/280, p. 32.
[20] Case C-317/93 *Nolte* [1995] ECR I-4625. Confirmed in Case C-281/97 *Krüger* [1999] ECR I-5127.
[21] For a detailed description of the new provisions see W. Boecken, 'Die Neuregelung der geringfügigen Beschäftigungsverhältnisse' (1999) *Neue Zeitschrift für Arbeitsrecht* p. 393 at 402.

to the statutory health insurance scheme and 12 per cent to the pension insurance scheme. In addition, it was considered important that workers' minor and non-minor employment relationships should be treated as a unity. That means that a worker has to pay social insurance contributions in respect of both types of employment relationship (the two incomes are added together for calculating contributions). By these means the legislature sought to render unattractive the former practice of engaging employees who already had a permanent job for certain types of employment. The negative employment effect which would otherwise have existed was to be avoided.

Furthermore, the Act grants workers in minor employment the option of waiving their exclusion from the pension insurance scheme. In such cases there is a contribution and insurance obligation arising under the statutory pension insurance scheme: the employer has to pay a share of 12 per cent and the employee a share of 7.3 per cent of the present contribution rate of 19.3 per cent. It is hoped through this rule that the pension levels of women will be improved.

Opinions differ on whether this legislation has had a positive effect on employment policy. Some employers criticise the Act as creating employment disincentives.[22] A study commissioned by the Ministry of Labour and Social Affairs of the *Bundesland* Nordrhein-Westfalen and undertaken by two social research companies[23] came to the conclusion that expectations for improved social insurance contributions were far surpassed. After the number of workers in minor employment had reached 5.6 million in 1997 and as many as 6.5 million in the first quarter of 1999, following the entry into force of the Act it decreased by 700,000 to 5.8 million in the period June to August 1999, thereby essentially returning to the 1997 level. In the medium term – according to the researchers' estimates – the number of employees engaged in minor employment and second jobs is likely to move to around 5.9 million, of which around 4 million will be exclusively engaged in minor employment.

4.2.2   Unemployment insurance

According to German law, anybody losing their job has a right to claim unemployment benefits if they have previously worked for a certain time.

---

[22] See, on the controversy, Deutsches Institut für Wirtschaftsforschung (1999) 37 *Wochenbericht* p. 661.

[23] See the study carried out by ISG Sozialforschung und Gesellschaftspolitik and Kienbaum Management Consultants. The findings of this study were published by the Ministry of Labour of the *Land* Nordrhein-Westfalen in 1999 under the title *Geringfügig Beschäftigte nach der Neu-Regelung des '630-DM-Gesetzes'*.

However, the right to unemployment benefits requires that the applicant is willing to take up new employment. This does not, however, necessarily have to be a full-time position. The law-maker has, for a long time now, regarded the search for a part-time job as sufficient if a position offering at least 18 working hours a week was being sought. This resulted in a conflict with those part-time employees who work less than 15 hours a week in accordance with the regulation of minor employment. For this reason the existing rule was seen as indirect discrimination and hence a violation of Art. 119 (now 141) ECT.[24] Nevertheless, as the European Court had not regarded minor employment as a violation of EC law, action by the law-maker was not absolutely necessary. The German law-maker recognised, however, that many women worked less than 18 hours a week and consequently sought a compromise by setting a threshold of at least 15 hours a week. Thus, anyone wanting a position offering at least 15 hours a week is regarded as looking for employment and therefore has a right to unemployment benefits.

A further fundamental condition for unemployment benefits is the availability of the applicant for employment under normal conditions on the relevant labour market. Anyone who is not in such a position is regarded as not being available and therefore not entitled to unemployment benefits. To take into account the particular situation of such part-time employees who look after a child in need of supervision or a relative in need of care, the Act states that availability is deemed to exist when at least 15 hours a week can be worked, even if the applicant makes special demands with regard to the duration, scheduling and distribution of the working time.

In creating unemployment benefits, the law-maker has also taken into account the special situation of those employees who hold more than one part-time job at the same time. Should such an employee lose one of his part-time jobs, he is regarded as partially unemployed by law. In this special case the Act has provided a so-called partial unemployment benefit, whereby the loss of income from the loss of one part-time job is compensated for.[25]

4.2.3 The promotion of part-time work combined with family duties under social security law

An important goal of the Commission of the European Communities has for many years been the compatibility of family and work, not least

---

[24] See above at 4.2.1.2.
[25] For further details see section 150 *Sozialgesetzbuch* III.

because of the implications of this goal for the realisation of equality of opportunity in women's working lives. This principle is also anchored in the Community Charter of the Fundamental Social Rights of Workers. Article 16(3) of this Charter states that measures are to be developed to enable men and women to reconcile their work and family obligations better. In the Federal Republic of Germany this demand is supported by all political parties and social partners.[26] Many businesses have begun to develop workplace models which allow for the reconciliation of business interests and the wishes of employees with regard to their family situation.

From the perspective of social insurance, we can see the theme of the compatibility of family and work as a problem related to the flexibility of working hours. As a rule it is women, but increasingly also men, who wish to reduce their working hours in order to assume family obligations. Of primary importance here are duties related to the raising of children. The care of dependants in need of care, however, which is becoming increasingly important, should also not be overlooked.

Since the late 1980s, the legislature has implemented numerous measures with the objective of promoting part-time employment at the same time as the fulfilment of family obligations. In the field of pension insurance, for instance, the loss of pension entitlements resulting from employment in part-time work and the payment of associated lower contributions is compensated, or even overcompensated, by a credit for the first three years of a child's life in the form of pension credits corresponding to the amount of an average employee income and, in addition, those contributions which are deducted for the part-time work.

In order to encourage people to take on caring duties, the legislature has provided that the pensions of those who care for a dependant for at least 14 hours a week in and around his home are guaranteed by law. It is the statutory care insurance scheme (*Pflegeversicherung*) that pays the contributions for this insurance. This rule, however, applies only when the carer works no more than 30 hours a week. Full-time workers must therefore reduce their working hours correspondingly.[27]

Also marked by efforts to achieve compatibility between family and work is the rule in unemployment insurance law according to which, in terms of their availability in the workforce, a person will be considered

[26] The whole range of problems in connection with the realisation of the family/work strategy is discussed in M. Fuchs, *Vereinbarkeit von Familie und Beruf* (Munich: Deutscher Juristentag, 1994).
[27] The legal provisions are described by S. Leitherer in B. Schulin (ed.), *Handbuch des Sozialversicherungsrechts*, vol. IV *Pflegeversicherungsrecht* (Munich, C. H. Beck, 1997), p. 501.

to be willing and able to work if they are available on the labour market, while not in an unrestricted sense, for at least 15 hours a week, if this is because of caring for and raising a dependent child.[28]

Lastly, an important promotional measure is contained in the Federal Parental Care Allowance Act (*Bundeserziehungsgeldgesetz*). This Act seeks to compensate the costs to parents of raising children through the payment of cash benefits. Cash benefits of DM 600 (now approximately €306) per month are paid for a period of two years from the birth of a child. The Act does not require that employment be relinquished entirely, but rather seeks to promote the continuation of an existing job as long as the hours worked do not exceed 30 hours per week. It can therefore be said that this scheme is intended to promote a model of the division of time between family and work.

4.3   The particular case of partial retirement (Altersteilzeit)

The regulation of partial retirement resulted from the Alliance for Work (see 2.2.1 above). It was a general objective in the Federal Republic of Germany, as in many other countries, to encourage the early retirement of older members of the workforce through measures which essentially ensured that the affected parties would retain their existing income levels. For this, however, comprehensive payments from the state pension funds as well as unemployment insurance were necessary. The practice came under increasing criticism.[29] For this reason, at the beginning of 1996 a new policy was adopted which sought to harmonise the interests of businesses in providing an incentive for older employees to take retirement so that their positions could be filled by younger employees and the interests of society in achieving acceptable conditions of retirement for employees. This resulted in the Partial Retirement Act (*Altersteilzeitgesetz*), which entered into force on 1 August 1996. The Act sets out a complicated mechanism which involves, on the one hand, important amendments to pension insurance and, on the other, new instruments for job creation.[30] In the end, successful implementation of the measures depended on the participation of the parties to collective agreements. The basic mechanisms of this statutory regulatory scheme will be presented here. The essential

---

[28] See section 119 para. 4 Sozialgesetzbuch III.

[29] For a description and the criticism of former measures see C. Oswald, 'Altersteilzeit: Nur "Frühpensionierung mit Vorlaufzeit"?' (1999) *Zeitschrift für Sozialreform*, p. 199.

[30] The Act is discussed in U. Preis and C. Rolfs, 'Das Altersteilzeitgesetz' (1998) *Die Sozialgerichtsbarkeit* p. 147 at 158.

subject-matter of the Act is as follows. The Partial Retirement Act is intended to facilitate a smooth transition from working life to retirement through a reduction in working time. A simultaneous objective was to help relieve the labour market through thereby freed-up labour requirements and recruitment of the unemployed and trainees. In order to achieve these objectives, it was necessary for the following to occur: employees, who on the commencement of the partial retirement scheme needed to be at least 55 years old, had to reach agreement with their employers to reduce their working hours to half of the regular working week stipulated in the applicable collective agreement. To make employees more prepared to take this step, in such cases the employer has to pay a supplementary amount of 20 per cent of the gross part-time pay in addition to the pay corresponding to the reduced working time, which means that the employees will still receive at least 70 per cent of their former gross pay. The employer also has to compensate for the disadvantages in respect of pension insurance which would result from the reduction in income, and must therefore pay additional contributions to the statutory pension insurance scheme. Contributions to be paid by employers are calculated as if the employees were earning 90 per cent of their former full-time pay.

Employers can avoid the additional costs imposed on them by this scheme by filling the newly released vacancies with unemployed workers registered with the Employment Office or with employees who have finished their training when the former full-time employee transfers to the partial retirement arrangement. In these cases, the Federal Employment Office will reimburse the employer with the additional wage costs which are paid to the now part-time employees as well as the cost of the extra pension insurance contributions. As a result, it is intended that employers can effect changes in personnel without having to relinquish the experience of the older employees.

The Act did not establish any individual rights for employees to enter the partial retirement scheme. It would in practice therefore be successful only if the parties to collective agreements (trade unions, employers' associations) arrived at supplementary agreements. In fact, such agreements were concluded very rapidly following the Act's entry into force. In this regard, a pilot agreement in the chemical industry became something of a model.

In its 1996 form, the Partial Retirement Act assumed that the scheme could be supported on a lasting basis. It soon became evident, though, that this was not in the interests of either employers or employees. The legislature therefore permitted working time to be divided in a different way over a period of up to five years, first under collective agreements and later also under individual contracts. This made it possible to reach agreements on the so-called 'block model'. Typically, this means that the partial retirement is divided into two blocks. During the first block of two and a half years, the employee continues working without any reduction of working time, but the changes to the income structure and the structure of pension insurance payment contributions apply immediately. During the second block the position is fully vacant, but the income payments and pension insurance contributions are continued.

In practice, the recruitment requirement stipulated by the Partial Retirement Act proved to be a problem. The 1996 Act required that the person hired should be an unemployed person registered with the Employment Office or a worker who had completed his training. Furthermore, this person had to be employed in the newly available position or in a position which had become vacant in connection with the other employee's change of employment status. This created problems for businesses and led to calls for amendments to the scheme. The legislature responded to these calls.[31] Since 1 January 2000, it has been possible to hire not only registered unemployed or newly trained persons, but also persons who are yet to complete their training. In workplaces with up to five persons it is also no longer necessary to comply with the same-job (or connected-job) requirement. Instead, the new employee may be employed in any position in the business.

Another objection raised against the Act in its 1996 form was that, in limiting opportunities for partial retirement to persons who had formerly been employed on a full-time basis, the resulting exclusion of part-time workers constituted a violation of European Community law. Because around 90 per cent of part-time workers are women, it was objected that the regulatory scheme amounted to indirect discrimination on the grounds of gender and therefore constituted a violation of Article 5 of Directive 76/207/EEC.[32] The legislature responded to this criticism as well. Since 1 January 2000 part-time employees are also able to claim partial retirement. They too must reduce their working hours by half. It is, however, also necessary that this halving of their working hours does not result in an employee relationship constituting 'minor' employment (see above at 4.2.1.2), for which there is no entitlement to participate in the partial retirement scheme.

---

[31] The former problems in this area and the Amendment to the existing Act are treated in S. Rittweger, 'Die Novelle des Altersteilzeitgesetzes' (2000) *Deutsches Steuerrecht* p. 161 at 163.

[32] See, for example, U. Preis and C. Rolfs, 'Das Altersteilzeitgesetz' (n. 30 above), p. 149.

4.4   Recent legislation: the Part-Time Work and Fixed-Term Contracts Act

4.4.1   Objectives of the Act

The Promotion of Employment Act discussed in sections 4.1 and 4.1.1 above was repealed on 31 December 2000. The replacement of its regulations came into effect with the Part-Time Work and Fixed-Term Contracts Act (*Teilzeit- und Befristungsgesetz*, or TzBfG) on 1 January 2001.[33] In as far as part-time work is concerned, the new Act implements 'Directive 97/81/EC on part-time work'.[34]

In its presentation of the draft of the Act, the Federal Government gave extensive reasons for the necessity of legal regulation.[35] In its view, all effective instruments for the promotion of employment must be used to achieve prolonged employment security. These also include sharing out the existing workload between more people by means of the reduction of individual working time in the form of part-time work. The quota of part-time jobs could be raised because many full-time employees show a willingness to reduce their number of working hours, a willingness that is constructive with regard to labour market policy. The demand for part-time work is rising steadily. The Government makes reference to the findings of the IAB, the Labour Market Research Institute of the Federal Labour Office, according to which exploitation of this potential demand for part-time work could trigger considerable alleviatory effects on the labour market.[36] The Government claims that those affected have often not been able to realise their desire for a part-time job because such jobs have just not been offered. Legal regulations that enable employees to realise their part-time job demands could, therefore, make an effective contribution to employment security and the promotion of employment.

The aspect of the 'work–life balance' is given great importance and attention in the law-maker's argumentation. To quote from the text:

> Additionally, part-time work has great importance in respect to emancipation and social welfare policies. With a share of 87 per cent, women account for the majority of part-time employees . . . More than half of part-time workers are engaged in part-time jobs because of family or personal reasons. Hence the major reason for reducing the number of working hours is the desire to have more time for the family. Other motives lie in the desire to

---

[33] See Bundesgesetzblatt (2000) I, p. 1966.
[34] For the impact of this upon the German Act, see section 5.3 below.
[35] See Bundestags-Drucksache 17/4374, p. 11.
[36] See (1999) 1 *Mitteilungen aus der Arbeitsmarkt- und Berufsforschung* 5.

take part in voluntary activities as well as to pursue non-professional interests. The wish to make use of the time gained by part-time employment for
further education is another motivation. The reasons for the latter are on
the one hand the possibility of 'lifelong learning' and on the other hand to
obtain extra qualifications outside the company. Thus the advancement of
part-time work not only promotes equal opportunities for men and women
and better reconciliation of work and family, it also takes into account the
different visions of life that employees have.

Lastly, the legislature turns its attention to the requirements of employers in its presentation of the draft. It is claimed that, as a rule, consideration
of the desire for a reduction in working hours also has positive effects for
employers, such as higher flexibility and productivity as well as better work
quality. In contrast, work regulations that bypass the needs and possibilities of employees can have considerable follow-up costs as a consequence,
owing to increased staff turnover or higher absenteeism. With reference
to the research of an eminent consultative institution, it is also stressed
that the expansion of part-time work need not lead to higher costs. There
is no general disadvantage as regards costs for part-time work compared
with full-time work. Additional costs for part-time work are often offset
by gains in productivity. The average initial costs for the introduction of
part-time work are often amortised within a year.

Thus the line of reasoning of the Act shows that the German legislature,
in passing the TzBfG, has taken into account all objectives that were shown
above[37] to be in discussion in political and social welfare policies, but
especially those objectives seen as relevant among the ranks of employees
and employers. The following deliberations will be concerned with the
question of how these objectives, emphasised by the government in its
draft, have been considered in the resultant legal regulation.

4.4.2   Content of the new Act

In general it can be said that the TzBfG has largely incorporated the regulations included in the Promotion of Employment Act.[38] A few innovations

---

[37] Under section 2.1.
[38] See above at section 4.1. For a detailed presentation of the new Act see W. Däubler,
'Das neue Teilzeit- und Befristungsgesetz' (2001) *Zeitschrift für Wirtschaftsrecht* p. 217;
W. Hromadka, 'Das neue Teilzeit- und Befristungsgesetz' (2001) *Neue Juristische Wochen-
schrift* p. 400; M. Kliemt, 'Der neue Teilzeitanspruch' (2001) *Neue Zeitschrift für Arbeitsrecht*
p. 63; U. Preis and M. Gotthardt, 'Das Teilzeit- und Befristungsgesetz' (2001) *Der Betrieb*
p. 145; M. Schmidt, 'The Right to Part-Time Work under German Law: Progress in or a
Boomerang for Equal Opportunities?' (2001) 40:4 *Industrial Law Journal* p. 335.

are due to the fact that the legislature was obliged to conform to 'Directive 97/81/EC on part-time work'. In part it wanted to realise ideas of a more far-reaching nature.

Fundamentally, section 2 TzBfG retains the existing definition of a part-time employee, choosing for the basis of its regulation the deviation from the regular weekly working hours of a comparable full-time employee. Also section 2 TzBfG now models its basis for comparison on Clause 3(2) of Directive 97/81/EC.

The creation of the ban on discrimination in section 4 TzBfG also adheres to the former legal provision. To this end, its being modelled on Directive 97/81/EC has led to clarity and precision to avoid legal disputes. A part-time employee may not be treated less favourably than a comparable full-time employee unless a concrete reason justifies different treatment. The law-maker has also put into practice the *pro-rata-temporis* principle recommended in the Directive. Accordingly, a part-time employee is entitled to pay or other divisible form of remuneration of at least the same amount as a comparable full-time employee receives for the same time. In accordance with the Directive, nor may parties to collective agreements diverge from the ban on discrimination to the disadvantage of the employee. This had already been ruled by the Federal Labour Court, however, in the past.[39]

The ban on discrimination is strengthened – again in conjunction with the European Directive – in that section 5 TzBfG rules that an employer may not put an employee at a disadvantage because the latter makes a claim based on this Act. A further guarantee for equality of treatment between full-time and part-time employees is ensured by the prohibition of dismissal in section 11 TzBfG: termination of employment is not binding in the case of an employee's refusal to change from full-time to part-time employment or vice versa.

Really new in the TzBfG are those regulations in which the law-maker was at pains to implement the programme for the promotion of part-time work to be found in Directive 97/81/EC. In detail this involves the following. Initially the concern was to create transparency in conjunction with Clause 5(3)(e).[40] Extensive information from employer and employee representatives regarding the possibilities of part-time employment in the company is a prerequisite for the increase of part-time work. Section 7 TzBfG thus includes the obligation on an employer to

[39] See BAGE (Official Report of the BAG) pp. 71, 29.
[40] For this see also Bundestags-Drucksache 14/4374, p. 12.

advertise vacancies also as part-time positions, should this be compatible with the position. Apart from this, an employer is obliged to give an employee information concerning relevant vacancies in the company or group when the employee has expressed the wish to make a change in the duration or scheduling of working hours that have been agreed by contract. Additionally, the employer is obliged to give the employees' representatives any information concerning part-time opportunities in the company or group, especially existing or planned part-time opportunities and the conversion of part-time into full-time positions or vice versa.

Moreover, the legislature based its regulations for the promotion of part-time work on the following arguments.[41] In order to exploit to the full the employment potential that arises from the expansion of part-time work, measures are necessary which, in compliance with recommendations in the Part-Time Directive, ensure that employee applications for a change from full-time to part-time employment are taken into account as far as possible. The concerns here are, firstly, to enable a clear expansion of part-time work and, secondly, to safeguard the legitimate organisational and planning interests of the employer. The presumption of the law-maker is that employer and employee will normally come to an agreement regarding the reduction of working hours. Directive 97/81/EC also makes the assumption that the development of part-time work will take place on a voluntary basis and in consensus between employer and employee.

The German legislature has adopted a more far-reaching position than that of the concept of voluntary agreement. It has included in section 8 TzBfG the individual right of an employee to a reduction in the working hours agreed by contract. This right had been much disputed during the deliberations in Parliament. Its introduction was fiercely contended, especially on the part of employers and their organisations. It was claimed that such a right would compromise a company's freedom of choice in staff placements to too great an extent and that in the long term it would not have a beneficial effect on the labour market. The additional administrative work often involved in the introduction of part-time work, which would put a strain on small and medium-sized enterprises especially, was stressed.[42]

---

[41] Ibid.
[42] Cf. statement of the Bund Deutscher Arbeitgeber (BDA) (= Confederation of German Employers' Associations) of 12 September 2000. See further the harsh criticism by B. Schiefer, 'Entwurf eines Gesetzes über Teilzeitarbeit und befristete Arbeitsverhältnisse und zur Änderung und Aufhebung arbeitsrechtlicher Bestimmungen' (2000) *Der Betrieb* p. 2118 at 2120.

The law-maker did not regard these objections as legitimate. Independently of the survey carried out by the McKinsey consultants already mentioned above,[43] which presumes initial short-term costs with the introduction of part-time work but a long-term increase in productivity, the following arguments were of interest for the law-maker when allowing an individual right to part-time employment. The wording of the arguments for the Act reads as follows:

> In Germany, according to the analysis of the IAB, the wishes of full-time and part-time employees are moving towards a reduction in weekly working hours of the order of between five and nine hours. The large majority of full-time employees (approx. 30 per cent) want a reduction in the working week of about eight hours. A similar conclusion was reached in a survey carried out for the EU and Norway (1999) by the European Foundation for the Improvement of Living and Working Conditions, which found that only approx. 15 per cent of the employees questioned wanted a reduction in the working week of 15 or more hours. A reduction of less than five hours was wanted by only 7 per cent. On average, the employees questioned preferred a reduction in working hours of about five hours. A survey carried out by the Institute for Research into Social Equality (ISO) for the Ministry of Labour and Social Welfare of the Land Nordrhein-Westfalen (1999) came to the following conclusions – which correspond to the above-mentioned findings – that the majority of full-time employees who express a wish for a reduction in working hours are not in fact looking for a part-time job but rather a reduction of 12, in their weekly hours, to 27 hours spread over a three or four day week. With this in mind, and to enable the realisation of the desire for a reduction in working hours, the law-maker allows employees to plan their weekly working hours individually. The planned regulations enable the meaningful use, with regard to labour market policy, of the existing potential for a redistribution of working hours as well as enabling a drastic increase in the effect of part-time work from an employment policy point of view.[44]

The law-maker has hereby acknowledged the precedence of individual employee interests over those of the employer. This does not mean, however, that the interests of the employer have not been taken into account in the concrete formulation of the right. The regulation of the right that is expounded in the subsequent passage is, rather more, a compromise between the interests of the employees and those of the employers. The right of an employee to a reduction in working hours that have been

---

[43] See above at section 4.4.1.   [44] Bundestags-Drucksache 14/4374, p. 17.

agreed by contract does not take effect until six months after conclusion of the contract. The employee must claim the reduction in his working hours and also state the extent of the reduction three months before it begins, including informing the employer of the desired distribution of working hours (section 8 para. 2 TzBfG).

That in principle the German law-maker is also interested in a voluntary concept for the introduction of part-time employment can be seen in the provision of section 8 para. 3 TzBfG. This provision provides for a period of negotiation between employer and employee. Both parties are required to discuss the employee's request with a view to reaching an agreement. Only in the case of failure to reach such an agreement is the employer obliged, according to section 8 para. 4 TzBfG, to agree to the desired reduction in working hours and to arrange their distribution accordingly. This, however, comes into force only in so far as there are no internal company reasons to hinder it. The intention with this regulation was to take the employer's interests into account. The internal company reasons that can impede the employee's right include the following particular cases: the reduction of the working hours concerned adversely affects the company organisation, the work process or safety aspects considerably, or comparatively high costs are incurred by the employer because of the introduction of part-time work. Further reasons for refusal can be determined by collective agreement. The objections of the employer to an employee's desire for a reduction in or redistribution of his working hours must be given in writing, at the latest, one month before the desired start. Otherwise the request made by the employee to the employer comes into force.

The argument brought forward by employers during the discussions in Parliament, namely that the introduction of part-time employment would especially burden small and medium-sized companies with great problems, has been given partial consideration by the law-maker. Section 8 para. 7 TzBfG rules that the right to a reduction in working hours is effective only in companies that generally have more than fifteen employees.

The TzBfG also regulates the return of a part-time employee to a full-time position. This topic is also mentioned in Clause 5(3)(b and c) of the Part-Time Directive. Accordingly, section 9 TzBfG rules that an employer must give preferential consideration to a request by a part-time employee for an extension of his contractually agreed working hours when filling a compatible vacancy requiring the same skills, unless urgent internal company reasons or the wishes of another part-time employee stand in the way of such a decision.

The intention with the ruling in section 10 TzBfG – again in concurrence with Directive 97/81/EC – was to fulfil the request of part-time employees for training and further education: the employer must ensure that part-time workers also have the opportunity to participate in training courses and further education schemes in order to promote their professional development and mobility, in so far as internal company reasons do not stand in the way.

In so far as it includes regulations that promote part-time work, the new Act has been warmly welcomed by academic lawyers.[45] However, opinions vary greatly where the principle of the individual right of an employee to a part-time position is concerned. Most authors express objections to the introduction of this right. Their arguments are divided into two categories. According to the first, the subjective right of an employee to a reduction in working hours results in serious disadvantages for the company organisation, disadvantages that lead to higher costs.[46] Whether or not the new regulation will have any beneficial effect from an employment policy point of view is doubtful: if at all, the effect could only be very modest. The second category of argumentation applied by critics is of a constitutional nature. It is maintained that the right to part-time work curtails the employer's right of ownership. It is even pointed out in the reasons for this that the BAG has already recognised the employer's freedom to organise his own company where duration and scheduling of working hours are concerned.[47] In a recent judgment, however, the Federal Labour Court saw no violation of this entrepreneurial right by Section 8 TzBfG.

5   The impact of European law upon the German part-time legislation

5.1   The role of the European Court of Justice (ECJ)

Even after the entry into force of the Promotion of Employment Act in 1985 and the ban on discrimination anchored in it, courts in the Federal Republic of Germany, including the Federal Labour Court, have scrutinised provisions negatively affecting part-time workers almost

---

[45] It is, however, generally remarked that the legislators were driven by too great a haste, reflected in numerous regulations in the Act which remain unclear: see U. Preis and M. Gotthardt, 'Das Teilzeit- und Befristungsgesetz', p. 145.

[46] See B. Schiefer, 'Entwurf eines Gesetzes', p. 2118.

[47] See M. Kliemt, 'Der neue Teilzeitanspruch', p. 63 at 65 with references to the settled case-law of the Bundesarbeitsgericht.

exclusively in terms of the standard set out in ex-Art. 119 of the EC Treaty. The so-called *Bilka*[48] decision of the ECJ was decisive in this respect. German labour courts and the Federal Labour Court, however, have frequently made preliminary references to the ECJ since the *Bilka* decision as well.

Two reasons may be suggested for this predominance of ex-Art. 119 EC as the legal standard. In the first place, judicial review in terms of the ban on gender discrimination is a natural result of the fact that part-time workers are overwhelmingly women. A further reason can be seen in one of the specific provisions of the Promotion of Employment Act. Under section 6(1) of this Act, it is possible to opt out of the statutory provisions on part-time work through a collective agreement even when the effect of this is to the disadvantage of the employee. With this provision, the legislature was continuing in a tradition of German labour law. As in many other areas, it was intended that here, too, priority was to be given to the autonomy of collective agreements. The assumption is that the parties to such agreements are better able than the legislature to arrive at objectively permissible deviations from statutory provisions and, moreover, that these parties are also sufficiently able to protect the interests of employees. In practice, therefore, collective agreements in Germany included numerous provisions confining particular payments and other benefits and advantages exclusively to full-time workers. Also the Federal Labour Court seemed to back the opinion that parties to a collective agreement were empowered to deviate from the principle of equal treatment contained in section 2(1).[49] Since many women part-timers objected to such discriminatory rules in collective agreements, numerous cases were brought in which the subject-matter of the proceedings was the review of such provisions. The ECJ was therefore presented with many such cases in the form of references for preliminary rulings. Once having determined that the principle of equal treatment contained in ex-Art. 119 also applied to collective agreements,[50] the Court had to overturn numerous provisions in collective agreements relating to the exclusion of part-time workers from particular benefits, on the basis of principles which it had developed in the context of ex-Art. 119 EC. The jurisprudence

---

[48] Case 170/84, [1986] ECR 1607.
[49] See for this the judgment by the Bundesarbeitsgericht in BAGE 61, 43 = AP Nr 2 for section 2 BeschFG 1985 and the critical remarks on this judgment by Reinhard Richardi, 'Das Gleichbehandlungsgebot für Teilzeitarbeit und seine Auswirkung auf Entgeltregelungen' (1992) *Neue Zeitschrift für Arbeitsrecht* p. 625 at 630.
[50] See Case 43/75 *Defrenne* [1976] ECR 455.

of the ECJ has without question had a decisive influence on the regulation of part-time work in the Federal Republic of Germany.[51]

In the course of time, however, the case-law, in particular of the Federal Labour Court, began to emphasise the discrimination ban set out in section 2(1) of the Promotion of Employment Act. Unquestionably an important step along this path was the decision of the Federal Labour Court that the parties to a collective agreement had to respect the ban on discrimination in relation to part-time work.[52] It was established in this case that the prohibition against disadvantaging part-time workers must be respected in every labour regulation, whether under a collective agreement or individual contract or even pursuant to the management rights of the employer. The case-law of the ECJ on Art. 119 EC has, moreover, also had an indirect influence on the interpretation of section 2(1) of the Promotion of Employment Act (now section 4 TzBfG). This provision likewise permits the unequal treatment of part-time workers when there are objective justifications for such treatment. Here the influence of the ECJ on the jurisprudence of German labour courts is unmistakable, since in the meantime a particularly high standard has been required with respect to the justification requirement as it also appears in Art. 2(1) of the Promotion of Employment Act.[53] The result is that, in principle, any form of difference in treatment between part-time and full-time employees is forbidden. Such difference in treatment can only be justified, on an exceptional basis, if objective reasons are present. Such objective reasons

---

[51] Leading decisions of the ECJ: Case 170/84 [1986] ECR 1607: exclusion of part-time workers from a workplace pension plan; Case 171/88 [1989] ECR 2743: exclusion from continuation of payment of wages in the case of illness; Case C-33/89 [1990] ECR I-2591: exclusion from payment of a transitional payment on the ending of an employment relationship; Case C-360/90 [1992] ECR I-3589: release from work of part-timers for staff council duties not counted as working hours, approved by the ECJ in Case C-457/93 [1996] ECR I-243; Case C-399/92 [1994] ECR I-5727: no violation of ex-Art. 119 EC where overtime premium rates are paid only in cases where the working hours set down for full-time workers are exceeded.
    For a detailed analysis of preliminary references made by German Labour Courts to the ECJ concerning discrimination against part-time workers, see C. Kilpatrick, 'Gender Equality: A Fundamental Dialogue', in S. Sciarra (ed.), *Labour Law in the Courts. National Judges and the European Court of Justice* (Oxford: Hart Publishing, 2001), p. 46. See further M. Körner, 'Der Dialog des EuGH mit den deutschen Arbeitsgerichten' (2001) *Neue Zeitschrift für Arbeitsrecht* p. 1046 at 1047.
[52] Bundesarbeitsgericht AP for section 1 BetrAVG Gleichbehandlung Nr 18.
[53] On the close relationship between the consistent jurisprudence of the ECJ and the principles laid down in section 2(1), see T. Dieterich, P. Hanau and G. Schaub (eds.), *Erfurter Kommentar zum Arbeitsrecht* (2nd edn, Munich: Verlag C. H. Beck, 2001), Section 2 BeschFG under VI.4.

can include performance, qualifications, professional experience or other job requirements.

The Federal Labour Court has had to consider the question of discrimination against part-time workers in numerous cases.[54] Most of the statutory and contractual provisions reviewed in these cases were found by the Court to have infringed section 2(1) of the Promotion of Employment Act. The Court has not accepted any differentiation in relation to basic remuneration, even when the part-time employment was only additional to a primary job. The Federal Labour Court has also prohibited any difference in the treatment of part-time workers in respect of supplementary employee benefits such as sickness benefits, occupational pensions, employer loans, Christmas bonuses, professional improvement possibilities or special protection against unfair dismissal under collective agreements. As a rule, only proportional reductions in remuneration are permissible. The Court has not accepted the lower motivation or commitment of part-time workers as sufficient reasons for discrimination.

5.2   The proposals by the EC Commission for reconciling work and family

The efforts of the EC Commission to achieve the reconciliation of work and family have also played a decisive role in the German debate. The demand for this reconciliation has long been a part of EC policy concerning the realisation of equal opportunities for women in the world of work.[55] The principle of reconciliation of work and family was already included in the medium-term programme for the promotion of equal opportunities for women (1986–90).[56] It was even recorded in the Community Charter of the Fundamental Social Rights of Workers, which was adopted by eleven Member States in Strasbourg on 9 December 1989.[57]

The initiatives of the European Commission and Council concerning the realisation of the principle of reconciliation of work and family have repeatedly helped as supporting arguments in political discussion and the law-making process. The sixtieth meeting of the German Law Congress in

---

[54] For a detailed documentation of the jurisprudence see K. H. Peifer, 'Die Teilzeitbeschäftigung in der neueren Rechtsprechung des Bundesarbeitsgerichts' (1999) *Zeitschrift für Arbeitsrecht* p. 271 at 298.
[55] See. S. Schunter-Kleemann, 'Die Familienpolitik der Europäischen Gemeinschaft' (1991) *Wirtschafts- und Sozialwissenschaftliches Institut Mitteilungen* p. 103 at 114.
[56] Doc. Nr 4 118-86, Bundestags-Drucksache 10/5235, II F1 a.
[57] See Nr 16 Para. 3 of the Social Charter.

1994 concerned itself in its labour and social welfare law section with this particular topic: 'What measures would be recommendable for improving the reconciliation between work and family?' The specialist reports put forward by Birk and Fuchs on this topic have made extensive reference to the EC recommendations.[58]

5.3   The transposition of Directive 97/81/EC on part-time work

In the presentation of its draft for a part-time employment law in October 2000, the Federal Government set down the objectives of the draft in the introduction:

> The guidelines for the lawmaking process concerning part-time employment have already been produced by Directive 97/81/EC on the subject. According to this Directive, which is based on a framework agreement between the European social partners, the regulations to be compiled by national governments should advance the acceptance of part-time employment, hinder discrimination against part-time workers and facilitate the transition from full-time to part-time employment and vice versa.[59]

When the text of Directive 97/81/EC and the provisions of the TzBfG are compared, it can be seen that the German legislature has adhered to the Directive down to the minutest detail. There is no single point or aspect appearing in the Directive that has not been taken into consideration, as is already clear from the description given earlier.[60]

Although the Act literally breathes the spirit of the Directive, it is nevertheless not just a systematic reproduction. This can be seen particularly in the concession of a right to part-time employment in section 8 TzBfG. The European Directive advocated the principle of free choice as a basis but the German legislature, in contrast, has gone a step further. It is true that it, too, relies on the principle of voluntary agreement between employer and employee for the introduction of part-time employment, but where this agreement fails there is a compelling legal right for the employee to a reduction in working hours.

5.4   EC Employment Guidelines and the German NAPs

In number 16 of the Employment Guidelines the modernisation of work organisation has become a topic on which the social partners are requested

---

[58] See *Verhandlungen des 60. Deutschen Juristentages*, vol. I: *Gutachten* (Munich: Verlag C. H. Beck, 1994). pp. E 24 and F 21.
[59] See Bundestags-Drucksache 14/4374, p. 1.   [60] See above at section 4.4.

to conclude appropriate agreements. These agreements should include the increase of part-time work. In its NAP 1999 the Federal Government underlines that the expansion and the promotion of part-time work is one of the central topics of the Alliance for Work.[61] Further, it is pointed out[62] that in the area of social insurance Germany has provided for better protection of part-time work by extending unemployment insurance protection to workers with a working time of at least 15 hours.[63] Moreover, in its NAP 2000 the government refers to the fact that the collective bargaining parties have concluded appropriate agreements in many areas in which the aim of flexibilisation of working time plays an important role. The most important example is the conclusion of collective agreements regarding partial retirement through which older employees are given the possibility of a smooth transition from working life into retirement.[64] An important step in this regard is claimed by the Federal Government to be the inclusion of part-time workers in the legal provisions on partial retirement.

In the efforts of the EC as expressed in the Employment Guidelines, part-time work is considered an element of the fourth pillar, i.e. the strengthening of measures for promoting equal opportunities for men and women. The Federal Government in its NAP 1999 has stressed the numerous efforts made in the world of work to promote 'family friendly' part-time employment conditions.[65] An examination was announced of the extent to which the possibilities for part-time workers to take parental childcare (*Erziehungsurlaub*) could be improved. In the NAP 2000 the Government was able to note the realisation of this proposal.[66] The Parental Care Allowance Act (*Bundeserziehungsgeldgesetz*) was amended in such a way that every parent has the possibility to take part-time employment of up to 30 hours a week without losing entitlement to parental care allowance (*Erziehungsgeld*).[67]

6 Conclusions

The history of part-time work regulation in Germany is more than fifteen years old. It began in 1985 with the Promotion of Employment Act. It was the legislators' intention to award part-time work legal recognition, and

---

[61] Nationaler Aktionsplan 1999, p. 58.
[62] Ibid., p. 59.   [63] See above at section 4.2.2.
[64] Nationaler Aktionsplan 2000, Bundestags-Drucksache 14/2950, p. 27.
[65] Nationaler Aktionsplan 1999, p. 67.
[66] See Nationaler Aktionsplan 2000, Bundestags-Drucksache 14/2950, p. 33.
[67] For this new provision see above at section 4.2.

above all the Act sought to do away with discrimination against part-time workers.

The years following its enactment, however, showed that this aim could be only partly achieved. Especially in collective agreements, discriminatory clauses continued to exist. Only the jurisprudence of the European Court of Justice changed discriminatory practices in collective agreements and employment contracts. This consistent jurisprudence of the Court in Luxembourg had a decisive impact on the rulings of the German Federal Labour Court which finally secured non-discriminatory treatment of part-time workers.

In the 1990s the Government and many public bodies began to make efforts for stronger promotion of part-time work. Political parties supported the generally recognised need for more part-time jobs. It was especially the aspect of compatibility between work and family obligations which was behind the manifold activities in the political arena and at the workplace to improve the employment situation for part-time workers. Initiatives and documents by the European Commission had made an important contribution to the debate in Germany. In the legislative field new regulations in the area of social security and social law in general mirror these requests.

During the second half of the 1990s the objective of furthering part-time jobs in order to allow women in particular to combine employment and family commitments was accompanied by a similar desire which had to do with new lifestyles and patterns of what we might call 'the work–life balance'. In addition these primarily private wishes met with positive reactions from employers, who saw in part-time arrangements an instrument of flexibility. The Government supported this general movement towards enhanced part-time strategies and tried to push implementation at the workplace by means of initiatives by the social partners within the context of the Alliance for Work.

Against this background it goes without saying that in Germany the Framework Directive on part-time work was greatly welcomed. It was guided by the various objectives mentioned above and favoured a clear-cut strategy for part-time work. The German Parliament fully transposed the Directive, but went even a step further by establishing an individual right to part-time work for employees. The conferment of this right, however, is highly controversial. Employers and their organisations in particular, but also numerous academic lawyers, regard this right as a job-killer rather than a job-creator.

Generally speaking, part-time work is loved by those who see in it the freedom of choice for shaping their private lives. Others regard it as a mere necessity since it is the only way to earn a living or add to the family income. The same is true for those employers who may regard it as a necessity to cope with production requirements. Beyond that, part-time work is met with complete hostility by employers if it can be forced upon them by workers, as is the case under the new Act.

6

Italy: adaptable employment and private autonomy in the Italian reform of part-time work

ANTONIO LO FARO

1 The 'eloquent silences' of the Italian legislation before 1984

When part-time work legislation was first introduced into the Italian system in 1984, adaptable employment, indirect discrimination and the reconciliation of work and family life were still obscure concepts to most Italian labour lawyers. Indeed, even at an institutional level, the major concern of legislators in the 1980s was to provide an initial rudimentary discipline for a type of work that was basically viewed 'in the negative', in terms of an atypical deviation from standard forms of employment, which at that time were still mainly represented by full-time, permanent contracts.[1]

Clearly, this is not to say that part-time contracts were considered as illegal before Law No. 863 of 1984 came to regulate them. However, it is unquestionably true that the extremely low rate of part-time work in Italy through the 1970s and the 1980s may not simply be considered as the straightforward result of hindering factors quite commonly found in all European labour markets, such as the social (and trade unions') wariness of the presence of part-time work and an actual entrepreneurial lack of enthusiasm towards it. Rather, it was the overall legislative and contractual context surrounding part-time work that was framed so as to render part-time jobs quite ill-matched with various pre-existing labour law rules which had been deliberated with regard to an ideal-typical employment relationship based on the assumption of permanent and full-time jobs. Rules such as those on public employment services, sick leave, notice and probationary periods, and particularly those related to social security

---

[1] The first liberalisation of fixed-term contracts, still subject to the intervention of authorising collective bargaining, was only to come about in 1987. Recently, at the end of 2001, the conservative Government fully liberalised fixed-term contracts, which may now be drawn up without any authorisation by collective agreements.

regimes, clearly clashed with the 'new' reality of part-time work. As concerns severance pay, for instance, the legislation in force until 1982 – even if not explicitly designed to hinder part-time work – clearly discouraged employees from entering into such a contract, since the amount of the severance pay was calculated on the basis of the wages being received at the time when employment was terminated. Another problem, related to the pension coverage of part-time contracts, was constituted by the so-called 'minimum hourly social security contribution', whose amount did not take into account the possible occurrence of daily working time less than the 'normal', full-time day. The result was that the employer was obliged to pay the minimum hourly social security contribution, even if the number of hours worked by part-timers did not justify such a contribution.[2]

Beyond the technicalities of social security legislation, the consistency of part-time work with the normative context surrounding it was also doubted with respect to basic constitutional rules related to the principle of just and fair wages. According to Art. 36 of the Italian Constitution, the amount of wage must be proportionate to the quantity and quality of the work and *in any case* sufficient to put the worker in a position to lead a free and decent life. The problem debated during a certain phase (essentially, the 1960s and early 1970s) was whether such 'sufficient' remuneration necessarily implied a minimum working time, i.e. a minimum number of working hours below which the worker could not attain a level of remuneration sufficient to assure him a free and decent life.

Lastly, even if not explicitly forbidden, part-time contracts had simply not been juridified in Italy until the mid-1980s, thus bringing about a situation that has been pertinently described as 'formal indifference but substantive dissuasion'.[3] With the exception of a few collective agreements providing scant rules for some specific sectors,[4] the regulation of part-time work was left entirely to the individual choices of employers and employees. Something that – in a national context where individual autonomy had traditionally been playing a secondary role in the regulation of employment relationships – led to a sort of spontaneous marginalisation of such contracts in the Italian labour market.

---

[2] See, on these issues, P. Ichino, *Il tempo della prestazione nel rapporto di lavoro*, Vol. II: *Estensione temporale della prestazione lavorativa subordinata e relative forme speciali di organizzazione* (Milan: Giuffrè, 1985), pp. 395–7.

[3] M. Brollo, *Il lavoro subordinato a tempo parziale* (Naples: ESI, 1991), p. 36.

[4] Typically, agriculture.

Following the entry into force of the 1984 legislation, and on account of a growing readiness on the part of the unions to accept employers' demands,[5] part-time work began to be spread through the Italian labour market, although without reaching the diffusion rates registered in other European countries.

In the last few years, however, the relatively recent and basically sluggish legislative existence of part-time work in Italy has undergone a series of shocks, the intensity of which does not seem to be abating: new legislation repealing the previous 1984 rules has been adopted in 2000, and the recent *Libro Bianco sul mercato del lavoro* (*White Paper on the Labour Market*), published by the newly installed Conservative Government in the Autumn of 2001, has already announced that a new reform will be implemented within 2002. Here is the complete story.

2 The part-time work reform in Italy (2000) and its demise foretold (2001): two different visions of the same EU Employment Strategy

In February 1999, while neo-liberal political forces (at that time, the Opposition party) were proposing a referendum to abrogate the 1984 legislation then in force, the Italian Parliament delegated implementation of European Directive 97/81/EC to the Government. It was clear to most at the time that intervention on the part of the delegated legislator – whatever its content – would not escape the troubled destiny of those emblematic legislative provisions around which, whether rightly or wrongly, all labour law dilemmas tend to be fastened together. Indeed, subsequent events in no way belied this initial impression.

The choice to implement EC Directives *via* a decree of the executive, rather than through the ordinary parliamentary route, is by no means a novelty essayed on the occasion of the Part-time Directive. On the contrary, this is the usual way in which EC directives are implemented within the Italian legal order. In the specific case at issue, however, the direct involvement of the Government in the outlining of a quite detailed and comprehensive form of part-time work regulation added to the impression that a crucial clash between different philosophies of labour market

---

[5] The 1984 Law heavily delegated to collective agreements the task of regulating not only the contractual terms between the two parties (tasks to be performed by part-timers, possibility of extra hours, elasticity clauses), but also the very possibility of entering into such a contract, since collective agreements could impose quantitative limits on part-time contracts through the introduction of quotas in each individual enterprise.

regulation was occurring in the wake of an EC Directive whose content was, at the end of the day, quite limited.[6]

As a matter of fact, in confirmation of the immanence of the 'political' dimension that with increasing frequency accompanies legal debates on part-time work, the decision-making process of the government decree[7] was closely linked to the succession of events surrounding the referendum *affaire*.[8] The new regulations governing part-time work were issued in February 2000, a few weeks after the judgment by which the Constitutional Court declared the referendum to be inadmissible:[9] voters, the Court declared, cannot be allowed to do what the State itself cannot do – i.e. leave a Communitarised issue without any domestic legislative regulation.[10]

This sort of chronological coincidence between the denied referendum and the new regulation of part-time work immediately triggered off reactions of perplexity, to say the least.[11] It is also no coincidence that one year later the Conservative Government, taking the place of the previous centre-left one, announced a thorough revision of part-time legislation as one of the main labour market issues on its political agenda.

At the time of writing, Italy is therefore going through a period of transition between the adoption (2000) and revision (probably 2002) of a reform on part-time work. One cannot help pointing out – given that the research project at hand aims at assessing the impact of EU measures upon the evolution of national systems – the singular circumstance that the promoters of both the reform and its more than likely revision have declared the reason behind their decisions to be the need to bring the

---

[6] As many commentators have pointed out. See, among others, M. Jeffery, 'Not Really Going to Work? Of the Directive on Part-time Work, "Atypical Work" and Attempts to Regulate It' (1998) 27:3 *Industrial Law Journal* p. 193; and S. Scarponi, 'Luci e ombre dell'accordo europeo in materia di lavoro a tempo parziale' (1999) *Rivista giuridica del lavoro* p. 399.

[7] Legislative Decree No. 61/2000.

[8] Twenty proposals for referenda were presented by the Radicals' political party in September 1999, which advocated, amongst other measures, a referendum on liberalisation of part-time work, fixed-term work and home-working.

[9] Constitutional Court, No. 49/2000, 3 February 2000.

[10] This would have been the result in the case of a successful referendum. The only legislation on part-time work would have been abrogated, leaving a legislative vacuum.

[11] See the critical earlier comments by A. Del Boca, 'Ingessato e costoso. Ecco il nuovo part-time'; L. Pelaggi, 'Sul part-time aperture a metà'; and M. Biagi, 'Mentre l'Europa corre l'Italia fa passi indietro' – all of them published in the Italian financial newspaper *Il Sole 24-ore*, respectively on 1 February, 18 March and 3 April 2000, at pp. 7, 13 and 14. One of the most critical authors is A. Vallebona, 'La nuova disciplina del lavoro a tempo parziale' (2000) 5 *Massimario di giurisprudenza del lavoro* p. 492; this author contributed arguments in support of the referendum during the admissibility proceedings held before the Constitutional Court.

national system into line with Community social legislation and employment policy. In the words of the *White Paper*, in fact, the foreseeable shelving of the 2000 reform is explicitly accounted for by the need to correct the interpretation of EC law and social policy made by the previous Government: bringing Directive 97/81/EC on part-time work into effect in Italy was, in the opinion of the present Government, 'an example of a transposition that did not reflect the wishes of the social partners at Community level'.

The particular time at which the Italian reform was brought about – at much the same time as a change in the political parties making up the Government coalition – therefore provides an opportunity to illustrate how a directive and a whole series of other EU documents can be called upon to support domestic legislative strategies that are to a great extent quite divergent.

The question of whether Europe mattered in the legislative evolution of part-time work in Italy can be answered by saying that it certainly did and that it continues to do so. With, however, the immediate rider that the particular formal and substantive structure of Community employment strategy makes it possible to use the political science notion of an 'EU framing policy',[12] that is, a European policy which, unlike both positive and negative integration, is 'highly dependent on the specific conditions which shape policy-making at the national level' and therefore 'may provide additional legitimisation for domestic leaders to justify the content and implementation of national reform policies'.[13]

3   The employment-promoting value of part-time work: making sense of comparative data and EU Employment Guidelines

Representing part-time contracts as one of the main ways to improve the employment performances of the labour market is a widespread practice in Italy.[14]

---

[12] C. Knill and D. Lehmkuhl, 'How Europe Matters: Different Mechanisms of Europeanization' (1999) 3:7 European Integration online Papers (EIoP); available at http://eiop.or.at/eiop/texte/1999-007a.htm.

[13] Ibid. What will probably happen with the reform of part-time work was presaged by the new regulations governing fixed-term contracts. Here again, the implementation of a Community Directive was a chance, and legitimisation, for a new Government to complete a process of total liberalisation of fixed-term work which was certainly not one of the aims of the EC legislation.

[14] Most recently, see R. Santucci, 'La riforma "europea" del part-time: cambiano le regole, rimangono i timori' (2000) 3 *Il diritto del mercato del lavoro* p. 563, and P. Reboani, 'Il terzo pilastro: l'adattabilità' (2000) 2 *Diritto delle relazioni industriali* p. 153.

It is normally based on well-known statistical data which would seem to prove that there is a connection between the spread of part-time work and a reduction in the unemployment rates. The Netherlands, which has the highest rate of part-time work and the lowest unemployment rate in Europe,[15] is often quoted as proof of this. The various EU documents adopted from 1997 onwards in the EE Strategy inaugurated by the Treaty of Amsterdam are also frequently called upon to support the employment-promoting value of a regulatory instrument that is seen as an excellent example of the 'adaptability' that enterprises and workers are required to possess.[16] As far as domestic legislative policies are concerned, these widespread representations of part-time work have led to a considerable drive towards the provision of incentives for it and, in the field of juridical analysis, a strong trend towards interpreting the relevant norms in the light of a single, all-embracing assessment criterion: whether and to what extent legislation makes it possible for part-time work to fulfil its beneficial task of decreasing unemployment rates.

The stance just mentioned suffers, however, from an excess of material rationality in its interpretation of the international data and subsequent analysis of EU regulations and policies, and is also based on grounds that are not to be so easily taken for granted. Analysing domestic regulations governing part-time work by verifying their compliance with an objective the EU is assumed to have set itself, that is, the maximum and unconditional spread of an employment policy based on flexibility on the demand side, is not fully acceptable if one takes into consideration a series of factors that will be outlined below.

3.1 Part-time work as a means to reduce unemployment

It is perhaps worthwhile clarifying certain misunderstandings regarding the employment-promoting value of part-time work.

It is without doubt true that there are countries where the correlation between spreading use of part-time work and reduction of unemployment rates appears to be evident: besides the Netherlands, for example, there are also Denmark and Sweden, even if the statistics are less striking.

However, it is also hard to deny that an exceptional improvement in the employment rate has been achieved in other countries where part-time

---

[15] For an interesting review of the correlation between low unemployment rates and the spread of part-time work in the Netherlands, see J. Visser, 'Piena occupazione fondata sul part-time: il "miracolo olandese"' (2001) 62 *Stato e Mercato* p. 293.

[16] On adaptability as a pillar of EU employment policy, see Reboani, 'Il terzo pilastro', and D. Meulders and R. Plasman, 'The Third Pillar: Adaptability' (1999) 4 *Transfer* p. 481.

work is not so widespread: in Ireland, for instance, the famous miracle that has brought the unemployment rate down from a 1988 level of 16 per cent to the current 4 per cent was not primarily based on part-time work, whose spread is still relatively limited (16 per cent).[17] A quick glance at European data also shows that there are countries where the same rate of part-time work corresponds to decidedly different unemployment rates, two cases in point being Italy and Portugal: in these two countries, quite different unemployment rates (10 per cent and 4 per cent, respectively) accompany quite similar part-time rates (about 10 per cent in both cases).

If it is true that for economic laws the exception does *not* prove the rule, one must conclude that the two-way correspondence 'more part-time jobs, less unemployment' does not always work, or at least not in a rigorously scientific fashion. One should, on the contrary, start from the realisation that unemployment rates can be reduced in various ways other than part-time work, as is demonstrated by the observation made in the *Joint Employment Report 2000*, where it is recognised that the improvement in employment rates in Europe in the last few years is not wholly due to the spread of part-time jobs: 'For the third year in a row, more full-time jobs than part-time jobs were created in 2000. Full-time jobs accounted for almost 70 per cent of the net jobs created, up from 60 per cent in 1999 and 54 per cent in 1998.'[18]

Relieved of the burdensome employment-promoting role that has been attributed to it, part-time work may therefore also be interpreted in ways other than mere verification of its suitability to reduce unemployment. More precisely, it could be opportune to begin to differentiate the notion of part-time work by asking what kind of part-time work we are talking about when speaking of its beneficial effects on employment.

First of all, closer observation of statistical data shows that the amount of employment created by the spread of part-time work is not always of good quality.

The reference here is above all to the 'real' discrepancy between male and female employment. It is undoubtedly true that the spread of part-time work causes an increase in the number of women in the labour market, an effect that is particularly noticeable in Italy, where the employment

---

[17] Outside Europe, American data confirms, albeit with different significance, that a high employment rate can be achieved without widespread part-time work, which reaches only levels of 13.2% in the USA.

[18] COM (2001) 438, 12.9.2001, p. 9.

rate among women is extremely low.[19] It is also true, however, that when different assessment parameters are used the situation alters, or at least can be represented in a different way. Statistical surveys carried out in the last few years have started to take into account a series of indicators that are different from and more refined than those used to measure the *amount* of employment alone. One of the most incisive as regards assessment of the *qualitative* effects of part-time jobs on employment is the so-called 'FTE', or Full-time Equivalent, which is obtained by dividing the total number of hours worked by the average number of hours worked in a year by full-time workers. Using the FTE index it is easy to show that the discrepancy between men and women is much greater in countries where there are more part-time jobs: the gap between the male and female FTE is 33 per cent in the Netherlands, for example, and 20 per cent in France.

Therefore, besides the possible on-the-job discrimination – the only aspect the Directive considers – the segregating effects of part-time work may become apparent at levels which are different from but still connected with the structure of the employed workforce. It is difficult to deny the fact that part-time work has two sides to it: it increases female participation in the workforce, responding to what some observers consider to be a negative feature of the Italian system.[20] The large-scale spread of part-time work, however, also helps to consolidate the segmentation of employment between men and women or, to leave considerations of gender aside, between good and bad jobs, the latter being unskilled jobs with few career prospects. As the Italian *Monitoring Report on Employment and Labour Policies* reveals, 'On the whole, the chances of future employment for part-time workers are fewer than those for full-time workers.'[21]

It would therefore be advisable to exercise extreme caution in recognising part-time work as having an unlimited power to improve the

---

[19] The female employment rate in Italy is just over 35%, as compared with 71% in Denmark, for example. The Italian gender-gap in labour market participation is the highest in Europe (27.6%, the lowest being Sweden with 3.8%). The European average of the gender-gap is 18.3%. Source: *Commission Report on Increasing Labour Force Participation and Promoting Active Ageing*, COM (2002) 9 final, 24.1.2002.

[20] See G. Rodano, *La disoccupazione* (Rome: Laterza, 1998), pp. 39–48.

[21] These are the words used by the *Rapporto di monitoraggio sulle politiche occupazionali e del lavoro* (*Monitoring Report on Employment and Labour Policies*), 2/2000, in particular at p. 52. The statement goes on to say that this difference 'is, however, due to the differences in age, sex and family position between the two groups and thus cannot be attributed to the inherently precarious nature of part-time work', thus seeming to ignore completely the existence of what is defined as indirect discrimination, which, as is widely known, may well be demonstrated by statistical data.

employment performances of a labour market, and consequently attributing to EU employment policy the intention of quantitatively increasing part-time work, no matter how 'good' or 'bad' part-time jobs are and, consequently, how their legal regulation is to be framed. The question is, in other words, to ascertain whether the three objectives usually ascribed to any legislation on atypical work – employment, firms' efficiency and workers' protection – are always and necessarily mutually inconsistent, or if, on the contrary, they could find some sort of genuine synthesis in the field of part-time work. The task now is to see whether any trace of this perception of part-time work is detectable in documents relating to the EU Employment Strategy.

3.2   Part-time work as a means to increase employment

Analysis of the latest versions of EU documents confirms that a quantitative increase in part-time work achieved by introducing measures aimed at increasing flexibility on the demand side is *not* the only index that can be obtained from the overall EES.[22]

It is well known that, on the occasion of the Spring 2000 European Council, the so-called 'Lisbon target' was agreed on: the objective is now to achieve an employment rate as close as possible to 70 per cent overall and exceeding 60 per cent for women by 2010.[23] Accordingly, in passing from the first to the more recent versions of the Community Guidelines for Member States' employment policies, the aim has shifted from a *decrease in unemployment* rates to an *increase in employment* rates.[24] Enlarging activity rates – this is the ultimate rationale of the Lisbon choice – will reinforce the sustainability of social protection systems.

This development of the EU objectives implies a radical change in how a consequential employment policy (and legislation) should be framed. In the light of the 'Lisbon target', the main goal of the European Employment

---

[22] On which see J. Goetschy, 'The European Employment Strategy: Genesis and Development' (1999) 5 *European Journal of Industrial Relations* p. 117, and J. Goetschy and P. Pochet, 'Regards croisés sur la stratégie européenne de l'emploi', in P. Magnette and E. Remacle (eds.), *Le nouveau modèle européen* (Brussels: Presses de l'Université Libre de Bruxelles, 2000).

[23] The 2001 Stockholm Council set intermediary targets of 67% overall and 57% for women by 2005.

[24] In statistical terminology, the unemployment rate is the proportion of the number of unemployed persons to the number of persons in the labour force, whereas the employment rate is the proportion of the number of employed persons to the number of persons of working age in the population.

Strategy shifts from an 'internal' modification of the existing labour force
to an increase in labour force participation. Indeed, whereas a policy aimed
at reducing unemployment tries to make people transit from searching
for a job to finding one, a policy aimed at increasing employment tries
to make people transit from not even searching for a job to beginning to
search and possibly to finding one.[25] In order to reach the EU objective
of a 70 per cent employment rate by 2010, it is therefore necessary to
increase labour force participation, i.e. the number of those to whom
the idea of starting to look for a job may appeal. It is therefore fully
understandable why the recent Commission report on the Lisbon (and
Stockholm) follow-up stresses that 'the overall aim must be . . . to attract
a substantial part of those currently inactive but able to work, particularly
women, to the labour market on a lasting basis, [and] to maintain the
participation of today's older workers; those over 50 being at high risk of
early retirement'.[26]

What has been said with regard to the 'Lisbon shift' in the EU Employment Strategy is decisive for a correct understanding of the labour market
function of part-time work regulations.

From a purely 'reduction of unemployment' perspective, part-time
work should serve as an instrument to allow people in search of a job to
find one. It would therefore be sufficient to frame its regulation in such a
way as to increase flexibility on the demand side.

On the contrary, from an 'increase the labour force participation' perspective, part-time work should serve as an instrument to encourage
people not searching for a job to begin to search and to find one that meets
their expectations. Consequently, its regulation should be structured in
such a way as to increase flexibility on the supply side. That is, a form of
regulation which – to recall another EU Employment Strategy formula –
could guarantee better (part-time) jobs rather than more (part-time)
jobs. Here, 'bad' part-time jobs may be essentially understood as those
governed by a legislation leaving to employers the right to unilaterally
vary their demand for (part-time) labour according to their economic

---

[25] People not looking for a job are not considered as 'unemployed' but rather as a population
'not in the labour force'. The typical case invoked when talking of the need to increase
labour force participation refers to women, whose difficulty in reconciling work and family
life often prevents them even looking for a job.

[26] Report from the Commission to the Council, the European Parliament, the Economic and
Social Committee and the Committee of the Regions – Report requested by Stockholm
European Council, *Increasing Labour Force Participation and Promoting Active Ageing*,
COM (2002) 9, 24.12.2002, p. 9.

exigencies. 'Good' part-time jobs would be those regulated so as to assure a 'work organisation that allows for a better balance between working and personal lives'.[27]

To conclude, it could be possible to illustrate the line of reasoning sketched in the above by delineating two different and mutually exclusive ways of linking EU employment goals and domestic part-time regulations. In the first sequence, the objective is a decrease of unemployment rates pursued through a policy of demand-side flexibility, postulating (or allowing) 'bad' part-time jobs. In the second sequence, the objective is an increase of activity and employment rates pursued through a policy of supply-side flexibility, postulating 'good' part-time jobs.

4 Post-Lisbon EU employment strategies and domestic policy targets in Italy: the connections between labour force participation and 'good' part-time jobs

This renewed perspective on the function of employment policy in part-time work regulation may prove particularly relevant to analysis of the Italian case.

Recent data confirms that the proportion of voluntary part-time workers in Italy is amongst the lowest in Europe, being less than half the European average.[28] The fact that part-time work is highly involuntary clearly reveals that such contracts in Italy mainly attract unemployed persons forced to accept part-time work as a second-best, rather than potential participants who would be ready to join the labour force so long as they could work on a part-time basis. In other words, the option to work part-time in Italy has more to do with a 'negative' choice made by workers reluctantly renouncing a full-time job, than with a 'positive' choice on the part of people willingly abandoning inactivity in search of a job compatible with family, study or training commitments.[29]

In short, the low proportion of voluntary part-time workers makes it clear that, up to now, part-time work in Italy has mainly been used – at best – in order to decrease unemployment rates, not in order to increase labour force participation and, therefore, employment rates: that is,

---

[27] To use the wording employed in Chapter 4 of the Commission Report on *Employment in Europe 2001: Recent Trends and Prospects* (Luxembourg: OOPEC, 2001), entitled 'Quality of Work and Social Inclusion'.

[28] See ibid., p. 70, graph 101. In Europe, the proportion of those who declare themselves satisfied with a part-time contract is about 60%, whereas in Italy it does not reach 30%.

[29] According to the Commission report quoted at n. 26, the major reasons for inactivity are personal or family responsibilities (almost 20% of the total inactive).

precisely the opposite of what a correct understanding of the EU employment strategy would imply.

Given such a national situation, it could be possible to infer that EU-compatible Italian legislation concerning part-time work should combine quantity and quality by making good use of the main blueprints of the EES, all converging on the legal space occupied by the regulation of part-time work – 'Lisbon target', 'better jobs' and 'gender mainstreaming' as horizontal objectives cutting through all four pillars; 'balance between flexibility and security' as the underlying inspiration of the third pillar on adaptability;[30] and 'reconciliation of work and family life' for the fourth pillar on equal opportunities.[31]

Is the Italian national legislation able to secure such a 'policy mix'[32] in the regulation of part-time work? Is it a form of legislation aimed at increasing the voluntary character of part-time work by making it 'appealing' to people who would otherwise remain outside the labour force? Is it aware of the fact that making part-time work a voluntary choice signifies increasing employment rates as the EU suggests Member States should do? Does it acknowledge that 'reconciliation of work and family life', 'better jobs' and 'balance between flexibility and security' are just semantic variations of a single policy aimed at increasing labour force participation as a necessary precondition for the achievement of the 'Lisbon target'?

As concerns Italy, the answer to these questions is a dual one, conditioned by the period of transition between two reforms at the time of writing, as mentioned previously.[33] Whereas the legislation currently in force may be considered as an acceptable trade-off between a quantitative spread and a qualitative increase in part-time work,[34] achieved by means

---

[30] The Commission evaluation on this point is not so encouraging: 'few initiatives relating specifically to the objective of improving the quality of employment are introduced under the Adaptability Pillar this year': see the *Draft Joint Employment Report*, COM (2001) 438 final, Brussels 12.9.2001, p. 35. The point of 'a renewed balance between flexibility and security' is stressed in the *Social Policy Agenda* as redefined by the Nice Council, COM (2000) 379 final, of 28.6.2000, and the final Council document in OJEC C-157 of 30.5.2001.

[31] It is certainly no mere chance that the main measures under the heading of 'Reconciling Work and Family Life' are indicated by the *Employment Guidelines* 2002 in the 'Policies on career breaks, parental leave and part-time work'.

[32] As the Commission recalls, 'In the context of the implementation of the Employment Guidelines, the term "policy mix" refers to the balance between the four pillars of the Guidelines': see the *Draft Joint Employment Report* (n. 30 above), p. 63.

[33] See above, section 2.

[34] A less favourable opinion is expressed in the *Monitoring Report* 1/2001; with reference to the reform brought into effect with Decree No. 61/2000, the report states that "The prediction that workers will be protected in their individual employment relationships by

of an innovative regulatory technique combining legislative obligations, collective autonomy and individual choice, the highly probable 'reform of the reform' announced by the *White Paper* seems to point to a step backwards towards a different concept which – in the name of the same EES – risks configuring part-time work as the subject of a policy aiming merely at a quantitative increase of part-time contracts and paying less attention to the request for quality from the supply side than to requests for flexibility from the demand side.

Nevertheless, let us take things in their proper order.

4.1   The aim of the EC Directive and its reinterpretation in the Government White Paper on the Labour Market: criticism of the instrumental use of supranational regulations

Immediately after the adoption of the reform in 2000, and with even greater vigour following publication of the Government's *White Paper*, harsh criticism has been levelled at the 'efficiency' of the part-time work legislation, which has been accused of not being a coherent application of the rather trite formula whereby 'flexibility cannot help but create employment'. In this context the most critical observers of the reform became convinced that greater liberalisation of part-time work would be more in line with the suggestions made by the EU,[35] if not quite a precise EC obligation.[36]

In fact, it would be senseless to deny that, in one way or another, the promotion of part-time work is mentioned in almost all the 'pillars' of the EU Employment Strategy. With the obvious exclusion of entrepreneurship, part-time work has a prominent role in the guidelines regarding employability, adaptability and equal opportunities. Indeed, it would be equally wrong to deny that behind the 1997 Directive there *also* lay a great desire to promote this type of employment. This, however, is a long step from claiming the existence of a legally binding EC obligation to promote its maximum and unconditional spread.

The main argument contested here is based on an instrumental interpretation of certain clauses in the Agreement attached to Directive 97/81/EC, which states that Member States 'should identify and review obstacles of a legal or administrative nature which may limit the

---

a (potential) improvement in the "quality" of part-time work, however, risks weakening actual flexibility of use by firms and reducing the "quantity" of such jobs', at p. 66.

[35] See Santucci, 'La riforma "europea" del part-time' (n. 14 above).

[36] A. Reale, 'Il lavoro a tempo parziale tra ordinamento comunitario e diritto interno' (2000) 12 *Massimario di giurisprudenza del lavoro* pp. 1262–3.

opportunities for part-time work and, where appropriate, eliminate them'
(Clause 5.1.a). Hence, in not having eliminated *all* the possible obstacles
to the spread of part-time work, Decree 61/2000 allegedly represents failure on the part of the Italian State to comply with obligations deriving
from its Community membership.

This kind of interpretation does not appear to be acceptable, in part
because it demonstrates too much and in part because it demonstrates
too little.

It demonstrates too little because it does not seem to consider that
in reality Community law does not impose any obligation concerning
unconditional promotion of part-time work. Claiming that the only balancing principle in the Directive is the prohibition against discrimination
between full-time and part-time workers[37] amounts to neglecting a whole
series of provisions that recur throughout the Directive and the accompanying Agreement, the aim of which is clearly to point out that reference
is being made to *voluntary* part-time work, given what has been defined
as 'mild flexibility'.[38]

Perusal of the *Consideranda* of the Directive reveals clearly that a maximum spread of part-time work – irrespective of the preservation of its
'quality' and 'voluntary' nature – was not the sole motive behind the adoption of the regulations. *Considerandum* 5, for instance, explicitly states that
the aim of the Directive is to favour 'a more flexible organisation of work
in a way which fulfils both the wishes of employees and the requirements
of competition'.[39] From this perspective, Clause 5 of the Agreement –
which the theses contested here view as placing Member States under
an unconditional obligation to promote part-time work – should be read
differently. That is to say, it should be read in its entirety, starting from the
beginning: the commitment of Member States to eliminate obstacles that
might limit opportunities for part-time work is in fact subject to the provisions made 'in the context of Clause 1 of this Agreement' (Clause 5.1).
Clause 1 – which comes well before the presumed obligation laid down by
Clause 5.1.a – only requires Member States 'to facilitate the development

---

[37] Vallebona, 'La nuova disciplina (n. 11 above)', p. 492.
[38] B. Caruso, 'Alla ricerca della "flessibilità mite": il terzo pilastro delle politiche del lavoro
comunitarie' (2000) 2 *Diritto delle relazioni industriali* p. 141.
[39] The dual strategy of promotion of part-time work to promote competitiveness on the
part of enterprises and the provision of limits to guarantee its voluntary nature is almost
explicitly stated in the foreword to the Agreement accompanying the Directive, where the
signatories themselves declare that the Agreement 'illustrates the willingness of the social
partners to establish a general framework for the elimination of discrimination against
part-time workers and to assist the development of opportunities for part-time work on
a basis acceptable to employers and workers'.

of part-time work on a voluntary basis and to contribute to the flexible organisation of working time in a manner which takes into account the needs of employers *and workers*. This is therefore by no means the gospel of unilateral flexibility that has been attributed to the EC legislators – and, behind them, the European trade unions.

Certainly, as a limit to the desired spread of part-time work, the references in the Directive to its voluntary nature may be accused of being excessively vague and generic. It is not difficult, however, to contend that the same vague and generic quality affects those Directive provisions which have been made out to be so precise and unconditional as to entail failure to comply on the part of any Member States that do not adopt national legislation unconditionally in favour of unconstrained part-time work. Therefore, unless we give different weight to words contained in one and the same text, the interpretation whereby the supranational regulations oblige Member States to introduce 'free' part-time work does not seem at all acceptable.

Lastly, the thesis that sees the Directive as imposing an unconditional and binding obligation, *ex* Art. 249 ECT, to remove all obstacles to absolutely free recourse to part-time work demonstrates too much, in that if this were true *any* national provision that in any way limited access to part-time work would be illegal under EC law. For example, even the national rule requiring written form for part-time contracts, of which the supranational rules make no mention whatever, would have to be considered as not complying with the EC Directive. The same applies to the procedural obligations prescribed by domestic regulations when a worker decides to change from a full-time job to a part-time one,[40] obligations which in principle could be considered as undue obstacles to the spread of this type of work.

The (mis)representation of part-time work as an EC-obligatory quantitative panacea for employment – by applying an instrumental interpretation of the Directive – has therefore become a basis for criticism from a significant number of authors, who make no mystery of their perplexity as to the by no means unconditional modalities with which part-time work is regulated under the 2000 reform. An echo of these criticisms – actually conducted through an instrumental use of the EC Directive, to which they

---

[40] The transformation of a full-time contract into a part-time one is viewed with some 'suspicion' by legislators: an employee's request to change to a part-time relationship must always be accompanied by the assistance of a union representative or, alternatively, ratified by the local labour inspectorate.

attribute regulatory intentions that only partially coincide with those of the parties who signed the Agreement – is to be found in the recent *White Paper on the Labour Market* released by the newly installed conservative Government, which reflects and even explicitly states many of the objections raised during scholarly debate on the issue. According to the *White Paper*:

> In Italy implementation of European Directive 97/81/EC regarding part-time work is an example of a transposition that does not reflect the wishes of the social partners at European Community level, as confirmed by the above-mentioned Directive. Whereas, in fact, the Directive invites Member States to remove any obstacles which may limit the full use of this type of contract, with a view to promoting employment, the decrees issued during the previous legislature introduce new constraints and thus undermine the promotional intentions of the EC legislators.

It is now time to verify whether the reform introduced in 2000 deserves this type of criticism.

4.2 At the basis of current Italian legislation on part-time work: employment as an 'institution' and private autonomy as a 'medium'

More than three years on from the adoption of the 2000 reform decree, a large number of commentators have already made an accurate analysis of it,[41] highlighting the divergence from or partial consolidation of previous legal requirements,[42] its direct descent from the EC Directive,[43] the

---

[41] V. Bavaro, 'La riforma del part-time', in M. Brollo (ed.), *Il lavoro a tempo parziale. Decreto legislativo 61/2000* (Milan: IPSOA Editore, 2001); G. Bolego, 'La gestione individualizzata dell'orario di lavoro nel "nuovo" part-time' (2000) *Rivista italiana di diritto del lavoro* p. 437; G. Bolego, 'La nuova disciplina del contratto di lavoro a tempo parziale' (2001) *Italian Labour Law e-Journal* p. 3 (www.labourlawjournal.it, ISSN 1561–8048); V. Pinto, 'Disciplina del part-time e autonomia collettiva' (2000) 19 *Lavoro informazione* p. 5; Reale, 'Il lavoro a tempo parziale' (n. 36 above), p. 1262; M. Roccella, 'Contrattazione collettiva, azione sindacale, problemi di regolazione del mercato del lavoro' (2000) 3 *Lavoro e diritto* p. 351; M. Roccella, 'Il rapporto di lavoro, nuove flessibilità e diritti' (2000) supplement 3 *Toscana lavoro giurisprudenza* p. 71; R. Romei, 'Prime riflessioni sulla nuova legge sul rapporto di lavoro a tempo parziale' (2000) 2 *Argomenti di diritto del lavoro* 247; Santucci, 'La riforma "europea" del part-time' (n. 14 above); Vallebona, 'La nuova disciplina' (n. 10 above).

[42] Respectively, requirements concerning the form of contracts and the re-proportioning of normative and economic rights of part-time workers.

[43] On the principle of non-discrimination, see A. Alaimo, 'Principio di non discriminazione e riproporzionamento dei trattamenti', in Brollo, *Il lavoro a tempo parziale* (n. 41 above).

total novelties it contains,[44] or the refinements introduced with respect to regulatory profiles that were already sufficiently well defined by previous legislation.[45]

It will not be possible to analyse in the following pages all the topics mentioned; and not all of them can be equally considered to be an expression of the fundamental policy aims on which legislators based the regulations introduced in 2000. It cannot be maintained, for example, that the principle of equal treatment – the main concern of the EC Directive – was one of the main driving forces behind the domestic legislation, which confines itself to consolidating trends that were already quite clearly defined. Nor can it be claimed that the use of part-time work in order to reconcile work and family life was a topic to which particular attention was paid, either during the public debate before and after the decree or while the decree itself was being formulated.[46] This circumstance can easily be accounted for by remembering that at the same time as the decree on part-time work was being prepared, the Government was conducting an exhaustive examination of parental leave regulations, which it was to adopt only a few weeks later.[47] Nor, to conclude, did Italy experience the heated debate that accompanied the introduction of a right to part-time work in other countries such as Germany and the Netherlands.[48]

On the other hand, an absolute priority in public discussion and academic debate was the employment dimension of part-time work, which was seen as the main parameter by which to assess the decisions made by national legislators. It therefore comes as no surprise that the most frequently debated issues following adoption of the 2000 decree were those directly connected with the flexible use of part-time work. In

---

[44] The criteria used to calculate the number of part-timers in order to apply the Workers' Statute (on which see A. Alaimo, 'Il computo dei lavoratori a tempo parziale per l'applicazione di normative specifiche', in Brollo, *Il lavoro a tempo parziale* (n. 41 above)), and the attribution of limited powers of equity to judges as a supplementation of contracts.

[45] The transformation of the employment relationship and priority rights of part-timers in the event of hiring full-time employees.

[46] In contrast with what is the case within the EU Employment Strategy, the text of the Directive does not seem to take much account of the reconciliation of work and family life, with the exception of a brief mention of the importance of 'measures which would facilitate access to part-time work for men and women in order to ... reconcile professional and family life', in General Consideration No. 5 of the Agreement.

[47] The part-time reform is dated 25 February 2000; the parental leave reform was introduced on 8 March 2000.

[48] See A. Jacobs and M. Schmidt, 'The Right to Part-time work: the Netherlands and Germany Compared' (2001) 17 *International Journal of Comparative Labour Law and Industrial Relations* p. 371.

particular, there have been two provisos that came under discussion and were strongly criticised: those related to the 'how much' and to the 'when' of part-time work, i.e. the possibility for an employer to impose extra hours (see below, section 5.1), and his power to vary the time at which the work should be done (so-called 'elasticity clauses', section 5.2).[49]

Beyond its potential employment effect, the recent Italian reform intersects with another important issue that has affected the entire evolution of national labour law in the last few years. By this I mean the progressive injection of increasing doses of individual autonomy into the regulation of atypical employment relationships,[50] such as to bring about a partial modification of a model of negotiated flexibility that was introduced in the late 1970s and firmly constructed around the two consolidated pillars of labour legislation and collective agreements.

The aim of the rest of this chapter will therefore be to view the legislative reform of part-time work against the background of a wider grid of observation which, starting from a careful analysis of the text of the national reform and the EC indications, will try to assess its coherence with the main trends in the domestic labour law debate in the last few years. Within this framework it seems that a possible approach to analysing the Italian part-time work reform would be to assess its consistency with respect to the two main issues which – together with federal decentralisation of public policies – have characterised Italian labour law in the transition from the twentieth to the twenty-first century: the employment-promoting significance of labour legislation and the restoration of individual autonomy in the regulation of employment relationships.

5 The real ground for assessment of the potential of part-time work to increase employment: flexible, individual organisation of working hours

The reference in previous sections to the need for 'balanced' promotion of part-time work was dictated by the intention to introduce a legal analysis of domestic legislation which will be conducted in the light of what seems to be the real economic function of part-time work, taking into account at the same time the need to guarantee competitiveness on the

---

[49] On these issues, see C. Alessi, 'La flessibilità della prestazione: clausole elastiche, lavoro supplementare, lavoro straordinario', in Brollo, *Il lavoro a tempo parziale* (n. 41 above).

[50] See M. D'Antona, 'Contrattazione collettiva e autonomia individuale nei rapporti di lavoro atipici', originally published in 1990 but now republished in B. Caruso and S. Sciarra (eds.), *Massimo D'Antona – Opere*, Vol. I (Milan: Giuffrè, 2000).

part of enterprises. That function is not one of reducing working hours in a distributive fashion so much as one of allowing enterprises to introduce flexible management of working hours. A firm that decides to take on two part-timers, each working 20 hours a week, instead of one full-timer working 40 hours certainly does not do so in order to distribute employment opportunities, but in order to exploit a certain amount of flexibility in the duration and scheduling of the work which, by definition, would be impossible with a full-time contract. In the rhetoric of part-time work seen as typical of a 'modern' labour market, the prototype of the part-time worker is one who voluntarily takes on several jobs, perhaps combining a part-time job with a series of semi-autonomous collaborations that provide professional and other forms of enrichment. In reality, however, the part-time worker that firms are looking for preferably has only one job and remains available for work in the rest of his/her time, if required.

From the entrepreneurial viewpoint, therefore, what qualifies part-time work as a resource for competitiveness is not a mere reduction in the number of working hours so much as the fact that this reduction allows for a certain amount of flexibility which would be impossible or difficult to achieve with a full-time contract. The economic rationale of part-time contracts, in other words, is not a reduction in working hours but a flexible use of working time, made possible by – but not identifiable with – the reduction itself. It is through the legislative criteria of a fair distribution of the 'doses' of flexibility required on both the demand and the supply side that one can measure the quality of part-time work and ascertain whether it is 'good' or 'bad'. Beyond the improbable threat of non-compliance with EC regulations, therefore, the suitability of domestic legislation to promote the real function of part-time work needs to be assessed with reference to its suitability to provide conditions whereby this type of contract can help in working out a flexible and individual organisation of working time: flexible on the demand side and individual on the supply side. Rather than providing incentives for recourse to part-time work *tout court*, this seems to be the most correct way to assess the adequacy of the domestic regulations.

The question to be answered is therefore whether it is possible to see the regime introduced by the 2000 part-time work reform in Italy as possessing legal mechanisms that will promote the real function of part-time work as defined above: whether, that is – to return to the issues mentioned in the introduction to this chapter – the regulations governing the duration (section 5.1) and scheduling of the work (section 5.2) are capable of favouring the balanced flexibility that is the real added value of part-time work and the only obligation that can be derived from the EC Directive.

5.1   The duration of part-time work and extra hours

Opinions expressed concerning regulations on extra hours have not been very positive: from the more openly hostile[51] to the more moderately perplexed,[52] most observers have charged the clauses in Decree 61/2000 introducing flexibility in the duration of work with excessive rigidity, in some cases even denying their capacity to ease previous constraints.

The opinion put forward here, on the opposite side, is that these clauses are one of the more innovative aspects of the new regulations, which clearly favour objectives of flexibility in the attempt to achieve a new balance between legislation, collective autonomy and individual autonomy.

5.1.1   Extra hours and collective autonomy

With reference to the possibility of extending the duration of working hours, the new regulations have entrusted collective bargaining with the task of identifying the causes for and maximum limits of any extra hours an employer can legitimately require.

The fact that under previous legislation it was possible for collective agreements to remove the legislative ban on extra hours for part-timers has created doubts as to the truly innovative character of the reform.[53] However, the analogy between a prohibition of extra hours that could be derogated from by collective bargaining (previously), and the possibility of extra hours within limits set by collective bargaining (today), is only an apparent one.

It was one thing to provide for collective bargaining having the faculty to 'seize' the individual right not to work extra hours (Art. 5 of Law 863/1984), a faculty that would preclude recourse to extra hours unless it was collectively agreed on.

It is quite another thing to provide, as in Art. 3 of Decree 61/2000, for bargaining which only has the task of establishing time limits on extra

---

[51] Vallebona, 'La nuova disciplina' (n. 11 above); Reale, 'Il lavoro a tempo parziale' (n. 36 above).

[52] Romei, 'Prime riflessioni sulla nuova legge' (n. 41 above), and Santucci, 'La riforma "europea" del part-time' (n. 14 above).

[53] See, in these terms, Pinto, 'Disciplina del part-time e autonomia collettiva' (n. 41 above), and Vallebona, 'La nuova disciplina' (n. 11 above).

hours that may *anyway* be requested by an employer, either in the form of exceeding the maximum limits set by applicable collective agreement or in the absence of any collective regulations.

5.1.1.1 Extra hours in the absence of an applicable collective agreement

In the event of a lack of collectively agreed regulations governing part-time work – a situation presumably, but not necessarily, destined to disappear in time – an employer has two choices.

First, he can decide to exploit the considerable 'cheap' flexibility margins provided by the new legislative exemption allowing a 10 per cent increase in individually agreed working hours, given that, within the limits of this exemption, extra hours are paid at the same rate as ordinary working hours.

The second alternative, in the absence of an applicable collective agreement, enables the employer to go even beyond the 10 per cent threshold allowed by legislation, as long as the hourly rate of pay is increased by 50 per cent, as Art. 3 of Decree 61/2000 explicitly provides.

5.1.1.2 Extra hours exceeding the limits set by applicable collective agreements

A slightly different case is when existing collective agreements are not applied. Although here again recourse to extra hours is not radically excluded, it depends entirely on calculation of the economic convenience to the employer. An employer who decides to reject collective negotiation can, in fact, no longer take advantage of the 10 per cent exemption – which can only be applied when no collective agreement regulations exist – and will have to pay for his decision with a 50 per cent increase in the rate of pay for *all* the extra hours he may ask for.

In other words, an employer wishing to remain a *free rider* with respect to application of a collective agreement would have to face one of the many choices that the logic of costs and benefits constantly poses: either to adhere completely to the collective bargaining system and thus be able to exploit the possibility of flexible working hours generally allowed for by collective agreements[54] or, if he decides to remain outside the system of negotiated flexibility, be ready to apply a 50 per cent pay increase for every extra hour he asks his part-time employees to work.

---

[54] Three years after the adoption of Decree 61/2000, the first collective bargaining experiences have moderated many of the initial fears expressed by enterprises. Almost all the collective agreements have, in fact, recognised the possibility of extra hours, up to the daily and/or weekly working hours of a full-time worker.

What Decree 61/2000 proposes with reference to the first kind of flexible use of part-time work is thus an explicit exchange between complete, effective application of the collective agreement and access to flexibility in the duration of part-time work. This is certainly one of the most significant systematic aspects of the reform and leads to the conclusion that, despite appearances, the new regulations governing part-time work have overcome the rigidities of the 1984 Law, which excluded any possibility of demanding extra hours beyond those provided for by collective agreement.

All things considered, there has been no tightening up of the collective constraints as compared with previous legislation. On the contrary: 'What was once formally prohibited (unless provided for by collective bargaining) is now expressly allowed for';[55] and extra hours requested by employers beyond the limits set down by collective agreements are no longer subject to administrative sanctions but merely have to be paid at a higher rate. This is not dissimilar to the so-called 'adult' logic of labour law on the basis of which the proposal was made a few years ago to abandon the logic of legislative prohibitions – including relative ones that could be derogated from by collective bargaining – in favour of generalised predetermination of the economic costs of flexibility.[56] The new rules concerning extra hours cannot be considered to be radically contrary to this prospect, as they have 'downgraded' collective bargaining from being a necessary condition for the legality of extra hours to simply an element that determines their cost.

Having thus qualified the role of collective autonomy in the regulation of extra hours, nothing decisive can be said about a radical change in direction introduced by the 2000 reform unless one highlights its real novelty. By this I mean the valorisation of individual autonomy achieved by the new regulations concerning extra hours in part-time jobs, which is discussed in the next section.

5.1.2 Extra hours and individual autonomy

The substantial monetisation of extra hours worked in part-time jobs is counterbalanced by the closing clause contained in Point 3 of Art. 3

---

[55] Bolego, 'La gestione individualizzata dell'orario di lavoro nel "nuovo" part-time' (n. 41 above).

[56] This was the logic applied, in the most widely discussed case, to flexibility in the termination of employment, with the proposal of so-called "firing costs"; see P. Ichino, *Il lavoro e il mercato* (Milan: Mondadori, 1996).

of Decree 61/2000, according to which 'the performance of extra hours requires in all cases the consent of the worker involved'.

This regulation can be interpreted in two ways. One way of reading it is that individual consent is necessary to complete the authorisation process for extra hours previously (and necessarily) initiated by the collective agreement. In order to have lawful extra hours, in other words, there must be both collective and individual consent.

There is also, however, another possible interpretation, which is more consistent with the above-mentioned possibility of extra hours worked beyond, or despite, the limits collectively agreed on. This interpretation removes any connection between individual consent and the prior exercise of collective autonomy: what the reform seems to allow for, in fact, is direct confrontation, not mediated by collective bargaining, between flexibility requirements on the part of an enterprise and a contractual choice by the two individual parties to the employment relationship. It is precisely in such a circumstance that the innovative nature of Decree 61/2000 appears most evident. The solution to this confrontation goes beyond collective autonomy to involve one of the pillars of labour law: the inderogability of collective norms. What, in fact, is the consent a worker gives to an employer's request for extra hours over and above the limits set by the trade unions, if not derogability *in peius* of the collective agreement? This derogability is, of course, accompanied by appropriate economic and normative guarantees,[57] but it is still depreciatory. Here it is also worthwhile pointing out the radical change in the protection mechanism adopted in the legislation: no longer an *ex post* annulment of individually negotiated clauses that are contrary to the collective agreement, but *ex ante* provision of economic and normative conditions allowing the expression of individual autonomy to be considered free, genuine and adequately remunerated.

Setting judgment aside, the novelty is worth highlighting owing to its systematic significance, which goes beyond the regulation of part-time work: there are, after all, very few provisions in Italian labour law that give the individual the faculty to renounce collective protection in exchange for forms of financial reward. Moreover, since extra hours worked over and above those allowed for by collective bargaining entail application of a higher rate of pay as established by the same collective agreements, it is as if the collective agreements were determining the price of their own violation.

---

[57] Respectively, a higher rate of pay, and no negative consequences for the worker who decides to refuse the request for extra hours.

This is of course neither a generalised nor a generalisable principle, not even with reference to the rest of the regulations governing part-time work,[58] but it must be stressed that the importance the legislation gives to individual autonomy in the context of extra hours is not all that far from the 'predetermination of the cost of flexibility' proposed some years ago in certain well-known analyses as the all-pervading principle of the regulation of working hours.[59]

We can therefore conclude that, despite critics who charge the 2000 reform with excessive rigidity, the new set of rules concerning extra hours in part-time contracts does in fact contain elements allowing for a more flexible use of the type of contracts involved; and it achieves this by means of an innovative combination of legislation, collective autonomy and individual autonomy.

Although it is impossible to speak of a real shift from collective to individual autonomy in handling the margins of elasticity present in part-time work, the remaining impression is that Decree 61/2000 has opened up prospects of flexibility that did not previously exist, setting them in the framework requested by an often neglected EC provision which requires Member States, as mentioned previously, to contribute towards the flexible organisation of working hours in such a way as to take into account the needs of both employers and workers.

It would therefore not be correct to claim – as has been done – that the requirement of individual consent to work extra hours constitutes a denial of the flexibility required by the EC Directive: it is, on the contrary, a faithful translation of the Directive clause which explicitly requires Member States to take the needs of both sides into account. If they had left it entirely to the unilateral decision of an employer willing to pay a higher rate, the national regulations would not have possessed the necessary counterbalance to allow us to state today that the margins of elasticity are really capable of 'taking into account the needs of employers and workers'.

The only obligation the EC Directive places on national legislators, therefore, is that of providing regulations that will allow both sides access to balanced flexibility. The Italian regulations on extra hours in part-time contracts do just that: they allow enterprises to ask for extra hours, if necessary even beyond collectively established limits, and they allow the worker the freedom to refuse the request or accept it in exchange for a higher rate of pay. The unilateral part-time regime that has found a certain

---

[58] As far as elasticity clauses are concerned, for example, the situation is slightly different. See below, section 5.2.

[59] Cf. Ichino, *Il lavoro e il mercato*, Chapter 4 (n. 56 above).

amount of support – flexible only on the demand side, thus neglecting any needs on the supply side – is another thing altogether. It may well be desirable to some, but representing it as an EC-imposed obligation is certainly unjustifiable.

5.2   The scheduling of part-time work and elasticity clauses

The comments made in the preceding section also apply in part to another aspect of flexibility in part-time work, i.e. identifying 'when' this type of work is to be done. I refer here to the issue of elasticity clauses, which in the 1980s and 1990s was at the centre of legal vicissitudes that were not only tempestuous but also highly revealing of the symbolic value of the issue for the different interests involved in the normative definition of flexible working hours.

Art. 3.7 of Decree 61/2000 grants collective agreements the 'faculty to provide for elasticity clauses referring to the scheduling of part-time work, establishing the conditions and modalities with which an employer may vary this scheduling'. In other words, elasticity clauses[60] are allowed only to the extent that collective bargaining authorises them.

Described in these terms, it would appear to be a highly 'traditional' provision, no different from many others that from the 1970s onwards gave rise to a series of 'relative' legislative prohibitions, i.e. ones that could be derogated from by collective agreements. However, the new rules concerning elasticity clauses are not confined to regulating the dialectics between legislative heteronomy and collective autonomy, thus demonstrating that twenty or more years and intense academic debate on the 'rediscovery of the individual'[61] have not gone by in vain. The rediscovery of the individual in the regulations governing elasticity clauses in part-time work contracts is manifest above all in the supersedence of collective bargaining as a necessary *and sufficient* condition for the clauses in question to be legitimate.

---

[60] Also known as *Kapovaz* clauses, according to German terminology.

[61] See S. Simitis, 'The Rediscovery of the Individual in Labour Law', in R. Rogowski and T. Wilthagen (eds.), *Reflexive Labour Law* (Deventer: Kluwer, 1994); the essay had been published in Italian in *Giornale di diritto del lavoro e di relazioni industriali* in 1990. See also D'Antona, 'L'autonomia individuale e le fonti del diritto del lavoro', originally published in 1991 but now republished in Caruso and Sciarra (eds.), *D'Antona – Opere*, Vol. I (n. 50 above); and Lord Wedderburn, 'Labour Law and the Individual: Convergence or Diversity?' The Sinzheimer Lecture 1993, now in Lord Wedderburn, *Labour Law and Freedom. Further Essays in Labour Law* (London: Lawrence & Wishart, 1995).

Here the classical model of collective derogability of legislative provisions is, in fact, modified in such a way as to consolidate in positive terms what had already been stated by the Constitutional Court in the 1992 judgment mentioned above. In the very well-known judgment by which it declared the illegitimacy of elasticity clauses in 1992, the Constitutional Court stated that 'it would be prejudicial to the freedom of the worker if a contract placed him under the power of the employer to require him to work not within a schedule that is or can be previously established by the contract but *ad libitum*, thus suppressing any freedom to organise his life'.[62] This is a condition of personal availability that is inadmissible, even if it is 'authorised' by a source – collective bargaining – that is not equipped to establish the limits of individual availability, which are by definition conditioned by personal circumstances and are therefore different and difficult to render homogeneous. In accordance with this position – and in contrast to the situation regarding extra hours, which a part-timer is allowed to work beyond and regardless of provisions made by collective agreements, provided they are paid at the higher rate established by law (see above, section 5.1) – the principle adopted for elasticity clauses could be likened to a door with two keys: a collective one and an individual one. An elasticity agreement cannot be entered into in the absence of collective clauses, but nor can the latter alone authorise an employer to vary a worker's schedule. For an elasticity clause to be added to a part-time contract, therefore, both collective authorisation and individual consent are required.

In the opinion of some critics of the reform, the constitutional requirement of the freedom to organise one's life would have been met simply by establishing the individual's right to refuse a request for elasticity from his employer. From this viewpoint, then, the second 'key' (or first in order of time), i.e. authorisation via collective agreements, is excessive for the purpose of guaranteeing individual freedom in the organisation of time outside the workplace.

However, developments following adoption of the decree allayed the fears connected with preservation of the authorising power of collective autonomy. All the collective agreements concluded since the decree was adopted have, in fact, granted the possibility of elastic work schedule modalities. This certainly comes as no surprise since the legislators almost took collective authorisation of elasticity clauses for granted. So if it was not realistically plausible to envisage collective agreements without

---

[62] Constitutional Court, No. 210/1992.

elasticity provisions, it would appear possible to conclude that the intention was not to assign collective autonomy the task of authorising individual choices that were in any case safeguarded, but rather to give the provisions another, twofold, significance.

First of all there is a problem of a practical nature: as all the regulations concerning elasticity clauses are essentially built around the principle whereby the availability to work is to be remunerated, it was first necessary to identify a technically suitable instrument to guarantee not so much the *an* of an elasticity but its *quantum*. In this sense, leaving it up to individual autonomy to establish the value of availability would have been ingenuous to say the least, considering that collective bargaining is much better equipped to quantify and safeguard the constitutional principle of the remunerability of the availability to work.

Secondly, it would not be far from the truth to say that the legislative provision of the two-key principle was not in order to entrust collective bargaining with the task of authorising elasticity clauses, so much as to use the clauses presumably introduced by collective bargaining in order to promote collective bargaining itself. It is, in fact, evident that the mechanism described above, which provides employers duly applying collective agreements with access to all the flexible modalities of part-time work,[63] is all the more effective if collective agreements are given the task of regulating the flexibility mechanisms.

Having thus accounted for the dual authorisation required by the 2000 reform, it is now necessary to describe how the reform decree based the application and effectiveness of the two-key principle on a series of 'accessory' provisions – judged by many critics to be too numerous – whose *raison d'être* is to guarantee the conditions in which a worker's individual decision to accept a request for elasticity – provided the collective agreement has also already authorised it – can be considered as the result of a free, potentially reversible, choice. It is in this context that we can account for the regulations that guarantee the worker who is willing to accept elasticity the right to adequate notice and a higher rate of pay, and the right to change his mind if his personal circumstances should alter, without any negative consequences for his job. Re-valuing individual autonomy without at the same time providing a series of safeguarding regulations would not have made much sense.

---

[63] Only a full and effective application of the entire collective agreement allows the employer to access the flexibility resources of the new legislation: 'cheap' extra hours (i.e. not paid at the legislative price of 50% more) and elasticity clauses.

It does not therefore seem possible to find justification for the explicit 'attack' launched in the Government *White Paper* against the Decree 61/2000 regulation which, more than any other, ensures the voluntary nature of elasticity in part-time work, i.e. the regulation which grants an 'elastic' worker the right to change his mind owing to family commitments, health reasons certified by the national health service, or reasons connected with the need to have another job. According to the position taken by the present Government, which will probably soon become law, 'it is hard to see the validity of a worker's right to denounce an agreement he has voluntarily entered into involving an elasticity clause. This exercise of a *jus penitendi* in a contractual agreement the worker has freely accepted seems quite incomprehensible and goes against the general principles governing contractual rights.'

These conclusions are neither acceptable nor in line with EC recommendations. An abrogation of the right to change one's mind about availability to accept employers' 'elastic' requests would be in contrast to the EC position – outlined in the opening paragraphs of this chapter – which views part-time work as an instrument to be used in order to increase labour force participation by providing flexibility rules that also take into account the needs of the supply side. How can an unconditionally elastic part-time job favour the participation of women in the labour market? What reconciliation between work and family life can be assured by a part-time contract that does not allow the worker to schedule either her working hours or the time she has to devote to looking after her children?[64]

Finally, a few closing remarks also need to be made concerning the balance of interests achieved through the elasticity clause regulations, which has become the battleground for the various ways of interpreting the regulations and the desirable balance between production requirements and workers' needs.

As happens with extra hours, the flexibility provided by elasticity clauses is limited to permanent part-time jobs. Criticism of this

[64] This type of observation generally aims to point out the impossibility of reconciling elasticity clauses and part-time work for women. The same applies, however, to men who decide to change over to part-time work in order to allow their partners to have a full-time job – for example, a father who decides to work only in the mornings so that he can look after his children in the afternoons, thus allowing the mother to continue with a full-time job or a part-time job in the afternoon. It is evident that if the father's part-time job is elastic, the whole family schedule – here again aiming at favouring labour force participation by women – cannot be established with the regularity it requires.

limitation, which precludes the accumulation of two flexibilities, and thus pre-empts the possibility of a contract that is both fixed-term and 'elastic', can be answered by objecting that a country like Spain, which can certainly not be charged with rigidity in its regulation of employment relationships, provides an excellent example of how the exclusion of dual flexibility is a manifestation of a common trend: by limiting the advantages of working time flexibility exclusively to permanent jobs, it tends to favour an explicit trade-off between steady access to employment and greater margins of flexibility in the performance of the employment relationship.[65]

6   Conclusions: the other side of flexibility

To conclude this chapter, it is worthwhile returning to the question on which this short analysis of the Italian reform of part-time work has been based: are the new regulations governing the duration (section 5.1) and scheduling (section 5.2) of part-time work capable of providing the balanced flexibility that is the real added value of part-time work, as well as being the only obligation imposed by the EC Directive?

Certain premises need to be repeated in connection with this, as correct identification of the interests the reform attempts to reconcile is an indispensable starting-point and conditions the answer to the question.

First of all, it is necessary to clear the field of interpretations that see part-time work as being objectively and fatally inevitable in a 'new economy' context, and to adopt an evaluative position which, far from supporting an incomprehensible 'eschatology of part-time work', confines itself to pointing out the presence of a more modest problem of conflicting interests.

In the perspective which I have contested, the ineluctability of part-time work – like other forms of departure from the traditional full-time permanent contract – is made to depend on the transformation of methods of production, and therefore of work, in the never sufficiently glorified post-Fordist era. Both internal diversification and the abandonment of the traditional subordinate employment model are seen as a necessary result of a new way of organising production.

---

[65] One of the main features of the 1997 Spanish labour market reform is the attempt to avoid excessive flexibility on commencement of a job, granting enterprises a greater amount of flexibility in cases of termination of permanent employment (by reducing the severance payment due to the worker in the event of withdrawal from a permanent employment contract). For Spanish regulations governing individual dismissal, see A. Lo Faro, 'Così fan tutti? Politica e politica del diritto nelle riforme dei governi conservatori in Italia e in Spagna' (2002) 3 *Lavoro e diritto* p. 505.

It is perhaps necessary to counter this increasingly widespread line of thought by discrediting what risks becoming a commonplace: it is without doubt true that some forms of organisation of labour require contracts other than permanent full-time ones. It is equally true, however, that these different forms of contract are also to be found in the organisation of production that has not changed at all in recent years. That is to say, it is not possible to claim that the standard employment model is always and necessarily inappropriate unless the organisation is based on a Taylor-type factory; nor is it possible to state that a post-Tayloristic organisation cannot work without contracts that are different from classical ones.

With more specific reference to the issues dealt with in this chapter, the allegedly inevitable causal connection between part-time work and post-Fordist organisation does not explain, for example, why part-time contracts have spread mainly in sectors which are totally unaffected by post-Fordism, such as services, agriculture and trade. In reality, part-time contracts are usually applied to 'Fordist' jobs, mostly unskilled in nature, the only kind that are really compatible with a reduced number of working hours. One rarely finds a qualified, responsible worker on a part-time contract; it is much easier to find hamburger sellers, shop assistants or farm workers.

Having excluded the objective indissolubility of the connection between part-time work and new production systems, there is, however, another common view that needs careful re-examination: the line of thought which, although it does not adhere to the above-mentioned eschatology of part-time work, views it as a necessary employment-promoting policy measure in consideration of its potential. Hence the charge of timidity on the part of the Italian legislators in laying down the new regulations: if part-time work serves to increase employment – it is said by the most critical observers of the 2000 reform – it should be equipped with strong incentives; obviously more than Decree 61/2000 has achieved, raising its spread by no more than 2 per cent in a year.

The undoubted employment-promoting potential of the spread of part-time work needs, however, to be seen in its proper setting: it can only achieve positive results from the point of view of an increase in employment if it is conceived and regulated with a view to 'dual flexibility', on both the demand and the supply side.[66] If this is so, the proper

---

[66] The logic of dual (demand- and supply-side) flexibility inscribed within the Part-time Directive is also pointed out by S. Deakin and H. Reed, 'The Contested Meaning of Labour Market Flexibility: Economic Theory and the Discourse of European Integration', in J. Shaw (ed.), *Social Law and Policy in an Evolving European Union* (Oxford: Hart Publishing, 2000).

balance in the promotional policy – and therefore in the juridical structure of any domestic system – of part-time regulation is to be sought in a balanced reconciliation of the conflicting interests involved. This means that it is first necessary to define those interests.

If, in fact, one considers part-time work only as a way of making the labour demand more flexible, it will inevitably be caught up in the notorious fight between insiders and outsiders on the labour market.[67] The obvious consequence of this will be pressure in favour of further liberalisation: if the value attributed to part-time work is a reduction in unemployment rates, it is easy to claim the need to sacrifice worker protection in the name of the right to work.

This position can be countered by stating that an increase in jobs is not a *passe-partout* for abdication from labour protection requirements, not least because the constitutional system still in force in Italy places labour protection and the right to work on the same plane.

This, though, is not the point. A representation of part-time work as an instrument able to reconcile the 'private' interests of workers and the 'public' interest in an increase in employment rates is not totally justifiable. The rhetoric surrounding part-time work which tends to shift the conflict of interests from its natural setting (an enterprise looking for flexibility *vs* a worker trying to safeguard his personal sphere), to a conflict between insiders and outsiders, does not recognise that – as the Constitutional Court has clearly stated – the conflict that part-time work regulations are called upon to resolve is not between the employed and the unemployed but, much less emphatically, between the employers' need for flexibility and the workers' right to safeguard their personal lives. Safeguarding the family life of part-time workers by reducing the margins of employers' requests clashes with the flexibility required by enterprises, not with the increase in employment that is in the public interest.

In short, the normative constraints clashing with unconditionally flexible use of part-time work cannot be represented as undue limits on the effort to promote employment, but merely as barriers against a certain way of handling the organisation of labour, which is a legitimate aspiration for entrepreneurs but cannot be said to be in the public interest. This is not without significance for juridical assessment. The idea that part-time work provides a form of flexibility on the supply side also, and not only on the demand side, seems to have been neglected by the harshest

---

[67] According to the renowned theory formulated by A. Lindbeck and D. Snower, *The Insider–Outsider Theory of Employment and Unemployment* (Cambridge, Mass.: MIT Press, 1988).

critics of the Decree, as well as the 'institutional' criticism of the reform contained in the Government *White Paper*.

It is not really surprising that the *White Paper* and the legislative innovations that will doubtless follow it declare themselves to be faithful interpreters of EC recommendations which, in all truth, appear to lead in quite another direction. The very nature of the Employment Guidelines[68] – defined as an 'open method of co-ordination' – leaves them open to widely diverging national interpretations, as sometimes happens with much more binding EC documents such as Directives. To predict an assessment of the content of the future reform of part-time work that is likely to be introduced in Italy, we can use the words that Knill and Lehmkuhl address to the reform of British Rail: a 'primarily domestically inspired reform that went far beyond European requirements'.[69]

Regarding the legislation currently in force, however, we can state that the recent Italian reform of part-time work does not seem to deserve the harsh criticism which it immediately earned and by which it will probably be crushed. The legislators of 2000 seemed to share the view that the policy of massive introduction of part-time work needed regulating in such a way as to render it appealing to both sides. If it is true that, in the light of post-Lisbon EC recommendations, the legal framework of part-time contracts should not discourage potential participants from joining the labour force, we may conclude that current Italian legislation is in line with this aim. Providing adequate normative conditions for part-time work to be considered as offering flexibility in the supply as well as the demand for labour increases rather than decreases recourse to this type of employment.

The '*renforcement de la logique du temps choisi*'[70] in regulating part-time work, in other words, fits in well with the aim of 'Quality of Work' expressly referred to in the most recent edition of the *Joint Employment Report* – a 'quality of work' that the European Commission views as being directly connected with the primary objective of attracting people into the labour force:

---

[68] For comments on the regulatory technique adopted within the EU Employment Strategy, see M. Barbera, 'Dopo Amsterdam. I nuovi confini del diritto sociale comunitario' (Brescia: Promodis, 2000).

[69] Knill and Lehmkuhl, 'How Europe Matters' (n. 12 above).

[70] The judgment expressed by M. Del Sol in 'Travail à temps partiel: le renforcement de la logique du temps choisi?' (2001) 7–8 *Droit Social* p. 728, with reference to French legislation, can be extended to the philosophy behind Italian legislation. The manifesto of this way of understanding the notion of flexible working time may be considered as Echanges et projets, *La revolution du temps choisi* (Paris: Albin Michel, 1980).

The quality of employment must be improved in such a way as to attract and maintain more people in employment. Better working conditions and better facilities to reconcile work and family lives are a key to increasing the participation of older people, women and the disabled. As a policy area which links the twin objectives of competitiveness and social inclusion, quality is a centrepiece of the European social model and a key to the success of the Lisbon strategy.[71]

In providing an opportunity for balanced individualised management of working and non-working hours, the current Italian legislation thus aspires to provide incentives for the spread of flexible work in the supply of labour *as well*, thereby complementing the Law on parental, family and training leave[72] which was passed at much the same time.

In conclusion, it seems appropriate to restore the part-time work regulations to their rightful dimension as a discipline regulating an employment contract between an enterprise requiring flexibility and a worker wishing to safeguard his/her family life, avoiding the absorption of the whole into a palingenetic framework of employment-oriented flexibility on the demand side that risks giving rise to increasingly hostile assessment of *any* regulation on part-time work. What seems to be preferable, in other words, is a sort of 'privatisation' of juridical analysis of part-time work, after having eliminated the ideological dross that views 'free' part-time work as a totem of the flexibility-creates-jobs theory. Greater attention to the needs of the two parties to the employment relationship is by no means contrary to the adoption of policies to promote this type of employment, and quashes those 'employment-promoting' representations which clearly mask less noble aspirations towards unacceptable unilateral flexibility.

Postscript

As previously stated, many of the provisos dealt with in this chapter were amended by the Government Decree implementing the *White Paper on the Reform of the Labour Market*. At the end of 2003, Legislative Decree No. 276/03 came into force, profoundly reforming the regulation of part-time work with specific regard to some of the issues raised in this chapter:

---

[71] *Draft Joint Employment Report*, COM (2001) 438 final of 12.9.2001, p. 88. In similar terms, see the call for a quantitative and qualitative improvement of employment in the *Social Policy Agenda*, cited in n. 30.

[72] For a comment on parental leave legislation, see R. Del Punta, 'La nuova disciplina dei congedi parentali, familiari e formativi' (2000) 2 *Rivista italiana di diritto del lavoro* p. 149.

namely, the 'flexible' use of part-time work, and the balance between collective and individual autonomy in the management of it.

In contrast to the previous situation, elasticity clauses can now be required by the employer even in the absence of a collective agreement authorising them. The consent of the employee is still required, and the worker cannot be penalised or dismissed if he refuses to enter into an elasticity clause. This, though, is hardly to be seen as the result of the noble intention of the legislator to shift the balance of labour regulation from the collective to the individual – as the Government tends to depict it. Rather, the rejection of the 'double key' principle as a requirement of elastic part-time work (see section 5.2) is to be understood as the result of the willingness to increase the flexible use of part-time work only on the demand side (section 6): indeed, when a collective agreement has already authorised the elasticity clause, individual consent is no longer required.

The legislator's disregard of supply-side flexibility in the new regulation on part-time work is further revealed by the abolition of one of the more significant provisos of the previous legislation: i.e. the reversibility of the employee's choice to enter into an elasticity clause. The employee's right to change his mind about elasticity clauses when personal circumstances change, and to return to working on the basis of a 'normal' part-time contract, has been repealed by the new Decree.

Moreover, the employers' claims to increase the flexible use of part-time work have been further enhanced by the introduction of zero-hours contracts, up to now unknown in the Italian legal system.

As far as supplementary hours are concerned, the same balance between individual and collective autonomy described above with regard to elasticity clauses applies, but the part-time worker's choice to accept extra hours even in the absence of an applicable collective agreement – also permitted by previous legislation (sections 5.1.1 and 5.1.2) – is no longer protected by the considerable increase in pay (50 per cent) which the old law granted.

If one considers that both extra hours and elasticity clauses, previously excluded in case of fixed-term contracts (section 5.2), are now allowed in such cases too, it is easy to conclude that the new Government regulation of part-time work pays less attention to the 'quality' of part-time work on the supply side than to the requests for flexibility on the demand side. Whether such an appraisal of the occupational role of part-time work is thoroughly consistent with the EU conception of 'good' part-time jobs as a means to increase activity rates in the context of the 'Lisbon target' (section 3.2) remains highly doubtful.

7

The Netherlands: from atypicality to typicality

JELLE VISSER, TON WILTHAGEN, RONALD BELTZER
AND ESTHER KOOT-VAN DER PUTTE

1 Introduction

In 2000 the European Council in Lisbon agreed to set targets concerning employment–population ratios. The EU target for 2010 is 70 per cent, meaning that seven out of ten people in the working age (15–64) population should be employed. The current figure for the Netherlands is 74 per cent, which ranks the country in third place, after Denmark and Sweden. Figure 7.1 shows that this was the result of above-average employment growth during the 1990s. Employment growth owed much to the rapid spread of part-time jobs. If employment is recalculated in Full-time Equivalent jobs, the employment record of the Netherlands is more modest. The full-time employment ratio would be just over 60 per cent, compared with 51 per cent for the EU as a whole, far short of the Lisbon target. An important feature of the Dutch labour market is the prevalence of part-time and temporary work. Figure 7.2 shows the share of part-time employment in the workforce as a whole. We see a remarkable difference between the Netherlands and the EU average. In the Netherlands almost 40 per cent of the employed labour force works part-time, while the figure for the European Union as a whole is less than 20 per cent. As Figures 7.1 and 7.2 show, part-time work is especially prevalent among women. An important issue is the reason why people work part-time. According to Eurostat surveys, in 1999 in the Netherlands 72 per cent of the people working in part-time jobs deliberately chose to do so. The European average was 60 per cent. We may conclude from these figures that Dutch part-time employment shares are higher than the EU average partly because of individual preferences, perhaps because the Dutch system of labour

The authors wish to thank Martijn Helmstrijd for his contribution to previous versions of this chapter.

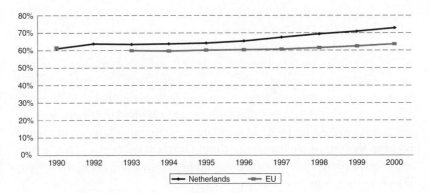

Source: Eurostat Labour Force Surveys

Figure 7.1 Employment rates, in persons

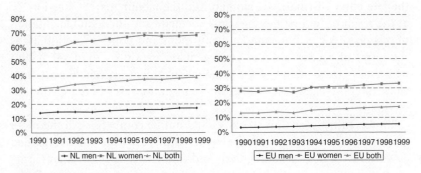

Source: Eurostat

Figure 7.2 Part-time employment in the Netherlands and the EU (as per cent of total employment in group)

law, employment relations and care is less accommodating to full-time employment, especially for women, and more facilitating towards part-time employment than most other systems in the EU. The Netherlands has been characterised as the first part-time economy in the world[1], perhaps becoming a model for other countries with a very gender-segregated labour market and large pockets of unemployment. Others have speculated about the potential of the part-time model as a new form of 'full'

[1] J. Visser, 'The First Part-time Economy of the World: a Model to be Followed?' (2002) 12:1 *Journal of European Social Policy* pp. 23–42; see also Richard Freeman, 'War of the Models: Which Labour Market Institutions for the 21st Century?' (1998) 5:1 *Labour Economics* pp. 1–24.

employment over the life cycle, within the framework of a 'transitional labour market'.[2] The Dutch 'miraculous' employment growth in recent times can to a large extent be attributed to the rise of part-time work and the entry of women into the labour force,[3] and the dynamics of transitions in the Dutch labour market largely revolves around part-time work.[4] We stress, once again, the role of working time preferences. As Bielenski *et al.* put it: 'If working time preferences in the Netherlands were realised, the hours worked by those in substantial part-time employment could become the "standard" working time. Only 58 per cent of Dutch men expressed a preference for full-time employment, while the figure among Dutch women is as low as 26 per cent.'[5]

In this chapter we seek to analyse the rise and significance of part-time work in the Netherlands as a result of a set of three separate though interrelated factors: as the result of a spontaneous process triggered by the late entry of (married) women into the labour market (section 2); as the result of (at first hesitant but) adequate and successful facilitation of this process by labour market institutions and policies (section 3); as the result of accelerated and consistent regulation by the legal system which has erased many of the unequal treatment aspects of part-time work (section 4). A brief conclusion and outlook is offered in the last section (5).

Importantly, 'part-time work' should not be confused with the more general term 'flexible work'. In the Netherlands, part-time work is regarded as work that is carried out regularly and voluntarily in employment, during working hours that are shorter than those generally customary in the sector or company concerned (i.e. the normal working hours for full-time workers). Employees with a fixed-term contract, temporary employment agency workers and on-call workers – except when they actually work part-time – are not classified as part-time workers.

---

[2] T. Wilthagen and R. Rogowski, 'Legal Regulation of Transitional Labour Markets', in G. Schmid and B. Gazier (eds.), *The Dynamics of Full Employment: Social Integration through Transitional Labour Markets* (Cheltenham: Edward Elgar, 2002), pp. 233–73.

[3] J. Visser and A. C. Hemerijck, '*A Dutch Miracle'. Job Growth, Welfare Reform, and Corporatism in the Netherlands* (Amsterdam: Amsterdam University Press, 1997).

[4] J. de Koning, G. Bijwaard, A. Gelderblom and H. Kroes, *Arbeidsmarkttransities en aanboddiscrepanties* ('Labour Market Transitions and Supply Discrepancies') (Tilburg: OSA, forthcoming).

[5] H. Bielenski, G. Bosch and A. Wagner, *Working Time Preferences in Sixteen European Countries* (Report for the European Foundation for the Improvement of Living and Working Conditions, Luxembourg, 2002), p. 61.

2   The growth of part-time work as a spontaneous process

As indicated in the Introduction, the Netherlands is an out-lier in Europe with regard to part-time employment, but it was not until the 1980s that the Netherlands took over the first place formerly occupied by Sweden, Denmark and the UK. During the 1980s the growth of part-time employment accelerated in tandem with the rise in female and service employment. The rapid expansion of part-time work in the Netherlands is sometimes presented as an outcome that was designed and shaped by public policy.[6] However, the rapid spread of part-time employment was mostly the outcome of a *spontaneous process* driven by the late entry of married women into the labour force, shaping, rather than shaped by, the policies of governments, unions and firms. The absence of facilities and support for childcare made part-time employment the dominant *coping* solution for mothers. The part-time option was reinforced by the labour market difficulties of the 1980s, then discovered and promoted by politicians and, after some hesitation, adopted by trade unions and feminists. Policy changes have been piecemeal, reactive and dictated by circumstances, but also innovative, with new goals being discovered along the way.

From 1860 till 1960 the level of labour force participation for Dutch men and women was almost constant.[7] With hardly any annual variation, 30 per cent of women and 90 per cent of men of working age participated in the labour market for paid jobs.[8] As late as 1971 the Netherlands had the lowest female participation rate in Europe – a fact that puzzled many who believed that this was an advanced industrialised society-cum-welfare state, with strong Protestant and workaholic roots. Change was under way, however, and in the next quarter century female labour participation increased more strongly than in any other European country. By 1999 the employment rate of women had risen to 59 per cent, above the EU average. Under the influence of education, early retirement and disability,

---

[6] CEC, *Employment in Europe in 1994* (Luxembourg: Office for Official Publications of the European Commission, 1994), p. 117. C. Hakim, *Key Issues in Women's Work* (London: The Athlone Press, 1996), p. 16.

[7] H. A. Pott-Buter, *Facts and Fairy Tales about Female Labor, Family and Fertility* (Amsterdam: Amsterdam University Press, 1993).

[8] P. W. Mol, J. C. van Ours and J. J. M. Theeuwes, *Honderd jaar gehuwde vrouwen op de arbeidsmarkt* ('A Hundred Years of Married Women in the Labour Market') (The Hague: OSA – *Organisatie voor Strategisch Arbeidsmarktbeleid*, 1988).

employment rates of males fell to 70 per cent in 1992 but rose again in the later 1990s.[9] The increase in female participation is due to *married* women. In 1971 only one in ten married women had paid employment outside the home; today, half of all married women have paid employment. In only one generation there has been a sea change in the labour participation of mothers. In 1973 one in ten mothers with children of pre-school age worked for pay; in 1998 more than half of these mothers did. The availability of a part-time option appears to be decisive. According to Eurostat, only 6 per cent of Dutch mothers with children under the age of ten worked full-time in 1996 – by far the lowest percentage in Europe (the EU average is 30 per cent). The flipside is that 41 per cent of these Dutch mothers worked part-time, nearly three times the EU average.

Panel data confirm the picture that Dutch women tend to switch from full-time to part-time jobs once they have children.[10] Unlike the pattern found (uniquely?) in Sweden,[11] few Dutch women return to full-time jobs when their children grow older.[12] These trends clarify why, despite 'the irresistible emergence of the working married woman',[13] the incidence of full-time employed women has hardly changed: around 18 per cent, the lowest percentage by far in Europe.[14]

On the demand side, the tight labour market, before 1973, fuelled union wage demands and improved job opportunities generally. Employers in services discovered the cheap and educated labour reservoir of married women. More women were encouraged to continue in a part-time job.

[9] OECD, *Employment Outlook 2000* (Paris: Organisation for Economic Co-operation and Development, 2000).

[10] C. M. Kragt, 'Arbeidsdeelname van jonge ouders' ('Labour Participation of Young Parents'), in *Centraal Bureau voor de Statistick* (CBS), *Sociaal-economische dynamiek 1997* (The Hague: Dutch Official Publications (SDU) 1997), pp. 37–43. See also C. Wetzels, *Squeezing Birth into Working Life. Household Panel Data Analysis comparing Germany, Great Britain, Sweden and the Netherlands* (Amsterdam: Thesis Publishers, 1999).

[11] D. Anxo and D. Storrie, 'Working-time Transitions in Sweden', in J. O'Reilly (ed.), *Regulating Working-time Transitions in Europe* (Cheltenham: Edward Elgar, 2003), pp. 46–83.

[12] R. Dekker, R. Muffels and E. Stancanelli, 'A Longitudinal Analysis of Part-time Work by Women and Men in the Netherlands', in S. Gustaffson and D. Meulders (eds.), *Gender and the Labour Market* (London: Macmillan, 2001).

[13] J. Hartog and J. Theeuwes, 'De onstuitbare opkomst van de werkende gehuwde vrouw' ('The Irresistible Emergence of the Working Married Woman') (1983) 68 *Economisch-Statistische Berichten* pp. 1152–7.

[14] OECD, *Employment Outlook 1998* (Paris: Organisation for Economic Co-operation and Development, 1998).

After 1973, when unemployment started its rise, the increase in part-time employment slowed temporarily.[15]

3 Institutional facilitation of part-time work

3.1 From collective towards individual working-time reduction

Institutional and normative changes have gradually reinforced and facilitated the spontaneous changes described in the previous section. The marriage bar for female civil servants, introduced in the 1930s, was withdrawn in 1957 but still applied in many municipalities ten years later.[16] Many private employers had followed, and most unions had condoned, the practice of terminating the employment contracts of married women; it was not until 1975 that this practice was made unlawful.[17] Under the regime of centrally guided wage policy in force between 1945 and 1962, women were paid less than men in the same jobs.[18]

The Netherlands came from a deeply socially and culturally entrenched model of housewifery.[19] In 1965 84 per cent of the adult Dutch population expressed reservations concerning working mothers of school-age children. In 1970 disapproval suddenly dropped to 44 per cent, decreasing to a mere 18 per cent in 1997.[20] It is useful to point out that the change in attitudes preceded the improvement in services and conditions facilitating the combination of work and childcare. The positive effect of such norm changes on women's decisions to participate in the labour market has been demonstrated.[21]

---

[15] K. Tijdens, *Zeggenschap over arbeidstijden* ('Co-determination over Working Hours') (Amsterdam: Welboom, 1998).

[16] H. A. Pott-Buter, *Veranderingen in de levensloop van vrouwen* ('Changes in the Life-course of Women') (Amsterdam: Welboom, 1998).

[17] I. Asscher-Vonk, 'The Legal Status of Female Labour in the Netherlands' (1978) 9 *Bulletin of Comparative Labour Relations* pp. 271–86.

[18] J. P. Windmuller, *Labor Relations in the Netherlands* (Ithaca, N.Y.: Cornell University Press, 1969).

[19] T. Knijn, 'Social Dilemmas in Images of Motherhood in the Netherlands' (1994) 1:2 *European Journal of Women's Studies* pp. 183–206. B. Pfau-Effinger, 'Culture or Structure as Explanations for Differences in Part-time work in Germany, Finland and the Netherlands?' in J. O'Reilly and C. Fagan (eds.), *Part-time Prospects* (London: Routledge, 1998), pp. 177–98.

[20] Sociaal en Cultureel Planbureau (SCP), *Sociaal en cultureel rapport 1998: 25 jaar sociale verandering* ('Social and Cultural Report 1998: 25 Years of Social Change') (Rijswijk: SCP, 1998).

[21] A. G. L. Romme, 'Projecting Female Labor Supply: the Relevance of Social Norm Change' (1990) 11 *Journal of Economic Psychology* pp. 85–99.

The same goes for institutional factors. Relative wages and returns from labour are influenced by institutional factors such as government and union wage policies, taxation, and employment bans. Legislation, labour-management bargaining and union work-sharing policies also shape supply and demand. The Dutch labour market is highly regulated and around 80 per cent of all Dutch employees are covered by collective agreements.

As regards part-time employment, Dutch trade unions initially shared the sceptical view of other European unions. In 1981 the main union federation published a position paper in which the inferiority of employment protection, pay and career prospects in part-time jobs and the lack of union membership among part-timers were highlighted. The union did not want to help create a secondary and non-unionised job market.[22] At that time, during a deep recession, unions wanted to fight unemployment and redistribute jobs through a *collective* reduction of the 40-hour working week. Dutch employers were adamantly opposed and advertised part-time work as a form of *individual* working-time reduction with a proportionate cut in pay.[23] European trade unions, including the Dutch ones, saw part-time employment as undermining their strategy.[24]

In the mid 1970s, the government, dominated by the Labour Party (*Partij van de Arbeid*, PvdA), wanted to bring more women into paid employment as part of its new 'emancipation' policy. The Ministry of the Interior promoted part-time jobs as a way of enabling female civil servants to continue their career after motherhood. Soon, this policy fell victim to the austerity policies of the centre-right government (1977–81). Ministers of Social Affairs and Employment invariably promoted part-time jobs as a job-rationing device in fighting youth unemployment, which reached dramatic proportions in the late 1970s and early 1980s. Employers received a subsidy if they split one full-time job into two part-time jobs. Workers switching to part-time jobs could qualify for a temporary

---

[22] FNV, *Een deel van het geheel* ('A Part of the Whole') (Amsterdam: Federatie Nederlandse Vakbeweging, 1981).

[23] Raad van Centrale Ondernemingsorganisaties (RCO), *De arbeidsduur* (The Hague: RCO, 1980).

[24] B. Casey, 'Staatliche Massnahmen zur Förderung der Teilzeitarbeit: Erfahrungen in Belgien, Frankreich, Großbritannien, den Niederlanden und der Bundesrepublik Deutschland' (1983) 16 *Mitteilungen aus der Arbeitsmarkt- und Berufsforschung* pp. 414–26. J. Visser, 'De langzame haast van de arbeidstijdverkorting in Europe' ('The Slow Pace of Working Time Reduction in Europe') (1985) 9:1 *Tijdschrift voor Politieke Eknomie* pp. 24–53.

wage supplement. In 1982 the programme was stopped for lack of success. The major Dutch study dealing with the 1976–83 period 'doubts whether, on balance, there is a government policy stimulating part-time employment'.[25]

3.2   The Wassenaar Agreement: a turning point

In November 1982 the central organisations of trade unions and employers, co-operating in the Labour Foundation (*Stichting van de Arbeid* or StAr, a joint institution founded in 1945 for the purpose of co-operation on wages and other labour issues), concluded, unexpectedly, a central agreement. This Wassenaar Agreement has been celebrated as the beginning of a new era in Dutch labour relations.[26] The trade unions offered wage restraint and employers' organisations lifted their veto against a general round of working-time reduction. The Agreement itself mentioned various options for work sharing, including early retirement and part-time employment. However, between 1983 and 1986 the unions obtained an average reduction of weekly working hours from 40 to 38. The reduction mostly took the form of extra days off per year and corresponded with a reduction of business hours.[27] In 1985, the central union leadership wanted a reduction to 36 weekly working hours in order to absorb the still high level of unemployment. Employers wanted no more, however, and the unions were divided.[28] Once the economy started to move out of recession their members wanted improved earnings.

As a result, the campaign for a collective reduction of working time died. Until 1993, when the unions launched a second campaign in response to the mini-recession of 1992–3, working hours hardly changed. Nearly all job redistribution took the form of part-time work, and part-time employment became the 'job motor' of the Dutch economy in the 1980s.[29]

We can interpret this outcome as reflecting the balance of forces between unions and employers. Unions had lost one-sixth of their

---

[25] F. Leijnse, 'Bevordering van deeltijdarbeid' ('The Promotion of Part-time Jobs') (dissertation, University of Nijmegen, Instituut voor Toegepaste Sociologie, 1985), p. 32.

[26] Visser and Hemerijck, 'A Dutch miracle' (n. 3 above).

[27] W. A. M. de Lange, 'De balans van ATV' ('The Balance of Working Time Reduction') (1988) 4 *Tijdschift voor Arbeidsvraagstukken* pp. 54–64.

[28] J. Visser, 'New Working-time Arrangements in The Netherlands', in A. Gladstone, R. Lansbury, J. Stieber, T. Treu and M. Weiss (eds.), *Current Issues in Labour Relations: an International Perspective* (Berlin and New York: de Gruyter, 1989), pp. 229–50.

[29] CPB, *De werkgelegenheid in de jaren tachtig* ('Employment in the Eighties') (The Hague: CPB, 1991).

members and more than 20 per cent of the remaining membership was unemployed or on benefits in 1985; mass unemployment had sapped union resources and confidence. Before and after the Wassenaar Agreement employers promoted part-time jobs as their preferred solution.[30] With the arrival of large cohorts of young and female workers, employers easily outplayed the unions. Especially where pay is closely related to experience and seniority, and new technologies favour new skills and devalue experience, there are large gains in productivity and costs to be had from the exchange of 'young' for 'old'. Fearing a lost generation, scarred by youth unemployment, this choice was backed by the centre-right governments of the 1980s. The labour supply decisions of (married) women were informed by the recession rather than by union policies or feminist preferences. Fewer women took the risk of temporarily withdrawing from the labour market. Consequently, more women tried to retain their jobs, possibly through reduced hours when confronted with the need to combine work and motherhood. Paradoxically, these supply forces were in accord with decreasing labour demand, especially in the public sector: local government, health and education.

The demand for flexibility and part-time jobs rose as an unintended consequence of the campaign for reduced working hours. When the economy recovered, employers tried to 'buy back' leisure time. The unions resisted attempts at monetarisation and rising overtime hours as best they could, but conceded the annualisation of working hours, offering increased flexibility throughout the month or year.[31] Working hours and business operating hours, having contracted in parallel movements until the mid 1980s, began to diverge. After a secular decline in business opening hours in services, a reverse movement set in during the 1990s, leading to longer opening hours including evenings, weekends and even Sundays. This development is itself stimulated by reduced working hours, part-time employment and the dual-earners economy. Increasingly, in the view of employers part-time jobs are needed as an 'optimising' manpower tool, i.e. as a means to meet extra demand, the tapping of a new labour reservoir, to help to match working and business hours and to limit costs related to overtime.[32]

[30] RCO, De arbeidsduur nader bekeken ('Working Hours Revisited') (The Hague: RCO, 1983).
[31] K. Tijdens, 'De balans van twee ronden arbeidsduurverkorting, 1982–85 en 1994–97' ('The Balance of Two Rounds of Working time Reductions, 1982–85 and 1994–97') (1998) 14 Tijdschrift voor Arbeidsvraagstukken pp. 212–25.
[32] SZW, Veranderende arbeidstijdpatronen ('Changing Working time Patterns') (The Hague: SZW, 1991).

In the 1990s the male breadwinner lost his once-dominant position in the Dutch labour market. With some delay, he was also losing ground in the unions. The fact that, in contrast to the situation in many European countries, part-time work in the Netherlands is mostly voluntary helps explain the singular position of the Dutch unions in the European Union spectrum. In Eurostat surveys, the Netherlands shows as the country with the lowest share of involuntary part-time work.[33] According to Eurobarometer data analysed by Schulze Buschoff,[34] part-time work is evaluated more positively by Dutch women than by their sisters elsewhere in Europe (with the exception of Denmark) as regards contractual status, tenure, perceived career opportunities, job satisfaction and social security, though on all these aspects part-time jobs attract lower scores than full-time jobs even in the Netherlands. In the 1990s the new union approach gained support from the centre-left (1989–94) and Lib.–Lab. (1994–8 and 1998–2002) governments, which saw the promotion of part-time jobs as a contribution to their newly discovered objective of an active welfare state based on increased labour market participation.[35]

In the Dutch consultation economy, central organisations, especially employers, have an incentive to stay ahead of legislation. That way they hope to wield more influence over the regulations that exist and to demonstrate their importance to member organisations and firms. In 1989 the Labour Foundation (StAr) published a 'joint opinion' and four years later a major agreement was reached, pre-empting legislation. Noting that part-time employment had expanded rapidly, the social partners agreed that 'a halt in this development should be prevented', such a halt being something that 'might happen if part-time work remains concentrated in a limited number of sectors and jobs, or if small part-time jobs, produce too limited income and career prospects'. The StAr recommended that collective bargainers 'improve standards' and 'that firms recognise a qualified right for full-time employees to work reduced hours, unless this cannot reasonably be granted on grounds of conflicting business interests'.[36]

[33] J. Rubery, C. Fagan and M. Smith, *Women and European Employment* (London: Routledge, 1999), table 7.5.

[34] K. Schulze Buschoff, 'Neue Arbeitsplätze durch Teilzeitarbeit – ein europäischer Vergleich' ('New Forms of Work through Part-time Employment – a European Solution'), Report for the Benchmarking Group of the *Bündnis für Arbeit* (Bonn, 1999).

[35] Visser and Hemerijck, 'A Dutch miracle' (n. 3 above).

[36] StAr, *Overwegingen en aanbevelingen ter bevordering van deeltijdarbeid en differentiatie van arbeidsduurpatronen* ('Considerations and Recommendations for Promoting Part-time

From 1990 to 1996 the percentage of firms with a *part-time clause* in the relevant collective agreement increased from 23 to 70 per cent.[37] Yet, the largest union federation, the Federation of Dutch Trade Unions (FNV) raised the criticism that too few firms had fully adopted the Foundation's recommendation. In some sectors *waiting lists* for employees who wanted to work part-time appeared.[38] An initiative bill to institute a statutory right to work part-time was narrowly rejected by Parliament in 1996, but new proposals resulted in legislation effective from July 2000, as will be described in the next section.

Since the mid 1990s part-time jobs have become common for women. Part-time jobs exist in two out of every three firms with ten or more employees. In the 1990s, owing to legal and contractual changes and public encouragement, part-time work has spread beyond the traditional occupations related to sales, cleaning, teaching, nursing and catering. In the 1990s the Dutch labour market combined a *high incidence* of part-time work with a comparatively *small divergence* in occupational profiles between full-timers and part-timers.[39]

In concluding this section, we observe that part-time jobs in the Netherlands are *neither atypical nor flexible*, though the spread of part-time jobs is likely to have increased the aggregate flexibility of the Dutch labour market, bringing in more women and leading to changing working patterns.[40] Flexibility may, however, be limited by the time schedules of schools, nurseries and day-care services. The great majority of part-time employees are covered by collective agreements and in 1998 81 per cent of all part-time jobs, compared with 91 per cent of all full-time jobs, were standard jobs of infinite duration enjoying full dismissal protection. Less protected, flexible part-time jobs, of fixed duration, are mostly those with very few hours (up to 20 hours weekly), located in catering, cleaning and

---

Jobs and Differentiating Working Hours'), Joint report of social partners (The Hague: StAr, 1993).

[37] StAr, *Evaluatie van de nota inzake deeltijdarbeid en differentiatie van arbeidsduurpatronen* ('Evaluation of the Report on Part-time Jobs and Differentiating Working Hours'), Joint report of social partners (The Hague: StAr, 1997).

[38] Tijdens, *Zeggenschap over arbeidstijden* (n. 15 above).

[39] C. Fagan, J. O'Reilly and J. Rubery, 'Challenging the "Breadwinner" Gender Contract: Part-time Work in the Netherlands, Germany and the United Kingdom', in J. O'Reilly, I. Cebrian and M. Lallement (eds.), *Working Time Changes* (Cheltenham: Edward Elgar, 2000), table 2.

[40] J. Visser, 'Negotiated Flexibility, Working-time and Transitions in the Netherlands', in O'Reilly, *Regulating Working-time Transitions in Europe* (n. 11 above), pp. 130–87.

retailing, and held by young people (male or female), re-entering women without formal education, and students. Slightly more part-time (52 per cent) than full-time (49 per cent) employees work irregular hours or during evenings, nights or weekends, but nearly all have a written contract stating how many and which hours are to be worked.[41] As a rule, part-time workers pay *pro rata* social insurance contributions in exchange for *pro rata* entitlements. We will return to this in more detail in the next section.

The 'normalisation' of part-time work is supported by the current process of 'negotiated flexibility' in working-time regimes, encouraged by the 'New Course' central agreement of 1993. That agreement combined wage moderation with tax reduction, rising labour market participation (of females and older males) and working time reduction by allowing more differentiation between workers or firms, and more decentralisation of decision-making.[42] Childcare facilities remain a crucial factor. Demand for childcare has grown steadily but it took until 1987 before unions, under pressure from their female members, began to negotiate childcare facilities in collective agreements.[43] However, notwithstanding enhanced government and private efforts, the demand for childcare still outweighs supply and will continue to do so in the coming years.

4 Legal regulation of part-time work

4.1 Statutory legislation

In current Dutch law, the *pro-rata-temporis* principle is strictly applied to part-time workers. This holds true not only for the position of the employee under civil law, but also for social security legislation. The Dutch regulation of part-time work at the end of the 1990s was ahead of legal developments in most other European countries. As a consequence, neither European legislation and policy – notably the EC Directive on part-time work[44] – nor the rulings by the European Court of Justice have

---

[41] J. Visser and C. van Rij, *Vakbeweging en flexibiliteit* ('Trade Unions and Flexibility') (Amsterdam: Elsevier, 1999).

[42] J. Visser, 'Two Cheers for Corporatism, One for the Market' (1998) 36 *British Journal of Industrial Relations*, pp. 269–92.

[43] K. Tijdens, T. van der Lippe and E. de Ruyter, *Huishoudelijke arbeid en de zorg voor kinderen* ('Household Work and Childcare') (The Hague: Elsevier, 2000).

[44] OJ.L14/9, Directive 97/81/EC. The Directive implements the Framework Agreement on part-time work concluded between the employers' organisations UNICE and CEEP and

led to major changes in Dutch law. However, note should be taken of the 1994 ILO Convention no. 175 and Recommendation 182 (also adopted in 1994) relating to part-time workers. The ILO's intention in concluding this Convention is to grant full status to part-time work. The Convention contains stipulations concerning matters such as legal protection for part-time workers, equal treatment, social security and leave. It also stipulates that steps must be taken to make part-time work more easily accessible. This could, for example, involve removing hindrances in legislation and regulation or introducing measures in the area of job seeking. Where applicable, steps must also be taken to enable adjustment of working hours (from full-time to part-time and vice versa). No more than nine countries have ratified this Convention to date. Contrary to what one might expect the Netherlands was not among the first countries to ratify the ILO Convention (as a matter of fact, Mauritius, Guyana and Finland were ahead). This was due to uncertainty about the implications for existing Dutch law. Ratification finally took place on 5 February 2001 in the process of drafting the new law on the adjustment of working hours, which will be discussed below.[45]

Two laws in particular are relevant to part-time workers: the Prohibition of Discrimination by Working Hours Act (*Wet Verbod onderscheid arbeidsduur*, WVOA) and the Adjustment of Working Hours Act (*Wet Aanpassing Arbeidsduur*, WAA).

4.1.1   The Prohibition of Discrimination by Working Hours Act (WVOA)

The Prohibition of Discrimination by Working Hours Act came into effect on 1 November 1996. One of the consequences of its introduction was the addition of Art. 7:648 to the Dutch Civil Code. Article 7:648 forbids employers to discriminate between employees, on the basis of a difference in working hours, as regards the conditions under which those employees enter, extend or terminate a contract of employment, unless there is objective justification for such discrimination. Clauses that conflict with

---

the European Trade Union Confederation (ETUC) in June 1997. The objectives of this Agreement are to promote equal treatment of part-time workers, to improve the quality of part-time jobs and to promote part-time work and the flexible organisation of working hours. Equal treatment is the norm; unequal treatment needs to be justified on objective grounds. The Member States and social partners will engage in identifying the existing obstacles to the growth of part-time work, and remove them where appropriate.

[45] See *Parliamentary Document* no. 27 512.

this ban are void. If the employer terminates the contract in contravention of the ban, or terminates it because the employee has invoked this ban, the termination is subject to annulment. The same ban also applies to government employers, now that a stipulation to the same effect has been incorporated into Art. 125g of the Central and Local Government Personnel Act.

The Equal Treatment Commission (*Commissie Gelijke Behandeling*), which already had the task of dealing with cases of discrimination on the grounds of race, sex, etc., is also responsible for supervising compliance with the ban on discrimination on the grounds of working hours. Some judgments of this committee will be discussed below.

4.1.2 Adjustment of Working Hours Act (WAA)

More important is the Adjustment of Working Hours Act, which came into force on 1 June 2000. This Act is the result of nearly nine years of political negotiation. It represents a very high-profile piece of legislation as it lends employees the right, albeit under certain conditions, to alter unilaterally the terms of an already existing employment contract. This deviation from conventional employment contract theory has provoked some severe criticism from labour lawyers.

The establishment of a statutory right to part-time work has played a very prominent role in parliamentary debate since June 1993, when the Green Left Party (*Groenlinks*, GL) sought to introduce a new legal right to part-time employment through a so-called 'initiative bill'.[46] This proposal was discussed extensively and it took until 1996 before a Lower House majority was prepared to support a watered-down version of the original proposal. When no Upper House majority could be obtained for this proposal, GL introduced a second initiative bill.[47] That proposal was presented to the Lower House in February 1998, and was quickly followed by a legislative proposal introduced by the Christian Democrats (*Christen-Democratisch Appèl*, CDA), the other main opposition party

---

[46] *Parliamentary Documents II* 1992–1993, no. 23216.
[47] *Parliamentary Documents II* 1997–1998 no. 25 902, nos. 1-3. This time the proposal was introduced in co-operation with the Labour Party (PvdA) and the Social Liberal Party (*Democraten '66*, D'66), both part of the governing coalition with the Liberal Party (*Volkspartij voor Vrijheid en Democratie*, VVD) since 1994. This time the bill included an amendment of the Working Hours Act (*Arbeidstijdenwet*, ATW), in connection with the desirability of encouraging part-time work and the further differentiation of working-hours patterns.

at the time, in April 1998.[48] That same year, after the general elections in May, it appeared that the new government, based on the same coalition as the outgoing government, wished to advance a legislative proposal on the right for an employee to adjust his or her working hours. Finally, on 23 December 1998, this proposal was passed in the Lower House.[49] Subsequently, the proposal was accepted on 19 February 2000 by the Upper House and the WAA came into force in June of the same year.

This law is part of the Work and Care Framework Act (*Wet Arbeid en Zorg*, WAZ), which came into force on 1 December 2001. It is generally acknowledged that the combination and balancing of work and care obligations is far from easy. The new WAA contains a right to the adjustment of working hours, a right that has a broader scope than just the right to part-time work. It includes the rights both to a reduction *and* to an extension of working hours. In this chapter the emphasis will be on the right to the reduction of working hours, since this can be seen as a right to work part-time.[50]

The Explanatory Policy Document to the WAA emphasises that, firstly, regulation of the new rights is expected to increase the supply of labour. Secondly, it should lead to improved scope for combining paid work with other responsibilities. This thought was expressed as follows by the Secretary of State: 'Therefore, it is about economic independence, the goal of equality of opportunity, to enhance the share of men in care, which is related to it, and about the necessity to strike a balance between work and private life in every life phase.'[51] This approach is different from the classical approach in Dutch labour law. Traditionally, compensation for social inequality was the main goal of labour law,[52] whereas now the possibility to combine work with care has been promoted into one of the leading principles. Of course, there is a connection with compensation for inequality, but the WAA is mainly about tailoring working

---

[48] *Parliamentary Documents II* 1997–1998 no. 26 009, nos. 1-3: a legislative proposal implying changes to the Civil Code and a number of other laws in order to lay down rules with respect to the combination of work and family life.

[49] *Parliamentary Documents II* 1998–1999 no. 26 358.

[50] S. W. Kuip and E. Verhulp, *Wet aanpassing arbeidsduur* ('Working Hours Adjustment Act') (The Hague: SDU, 2000), p. 5.

[51] *Parliamentary Documents I* 1998–1999 no. 26 358.

[52] L. Betten (ed.), *Ongelijkheidscompensatie als roode draad in het recht* ('Inequality Compensation as a Leading Principle in Law') (Deventer: Kluwer, 1997).

hours to the wishes of the employee, taking into account his or her personal circumstances, which include care and family obligations.[53] Finally, the government contends that the emergence of more differentiated patterns of work '(can) fit in very well with companies' need for greater flexibility'.[54]

The 1996 Working Hours Act (ATW), which replaced the 1919 Labour Act, was based on similar arguments. The 1996 Act sets wider margins for normal and maximum working hours and allows deviation from statutory norms, within given boundaries, if there is a formal agreement with the unions or the works council (existing in firms with fifty or more employees). In its introduction the Act considers that, in a dual-earners economy, employees must be able to combine work and care and therefore find variable and personal solutions in matters of working time.

One may wonder why a legal and basically unilateral right to adjust working hours was established in a country that already displayed the highest part-time work rates in the world. The main explanation lies in the fact that part-time work rates among Dutch men are still significantly lower – despite men's wishes for reducing working time – than among Dutch women and that this imbalance was believed to restrict the possibilities for women in combining work and care commitments, developing their careers and creating greater gender equality. Furthermore, legal regulation often operates as a 'sag wagon' that extends rights to groups that have not already been granted these rights by collective or other agreements. Strengthening the hand of men in negotiating shorter hours with their line managers was believed to help women in their negotiations at home.

The new WAA applies to employees who are employed on the basis of a contract of employment as defined in Art. 7:610 of the Civil Code, and also to those who are employed in the service of an administrative body by virtue of an appointment under public law (Art. 1 of the WAA). The essence of this regulation is that an employee's request for modification of his or her working hours must be granted by the employer, unless conflicting business or departmental interests apply.[55]

The WAA is remarkable for its detailed nature regarding terms and procedures. The employee is to file a request four months before the

---

[53] Kuip and Verhulp, *Wet aanpassing arbeidsduur* (n. 50 above), p. 6.
[54] *Parliamentary Documents II* 1998–1999 no. 26 358, n. 3, p. 7.
[55] Article 2 of the WAA.

expected date from which the employee wants to work part-time; he or she must have been employed for at least one year; the request can be repeated once every two years; the request must be in writing; the employer must consult the employee and give a written and well-reasoned response, etc. In addition to the norm on conflicting business or departmental interests the law contains two more general or 'open' norms, i.e. one on fairness regarding the division of hours (Art. 2, s. 6) and, lastly, the one on 'good employership' and 'good employeeship' stemming from general labour law.

The law is also complicated. With respect to the shortening of working hours, fewer possibilities exist to deviate by collective agreement from the legal rule than in the case of the extension of working hours. Should a collective agreement *not* contain *any* provision on the extension of working hours an individual employer in this sector may agree with the works council or personnel representation to exclude or alter the right to extension of working hours. Therefore trade unions may wish to include a provision in collective agreements stipulating that it is not permissible to deviate from the legal regulation of extension of working hours. In that case the works council is no longer competent in this area.

Lastly, Art. 2, s. 12 stipulates that this article does not apply to firms, establishments or organisations with fewer than ten employees. This does not mean that there is no right to shorter or longer working hours in these workplaces; they must establish their own regulation regarding the adjustment of working hours. According to the Minister this implies that such company regulation cannot deviate from the legal regulation pertaining to shorter working hours. However, requests for shorter working hours could be excluded by the company collective agreement (if the company has such a collective agreement, as opposed to a sectoral collective agreement).[56] It is not unlikely that the courts will adopt a different interpretation, since Art. 2, s.12 leaves small businesses entirely free in determining the content of their company regulation by stating that Art. 2 does not apply. As no requirements apply to the *content*, a regulation that simply states that there is no regulation does seem legitimate.

As regards the interpretation of the norm 'unless conflicting business or departmental interests apply', the law does not include a restrictive list. For reasons of clarification the Secretary of State has made a selection of

---

[56] *Parliamentary Documents I* 1999–2000, pp. 634–5.

relevant case-law, included in a letter to the Lower House of Parliament.[57] One of the cases concerned the request by a pilot, working for KLM, to reduce his working week to 50 per cent of full-time. The Amsterdam Court decided that KLM had rightly refused the pilot's request, since for the safety of the pilot and the passengers it was necessary for the pilot to fly on a regular basis. According to KLM, a working week of 80 per cent of full-time would be the absolute minimum.

Box 1 contains a short overview of the legally regulated terms of employment and social security for part-time work in the Netherlands. From this overview it can be deduced that the legal position of the part-time worker is similar to that of a full-time employee.

Box 1

Legally regulated terms of employment and social security for part-time work in the Netherlands[58]

Pay

Persons who do the same kind of work should receive the same (gross) hourly wage regardless of working time. As from 1 January 1993 all employees are entitled to (proportional) pay based on the legal minimum wage regardless of working time.

Holidays

A part-time worker is entitled to the same number of days off as full-time workers, in proportion to the hours he or she works. For example, if somebody working full-time gets twenty full days off a year, somebody working half-time gets twenty half-days off a year. According to the Civil Code the minimum holiday entitlement is four times the average working hours per week, which amounts to twenty days for a full-timer; collective agreements generally grant approximately twenty-five days a year.

---

[57] *Parliamentary Documents II* 1998–1999 no. 26 358, n. 25.
[58] Taken from the Ministry of Social Affairs and Employment (SZW, *Part-time Work in the Netherlands*, 1997, pp. 17–20) and adapted by the authors.

Probationary period

The maximum is two months for permanent contracts and possibly shorter for fixed-term contracts, but this is regardless of working time.

Dismissal law

This is exactly the same for all workers regardless of working time.

Special leave

In principle a part-time worker is entitled to special leave in the same cases as full-time workers. Divergence from this principle could be justified if the activities concerned could also be planned in the free time of the part-time worker. If a bank holiday falls in the time that a part-time worker is not working, he or she cannot claim a free day at some other time.

Parental leave

On the basis of the Parental Leave Act persons employed by the same employer for a year or more are entitled to unpaid part-time leave. As a consequence of the 2001 Work and Care Framework Act employees working twenty hours or less are no longer excluded from this possibility (employees, part-time workers included, may reduce their weekly working hours by up to 50 per cent).

Overtime

There is no law on working overtime. Most collective agreements contain clauses regarding overtime and overtime pay. In accordance with European jurisprudence,[59] it is not considered unequal treatment if, on the basis of these clauses, overtime pay is granted only if full-time working hours are exceeded. Nevertheless, social partners may have good reasons to grant overtime pay as soon as work is being done above the contractually agreed working hours (whether full-time or part-time).

[59] ECJ 15 December 1994, C-399/92, *Jur.* 1994, p. I-5727.

Pensions

Under the General Old Age Act every person is provided with a monthly pension. On top of that, employees can, as a rule, build up additional pension within their company. There are about 1,000 private pension schemes. In the first tier of the Dutch pension system, entitlements were individualised, unrelated to earnings (covering about 40 per cent of average wages) and based on citizenship, which is the system in which part-timers fare best. Hours limits for admittance into occupational pension funds guaranteeing earnings-related pensions – the second tier – have been outlawed under the 1990 Pensions and Savings Funds Act. If an earnings limit is applied in pension schemes, the pay of a part-time employee has to be converted to full-time level. A part-time employee acquires pension rights in proportion to the number of his/her working hours. In 1996, 91 per cent of all Dutch workers were covered by occupational pensions which, when fully matured, guarantee 70 per cent of earnings. The 'white spots', without coverage, are seasonal workers, young people and women working flexible hours in low-pay occupations.

Unemployment (Unemployment Insurance Act)

Part-time employees receive unemployment benefit for the same period of time and under the same conditions as a full-time employee based on 70 per cent of their last-earned gross pay.

Sickness (Article 629 Civil Code)

Both part-time and full-time employees (having either a permanent or a fixed-term contract) receive at least 70 per cent of their gross pay in the event of illness (but not less than the minimum wage, calculated proportionally for part-timers), paid by the employer for a period of one year.

Disability (Invalidity Insurance Act)

Part-time employees receive disability benefits for the same period of time and under the same conditions as a full-time employee, based on 70 per cent of their last-earned pay (if fully incapacitated) and depending on the age at which the said employee starts receiving this benefit.

Social security contributions

The contributions paid for social security insurance are usually calculated on the basis of a fixed percentage of pay or income. Working time does not play a role.

Health insurance

Up to a certain earnings limit (in 2002, €59,700 a year) all employees are insured under the terms of the Compulsory Health Insurance Act, which provides medical and dental care, hospital, nursing and other services. Above this limit employees have to insure themselves privately. There is no difference in the conditions that apply to part-time and full-time employees. Both pay the same percentage of their income plus the same nominal contribution.

Working conditions

Employers are legally obliged to apply the same safety regulations and measures at work for both part-time and full-time workers.

Working hours

The ATW, which came into force on 1 January 1996, includes an article regarding the obligation on employers to take into account the care commitments of their employees. This means that, within reasonable limits, employers have to take into consideration the wishes regarding working hours and patterns of the individual employee in their work planning. The importance of this Act has diminished since the WAA came into force in 2000.

Taxes

There are no specific or special measures in the tax system to encourage (or discourage) part-time work. As the tax system is based on progressive taxation for higher incomes, the net income losses in the case of part-time jobs are smaller than the gross reduction of income. The 1990 tax reform already reduced the basic tax allowance for breadwinners and integrated social security charges, thus lowering disincentives for second earners to take up more hours. The 2001 tax reform removed the remaining shared taxation components.

In addition, statutory minimum wages also help to narrow wage differentials between men and women.[60] The 1/3 rule, under which employees working less than one-third of full-time hours were denied coverage under the national minimum wage (and holiday payments) law, was repealed in 1993. Similar exclusionary clauses in collective agreements have become unlawful under the WVOA (see above). Traditionally, fringe benefits and premium pay for overtime have been structured around full-time thresholds. In most collective agreements negotiators have agreed to remove or reconsider these thresholds.

4.2   Case-law on part-time work

As we stated before, neither European law nor European employment policy has played an important role in establishing the rights of part-time workers in the Netherlands. On a national level, some judgments have been passed on the WVOA and the WAA. Besides those, the courts have been willing to grant a request to work part-time on the ground that the employer should behave like 'a good employer' (Art. 7:611 of the Civil Code). There are almost no legal precedents based on the Prohibition of Discrimination by Working Hours Act (WVOA). In two cases where discrimination on the grounds of working hours was tested against the WVOA, the sub-district court concluded that the discrimination that had taken place on the grounds of working hours was unjustified. One case concerned the continued payment of wages during illness, while the other concerned payment for overtime incurred by part-time workers for the purposes of employee participation in consultation with management. The Central Social Security Tribunal, the highest judicial authority in the area of social security, issued a judgment on the question of contributions to medical expenses in proportion to working hours. The tribunal concluded that this did not contravene the WVOA.

Although the Adjustment of Working Hours Act (WAA) was introduced in the year 2000, the few cases that have been brought to court are consistent in their results. In almost all cases, the request to work part-time could not be refused by the employer. Judges seem to be aware of the meaning of the law as expressed by the government in the parliamentary

---

[60] F. Blau and L. Kahn, 'International Differences in Male Wage Inequality: Institutional versus Market Forces' (1996) 104 *Journal of Political Economy* pp. 791–837; W. Roorda and E. Vogel, *Income Policy, Minimum Wages and Labour Relations* (The Hague: SZW / Ministerie van Sociale Zaken en Werkgelegenheid, 1997).

documents. One could argue that the WAA leaves so little room for refusal of a request to work part-time, that consistency is inevitable.

In a few cases, the sub-district court explicitly stated that the fact that granting the request of an employee to work part-time would impose extra costs on the employer (i.e. the costs of employing another person for the available hours) is not a ground for refusal.[61] The argument that the employee – in this case, the director's personal assistant – is 'the spider in the web' who cannot be spared any day of the working week was of no avail for the employer. Creating a shared job would undoubtedly be a major switch and cause inconvenience and financial sacrifices, but would not be impossible. According to the parliamentary documents this is exactly the kind of request that should be granted.[62] In several cases, the female employee who had made the request to work part-time had already worked part-time during her maternity leave or parental leave. Therefore, the employer had already been obliged to make arrangements to fill in the available hours. In all these cases, the court found that the employer had no reason to refuse a request from the employee to work part-time after her leave.[63]

The WAA does not entail the right merely to change the organisation or distribution of working hours without increasing or reducing the total working hours per week. Therefore, a request to spread the 36-hour working week over four days of 9 hours each (instead of five days of just over 7 hours each) did not have to be complied with by the employer.[64] Reducing the number of hours worked on a weekly basis also has consequences for the distribution of the remaining hours. As far as the latter is concerned, it seems that courts are willing to leave the employer a certain amount of discretion.[65]

4.2.1   Good employership

Another way of effectuating the right to part-time work is to test an employer's refusal of an employee's request to work part-time against the

---

[61] Sub-district Court of Zwolle, 12 October 2000, *KG* 2000, 235.

[62] Sub-district Court of Haarlem, 12 May 2001, *JAR* 2001/117.

[63] See, for example: Sub-district Court of Groningen, 23 March 2001, *JAR* 2001/87.

[64] Sub-district Court of Amsterdam, 2 May 2001, *JAR* 2001/113.

[65] See, for an overview of the case-law with respect to the WAA, E. van der Putte, 'Eeste verjaardag wet aanpassing arbeidsduur' (2001) 30 *Rechtshulp*; J. J. Willemsen, 'Wet aanpassing arbeidsduur, cen updating' (2001) 12:64 *Arbeidsrecht*; and P. F. van der Heijden, 'Aanpassing arbeidsduur' *JAR Vestelaard* 9 November 2001, pp. 15–17.

norm of good employership specified in Art. 7:611 of the Civil Code. Testing against this norm as far as part-time work is concerned is carried out when employees request partial dissolution of their contract of employment on the grounds of Art. 7:685 of the Civil Code. This testing is also carried out when employees request the conversion of their existing full-time contract of employment into a part-time contract on the grounds of changed circumstances under Art. 6:258 of the Civil Code. For example, in a case submitted to the Groenlo Sub-district Court, a female employee wanted to change her working hours in view of changed family circumstances. Her employer insisted on the agreed working hours. In this context, the Sub-district Court took the position that the requirements of good employership imply that if an employee makes a request to change his or her conditions of employment (such as working hours) in connection with changed family circumstances, the employer can be expected to look into this request seriously and to provide justification if the request is refused. However, it would appear from the judgments available that changes in working hours based on the principles of good employership and/or invoking of unforeseen circumstances under Art. 6:258 of the Civil Code are not easy to enforce.

4.2.2 The Equal Treatment Commission

The Equal Treatment Commission is not a court of justice and therefore cannot give any legally binding judgments. However, its opinions are highly valued and often followed. Between 1 November 1996 and 1 November 1998 – the first two years following the introduction of the WVOA – the Equal Treatment Commission dealt with twenty-five cases in which it was required to arbitrate on discrimination on the grounds of working hours.[66] In seventeen cases, the Commission was asked to arbitrate by an employee; in five cases, the request for arbitration came from the employer; in two cases, it came from a works council; and in just one case, the Commission initiated a study of its own accord.

The Commission is of the opinion that where the conditions of regular salary payments are at issue, these payments should be made on a pro rata basis. Where exceptional financial benefits are at issue, the

---

[66] In the year 2000, only seven cases came before the Commission.

most appropriate treatment will depend on the condition of employment in question. To date, the Commission has not accepted purely financial arguments as grounds for objective justification. In principle, therefore, part-time workers should not be treated less favourably than their (comparable) colleagues in full-time employment. This rule also implies that (female) part-time workers no longer have to rely on the indirect legislation provided in the Equal Opportunities Act (Arts. 7:646 and 7:647 of the Civil Code). However, this does not mean that the legal precedents that have emerged under this law have lost their relevance to part-time workers. Discrimination on the grounds of working hours that is deemed to be discrimination between men and women will usually also constitute unlawful discrimination on the grounds of working hours. However, not all unlawful discrimination on the grounds of working hours also constitutes a breach of the Equal Opportunities Act. Male employees can now also invoke Art. 7:648 of the Civil Code (or Art. 125g of the Central and Local Government Personnel Act) if their employers maintain an unlawful distinction on the grounds of working hours between them and their colleagues in full-time employment.

5   Conclusions

In the Netherlands it was as a *latecomers' advantage* that part-time work was appreciated by most women, notably married women, who saw this choice as progress compared with the alternative of withdrawal, since it generated extra earnings and household spending power, some (limited) economic independence and the possibility of providing personal care for their children (rather than relying full-time on external childcare facilities). In countries like France and Belgium, where a tradition of full-time working married women existed, part-time work, proposed as a means to redistribute jobs in a period of high unemployment, was more probably evaluated as a retrograde step. Remarkably, women's changing preferences matched labour market and business needs, not only in times of economic upturn but also in times of economic downturn in the 1980s and 1990s.

Institutions and policy-makers were at first slow and reluctant to support and facilitate the rise of part-time work, but this changed in the early 1980s. Regulations, including collective bargaining agreements, which had been favouring the traditional breadwinner model over a period of fifty to a hundred years, likewise started to catch up in the same period and went 'all the way' in removing labour law and social security barriers to part-time work, thus bringing part-time workers onto an equal footing with their full-time colleagues. A major shift occurred from the traditional breadwinner model towards a so-called dual breadwinner / dual career model.[67]

Nowadays, part-time work in the Netherlands is regulated, both in statutory law and in collective agreements, in such a way that it can more accurately be described as typical rather than atypical employment. In fact, the upshot of this chapter is that in the Netherlands part-time employment has become more or less normalised. The Netherlands can indeed be referred to as a part-time economy.[68] Part-time work is seen as an instrument for obtaining a fairer division of paid and unpaid work between men and women. A part-time economy, however, does not constitute a part-time *paradise*. Institutions, policies and new entitlements and legal regulation have so far not fundamentally altered company cultures and human resource management practices. Nor has the division between paid and unpaid work become equal yet. Many men are still hesitant about reducing or adjusting their working hours[69] and many women are facing limited prospects and find it hard to build up a high-profile career. The number of women in the highest job ladders within companies has only slightly increased over the last two years, with the health care sector and the judiciary as prominent exceptions.[70]

Appendix

Part-time employment in business practice

The facts and figures stated below are mainly based on the results of the 1996 Workforce Survey conducted by the Central Statistical Office (CBS) and the tables compiled by the CBS for this assessment. An analysis of the tables has already been published by the Dutch Foundation of Labour (*Stichting van de Arbeid*, StAr).

---

[67] B. Pfau-Effinger, 'Culture or Structure as Explanations for Differences in Part-time Work in Germany, Finland and the Netherlands?' in J. O'Reilly and C. Fagan (eds.), *Part-time Prospects* (London: Routledge, 1998), 177–8.

[68] J. Visser, 'The First Part-time Economy of the World' (n. 1 above).

[69] M. Grunell, *Mannen zorgen* ('Men Care') (Utrecht: Jan van Arkel, 2002).

[70] Opportunity in Bedrijf, *Toptelling 2002* (Amstelveen / The Hague: SCP, 2002).

Table 7.1 Classification of employees by weekly working hours and gender, 1992/1996

Weekly working hours	Men		Women		Men + Women		In absolute numbers × 1,000		
					as a %				
	Total	Only with working hours >12 hrs	Total	Only with working hours >12 hrs	Total	Only with working hours >12 hrs	Men	Women	Total
1992									
<12 hrs	5.4	–	18.0	–	10.5	–	192	415	607
12–19 hrs	1.3	1.4	11.9	14.5	5.5	6.2	45	278	323
20–34 hrs	6.7	7.1	31.6	38.6	16.7	18.6	237	741	978
total part-time	13.4	8.5	61.5	53.1	32.7	24.8	474	1434	1908
35 hrs and >	86.6	91.5	38.5	47.0	67.4	75.2	3053	903	3956
Total	100	100	100	100	100	100	3527	2337	5864
1996									
<12 hrs	5.7	–	18.4	–	11.1	–	205	474	679
12–19 hrs	1.7	1.8	12.4	15.3	6.2	7.0	61	318	379
20–34 hrs	8.2	8.7	35.1	43.1	19.5	21.9	293	901	1194
total part-time	15.6	10.5	65.9	58.4	36.8	28.9	559	1693	2252
35 hrs and >	84.4	89.5	34.0	41.7	63.3	71.2	3013	872	3885
Total	100	100	100	100	100	100	3573	2565	6138

Table 7.2 *Percentage of male and female part-timers in EU Member States*

	Netherlands	Germany	France	UK	Italy	Greece	Spain	Portugal	Ireland	Denmark	Luxembourg	Finland	Austria	Sweden	EU
	Part-time employment as a % of the total number of job-seekers														
1990															
M	15.0	2.6	3.3	5.3	2.4	2.2	1.6	3.5	3.4	10.4	1.9	4.4	1.8	7.3	
F	59.6	33.8	23.6	43.2	9.6	7.6	12.1	9.4	17.7	38.4	16.5	10.2	18.9	40.0	
1993															
M	15.3	2.9	4.1	6.6	2.5	2.6	2.4	4.5	4.8	2.3	–	6.2	1.9	8.9	4.5
F	64.5	32.0	26.3	43.9	21.3	7.7	14.8	11.1	21.3	37.4	18.3	11.2	20.3	40.9	29.6
1995															
M	16.8	3.6	5.1	7.7	2.9	2.8	2.7	4.2	–	2.8	–	5.5	–	9.1	5.1
F	57.2	33.8	28.9	44.3	12.7	8.4	16.6	11.8	–	35.5	20.3	11.1	–	39.8	31.0

– = no figures available.
Source: Eurostat Yearbook 1996: a Statistical View on Europe 1985–1995.

Table 7.3 *Part-time employment in the EU, 1996*

	As a % of total employment	% part-timers aged 25 or older who want to work full-time	% part-timers aged 25 or older who do not want to work full-time
EU	16	18	63
Belgium	14	24	12
Denmark	21	18	69
Germany (1995)	16	9	64
Greece	5	37	39
Spain	8	21	4
France	16	37	63
Ireland	12	28	25
Italy	7	34	28
Luxembourg	8	6	61
Netherlands	38	6	88
Austria	15	9	16
Portugal	9	21	11
Finland	12	46	30
Sweden	23	28	57
UK	24	12	84

Source: Eurostat press release no. 6597, 18 September 1997.

Table 7.4 *Percentage and absolute classification of employees by weekly working hours, gender and age, as a % / absolute numbers (× 1,000)*

Weekly working hours	Men				Women			
	15–24 yrs	25–44 yrs	45–64 yrs	Total	15–24 yrs	25–44 yrs	45–64 yrs	Total
1992								
<12 hrs	25.7 / 158	0.9 / 19	1.7 / 15	5.4 / 192	25.4 / 151	13.1 / 173	21.5 / 91	18.0 / 415
12–19 hrs	3.4 / 21	0.6 / 12	1.4 / 12	1.3 / 45	5.2 / 31	12.9 / 171	18.0 / 76	11.9 / 278
20–34 hrs	9.3 / 57	5.9 / 119	6.9 / 61	6.7 / 237	18.7 / 111	35.8 / 473	37.1 / 157	31.6 / 741
total part-time	38.4 / 236	7.4 / 150	10.0 / 88	13.4 / 474	49.3 / 293	61.8 / 817	76.6 / 324	61.5 / 1434
35 hrs and >	61.9 / 381	92.6 / 1874	90.0 / 798	86.5 / –	50.6 / 301	38.1 / 503	23.4 / 99	38.5 / 903
Total	100 / 617	100 / 2024	100 / 886	100 / 3527	100 / 595	100 / 1320	100 / 423	100 / 2337
1996								
<12 hrs	30.4 / 171	0.9 / 19	1.6 / 16	5.7 / 205	33.6 / 180	12.6 / 186	19.6 / 108	18.4 / 474
12–19 hrs	6.4 / 36	0.7 / 15	1.0 / 10	1.7 / 61	6.9 / 37	12.7 / 188	16.9 / 93	12.4 / 318
20–34 hrs	12.3 / 69	7.0 / 142	8.3 / 82	8.2 / 293	20.8 / 111	37.8 / 558	42.0 / 232	35.1 / 901
total part-time	49.1 / 276	8.6 / 176	10.9 / 108	15.6 / 559	61.3 / 328	63.1 / 932	78.5 / 433	65.9 / 1693
35 hrs and >	50.9 / 286	91.4 / 1851	89.0 / 877	84.3 / 3013	38.7 / 207	36.9 / 546	21.6 / 119	34.0 / 872
Total	100 / 562	100 / 2026	100 / 985	100 / 3573	100 / 535	100 / 1478	100 / 552	100 / 2565

– = no figures available.

Table 7.5 Classification of employees by weekly working hours, gender and level of education, 1992/1996* (as a % / in absolute numbers (× 1,000))

Weekly working hours	Men				Women			
	primary education	secondary education	higher education	Total	primary education	secondary education	higher education	Total
1992								
12–19 hrs	2.2 / 25	0.4 / 6	0.8 / 7	1.2 / 38	19.9 / 141	10.9 / 77	8.2 / 34	13.8 / 252
20–34 hrs	8.1 / 91	5.5 / 67	7.3 / 64	6.7 / 222	40.8 / 290	37.1 / 261	38.3 / 160	38.8 / 711
total part-time	10.3 /116	5.9 / 73	8.1 / 71	7.9 / 260	60.7 / 431	48.0 / 338	46.5 / 194	52.6 / 963
35 hrs and >	89.8 /1019	94.1 / 1154	91.9 / 808	95.4 / 3092	39.2 / 279	52.0 / 366	53.2 / 223	47.4 / 868
Total	100 / 1134	100 / 1227	100 / 879	100 / 3352	100 / 710	100 / 704	100 / 417	100 / 1831
1996								
12–19 hrs	3.9 / 45	0.7 / 9	0.6 / 60	1.8 / 60	22.3 / 165	12.7 / 107	9.0 / 45	15.2 / 317
20–34 hrs	10.8 / 124	7.1 / 89	8.2 / 76	8.7 / 289	44.4 / 329	42.3 / 356	42.2 / 211	43.1 / 869
total part-time	14.7 / 169	7.8 / 98	8.8 / 136	10.5 / 349	66.7 / 494	55.0 / 463	51.2 / 256	58.3 / 1186
35 hrs and >	85.2 / 976	92.2 / 1162	91.3 / 846	89.5 / 2984	33.3 / 247	44.9 / 378	48.6 / 242	41.7 / 867
Total	100 / 1146	100 / 1260	100 / 982	100 / 3333	100 / 741	100 / 841	100 / 498	100 / 2053

* Excluding part-time jobs < 12 hrs

NB. The absolute numbers do not correspond exactly with those in the categories concerned in the other tables, because some levels of education were not known and/or impossible to ascertain.

Table 7.6 *Development in the number of part-time employees by gender and age, 1992/1996 (1992 = 100)*

Weekly working hours	Men				Women			
	15–24 yrs	25–44 yrs	45–64 yrs	Total	15–24 yrs	25–44 yrs	45–64 yrs	Total
<12 hrs	108	100	107	107	119	108	119	114
12–19 hrs	171	125	83	136	119	110	122	114
20–34 hrs	121	119	134	124	100	118	148	122
Total part-time	117	117	123	118	112	109	120	118
35 hrs and >	75	99	110	97	69	114	134	97
Total	91	100	111	101	90	112	130	110

Table 7.7 Classification of workforce (incl. self-employed) by weekly working hours and sector, 1994/1996* as a %

Sector	1994				1996			
	12–19 hrs	20–34 hrs	35 hrs and >	Total × 1,000	12–19 hrs	20–34 hrs	35 hrs and >	Total × 1,000
agriculture and fisheries	4.2	15.7	80.1	236	5.2	16.0	78.9	232
mineral extraction	–	–	100	9	–	–	100	10
industry	2.4	11.5	86.1	1003	2.2	12.3	85.5	1022
public utilities	–	–	100	42	–	12.2	87.8	41
construction	–	6.6	93.2	396	–	7.5	92.5	415
commercial	7.9	18.6	73.6	911	8.8	19.4	71.8	986
hotel, restaurant and catering	14.2	25.4	60.4	167	15.6	25.2	59.3	167
transport/ communication	3.9	13.4	82.7	396	3.6	14.4	81.8	396
financial services	3.3	16.0	80.7	212	3.9	19.1	77.1	231
other business services	6.5	16.5	77.1	541	6.1	18.0	75.9	640
public administration	3.8	14.8	81.4	528	3.2	17.7	79.1	497
education	9.3	28.4	62.3	387	8.5	29.5	62.0	410
health/welfare	13.4	43.0	43.7	756	14.4	45.2	40.4	812
culture	10.1	30.7	59.2	228	10.7	29.6	59.7	243
Total	6.5	19.8	73.7	5810	6.6	21.3	72.0	6102

* Including employees with a working week < 12 hrs.

Table 7.8 *Percentage of organisations with part-time employees by sector and size of the organisation, 1989–1995*

Sector	% organisations with part-time employees		
	1989	1993	1995
industry and agriculture	39	61	62
construction	–	37	29
commercial, hotel, restaurant and catering, repairs	42	61	61
transport	15	58	48
business services	60	76	74
health-care	91	93	89
other services	88	90	85
government and public utilities	90	99	96
education	99	97	100
Size			
5–9 employees	–	–	–
10–49 employees	43	63	62
50–99 employees	64	74	79
100 or more employees	83	92	90
Total	50	69	67

Source: OSA report on labour demand trends in 1996, May 1996.

8

Spain: the difficulty of marrying flexibility with security

FERNANDO VALDÉS DAL-RÉ

1 Introduction

Working shortened hours is not a form of work that can be described as anything new. For as long as can be remembered contractual arrangements have been made under which the working time fell short of whatever happened at the time to be specified as the statutory or collectively agreed normal working hours. As a long-established practice, throughout much of the history (or perhaps sub-history) of industrial relations in Europe, part-time work remained confined to areas of social marginalisation and exclusion from legal regulation; it attracted no attention from the public authorities or interest from the actors of industrial relations, who were at one in being preoccupied with constructing a system of employee guarantees based on full-time work.

First 'discovered' in the 1960s as a solution to labour shortages by facilitating access to the labour market for groups unavailable for full-time work (young people still completing their studies and, most of all, women with family commitments), during the 1970s part-time work took on an additional new function as an instrument of demographic policy: by making it possible to reconcile family and professional life it came to be used as an incentive in order to offset falling birth rates. Only in the decades since then, however, has part-time work become a prominent feature of European industrial relations systems as a result of the sweeping changes of every kind (economic, technological, social and cultural) taking place in our societies.

Whilst still retaining its former functions in relation to family arrangements, part-time work is nowadays acquiring a high profile on two main fronts: first, as an element of active employment policies and, second, as an instrument of flexibility in the organisation of work. That versatility explains its recent elevation to a starring role in the firmament of industrial relations, but is also the reason why the subject cannot be approached from the point of view of just one of its many functions.[1]

Part-time work is relevant to formulas for the distribution of employment, has a bearing on new patterns of working time regulation, facilitates the flexible management of forms of work organisation, makes it easier to reconcile family life and working life, plays a part in the effective staffing of so-called 'new areas' of employment, and assists the integration of particular groups into the labour market. However, no single function, if considered in isolation, fully illustrates the varied and complex set of problems that can accompany this form of work, in which a good many of the issues shaping current debate in European industrial relations systems also converge: maintenance of professional skills and competence, gender-based discrimination, erosion of uniformity in the basic legal status of employees, forms of collective representation and guarantees of adequate social protection, to name just some of the most important.

This is neither the time nor the place to attempt to discuss the concept of part-time work as a unitary phenomenon. The less ambitious purpose of the present study is to analyse the legal policy decisions that have informed the regulation of part-time work in Spain's industrial relations system since the early 1980s. In adopting that approach, after an initial account of the social and employment-related context of part-time work in Spain, the study swiftly moves on to a dialogue, with reference to many different points in time, between the two major functions traditionally attributed to part-time work (creation of employment and flexibility in the organisation of work) and the way in which those functions have actually been utilised by the public authorities and the social partners in Spain. The focus is then placed on instruments, in presenting a comparison between the policies adopted to encourage part-time work and the mechanisms used to implement them, while in the concluding section a systematic approach is used in identifying the reasons for the social and employment-related context within which developments regarding part-time work are taking place in Spain's industrial relations system.

---

[1] The dangers of doing so are pointed out by M. Rodríguez-Piñero, 'El trabajo a tiempo parcial, entre normalización e incentivación' (1998) 15/16 *Relaciones laborales* p. 2.

2 The context of part-time work

2.1 The quantity variable: a statistical approximation

Within the structure of work for an employee under a contract of employment, since the mid 1980s part-time work has experienced a significant increase in both absolute and relative terms.[2] Close examination of the statistical series for part-time employment over the period 1981–2000 reveals a direct relationship between growth in the part-time employment rate and legislative intervention. The first qualitative jump in these series occurs as a result of the first legislative amendment of Art. 12 of the Workers' Statute (ET) implemented through Law 32/1984 (prior to 1984, as a proportion of the total number of employees part-timers represented barely 2 per cent).[3] A gradual and steady increase is then maintained during the period 1986–93, with a second qualitative jump occurring in 1994 when the rate reaches 6 per cent,[4] after which it remains constant from 1997 to the present day, with minor upward and downward fluctuations, at around 8 per cent.[5]

Despite that growth, Spain's part-time employment rate is still well below the EU average of 16 per cent: far removed from the North European countries with their figures of over 20 per cent and, in the case of the Netherlands, more than 35 per cent, although reasonably similar to the figures for the Mediterranean countries (Portugal, Italy and Greece).[6]

As in the majority of European countries, however, part-time work is a 'predominantly female phenomenon'[7] in Spain as well. Its growth has been due to the increase in the part-time employment rate among women.

---

[2] The statistics cited here have been extracted from the following sources: Consejo Económico y Social (CES), *El trabajo a tiempo parcial* (Madrid: CES, 1996), pp. 58–72; Ministerio de Trabajo y Asuntos Sociales, *Anuario de estadísticas laborales y de asuntos sociales 1997* (Madrid: Ministerio de Trabajo y Asuntos Sociales, 1998), *1998* (Madrid: Ministerio de Trabajo y Asuntos Sociales, 1999), *1999* (Madrid: Ministerio de Trabajo y Asuntos Sociales, 2000) and *2000* (Madrid: Ministerio de Trabajo y Asuntos Sociales, 2001); CES, *Economía, trabajo y sociedad. España 1998. Memoria sobre la situación socioeconómica y laboral* (Madrid: CES, 1999), pp. 216–19, . . . *España 1999* (Madrid: CES, 2000), pp. 236–9, and . . . *España 2000* (Madrid: CES, 2001), pp. 219–22.

[3] The number of part-time contracts leapt from 47,665 in 1984 to 121,905 in 1985.

[4] The number of part-time contracts finalised during that period was as follows: 177,449 (1986), 220,846 (1987), 293,245 (1988), 356,968 (1989), 410,953 (1990), 470,884 (1991), 539,682 (1992), 635,880 (1993) and 935,428 (1994).

[5] CES, *Economía, trabajo y sociedad. España 2000*, p. 220.

[6] For more details see Ministerio de Trabajo y Asuntos Sociales, *OCDE, perspectivos de empleo 1998* (Madrid: Ministerio de Trabajo y Asuntos Sociales, 1998), pp. 384–7.

[7] CES, *El trabajo a tiempo parcial* (n. 2 above), p. 59.

Over the period 1991–2000 the number of men working part-time as a proportion of the total male employee population fluctuated between very low percentages, with a declining trend during more recent years,[8] whereas in the case of female employment the proportion of part-timers rose steadily over the same period to reach a value of around 18 per cent in 2000. To put it differently, eight out of every ten part-time employees are women.[9]

Another characteristic of part-time work is its much-criticised temporary nature, a feature which marks out Spain as singular among the EU Member States. In 2000, while the proportion of all full-time employees who were on temporary (i.e. fixed-term) contracts amounted to the already scandalous figure of 30.1 per cent, in the case of part-time work the figure had reached 54.9 per cent, meaning that almost six out of every ten part-time contracts had been concluded in accordance with one of the mechanisms permitting fixed-term contracts and were subject to its regulation.[10] This high incidence of temporary contracts among part-timers was not, however, distributed proportionately between the sexes but was greater for men than for women.[11] At any rate, the legislative reform implemented in 1998 on this form of work and the introduction of a system of social security incentives to encourage permanent contracts, both full-time and part-time, reduced the proportion of fixed-term contracts among part-timers and slightly modified the pre-existing trend.

From a different point of view, and in this case one common to all EU Member States, part-time work is fundamentally a feature of the service sector: in the case of men, in agriculture, the hotel and catering industry and, to a lesser extent, commerce; and in the case of women, in domestic work, recreational, cultural and sporting activities, the hotel and catering industry and teaching.[12]

---

[8] The lowest value (1.8%) was recorded in 1991 and the highest (3.2%) in 1996. Since then, the rate has been gradually declining (2.7% in 1999 and 2.5% in 2000): CES, *Economía, trabajo y sociedad. España 2000* (n. 2 above), p. 220.

[9] Following a steady decrease in female part-time employment starting in 1987, the trend changes in 1991: the part-time employment rate for that year was 11.4%. Over the period 1991–2001 the female part-time employment rate then underwent an almost 6% increase. See ibid., p. 220.

[10] Following a steady increase over the period 1987–95, from 1996 the proportion of fixed-term contracts for part-timers began to fall (57.6% in 1995, 56.5% in 1996, 60.2% in 1997, 49.9% in 1998), rose in 1999 (54.0%) and then fell again in 2000 (51.3%). See ibid., p. 222.

[11] For men, the incidence of fixed-term contracts among part-timers fluctuated around 70% over the period 1996–2000, while for women it varied around 50% (51.3% in 2000). *Ibid.*, p. 22.

[12] CES, *El trabajo a tiempo parcial* (n. 2 above), p. 67.

In terms of age, when both men and women are taken into account, part-time work is concentrated among younger workers. However, whereas men who work part-time are younger than those in full-time jobs, in the case of women those who work part-time are older, on average, than those in full-time jobs. A gender-based difference is also discernible as regards educational level. Female part-time employment is highest among women with low educational levels, whereas in the case of men part-time employment is highest among those with higher educational levels, which seems to suggest a supply of skilled part-time jobs that are predominantly occupied by male employees.[13]

2.2 The quality variable: a socially discredited form of work

In 1997 the European Commission published an interesting document with the expressly stated purpose of inviting the social partners and public authorities to seek to build a partnership for the development of a new framework for the modernisation of work: a framework offering scope for improving employment and competitiveness through a more appropriate organisation of work at the workplace.[14] In it, the Commission warns of the inherently ambiguous nature of part-time work, which it describes as a form of work that represents both 'opportunities and risks'. The opportunities centre on offering employers 'the flexibility which is necessary to meet changing consumer demands' and also providing employees with 'a flexibility that makes it easier to combine work with other responsibilities, for example studies or housework'. The risks are summed up in the fact that 'conditions of employment, for example social protection, for part-time workers are often limited when compared with those for full-time work'. On the basis of that acknowledgment of the serious disadvantages attending part-time work, the Green Paper goes on to assert the need for a new form of regulation that provides a better balance between the interests of employers and employees: a legal framework, in short, which makes part-time work 'less precarious'.[15]

In Spain, probably more than in any other country, the difficult balance between 'opportunities and risks', within which part-time work functions, became weighted down, heavily, on the risks side, where it remained

---

[13] Ibid.

[14] Commission of the European Communities, *Green Paper: Partnership for a New Organization of Work* COM (1997) 128 final, Brussels, 16.4.1997.

[15] The passages enclosed in quotation marks are all taken from the *Green Paper* (see n. 14), para. 52, p. 10.

stuck fast for nearly twenty years. Until very recently, part-time work signified none of the advantages of its use from the employee's point of view; instead, it embodied almost all of its conceivable disadvantages. The potential risks inherent in this form of work, to which the Commission's Green Paper draws attention, were translated, in the case of Spain's industrial relations system, into real and tangible disadvantages that were measurable and identifiable in terms of quality of employment. To use the terminology of game theory as widely applied in economics, social and economic policies (both public and private) relegated part-timers to a 'zero-sum' scenario – a scenario carrying no advantages whatever or, to put it bluntly, of maximum precariousness of employment.

Working under a part-time contract in Spain combined 'all the elements of what is regarded as precariousness'.[16] These are, very briefly: (i) widespread use of individualised formulas (across-the-board conclusion of contracts or unilateral employer powers) in the definition of terms and conditions of employment, with a resultant lack of protection through collective bargaining; (ii) the predominantly temporary nature of part-time contracts – many of them, furthermore, of very short duration and hence involving a high rate of turnover;[17] (iii) an over-representation of women among part-timers, with all the consequences of such a situation from the point of view of indirect discrimination; (iv) an excessive concentration of part-time employment among young people with a very low level of qualifications; (v) the 'involuntary' nature of most part-time employment;[18] (vi) a total lack of equivalence in the application of the *pro rata temporis* principle to the remuneration of part-timers, resulting in some cases (particularly among women) in rates of pay far below those corresponding proportionately to the reduction of working hours; and (vii) a weak and inequitable system of social protection stipulating very lengthy qualifying periods as a condition of eligibility for social security benefits.

When we add to this catalogue of social and economic manifestations of precariousness those elements of its precariousness which are directly

[16] R. Escudero Rodríguez, 'Los incentivos a la contratación estable a tiempo parcial: un significativo y polémnico cambio de rumbo', in M. E. Casas Baamonde and F. Valdés Dal-Ré (eds.), *Los contratos de trabajo a tiempo parcial* (Valladolid: Lex-Nova, 1999), p. 256.

[17] In 1998, for example, the duration of 48% of temporary part-time contracts was less than one month. See CC.OO/UGT (Trade Union Confederation of Workers' Commissions / General Workers' Confederation), 'Evaluación del Acuerdo Interconfederal para la estabilidad en el empleo' (2000) 24 *Relaciones laborales* p. 96.

[18] For 1999, only 4.5% of part-timers stated that they were happy with their type of employment: ibid., p. 95.

imputable to the successive legislative measures that will be discussed later, it is easy to understand the discredit and lack of regard, in the industrial relations context, shown towards part-time work in Spain, which explains the entrenched lack of social status for this form of work.

Later sections of this study will examine the successive and not always consistent measures which, since November 1998, have been adopted by the social partners and the Government in order to improve the quality of part-time work, and will attempt to assess whether those measures have achieved their objectives. In this introductory section the purpose has been to demonstrate the social evaluation of part-time work and its ranking in one of the lowest positions as regards social and employment-related precariousness. That high degree of precariousness is very probably the explanation for the social and trade-union rejection that has traditionally accompanied part-time work, in which the possibility of an employee possessing the right to make a voluntary and deliberate decision to work less than the normal working hours is seen rather as an *ultima ratio* solution.

Any reflection on part-time work in Spain, however superficial, cannot avoid confronting that reality – a reality that evokes the most perverse effects of policies on the deregulation and flexibilisation of the labour market.

3 Legal policy choices on the regulation of part-time work

During the late 1970s and practically the whole of the 1980s the European debate *par excellence* in the field of industrial relations was centred on 'new forms of employment': forms of work in which the permanent full-time contract of employment 'is no longer the pole star of labour law'.[19] The legal presumption of the open-ended contract of employment as the socially typical contractual model for the performance of work on another's behalf in a position of dependence, which had been applied in conceiving the employment relationship as a 'stable, long-term, exclusive and full-time relationship',[20] was thrown into crisis by the emergence of a whole range of 'atypical' contracts which were tending to blur the outlines of the employee prototype used as the statutory reference point – as the social pattern or standard in regulating the mandatory employment relationship.

[19] See Umberto Romagnoli, *El Derecho, el trabajo y la historia* (Madrid: CES, 1997), p. 170.
[20] Gino Giugni, *Lavoro, leggi, contratti* (Bologna: Il Mulino, 1989), p. 307.

Suddenly, the legal figure of the employee that for many decades had been viewed in singular terms had to be viewed as one with numerous different facets. As a result of this segmentation of the labour market, the labour legislation of most EU Member States lost much of its traditional vocation of establishing minimum and uniform legal provisions in favour of employees as a body and became adapted, instead, to making substantively diverse provisions attuned to the incorporation of these new forms of employment.

Ever since that fragmentation of 'work' into 'forms of work', the resultant main preoccupation from the industrial relations perspective has been the achievement of an appropriate balance between flexibility and security, i.e. a regulatory framework that simultaneously provides employers with reasonable levels of flexibility to accommodate the changes accompanying a progressively more open and competitive market and employees with equally reasonable levels of job security and social protection.

The achievement of such a balance forms part of the European Employment Strategy that has been in the process of construction since the Essen European Council. Ever since the above-mentioned Green Paper, following the earlier guidelines laid down in the so-called 'White Paper',[21] dedicated one of its chapters to the subject, references to the necessity of combining 'flexibility and security' have been a constant factor in Community employment policy. This can be confirmed simply by reading the statements on the third pillar, regarding the adaptability of businesses, contained in the successive Employment Guidelines adopted to date by the Council.[22]

In all of these the Council, in order to promote the modernisation of work organisation and diverse forms of work, invites the social partners to negotiate agreements aimed at achieving that objective in which, in addition to increasing productivity and competitiveness, employees are ensured 'the required balance between flexibility and security'.[23] It also

---

[21] European Commission, *Growth, Competitiveness, Employment: The Challenges and Ways Forward into the 21st Century*, White Paper (Brussels, 5.12.1993, COM(93) 700 final).

[22] Council Resolution (98/C 30/01) of 15 December 1997 on the 1998 Employment Guidelines (OJ C 30/1 of 28.1.1998); Council Resolution (1999/C 69/02) of 22 February 1999 on the 1999 Employment Guidelines (OJ C 69/2 of 12.3.1999); Council Decision 2000/228/EC of 13 March 2000 on Guidelines for Member States' employment policies for the year 2000 (OJ L 72/15 of 21.3.2000) and Council Decision 2001/63/EC of 19 January 2001 on Guidelines for Member States' employment policies for the year 2001 (OJ L 22/18 of 24.1.2001).

[23] See, in each year's Guidelines: pillar III (1998); pillar III, guideline 16 (1999); pillar III, guideline 15 (2000); and pillar III, guideline 13 (2001).

instructs the Member States to examine the possibility of incorporating in their national legislation 'more adaptable types of contract' while guaranteeing that those working under contracts of this kind 'enjoy adequate security'.[24]

It is precisely from the point of view of the 'flexibility/security' pairing that the observations set out below attempt to appraise Spanish policies on part-time work, analysing in turn the limits of that pairing in the light of the three main functions which can, in theory, be served by working shortened hours: creation of employment, adaptability of work organisation and satisfaction of the employee's personal interests (reconciling working life and family life or engaging in training activities, for example).

That being so, it will perhaps be pertinent to start with two preliminary explanations that make it easier to understand the methodology adopted in the present account. The first is that policies on the regulation of part-time work have combined, as equally constant factors, not only the use of this form of work by the Spanish public authorities as an instrument of employment policy but also its use as a means of enabling employers to adapt working time to the changing needs of business organisation and enabling employees to fulfil their personal interests.

The Preamble to Law 32/1984, which implemented the first amendment of Art. 12 of the Workers' Statute (1980 version), shows that the ambitious intention of the legislators of the time was, at least nominally, to shape the regulation of part-time work to serve both objectives. Thus, it stated that the purpose of the legislative reform being introduced was: 'to foster the creation of the greatest possible number of jobs' (creating jobs), to cater for 'the wishes of a section of the working population available to work for only less than full-time hours' (satisfying employees' personal interests) and, lastly, 'to give the legal framework greater clarity and stability in order to reduce employers' hesitancy in taking measures leading to the creation of new jobs' (promoting the adaptability of forms of work organisation).

These are, however, generalised functions allocated by the legislators which do not always pass even the rudimentary test of comparison with the real situation as eventually regulated. Setting aside the professed *voluntas legislatoris*, developments in the regulation of part-time work in Spain cannot be assessed purely in terms of a series of successive policy decisions aimed at achieving balanced results from the various functions that this form of work can potentially fulfil. In addition to a lack of firm

---

[24] See, in each year's Guidelines: pillar III (1998); pillar III, guideline 17 (1999); pillar III, guideline 16 (2000); and pillar III, guideline 14 (2001).

and consistent policy approaches, the statutory regulation of part-time work has been characterised even more, at least until relatively recently, by a manifest lack of correspondence between the rhetorically professed objectives being pursued and the techniques used to put them into practice.

It is that lack of correspondence (or of what might also be called political sincerity) in the regulatory treatment of this form of work which is, ultimately, the possible reason for the low part-time employment rate in Spain's industrial relations system. To put it another way, part-time work has not been given a 'chance' to develop its functional potential. It has never counted among the policy priorities of the public authorities or the bargaining priorities of the social partners.

The second explanatory observation that seems indicated at this point is actually an anticipatory one and relates to the pre-eminence accorded, in the national regulation of part-time work, to flexibility at the cost of security – a hypothesis that will be developed and justified later. That pre-eminence persisted as an absolute until relatively recently, when there was a discernible change of direction in legal policy decisions, largely prompted by the requirements of complying with European agreements relating to employment. The transposition into national law of the content of the Framework Agreement on part-time work concluded by UNICE, CEEP and the ETUC, as implemented under Council Directive 97/81/EC of 15 December 1997, would seem to have marked a turning-point, albeit tardy, for developments in the regulation of part-time work in Spain.

3.1   A stability lost

In its 1980 version Spain's Workers' Statute enshrined a principle of neutrality in the regulation of part-time work, adopting a *laissez-faire* stance from the point of view of the policy underlying, or claimed to underlie, the organisation of this contractual form. The hoped-for effectiveness of part-time work in encouraging employment or allowing more flexible organisation of work remained exposed to the mercies of the market, i.e. to the often conflicting interests of the contracting parties. Aside from the advantages that can generally be attributed to part-time work (reduction in absenteeism, higher productivity), counterbalanced by its equally well-recognised general disadvantages (lack of integration within the company structure, greater problems of control, higher organisational costs), this first legal text of the constitutional era lacked any clear and decisive policy direction. All it really did, in fact, was to establish legal 'citizenship credentials' for part-time work and regulate its effects on social security rights and obligations while, however, restricting access to a part-time contract exclusively to certain sections of the working population (the unemployed and young people aged under twenty-five). Such treatment as an exceptional case explains the almost marginal use of this form of work: the rates were less than 2 per cent of the employee population.

The year 1984 saw the first statutory reform of part-time work. In line with the idea of 'normalising' this type of contract, the legislators of the day merely abolished the restrictions on eligibility imposed by Art. 12 of the Workers' Statute in its 1980 version and opened up the possibility of entering into a part-time employment relationship to the entire working population.[25]

At first sight that reform could be construed as a decision aimed at using this new form of work as a means of promoting employment. What is more, the increase in the part-time employment rate discernible from 1984 onwards could even lead to the conclusion that part-time work really did serve to promote employment or, at least, contain unemployment rates.

However, actually being able to attribute any incentive effects on part-time work to the legislative reform of 1984 would call for the use of a set of tools more refined than mere statistics. It is true that, in absolute numbers, the level of part-time employment in Spain tripled during the period 1984–93.[26] It is truer still, however, that the increase was not the result of an independent employment policy aimed at encouraging part-time work *per se*, i.e. in view of the employment opportunities which this form of work can offer for integrating particular groups into the labour market. On the contrary, it was the direct consequence or simple reflection of the employment policy prevailing in Spain during that period, a policy that revolved entirely around one single element: establishing maximum flexibility in the use of fixed-term contracts in their various forms, whether full-time or part-time.

---

[25] On the statutory rules of 1980 and their reform in 1984, see: A. Ojeda Aviles, 'Los contratos a tiempo parcial y de empleo compartido' (1984) 14 *Documentación laboral* pp. 29–52; F. Durán López, 'Trabajo a tiempo parcial y el contrato de relevo', in Miguel Rodríguez-Piñero (ed.), *Comentarios a la nueva legislación laboral* (Madrid: Tecnos, 1985), pp. 65–83; and J. M. Ramírez Martínez, 'El trabajo a tiempo parcial y el contrato de relevo', in E. Borrajo Dacruz (ed.), *Comentario a las leyes laborales. El Estatuto de los Trajadores III* (Madrid: Edersa, 1985), pp. 253–310.

[26] See n. 4 above.

The real contribution of Law 32/1984 was confined to burying the principle of causality that formerly governed the use of temporary contracts and, consequently, to elevating temporary work to the status of a formula capable of promoting employment. Or, to put it in less legal terms, the 1984 Law concentrated all its efforts to renovate labour legislation on the narrow issue of making forms of entry into the labour market flexible. Within a short period of time, barely six years, Spain's industrial relations system switched from a regulatory framework embodying a clear and deliberate preference in favour of the permanent, open-ended contract of employment to one with quite the opposite emphasis.

This is the context within which the quantitative jump in Spain's part-time employment rate has to be viewed. Rather than being conceived as a form of work incorporating a degree of functional autonomy, part-time work represents a mere by-product of the use of temporary or fixed-term contracts: just another of the possibilities made available by the legislators to employers for the flexible management of labour. The total dependence of part-time work on the logic which informs government employment policies and, because of that, underlies policies on human resource management accounts for the temporary nature of part-time contracts, which is greater even than that of full-time fixed-term contracts. It also explains why the vast majority of such contracts are concluded on an involuntary basis.[27]

The conclusion to be drawn from all this is an immediately obvious one: the 'normalisation' of part-time work brought about by Law 32/1984 consisted in its 'normalisation' as a non-permanent and precarious type of contract. The national legislators of the time did liberate it from its former situation of marginality and convert it into a socially typical form of work. The process of liberation was not painless, however; on the contrary, the price that part-time work had to pay for that conversion was the loss of stability.

3.2   A flexibility imposed

The slowdown in Spain's economy which set in from 1990 onwards was to highlight the limits, together with the unwanted effects, of the flexibility model that had been functioning during the second half of the 1980s.

---

[27]   See n. 18 above.

The first aspect to be noted is the 'high sensitivity of employment to developments in the economic cycle'.[28] It was noticeable that in the recessionary phase which began in 1991 Spanish companies adapted the size of their workforces to the new market conditions more quickly than in the past by making use of the opportunities offered by passive adjustment of employment coupled with the large proportion of employees on temporary contracts. A second, 'somewhat paradoxical', circumstance is that the reduction in employment took the form of a disproportionate decline in the number of employees on open-ended contracts, with more of the latter being affected by the adjustment than those on temporary contracts. The third feature is the massive increase in labour turnover rates, which rose from 20 per cent in 1982 to 54 per cent in 1991.

Alongside the above aspects we also need to add the dualisation which took place in the labour market. The latter was split into two core elements: one made up of young people with a good initial educational level who, however, became progressively devalued and unable to achieve integration into the world of work; and the other made up of existing employees on permanent contracts, normally older workers, with fundamental skill deficiencies that hindered their ability to adapt and their retraining. The increased use of precarious contracts, including part-time contracts, fostered the emergence of social inequalities. It also led to noticeable dysfunctions in a production system already beginning to make growing demands for a labour force which was not only flexible but, above all, skilled and motivated.

A document addressed to the Consejo Económico y Social by the Spanish Government in May 1993 gave an accurate diagnosis of the situation produced by the legislative decision to centre flexibility exclusively on the use of temporary contracts. That situation, stated the Government's report, was not only prejudicial to 'employees and their employment and career prospects'; it was also damaging 'to the economy as a whole and to businesses',[29] at least in two respects: first, because it resulted in companies basing the way in which they dealt with the problems of adjustment on criteria that were 'out of step with economic and productive rationality'; and second, because a flexibility strategy focussed on the use

---

[28] *La reforma del mercado de trabajo* (Document addressed by the Government to the Consejo Económico y Social requesting its opinion) (Madrid: Ministry of Labour and Social Security, 1994), p. 21.

[29] Ibid., p. 25.

of temporary contracts contradicts the most rudimentary techniques of human resource management, which place a high value on the stable contractual bond as an instrument of employee motivation and active commitment to company objectives.

On the basis of that diagnosis, which dismissed a labour flexibility based on the continual rotation of a major segment of the employee population as an inappropriate scheme for coping with the changes of every kind that were bound to occur during the 1990s, the proposal advanced by the Government was for an overall reform of the labour market's institutional framework. That reform, the most deep-reaching and extensive of all those made to the Workers' Statute from its introduction in 1980 up to the present day, took place in two phases at successive points in time, each presenting different scenarios. Only the first of those phases will be discussed here, leaving an examination of the second until section 3.3 below.

This first process, which involved a scenario of open trade union confrontation, began at the end of 1993 with the proclamation of Royal Decree-Law 18/1993 and culminated in the following year with the promulgation of Law 11/1994.[30] Both enactments left their reforming mark on the regulation of part-time work.

In the Preamble to Royal Decree-Law 18/1993 the objectives being pursued were, this time, explained quite clearly: they were 'to convert part-time work, as is the case in our neighbouring countries, into a factor that favours an increase in employment rates as far as is possible, . . . , to adapt systems of work organisation in companies to production requirements . . . '. Leaving aside ambiguous justifications deriving from comparative law, which always tend to be only partly relevant, the underlying idea which emerges from the passage cited above and was given concrete expression in the provisions concerned is clear: to utilise part-time work as an effective instrument placed at the disposal of employers with a view to making management of the quantitative and qualitative aspects of working time flexible. Part-time work ceased to be viewed merely as a 'scaled-down' replica of full-time work, as had been the case in the first two versions of Art. 12 of the Workers' Statute (1980 Workers' Statute and Law 32/1984) and progressed to having a substantive identity of its own for the purposes of a policy which entrusted the capacity to generate

---

[30] For a lucid overall view of the 1994 reform, see J. Matía Prim, 'Sentido y alcance de la reforma de la legislación laboral', in Fernando Valdés Dal-Ré (ed.), *La reforma del mercado de trabajo* (Valladolid: Lex-Nova, 1994), pp. 13–35.

employment to the establishment of a flexible system of organising the workforce.

This meant that the advantages which part-time work now brought for employers were no longer those obtained from making use of temporary part-time employees. For the first time, this form of work acquired an independent logic of its own. Full-time contracts and part-time contracts were no longer instruments to be used interchangeably in step with the requirements of labour supply and demand. Part-time work ceased to be conceived as a tool serving a policy which had entrusted the capacity to generate employment exclusively to encouraging the use of temporary contracts and became perceived as a means of achieving a flexible organisation of work.

Endowing part-time work with that functional dimension, which until then had been ignored by the public authorities, produced a new qualitative jump in the part-time employment rate accompanied, for the first time, by a slight decrease in temporary part-time work.[31] Nevertheless, the effects of the new provisions proved to be low-key. In the first place, the part-time employment rate achieved only a two-point increase over the values reached prior to these legislative changes and remained at a modest 8 per cent, i.e. well below the EU average. In other words, employers still did not use part-time work as an instrument of flexible work organisation, preferring to use other more straightforward formulas such as overtime, variable distribution of working hours for full-time employees and, of course, temporary contracts.[32] Secondly, however, Law 11/1994 not only failed to rescue part-time work from the context of instability and lack of social protection to which it had been consigned under Law 32/1984; on the contrary, as a result of the considerable flexibility of its provisions the 1994 Law introduced additional elements of precariousness.

What the above-mentioned Royal Decree 18/1993 and, subsequently, Law 11/1994 actually contributed to the statutory regulation of part-time work involved two major new elements. The first of these concerns the very definition itself of part-time work and consisted in freeing it from the former stipulation that it should not exceed two-thirds of normal working hours: all that was now required was that the agreed working hours should be 'less than' those regarded as normal in the occupation concerned. The second new element concerns the distribution of working time in the case of part-time work. Whereas under the former statutory provisions, as laid down in 1984, the modules of distribution were 'hours', with working time

---

[31] See n. 10 above.   [32] See CC. OO/UGT (2000) (n. 17 above), p. 99.

calculated on a daily or weekly basis and 'days', in their turn, defined in terms of weeks or months, the new legal provisions established the 'hour' as the sole unit on which the agreement of working time can be based, for all the possible modules: day, week, month or year.[33]

These regulatory changes constituted the technical means used by the 1993–4 reform to establish part-time work as an instrument to promote employment through policies on increased flexibility. Such legislation not only broadened the opportunities for part-time contracts; it also allowed 'wider scope for establishing an irregular and variable distribution of daily working hours, with scheduled hours differing from one day to another.'[34] Thus, for example, whereas under the former legislation there had been little legal accommodation for formulas in which the duration of working time can vary between a minimum and a maximum, the new provisions opened up the way for the use of such formulas 'at a stroke'.[35]

With the 1993–4 reform, the function of part-time work as a mechanism especially suited to offering the employers' organisations broad scope for adapting working time to market requirements was recognised and given prominence through the establishment of the fundamentals of an independent regulatory system for this form of work. In the legislative development of part-time work the reforms implemented during that period elevated its function as an instrument of flexibility to the top of the list, ultimately overshadowing its other features.

3.3   Ups and downs in the quest for security

Following the hiatus in social concertation policies with respect to the issue of flexibility as marked by Law 11/1994 and other reforms of labour market legislation, the trade-union and employers' organisations possessing 'most representative' status at national level reopened negotiations both at their strictly bilateral level and in the context of tripartite negotiations involving government participation. Within the framework of these renewed processes of social dialogue a number of National Cross-Industry Agreements were concluded, some of them accompanied by tripartite agreements in order to guarantee their operative effect. In any event, the underlying motivation for the new phase of social dialogue was the need

---

[33] For a more detailed study of that reform, see I. García-Perrote, 'El contrato a tiempo parcial' (1994) 5/6 *Relaciones laborales* pp. 82–107; and A. Pedrajas Moreno, 'Nuevo diseño del trabajo a tiempo parcial' (1994) 8 *Relaciones laborales* pp. 9–42.
[34] Pedrajas, 'Nuevo diseño del trabajo', p. 16.
[35] H. Merino Senovilla, *El trabajo a tiempo parcial* (Valladolid: Lex-Nova, 1994), p. 185.

to correct the chronic distortions of Spain's labour market resulting from the excessive use of temporary contracts – in other words, caused by a noticeably low proportion of permanent contracts of employment.[36]

In this renewed climate of social dialogue that set in from 1997 onwards, the most representative trade-union and employer confederations signed what was called the 'National Cross-Industry Agreement on Stability in Employment', in which the signatory parties called on the Government to introduce a series of legislative measures on, among other things, part-time work.[37] As a result of the process of social concertation the Government accordingly promulgated Royal Decree-Law 8/1997,[38] an enactment subsequently described, quite rightly, as 'a wasted opportunity'[39] to make provision for part-time work on a more evenly balanced basis as regards its substantive guarantees and social protection.[40] This was acknowledged by the Government itself when it expressly recognised, in its first National Action Plan for Employment (NAP), the need to 'provide a new regulatory framework' for part-time work, as indicated by the opening-up of 'an area of dialogue with the social partners in which a range of incentives are also examined that will enable this contractual concept to be developed'.[41]

This compromise in domestic policy, to which other compromises of a European nature were added later, was implemented through a further amendment of Art. 12 of the Workers' Statute, this time in the form of Royal Decree-Law 15/1998. Far from meriting dismissal as a more or less

---

[36] The high percentage of temporary employment has been cited on more than one occasion by the EC Council as one of the basic problems of employment in Spain. See Council Recommendation 2000/64/EC of 14 February 2000 on the implementation of Member States' employment policies (OJL 52/32 of 25.2.2000) and Council Recommendation 2001/64/EC of 19 January 2001 on the implementation of Member States' employment policies (OJL 22/27 of 24.1.2001).

[37] National Cross-Industry Agreement on Stability in Employment of 28 April 1997, signed by the UGT and CC.OO and the CEOE and CEPYME (Spanish Confederation of Employers' Organisations and Spanish Confederation of Small and Medium-Sized Enterprises). The specific proposals on part-time work are contained in its section 3. The complete text can be consulted in *Diálogo social y estabilidad en el empleo* (Madrid: Ministerio de Trabajo y Asuntos Sociales, 1997), pp. 25–37.

[38] Transformed soon after into Law 63/1997.

[39] M. D. C. Ortiz Lallana, 'Algunos problemas del regimen jurídico del trabajo a tiempo parcial' (1998) 15/16 *Relaciones laborales* p. 101.

[40] For a more detailed examination of the scope of this reform, see H. Merino Senovilla, 'Los contratos formativos y el trabajo a tiempo parcial', in F. Valdés Dal-Ré (ed.), *La reforma pactada de las legislaciones laborales y de seguridad social* (Valladolid: Lex-Nova, 1997), pp. 86–95.

[41] *Plan de acción para el empleo del reino de España* (Madrid: Ministerio de Trabajo y Asuntos Sociales, April 1998), p. 32.

passing episode in the chequered history of the regulation of part-time work, this enactment occupies a key position as representing the most serious attempt, in legislative terms, to give part-timers a legal status on an equal footing with that of full-time employees.

The new reform was governed, albeit imperfectly, by the same logic that underlies the most recent labour market reforms brought about both in Spain and in the European Union as a whole: the logic of social dialogue and social concertation. For the 1998 provision not only transposed the social contract signed between the Government and Spain's two most representative trade-union confederations, endowing it with the effectiveness of a statutory rule;[42] it also transposed into national law Council Directive 97/81/EC of 15 December 1987 implementing the Framework Agreement on part-time work concluded at European level by UNICE, CEEP and the ETUC.

However, the significance of Royal Decree-Law 15/1998 does not rest solely on its status either as a 'negotiated' law or as the vehicle of the compromises made by the Spanish Government to shape its employment policy to the European Employment Strategy. It is also due to the undeniable fact that this enactment introduced a change of direction in the statutory regulation of part-time work.

The 1998 reform clarified and improved the status of part-time employees, by endeavouring to lay down a legal regime which reconciled (or at least balanced more evenly) employers' interests in having the regulatory means allowing them to deal with their company's adaptability requirements and employees' interests in performing work within a reasonable framework of certainties and guarantees regarding the essential elements of their work obligation. This was undoubtedly the most significant contribution of the reform – the legal policy decision which at any rate marked a turning-point in the direction followed by the previous legislation.

Despite its deficiencies and shortcomings, the new legislation combined a good many technical mechanisms aimed at helping to rectify the status of part-time work in a practical and effective manner. These included, most notably, enshrinement of the principles of voluntariness in access to this form of employment and equality of treatment with full-time working, and the encouragement of 'voluntary mobility' from

---

[42] 'Acuerdo sobre Trabajo a Tiempo Parcial y Fomento de su Estabilidad' of 13 November 1998, signed between the Spanish Government and the UGT and CC.OO. Its complete text can be consulted in Casas and Valdés Dal-Ré, *Los contratos* (n. 16 above), pp. 301–11.

full-time to part-time contracts and vice versa. The new regulations on social protection also illustrated the favourable course set by the reform towards normalising and improving the employment-related legal status of part-timers.[43] Moreover, the same approach is also evident in the establishment, for the first time in Spain's legislative system, of incentives for using open-ended part-time contracts in order to combat the hitherto predominantly temporary nature of this form of work.[44]

With the 1998 reform the Spanish legislators installed part-time work in a regulatory scenario conforming to the European Employment Guidelines, by providing for the first time a legal regime that was better balanced between flexibility and security – between the necessary adaptability of companies to consumer demand and social and employment-related guarantees for the part-time employee category, which in the circumstances prevailing in Spain comprised groups whose position in the labour market was, furthermore, a weak one (women and young people).

This legislative change, the outcome of a social contract agreed exclusively between the Government and the most representative trade-union confederations, was the target of strong criticism from the organisations representing employers' interests, which branded the amended version of Art. 12 of the Workers' Statute as 'a retrograde step, in terms of flexibility, as compared with the previous rules'.[45]

In this climate of disaccord between the social partners, causing a downward trend in the use of part-time work, a new round of social dialogue was initiated at the end of 2000 which was to end without a social contract. It was then that the Government promulgated Royal Decree-Law 5/2001, which again amended, for the Nth time, the regulatory framework of part-time work, but now in a direction essentially coinciding with the positions adopted by the employers' organisations in the closing stages of the above-mentioned dialogue.[46] Or, as the Government put it plainly in presenting its 2001 NAP, this new legislative change was intended to

---

[43] See I. García-Perrote, 'La protección social de los trabajadores a tiempo parcial', in Casas and Valdés Dal-Ré, *Los contratos* (n. 16 above), pp. 221–47.

[44] Escudero Rodríguez, 'Los incentivos' (n. 16 above).

[45] 'Consideraciones de la CEOE, de 10 de noviembre de 1998, al principio de Acuerdo entre el Gobierno y las organizaciones sindicales UGT y CC.OO sobre contrato a tiempo parcial', in Casas and Valdés Dal-Ré, *Los contratos* (n. 16 above), pp. 313–22 at 317.

[46] M. Rodríguez-Piñero, F. Valdés Dal-Ré and M. E. Casas Baamonde, 'La reforma del mercado de trabajo (para el incremento del empleo y la mejora de su calidad)' (2001) 7 *Relaciones laborales* p. 4.

'remove the rigidities of the 1998 rules' and give this form of contract 'greater flexibility'.[47] The logic of the 2001 reform was therefore that of rectifying the 1998 version of Art. 12 of the Workers' Statute; it was its 'counter-reform', the purpose of which was none other than to shift those aspects aimed at providing a framework of legal security for part-timers into a direction more in line with employers' interests.

To that end, it removed the percentage limit (77 per cent of full-time working hours) that from 1998 onwards had marked the boundary between part-time and full-time work; it abolished the requirement that the contract should specify the actual monthly, weekly and daily pattern of regular contractual working hours and identify the days on which the employee was obliged to work and, instead, made a constant annual distribution of those hours sufficient; and it made fundamental changes to the regime of what the 1998 law had referred to as 'extra hours' (*horas complementarias*). The difficult balance between flexibility and security arrived at by that Law was disrupted, with the legislation again coming down on the side of flexibility.

The promulgation and entry into force of Royal Decree-Law 5/2001[48] concludes the chequered legislative history of part-time work in Spain. However, it is safe to assume that this represents no more than a temporary state of affairs – just one link in a chain that is bound to be extended in the near future with new regulatory measures, either as a result of state intervention or through collective bargaining. The most recent example of cross-industry collective bargaining at national level would appear to suggest this.

In the closing days of 2001, on 20 December, the most representative Spanish trade-union and employers' confederations signed what they called the *Acuerdo Interconfederal para la negociación colectiva del año 2002* ('National Cross-Industry Agreement on Collective Bargaining in 2002'), in which special attention is paid to the subject of employment. Without embarking here on an analysis of the content of this *au sommet* agreement,[49] it is useful to note that for the first time in Spain's industrial

---

[47] *Plan de acción para el empleo del reino de España* (Madrid: Ministerio de Trabajo y Asuntos Sociales, May 2001), p. 34.

[48] Subsequently repealed by Law 12/2001, which retains many of the provisions of the enactment it replaces.

[49] For more details, see M. Rodríguez-Piñero, F. Valdés Dal-Ré and M. E. Casas, 'El Acuerdo Interconfederal para la negociación colectiva del año 2002' (2002) 2 *Relaciones laborales* pp. 1–22.

relations system the social partners have exhibited a basic consensus on the import of the notions that make up the flexibility/security pairing in the work context.

The relevant point here is that the signatories to the Agreement were at one in categorising stability in employment as 'an element to be borne in mind in collective bargaining as a guarantee of competitiveness for businesses and security for employees'. They also concurred in stating that 'the need for businesses to be able to respond to an environment that alters rapidly calls for the development of their capacity to adapt through applying internal flexibility mechanisms'.

Consensus between the social partners on the major concepts governing the regulation of 'atypical' forms of employment is, of course, an essential guarantee if reasonable and equitable standards of security and quality of employment are to be restored to part-time work; however, the consensus as it exists so far is not enough of a guarantee to achieve that objective. In addition to a convergence of opinion on the formulation of strategies there is also an unavoidable need for substantial agreement on the nature of the technical measures adopted; that is, the establishment of the technical means that (to use the wording of the Guidelines for EU Member States' employment policies for the year 2001) guarantee part-timers 'adequate security . . . compatible with the needs of business'.[50]

Nevertheless, that must not detract from the significance of the consensus reached between the social partners, which opens up the prospect of a future form of regulation that will bring the eventful history of rules on part-time work to a more satisfactory and less transitory end.

4 Heteronomy and autonomy in the statutory regulation of part-time work

The legal structure of the provisions regulating part-time work (the successive versions of Art. 12 of the Workers' Statute) has followed, and to a large extent still follows, the general principles that characterise the Spanish system of sources of regulation and, for the most part, the labour law system itself. It is the state which decides, in every instance and with respect to every institution forming the subject of regulatory action, the respective role falling to the sources of regulation of the employment relationship: both to the sources of law (legislation and collective bargaining)

[50] Council Decision 2001/63/EC of 19 January 2001 (see n. 22 above), Guideline 14.

and to the sources of obligation (individual autonomy). To put it another way, it is the state's norm which defines the type of relationship (legal structure) that the collective agreement and individual contract of employment have to maintain with each other, thereby marking out the areas (topics and limits) within which each source of law can fulfil its regulatory function.

However, this function of Art. 12 of the Workers' Statute in programming the interplay of collective autonomy and individual autonomy in the legal regulation of part-time work has undergone a number of changes, far from negligible in historical terms, which are largely in line with the logic followed in Spanish labour law since the deep-reaching and extensive reform of the Workers' Statute implemented by Law 11/1994: a progressive withdrawal of the state's regulatory powers and strengthening of collective bargaining powers. These are the obverse and reverse of the same phenomenon, in that an increase in the scope of collective bargaining (or, although to a lesser degree here, individual contract negotiation) tends to facilitate the adaptation by collective agreements (or contracts of employment) of legal regulation. Hence the preferred technique for achieving that objective: conversion of the legal structure of the state norm, which from (absolute or relative) mandatory law moves on to operating as discretionary law. As in the majority of EU Member States and in the Community legal order itself, *soft law* is gradually but implacably replacing *hard law*.

If we consider that process in the specific context of interest to us here, the first sets of provisions on part-time work (1980 and 1984) were characterised by instituting a legal regime which left barely any opportunities for regulatory action to collective bargaining. The bulk of the rules governing the part-time contract fell into one of the two categories of mandatory law: either they could not be departed from by agreement in any way at all (absolute mandatory law), or they could only be departed from by agreement if that had the effect of creating more favourable conditions (relative mandatory law). It was state norms (statutes and non-statutory instruments) which defined the group of employees for whom a part-time contract was permissible, laid down the concept of part-time work, stipulated the formal requirements for finalising such a contract and established the rights and obligations of employees working on part-time contracts.

Alongside the noticeable elements of continuity in the part-time regime during the period that elapsed between 1980 and 1993, the 1984 reform did nevertheless introduce some measure of innovation in the system of regulatory sources governing this form of work and, more generally, other forms of contract aimed at promoting employment (temporary and work-experience contracts). That innovation, which was not unconnected with legal policies moving in the direction of greater flexibility, consisted in allocating a more extensive role to individual autonomy. The regulatory function of the contract of employment, previously relegated to a subordinate and second-stage role, regained ground as much in strategic terms as in relation to negotiated agreements on the reduction of working hours.[51] From that point of view, the 1984 legislation had the effect of instituting a flexibility model of a deregulatory nature.

The 1993–4 reform brought an initial, albeit modest, change of direction from this marginalisation or exclusion of collective autonomy in the regulation of part-time work. Although the regulatory model basically perpetuated a legal model, including emphasis on the 'statutory provisions' for the finalising and performance of the part-time contract, the state norm did open up, even if to only a rudimentary degree, some scope for regulatory action through collective bargaining. The 1998 reform then strengthened that trend, so much so that legal regulation on the subject of part-time work nowadays offers an excellent platform from which to gain a true insight into the heterogeneity of the relations currently existing between the typical regulatory instruments governing the labour market, and to assess, more generally, the extent of the changes that have taken place in the system of sources of Spanish labour law.

This is not the place for a detailed discussion of the dialogue established between the law and collective bargaining in the regulation of part-time work; for the purposes of this study, a few general observations will suffice. The first point to mention is that the more vigorous role attributed to the collective agreement has not brought any curtailment of the contract of employment's regulatory function, which 'comes out strengthened' in the new legal context.[52] There is, however, a change in the hallmark of that function, which is not always used as a means of shifting its regulation towards market influences, ultimately with a view to offering a contractual advantage for employer authority in the name

---

[51] A. Martín Valverde, 'Las transformaciones del Derecho del Trabajo en España (1976–1984) y la Ley 32/1984 de reforma del Estatuto de los Trabajadores', in M. Rodríguez-Piñero, *Comentarios* (n. 25 above), p. 36.

[52] M. E. Casas Baamonde, 'Ley, negociación y autonomía individual en la regulación de los contratos de trabajo a tiempo parcial', in Casas and Valdés Dal-Ré, *Los contratos* (n. 16 above), p. 110.

of all-important adaptability. Sometimes, the function fulfilled by referral or delegation to the contract of employment is one of guaranteeing individual rights, as is the case with, for example, agreed extra hours or the principle of a voluntary basis for part-time work.

Another aspect is the very varied nature of the functions that the legislation entrusts to collective bargaining. In addition to the typical and traditional function of departing from the rules of relative mandatory law to make them more favourable, collaboration between the law and the collective agreement in the regulation of part-time work can also take the form of a supplemental function, i.e. in adjusting the rules of discretionary law, or a complementary function, i.e. in integrating the basic rules laid down by statute. Lastly, it can also be manifested in the exercise of an autonomous normative function,[53] independently of the law, in those cases where the provision in question expressly delegates the regulation of a particular issue or simply omits to regulate it at all.

Traditionally, 'activism' in the regulation of part-time work has been exercised through the two channels available to the state for expressing its normative powers: the statute and the non-statutory Regulation. The regulatory history of part-time work, and indeed other contractual forms, actually demonstrates that in exercising its constitutional regulatory powers the Government has not always confined itself to stipulating rules that represent development of the law; often, those powers have entailed acts which are manifestly ultra vires, encroaching on matters for whose regulation there is no proper authority without infringing the principle of legitimacy or skirting the limits of its application. Apart from their pathological aspects, however, regulatory powers have had an additional effect of a perverse kind. The non-statutory Regulation, in sealing off the porosity of the legal framework of part-time work, blocked or at least discouraged collectively agreed rules. The 1998 reform has brought about a change of tendency on this point as well, making the collaboration between statute and non-statutory Regulation unnecessary. The functions of developing or integrating the legal rules are now left exclusively to autonomy, either collective or individual, without needing complementary non-statutory Regulations.

One further point in this catalogue of observations remains to be made. The opening-up of greater scope for collective bargaining is not as yet matched by concrete results and a critical mass of rules on part-time

---

[53] See, for more details, ibid., pp. 121–6.

work has still not been reached in Spain's bargaining system, either quantitatively (number of agreements dealing with this form of work) or qualitatively (innovative nature of the clauses contained in agreements that deal with any of the concepts of part-time work).[54] The protracted course of legislative intervention in the matter, the slowness of the bargaining system to extend its content to new topics, the reluctance of employers to negotiate in flexible terms on institutions already covered by earlier legal rules and the short period of time that has elapsed since the last reform are all possible explanations for the lack of attention or indifference exhibited in bargaining practice towards a contractual form that is coming into growing use and, furthermore, necessitated by developments in bargaining.

5 Some aspects of the part-time contract's legal regime

5.1 Unity and diversity in the form of the part-time contract of employment

As already noted,[55] the 1980 version of the Workers' Statute conferred 'legal citizenship' on the part-time contract of employment, with the latter interpreted as a contract under which work is performed 'on a specified number of days a year, month or week, or for a specified number of hours, respectively less than two thirds of those regarded as normal in the industry concerned for the same period of time'.

Over the years, however, that initial unity gave way to a diversity in the typology of the part-time contract, with changes occurring in line with successive developments in the regulation of this form of work. The 1984 reform, for example, introduced a new form of part-time contract called a 'hand-over contract' (*contrato de relevo*). Envisaged as a manifestation of solidarity or work-sharing, the hand-over contract embodies the division of full-time working hours between two employees: one approaching retirement age who has opted for partial retirement and another, recruited from the unemployed, who is hired to work for hours at least equivalent to those no longer worked by the employee being replaced. The hand-over contract therefore fulfils a dual purpose: easing the gradual path towards

---

[54] I. González del Rey, 'Ordenación del tiempo de trabajo: trabajo a tiempo parcial', in J. G. Murcia (ed.), *Condiciones de empleo y de trabajo en la negociación colectiva* (Madrid: Consejo Económico y Social, 1998), p. 337.

[55] See section 3.1 above.

retirement of employees approaching the end of their working life and, at the same time, helping to create employment.[56]

The 1993–4 reform added to the trend away from the typological unity of part-time work. First, it brought within the scope of the legal rules governing part-time work the group classed as 'intermittent permanent employees' (*trabajadores fijos-discontinuos*) in the context of regular seasonal or casual work. Second, it created a sub-category of the usual part-time contract of employment as defined in quantitative terms: the performance of working hours of less than 12 hours a week or 40 hours a month. Or, in the words used by the legislators, a form of economic activity 'which, because of the short working hours concerned, has to be classed as a marginal or insufficient means of livelihood'.

Since then, and up to the present day, the sub-types of part-time work have followed a separate path. As a result of the strong criticism from the union side which greeted the establishment of 'marginal' part-time work as a paradigm of social sub-protection, 'marginal part-time work' was then abolished under the mini-reform implemented in 1997.[57] Accordingly, the legal family of forms of part-time employment is now structured on the basis of an ordinary part-time contract plus two special forms: the hand-over contract[58] and intermittent permanent employment.

5.2   The legal concept of part-time work

By its very nature, the notion of part-time work carries a relational or comparative dimension. A job is classed as part-time with reference to the working hours that are classed as constituting full-time employment. However, setting a precise limit on what is to be interpreted as part-time work involves more than merely stipulating the *quantum* of its reduction in working hours as compared with full-time work. The whole range of factors entering into the definition of full-time work, i.e. the various

---

[56] On the convergences and divergences of the hand-over contract with respect to allied contractual forms (job-sharing or job-splitting), see I. González del Rey, *El contrato de trabajo a tiempo parcial* (Pamplona: Aranzadi, 1998), pp. 43–7.

[57] Section 3.1 of the National Cross-Industry Agreement on Stability in Employment (see n. 37 above) expressed the need to place marginal part-timers on an equal footing with other part-time employees in matters relating to social protection.

[58] The legal regime of the hand-over contract was revised under Royal Decree-Law 15/1998 and, more recently, was fundamentally amended under Law 12/2001. See M. Rodríguez-Piñero, F. Valdés Dal-Ré and M. E. Casas Baamonde, 'La Ley 12/2001 y la consolidación de la – reforma del mercado de trabajo (para el incremento del empleo y la mejora de su calidad)' (2001) 17 *Relaciones laborales* pp. 1–18.

chronological units into which it can be broken down (day, week, month or year) and the diversity of its regulatory sources, means that the concept of part-time work has to be formulated on the basis of three temporal elements: the reduction that constitutes part-time hours, the duration of full-time hours and the reference periods within which both may be worked.[59]

That methodology will be followed below in explaining the notion of part-time work in Spain's legal system, where an attempt will be made to show clearly the constant changes that the notion has undergone. In the final analysis, the contingent nature of the concept reflects fairly accurately the predominant functions assigned to part-time work by the legislators at each point in time.

In its first versions (1980 and 1984) Art. 12 of the Workers' Statute defined part-time work as work where the hours did not exceed two-thirds of the maximum full-time or normal working hours. That quantitative limit, a real de facto basis for classing a reduction in working hours as part-time work, was abolished by the 1993–4 reform, which held that any work whatever performed for a number of hours less than those regarded as normal could be categorised as part-time work. Hence, under the new version of the rules the contractual work performance needed only to be 'simply less'[60] than normal during the reference period (day and week, but also month or year) for it to be classed, formally, as part-time – without, moreover, any minimum number of hours being set. The possibilities for agreeing part-time contracts became practically unlimited, ranging from hours only 'slightly' less than the normal working hours (one hour less, for example) right down to marginal working hours (of one hour, for example).

That legislative change, adopted for the sake of maximising the flexible use of this form of contract, was greeted with strong and widespread criticism from national experts in the field, who were of the opinion that the new legal concept weakened the boundaries between part-time and full-time jobs, blurred the differences between the part-time contract and arrangements for reduced working hours that did not constitute part-time (such as permitted reductions in working hours to care for dependent children or nurse infants) and, lastly, groundlessly accentuated the distinction between 'horizontal' and 'vertical' forms of part-time work.

---

[59] Merino Senovilla, *El trabajo* (n. 35 above), pp. 115–125, and González del Rey, *El contrato* (n. 56 above), pp. 63–77.
[60] Pedrajas, 'Nuevo diseño del trabajo' (n. 33 above), p. 16.

The 1998 reform restored the concept of the upper limit as an element of the legal notion of part-time work, with the reworded Art. 12(1) of the Workers' Statute stipulating that the contract of employment was deemed to be a part-time contract 'where it provides for the performance of work for a number of hours per day, week, month or year *less than 77 per cent* of the full-time working hours'. The 2001 reform then abolished that controversial upper limit, leaving the part-time contract now defined as one providing for working hours 'less than the working hours of a comparable full-time employee'.

The second temporal element in the make-up of the legal concept of part-time work is the duration of full-time working hours as a point of comparison, an aspect on which the 1998 reform also intervened with a view to endowing that concept with greater legal certainty and technical straightforwardness.

Under the legislation prior to the 1998 reform, the reduced working hours – less than two-thirds (1980 and 1984) or simply less (1993–4) – which constituted part-time work had to be compared with the 'normal working hours in the industry concerned'. That statutory requirement, rightly dismissed as 'woolly',[61] was revised in the 1998 version of Art. 12(1) of the Workers' Statute, which used as the term of comparison for the purposes of classifying a reduction in working hours as part-time work the 'full-time working hours specified in the applicable collective agreement or, where none exists, the statutory maximum working hours'. Most recently, the 2001 reform incorporated as the element of comparison the notion used in the EC Framework Agreement: a 'comparable full-time employee'.

The third and last temporal element involved in defining the legal notion of part-time work concerns the reference periods within which the respective work performances to be compared (part-time and full-time) must take place. Here too, the keynote of the legislation had been a constant change of criterion.

Without going into wearisome detail on the different chronological units of reference that have successively been used under each legislative reform, it is nevertheless important to point out that the most awkward aspect of this development has centred on whether or not the year is accepted as a unit for calculating working hours that are shorter than full-time hours. Debate has, in short, centred on whether the pattern

---

[61] C. Palomeque López, 'El [nuevo] contrato de trabajo a tiempo parcial', in Casas and Valdés Dal-Ré, *Los contratos* (n. 16 above), p. 54.

of the distribution of working time in part-time work is predominantly horizontal or vertical.

After being initially accepted under the 1980 version of Art. 12, the annualised dimension was excluded under the 1984 reform, then restored under the 1993–4 reform and since maintained under the subsequent provisions. As provided for under the present Art. 12(1) of the Workers' Statute, the working hours that constitute part-time work can be calculated 'on the basis of a number of hours per day, week, month or year'. Two comments are called for in regard to the legal formula currently in force.

First, whatever the reference period used (day, week, month or year), the unit of calculation is necessarily the hour: the number of hours per day, per week, per month or per year. The use of different units (days per week or month, or weeks per month, for example) remains excluded.[62] Second, the list of reference periods as represented in the statutory provisions (the day, week, month or year) should be regarded as purely indicative, since others (the fortnight or semester) can be used provided they do not exceed the upper limit of one year.[63]

5.3   The principle of voluntariness and part-time work

One of the major preoccupations of the legislative texts on part-time work enacted during the 1990s was to establish a framework of measures intended to guarantee that not only access to part-time work but also the conditions relating to its performance should be on a voluntary basis. This preoccupation was one that was echoed by the relevant ILO regulatory instruments adopted in 1994[64] and elevated by the EC Framework Agreement on part-time work to the status of a purpose of its specific regulation (Clause 1(b)).[65]

After being ignored by the national legislators in the context of the 1993–4 reform, the principle of voluntariness has been restored under the current version of Art. 12 of the Workers' Statute as one of the principal axes underlying the regulation of part-time work, adapted very faithfully

---

[62] Merino Senovilla, El trabajo (n. 35 above), pp. 192–4.

[63] In accordance with this thesis, see González del Rey, El contrato (n. 56 above), p. 78.

[64] The relevant instruments are ILO Convention No. 175 and Recommendation No. 182, adopted at the 81st ILO Conference held in Geneva on 24 June 1994.

[65] Clause 5 of the Framework Agreement then goes on to develop the principle of voluntariness.

to the compromises made at Community level. The objective pursued is also to 'reinforce the principle of voluntariness in the conclusion of part-time contracts'.[66]

Viewed schematically, the principle of voluntariness has practical effect in successive contractual phases: first, in that of access to part-time employment; later, at the time when the work performance is provided; and lastly, in the termination phase. All three will be mentioned below, although necessarily briefly.

The principle comes into play, to start with, at the time when the relevant employment relationship is established. The fact that a contract of employment provides for reduced working hours is not in itself enough for it to be classed as a part-time contract. It is also a requirement that the reduction is *agreed* between the parties as being governed by that particular form of contract. Hence, instances of a straightforward cut in working hours, either because the contractual intention was to draw up an ordinary full-time contract of employment with shortened working hours or because there was no such voluntary element involved, cannot be classed as part-time contracts. Examples of this excluded category include reductions in working hours due to suspension of the contract of employment for economic or technological reasons (i.e. short-time working under Art. 47 of the Workers' Statute), circumstances resulting from the employees' exercise of a legally recognised right (legal custody or direct care of minors under Arts. 37(5) and 37(6)) and special (shorter) working hours in occupations involving health hazards (Article 34(7)).

However, the requirement for mutual agreement between employee and employer is not confined to the initial contractual phase when the contract of employment is being finalised; it continues to apply later, during the phase when the agreed employment relationship is being performed. Under Art. 12(4)(e) of the Workers' Statute, 'the conversion of a full-time job into a part-time job and vice versa' cannot be imposed unilaterally by the employer, even through the existing procedure for major changes to terms and conditions of employment. In making that provision the legislation put an end to the heated polemic previously waged by scholars and legal practitioners as to the legitimacy of a change of contract based

---

[66] Cf. s. 2(1) of the 1998 social contract (see n. 42 above). As stated in the Preamble to Royal Decree-Law 15/1998, the three main axes of the reform, aimed at 'improving the quality of part-time work', are its voluntary nature, the right to equality and non-discrimination, and the right to adequate social protection.

on the powers granted to employers under the legal system, by expressly decreeing the unlawfulness of such an action.[67]

The requirement that the conversion of a full-time contract into a part-time contract and vice versa must be on a voluntary basis applies not only with respect to the employer but also, as an additional element, with respect to collective bargaining. In this latter context the requirement for voluntariness operates exclusively in relation to anything detrimental to the employee, which means that collective agreements can recognise a perfect right to a change of contract where it is in the employee's favour, i.e. for family reasons or training purposes.[68]

Observance of the principle that changes of contract must be on a voluntary basis is compatible with the establishment of a framework of measures intended to foster the 'voluntary transfer' of full-time employees to part-time jobs and vice versa, whose implementation is largely entrusted to collective bargaining. On this point the Workers' Statute has been meticulous in its transposition of the content of Cl. 5(3) of the Framework Agreement as implemented under Directive 97/81/EC. Thus, employers are under an obligation to 'inform' employees in their service of any posts that become available so that the latter are able to request a transfer of contract 'in accordance with the procedures established by collective agreement' (Art. 12(4)(e) of the Workers' Statute). However, the statutory provision does not embody, in itself and exclusive of what may have been established by collective agreement, an automatic right to a transfer when posts become available, but merely a right to request such a transfer. Nevertheless, inasmuch as the provision does require the employer to justify refusing such a request by stating the express grounds for doing so, transfer from full-time to part-time work and vice versa can ultimately be conceived as a right, subject to the condition that there is no other employee who possesses a stronger claim to the vacant post and asserts that claim before the courts.[69] Apart from this, employees who have agreed with the employer on the conversion of their contracts have a priority right to return to the situation *quo ante* in vacant posts in the same occupational group or equivalent occupational category in accordance with collectively agreed requirements and procedures.

Lastly, voluntariness also applies in connection with termination of the employment relationship: the rule provides, for that purpose, that

---

[67] On the terms of that debate, see T. Sala Franco, 'Los principios de ordenación del contrato a tiempo parcial', in Casas and Valdés Dal-Ré, *Los contratos* (n. 16 above), pp. 79–81.
[68] Ibid., p. 86.   [69] See, in accordance with this thesis, ibid., p. 90.

the decision to refuse an employer's proposal to convert a full-time contract into a part-time one and vice versa must not cause the employee any
detriment. This guarantee of indemnification for the employee covers
disciplinary dismissal (or sanction) which, for disciplinary dismissal to
take place, has to be classed by the courts as void rather than wrongful
dismissal,[70] resulting in the employee's immediate reinstatement. It does
not, however, include forms of termination that may be based on economic or technological grounds (collective dismissals or dismissals for
objective reasons).

5.4   Equality and proportionality in the recognition and exercise of rights

Both at the level of its statutory formulation and at that of its practical
application, the definition of the legal status of part-time employees
involves the operation of a dual principle: equality of treatment and
diversity of treatment, as compared in both cases with the legal status
of full-time employees.

In their capacity as individuals working on another's account and parties to an employment relationship combining each and every one of the
features which typify, in law, that particular and mandatory legal relationship, part-time employees are bearers of the general catalogue of rights
and obligations formally recognised as applying to employees under the
ordinary rules. The principle of equality of course prohibits unequal treatment of equals. However, equality is not the same thing as egalitarianism:
it does not proscribe diversity in the treatment of what is unequal, always
provided that diversity is based on a differentiating factor which is found
to be objective, reasonable and non-arbitrary. From that point of view, the
major problem that arises in the definition of the legal status of part-time
work is that of determining in what cases, and under what conditions,
the element characterising such an employment relationship (shortened
working hours) can moderate application of the principle of equality or,
to put it more precisely, can justify application of a principle of diversity.
The fact of performing shortened working hours is therefore the element
that operates as a possible differentiating factor. Consequently, judgment
as to the presence or otherwise of objective and reasonable justification
for a difference in treatment boils down to a judgment as to the real
and effective influence of shortened working hours on the recognition

---

[70] Casas Baamonde and Valdés Dal-Ré (1999), *Los contratos* (n. 16 above), p. 104.

and exercise of a particular right or employment condition in terms of equality or diversity.

The history of the regulation of part-time work in Spain's legal system has followed that logic, as it was bound to do. The very first statutory rules on this form of work, as laid down in the development of the 1980 version of Art. 12 of the Workers' Statute, enshrined a principle of equivalence of rights between part-time and full-time employees although, firstly, stipulating that such equivalence refers to rights 'which are compatible with the inherent nature of the contract' and, secondly, introducing a criterion of proportionality in the case of rights with a monetary content.[71] Apart from various amendments of a semantic or technical nature the later versions of the rules retained the essence of the same approach, with the labour courts left to play an active role as regards the practical application of the principle of equivalence modulated by that of proportionality.[72]

Prompted directly by Cl. 4 of the European Framework Agreement implemented under Directive 97/81/EC, the current version of Art. 12 of the Workers' Statute proclaims the principle of equality or equivalence of rights of part-timers with full-time employees. Moreover, in line with what the Agreement also establishes, Spanish legislation permits that principle, 'where appropriate in view of their nature' (i.e. the nature of the rights in question), to be moderated by the principle of proportionality as a function of the amount of time worked, entrusting the practical application of the *pro rata temporis* rule to statutory provisions, non-statutory Regulations and collective agreements (Art. 12(4)(d) of the Workers' Statute).

Thus, the rules now embody the principle of equality, albeit in a dual version: one strong and the other weak. Under the strong version, part-timers possess the same rights as full-time employees and exercise them in a context of identical conditions and content. Nevertheless, the operation of that general rule can be modulated by statutory provisions and collective agreements, subject to certain limits and requirements. First, any departure from the principle of equivalence of rights has to rely on an

---

[71] J. García Murcia, 'El trabajo a tiempo parcial y su regimen jurídico en el ordenamiento laboral español', in F. Durán López (ed.), *Las relaciones laborales y la reorganización del sistema productivo* (Córdoba: Publicaciones del Monte de Piedad y Caja de Ahorros, 1983), pp. 151–3.

[72] For example, since they relate to the employee's physiological needs, the actual length of daily, weekly and annual rest periods is governed by a strict principle of equivalence, regardless of the fact that the accompanying pay is proportional to the amount of time worked in the period attracting remuneration. Monetary rights, by contrast, are subject to the principle of proportionality. For more details on the various conditions, see González del Rey, *El contrato* (n. 56 above), pp. 229–44.

objective and reasonable ground deriving from the particular nature of the right in question. Second, any moderation of this same principle must necessarily be expressed through a criterion of proportionality, measured as a function of the time worked. Otherwise, and failing any explicit provision, the legal presumption favours applicability of the general rule, not the exception.

One final observation remains to be made. The regulatory expression and practical application of the weakened version of the principle of equality (proportionality) cannot be isolated from the social context in which part-time work takes place. The predominantly female nature of this form of employment fosters or at least favours a situation where the *pro rata temporis* reduction of pay and related matters disguises hidden indirect discrimination, not always easy to detect – something which is borne out by Community case-law.

9

Sweden: part-time work – welfare or unfair?

RONNIE EKLUND

1 Introductory remarks

The frequency of part-time work in Sweden is high, one of the highest in Europe. The Netherlands is reported to have the highest number of part-timers in Europe, followed by the UK, Sweden and Denmark.[1] The current trend in Sweden, however, is that the number of part-timers is on the decrease. It is current government policy to reduce the large number of involuntary, i.e. underemployed, part-timers.[2] The Swedish unemployment insurance scheme, as applied to the underemployed, has inherent defects particularly with regards to part-timers; in another context a Government Commission Report calls part-time work a 'women's trap'.[3] A huge number of part-timers is not necessarily a good omen. The EC Part-time Directive, whose basis is in part intended to encourage the growth of part-time employment, has received a cool reception in Sweden that is reflected in the Government Bill submitted to Parliament on 20 February 2002.[4]

All translations from the Swedish in this chapter are by the author, Ronnie Eklund.

[1] Eurostat, *Eurostat Yearbook 98/99* (Luxembourg: OOPEC, 1999), p. 136. The figures relate to 1997: Netherlands 38%, UK 24.9%, Sweden 24.5% and Denmark 22.3%. Other Member States are quite far behind.

[2] See, in particular, Government Yearly Budget Bill 2001/02:1 App. 13, pp. 21, 34–5, and App. 14, p. 29. The same concern is voiced in the Swedish National Action Plans of 1999 (p. 30), 2000 (p. 22) and 2001 (p. 22).

[3] SOU 1999:27. *DELTA. Utredningen om deltidsarbete, tillfälliga jobb och arbetslöshetsersättning* ('The Investigation into Part-time Work, Temporary Jobs and Unemployment Benefits'), p. 283.

[4] Government Bill 2001/02: 97. *Lag om förbud mot diskriminering av deltidsarbetande arbetstagare och arbetstagare med tidsbegränsad anställning, m.m.* ('Prohibition of Discrimination against Part-time workers and Workers with Fixed-Term Employment Act').

2   Why did part-time work reach high levels?

2.1   Tax reform

The impetus for part-time employment in Sweden was the tax reform of 1970, when it was declared that, if both were employed, husband and wife were to be taxed separately, i.e. independently of the other spouse's income. A discussion related to the independence of women had started in the 1960s, the tenor of this debate being that women should have jobs with an income and their own identity outside the home, which would give them a better pension. The Sweden of the 1960s was also characterised by a shortage of manpower. It was in addition a time marked by the expansion of the public sector, which absorbed many of the women seeking part-time work.[5] The 1970 reform produced a major increase in the number of women on the Swedish labour market, often employed on a part-time basis. At the same time, a deliberate debate with respect to gender equality was launched. It is fair to say that the main motive of this campaign was the *emancipation* of women, in the sense that they were given a chance to earn their own living and thus become less dependent upon their husbands. Experience shows, however, that it has been more difficult to emancipate the men, i.e. to make them participate in the performance of household duties. Forcing people to do something forms no part of the Swedish liberal heritage.[6]

2.2   Abolition of the closing hours laws

In 1972, there occurred an event of major importance: the rather strict Swedish closing hours laws relating to the retail trade were finally abolished. The issue had been regulated by statute since 1909 in an often detailed way, requiring exceptions in specific cases involving either state or local government authorities. After several amendments to the closing hours laws, the final and major step was taken with the 1966 Government Bill on closing hours.[7] Marking the end of an era, it proposed the abolition

---

[5] Comments from SOU 1999:27 (n. 3 above), at pp. 124–6.

[6] A Southeast Asian experience is that successful women do not argue with their husbands about who will do the washing-up after a hard day at work; a successful woman is backed up by domestic help, which is a major contribution to their professional success; see an account by the Australian journalist L. Williams, *Wives, Mistresses and Matriarchs. Asian Women Today* (London: Weidenfeld & Nicholson, 1998), p. 130.

[7] Government Bill 1966:144 with respect to closing hours in the retail trade.

of the former regulations at the end of 1971. The then Minister for Home Affairs held first and foremost that consumer interest dictated the abolition of the closing hours laws; also, involvement of local and other agencies in setting the exceptions to the rather strict regulations was cumbersome and could easily be dispensed with. The Minister also hinted, however, that the abolition might imply that an increase in part-time employment could be achieved, which would be regarded as a desirable development. In its comments on the pending legislation, the National Labour Market Board had held that the reform was to be welcomed, since it opened up more opportunities for women to find part-time employment. This is something beneficial to both employers and employees, it was said.[8] However, the trade unions that represented retail trade employees were sceptical, basically because the union organisation rate among these employees was low. A great number of small shop-owners were not bound by a collective agreement (CA); their organisation rate was also low. Therefore, the trade unions feared that many employers would not honour the Sector CA's rules on compensation for unsocial working hours. The Minister discounted these fears and argued that current developments in the retail trade showed unequivocally that the sector was undergoing a structural reorganisation that meant that even larger establishments were being formed, and there CAs usually secured the terms and conditions of employment.[9]

Accordingly, since 1972 the retail trade had had the option of setting its own closing hours. This meant that if proprietors found a market for their goods during unsocial hours, they were free to have the shop open and employ anybody.

2.3   Past developments in figures

To start with, it must be said that in Sweden the frequency of part-time work is not exclusively a 1970s phenomenon. Part-time employees were registered in the statistics on a more comprehensive basis for the first

---

[8] Ibid., p. 43.

[9] Ibid., pp. 47–8. A more comprehensive account of the tug-of-war relating to the closing hours laws in the 1950s and 1960s is given in a recently published doctoral thesis by an economic historian, C. Gråbacke, *Möten med marknaden. Tre svenska fackförbunds agerande under perioden 1945–1970* ('Meetings with the Market. The Actions taken by Three Swedish Trade Unions during the Period 1945–1970') (Ph.D. thesis, University of Gothenburg, 2002), pp. 279–304. The resistance from the trade unions in question ultimately concerned opening hours on Sundays.

time in 1963.[10] At that time there were 456,000 women in part-time employment (women aged 16–74); in 1970 there were 594,000 women in a similar situation, which is a significant increase of 30 per cent in only five years. During the same period the number of women employed full-time increased by only 3 per cent, i.e. 27,000 (from 898,000 to 925,000).[11]

The first comprehensive study on part-timers' employment conditions was made in 1976.[12] In 1974 the Swedish labour force was composed of 3,165,000 full-time employees and 657,000 part-time employees.[13] Of those in part-time employment, 226,000 had a working week of 1–19 hours ('short part-time'), while 431,000 had a working week of 20–34 hours ('long part-time').[14] Some 91 per cent of all part-time employees were women (601,000). At the same time 943,000 women were reported as working full-time.

Breaking down the statistics will highlight two features of the Swedish labour market.[15] The first aspect has to do with the *activity rate* among women, i.e. the proportion of women in the active labour force out of all the women in different age brackets, as compared with men (Table 9.1). The statistics show clearly that the proportion of women in the total labour force is lower in all age brackets as compared with men, and far lower after the age of 24. The activity rate among women has been gradually

---

[10] In another report, *Utredning angående industriarbetande kvinnors deltidsarbete. Arbetsmarknadens kvinnonämnd* (1957; report from the Labour Market Committee for Women), p. 13, some figures were given applying to industry during the years 1948–52. Only slightly more than 1.5% of the women employed in industry were reported to be part-timers then; in nominal numbers they accounted for no more than 6,000 persons. At that time, employers favoured women part-timers for strictly labour market reasons, i.e. because there was a growing shortage of manpower. Part-time employment was also found among employees who were to some extent disabled or who were older. The committee recommended that the social partners should consider establishing more comprehensive CAs relating to part-time employment; no such CA ever saw the light of day.

[11] M. Pettersson, *Deltidsarbetet i Sverige. Deltidsökningens orsaker. Deltidsanställdas levnadsförhållanden* ('Part-time Work in Sweden. The Causes of the Increase in Part-time Work. The Family Situation for Part-time Employees') (Arbetslivscentrum report No. 23, Stockholm, 1981), p. 52.

[12] SOU 1976:6. *Deltidsanställdas villkor. En utredning från delegationen för jämställdhet mellan män och kvinnor*, and SOU 1976:7. *Deltidsarbete 1974. En undersökning av statistiska centralbyrån.*

[13] SOU 1976:7 (n. 12 above), at pp. 20–1.

[14] The concepts of 'short part-time' (1–19 hours per week) and 'long part-time' (20–34 hours per week) are used in the official statistics. It is quite unclear why the upper limit for part-time work had been set at 34 hours per week; see SOU 1976:6 (n. 12 above), p. 13, and SOU 1999:27 (n. 3 above), pp. 116, 334.

[15] SOU 1976:7 (n. 12 above), pp. 7–11.

Table 9.1 *Activity rates for men and women (%; taken from SOU 1976:7)*

Age	16–19	20–4	25–34	35–44	45–54	55–64
Activity rates of women	48	69	67	73	71	46
Activity rates of men	54	79	93	95	93	80

Table 9.2 *Percentage of men and women in full-time employment (taken from SOU 1976:7)*

Age	16–19	20–4	25–34	35–44	45–54	55–64
Women in full-time employment	81	81	59	50	51	48
Men in full-time employment	88	96	98	99	99	98
Women in part-time employment	19	19	41	50	49	52
Men in part-time employment	12	4	2	1	1	2

increasing, however. In 1970, 52.8 per cent of all women aged 16–74 were found in the active labour force; in 1974 the equivalent figure was 57.1 per cent. The figure for men in 1970 was 80.6 per cent; in 1974 it was 79.7 per cent.[16]

The second aspect will highlight the *percentage of full-time/part-time employment* among women, as compared with men (Table 9.2). Actually, the figures speak for themselves. A high percentage of working women are part-timers throughout the entire active working life, i.e. from the age of 24 until they retire. Men work full-time practically from the age of 20 until retirement.

Up to 1980 the number of women in part-time employment increased dramatically, from 570,000 (1970) to 873,000 (1980). This is an increase of 53 per cent over the period of ten years, as against a rather moderate increase in the number of women employed full-time during the same period (from 917,000 to 1,016,000). In 1980 some 73 per cent of all women aged 16–64 years were part of the active labour force.[17] Thus, previously non-employed women now comprised the major proportion of women in part-time employment.[18]

---

[16] Ibid., p. 25.   [17] Pettersson, *Deltidsarbetet i Sverige* (n. 11 above), p. 55.
[18] Ibid., pp. 58–9.

In 1989 another assessment of part-time work in Sweden was made.[19] In 1988, 1,073,000 persons (male and female) worked part-time, while 3,325,000 worked full-time. It was now reported that the number of women in the Swedish labour market in 1988 constituted 48 per cent of the entire labour force. As a comparison, in 1970 the same figure was 40 per cent. It is also interesting to note that women account for almost the whole increase in the entire labour force between those years. Again, the primary explanation is the tax reform of 1970, which made it more profitable for women to enter the labour market.

The number of employees working part-time for 20–34 hours per week ('long part-time') showed a gradual increase. In 1988 they numbered some 900,000, whereas those working 'short part-time' accounted for some 170,000 persons. Of all part-time employees 85 per cent were women. Only 7 per cent of all men worked part-time. Men who worked part-time did so because of studies (in the case of younger men) or because they were close to retirement age. On the other hand, women part-timers were more or less evenly spread over all age brackets, with the exception of women aged 20–4, where full-time employment dominated.

To sum up, the picture presented seems to support the conclusion that for women part-time work was a means of entering the labour market. If in the 1970s women made a move from non-employment to part-time employment, in the 1980s a gradual shift to full-time employment occurred. Another significant feature of the 1980s is the increase in the so-called 'long part-time' group.

3   Present statistics on part-time work in Sweden

I have chosen the year 1999 as the basis for the most recent statistics on part-time work.[20] In 1999 the total labour force was composed of 4,308,400 persons (aged 16–64), of whom 2,254,500 were men and 2,053,900 were women. Of this total 240,600 persons were reported as unemployed. Accordingly, 4,067,900 were employed. However, 611,400 of these workers were absent from work for legitimate reasons (such as illness, vacation, childcare). Thus, only 3,456,600 were found in the active

---

[19] Data in the following is taken from SOU 1989:53. *Arbetstid och välfärd*, pp. 56–7, 61–3.
[20] The Swedish Bureau of Statistics has conducted both annual and monthly surveys on the use of manpower for quite some time. The figures given here are taken from Arbetskraftsundersökningen (AKU, The Swedish Labour Force Survey). Arsmedeltal ['Averages'] 1999, Tables 1A, 2A, 3A, 3B, 3D, 4, 7, 15A.

labour force. The activity rate for the whole population aged 16–64 was 77.2 per cent (male rate: 79.5 per cent; female rate: 74.8 per cent).

How many were employed full-time and part-time in 1999?

Of the entire labour force, 78 per cent (3,168,000 persons) had full-time employment, while 22 per cent (896,000) were employed part-time, which, in the light of previous figures, is quite a significant decrease in the number working part-time. It has been assessed that this is a trend that will continue during the next five to ten years.[21]

Only 9.3 per cent of all men in the active labour force worked part-time. The corresponding figure for women is different: 36 per cent of all women in the active labour force worked part-time, which is a far lower figure than found during the previous years. In 1989, for example, women working part-time amounted to just on 45 per cent. In 1999, it is reported that 83 per cent of the women worked 20–34 hours per week while only 17 per cent worked 1–19 hours. The increase of so-called 'long part-time' work among women, compared with past statistics, therefore seems to be a stable trend.

Most types of part-time employment for women are found in the areas of healthcare and social work, which has been the case previously as well; 46 per cent of all women active in these branches work part-time. If, however, the statistics are broken down to more specialised areas, the highest rate of part-time work among women is found in department stores with a broad range of goods (66 per cent work part-time), as well as in social work and home care for elderly people (62 per cent of the women work part-time). Women tend to work part-time in areas where they dominate in the labour force.[22] However, very few women working part-time are found in professions which require a high level of competence or some university or college education,[23] such as: management work in large and

---

[21] SOU 1999:27 (n. 3 above), p. 227.

[22] In a report from the EC–S. McRae, *Part-Time Work in the European Union. The Gender Dimension* (Luxembourg: European Foundation for the Improvement of Living and Working Conditions, 1995), p. 25 – it is claimed: 'Women who work part-time tend to work in establishments with many women workers, rather than in ones where women are poorly represented: which is to say that establishments with a large number of women employees are also likely to use part-time arrangements.'

[23] In quite another context I have found that in the Philippines the more qualified women on the labour market, i.e. those having at least a high-school education or a college degree, give birth to fewer children. In a country like the Philippines, where the birth rate is very high, the most promising measure to keep it low is to encourage women to enter higher education, which seems to be a better instrument than any of the other family planning programmes practised in that country (source: materials on gender law in the Philippines not yet published by the author).

medium-sized enterprises and public agencies (only 5 per cent of these women work part-time), among psychologists and social welfare secretaries (9 per cent), among physical therapists and dental hygienists (6 per cent) and among electrical installation workers and military officers (both professions 0 per cent).

One may ask: how many employees want to work more than they actually do? The answer may indicate that many part-timers are trapped between part-time employment and unemployment.

The total number of persons who want to work more than they actually do is estimated at 310,500, which is just about one-third of all part-time employees (896,000) in Sweden in 1999. A fairly large number are accordingly relegated to under-employment for labour market reasons; they cannot obtain more working hours. It is basically women who want to work more: 200,600 women work less than they would like to for labour market reasons, while the same figure for men is 76,900. Some 10 per cent (28,700) work less for personal reasons. Personal reasons for part-time work relate, *inter alia*, to: childcare, studies, health reasons, leisure time, etc. The number of men who work less than they would like to for personal reasons is almost negligible (8,800).[24]

However, one should not forget that, overall, well over half a million Swedish part-time employees are content with their part-time work.[25] In late 2001, a UK report brought up another facet of part-time work: mothers who work part-time are more likely to stay married.[26] Professor Susan McRae reported that only 8 per cent of mothers who had continued in part-time work after having babies had separated or divorced from their husbands. In contrast, 16 per cent of mothers who had stayed at home all the time looking after the house and the family were separated or divorced, while 27 per cent of mothers working full-time saw their marriages collapse. Professor McRae noted: 'Mothers who keep going to the workplace may become more emotionally balanced, by meeting colleagues and by being stimulated by the challenges of work. The extra income to help the family is also obviously a major factor in keeping a

---

[24] The above-stated figures for women indicate strongly that a shift in preferences among women has occurred since the time of the previous studies; see in particular, Pettersson, *Deltidsarbetet i Sverige* (n. 11 above), pp. 113–18, where a dominant theme was that women part-timers were more satisfied with their part-time work and where labour market reasons (difficulty in getting a job, partial closures, maintenance or repair work, etc.) accounted for only a very small number of women who worked part-time.

[25] See SOU 1999:27 (n. 3 above), p. 129.

[26] A. Lee, 'Mums who Work Part-time Likely to Stay Married', *Straits Times*, 11 December 2001.

marriage successful.' I have no opinion as to whether these findings apply to other countries as well.

4   Ideologies and interests at stake with respect to part-time work

Since 1976 part-time work has been the subject of several investigations in Sweden. The main aim of the studies has been to determine the advantages and disadvantages connected with part-time work, especially regarding women.

A crucial issue concerns the reasons why part-time work is considerably more frequent in some sectors of the labour market than in others.[27] This is a question of the *economics of part-time work*. To start with, it is clear that there is no economic motive on the part of employers to favour part-time work, since employers in Sweden pay flat-rate social charges for their employees irrespective of the number of hours they work per week.[28] The fact that some part-time employees are not entitled to social benefits, since they work too few hours per week, is another matter.

Part-time work is also more frequent in the service sector than in manufacturing industry. The highest rate of part-time employment is found in the retail trade, but high rates of part-time employment are also found in the hotel and restaurant business, in education, healthcare and social work – in all of which close to 50 per cent of the labour force is employed part-time. These sectors are characterised by great variations in *consumer demand*, on both a daily and a weekly basis.

On the other hand, *high capital costs* per employee signal a low rate of part-time work. Such sectors include, for example, electricity, gas and waterworks, transport, postal and telecommunication services, agriculture, mining, iron and metal works, and the engineering and chemical industries. Less than 10 per cent of the labour force in these sectors is employed part-time. Hence, part-time work is not a first choice for employers when the *learning process* connected with the job is demanding, or when the work is *team-related*, requiring supervision and co-ordination between employees as well as between employees and their supervisors. In such cases the employer wants to keep as few employees as possible for as many hours as possible at the workplace. Too many people doing

---

[27] For what follows, see Pettersson, *Deltidsarbetet i Sverige* (n. 11 above), pp. 124–34.
[28] See M. Tam, *Part-Time Employment: a Bridge or a Trap?* (Aldershot: Avebury, 1997), pp. 112–18, who reports that UK employers seem to take advantage of part-timers, giving them a lower wage and fewer fringe benefits as compared with full-time employees.

the same work in a co-ordinated way increases the indirect costs, which is why *transaction costs* come into the picture.[29] It is a notorious fact that employers seek to reduce transaction costs by all means possible. As a result, women, who also have other commitments, are not wanted in these segments of the labour market.[30]

It is a sad fact that part-time employment is frequent in those segments of the labour market in which job-seekers are less qualified, the wages are low and the demand for services varies. Women part-timers usually have only compulsory-school education; this has a negative effect on the level of sick pay, parental allowance and pension benefits.[31] Employers have taken advantage of this situation: it has given them an opportunity to adjust the number of staff to the demand for services by their clients and customers. Hence, women part-timers are a flexible and cheaper source of labour.[32]

A vexing problem is that many women also tend to stay in part-time employment against their will.[33] Part-time work may be considered a 'women's trap',[34] the reason being that for many badly paid women part-timers there is in Sweden at the moment no economic disadvantage in working part-time. The reason is as follows. In the Swedish unemployment scheme, part-time employees are handsomely compensated. The partially unemployed receive benefits according to a special formula, containing certain restrictions that were introduced in 1995.[35] The restrictions state that a person who performs part-time work on a *continuous basis* within the range of her/his regular employment can no longer claim partial unemployment benefit, if that same person has already exhausted the benefit entitlement in the past, i.e., as a rule, during the

---

[29] The rich literature on the importance of transaction costs in modern law and economics dates from the seminal article by 1991 Nobel laureate R. H. Coase, 'The Nature of the Firm' 1937 *Economica* pp. 386–405.

[30] In a recent study, SOU 1998:6. *Ty makten är din . . . Myten om det rationella arbetslivet och det jämställda Sverige* ('The Power is Yours . . . The Myth of Rational Work Life and Equality in Sweden'), pp. 76–85, it is even argued that it was never intended that women should compete with men when they entered the labour market in the 1970s in large numbers; the women were supposed to take up employment created by the public sector, or in those segments of the labour market which already contained typically 'female' jobs found, for example, in the local government sectors, such as healthcare and social work.

[31] Ibid., p. 85.   [32] SOU 1999:27 (n. 3 above), p. 127.

[33] Similar conclusions are found in Tam, *Part-Time Employment* (n. 28 above), p. 110. Female part-timers are more often found in dead-end jobs where promotions do not materialise.

[34] See also Tam, ibid., p. 243, who talks about a 'trap' for women working part-time.

[35] See SFS (*Swedish Official Gazette*) 1995: 997.

preceding 300 days (the maximum compensation period in the context of unemployment according to the Unemployment Insurance Act (*Lag om arbetslöshetsförsäkring*) 1997). This does not apply, however, to persons who have only *temporary* part-time employment. An example will illustrate how the scheme works. If a part-timer works 80 per cent of full-time, unemployment benefits will be due for one day each week. Since only 52 days are used up in a year, the benefits may be due for as long a period as almost six years (52 × 6 = 310 days), provided the employee continues to work part-time on a continuous basis. This is hardly a scheme that will give part-timers an incentive to take action in order to increase the amount of their working time. The scheme is counterproductive from a gender equality point of view.

The trap gives rise to a 'locking-in effect'. In the past, both employment offices and employers seemed to treat the underemployed group of employees as a secondary source of labour. Experience has also indicated that it is difficult to offer education or training to female employees in part-time employment, taking into consideration their other commitments. Their employers therefore seldom offer such employees opportunities to participate in competence/skills programmes, and they are less inclined to take another job or change employers.[36] The Swedish Government is obviously deeply concerned about this situation applying to partially unemployed individuals.[37] The present activities on the part of the Government and the responsible authorities are intended instead to enhance the number of full-time employed.[38]

5 Part-time work as defined

First of all, no legal definition can be found relating to part-time employment.[39] However, from the practical point of view, part-time employment means that an employee works fewer than the full-time hours as defined by law or the pertinent CA. Secondly, one can say that, overall, part-time employees enjoy the same rights as full-time employees, unless otherwise stated. The wages are, for example, usually proportional to the working time of a part-time employee, as compared with what a full-time employee receives. From this point of view, a part-time employee has probably never

---

[36] See SOU 1999:27 (n. 3 above), p. 283.
[37] See Government Yearly Budget Bill 2000/01:1, App. 13, pp. 31–2.
[38] Ministry of Industry press release 2002-02-14.
[39] This will change with the implementation of the EC Part-time Directive; see Government Bill 2001/02:97 (n. 4 above).

been treated as an inferior employee category.[40] However, a slightly different picture emerges when other benefits are taken into consideration, such as pension benefits.[41]

A part-time employee may be a person working on a daily basis for fewer total hours per week (horizontal part-time) or a person working, for example, only three days in a five-day week (vertical part-time). It is up to the employer and the employee to decide upon the scheduling of working hours. If no agreement can be reached, it is ultimately the employer who decides the employee's working time when initiating the contract of employment. The employer has no right to amend unilaterally the agreed number of hours while the contract is in force; this is something that can be done only with the consent of the respective employee.[42]

At present, it is also noteworthy that under Swedish labour law no employee can demand to be shifted from full-time to part-time employment. It is up to the parties concerned to decide jointly upon such an amendment of the contract. Freedom of contract prevails. Freedom of contract has implied that employers and employees have freedom to decide upon the amount of work to be performed, and they are also free then to agree jointly to modify that amount. Consequently, the contract of employment is treated essentially like any other contract of law that can be modified only with the consent of the other party. The State has left it to the parties concerned to conclude a contract that is best suited to them. Neither have there been bans on part-time work in the past. Nor has the Government contemplated adopting a labour policy that would encourage men or women to enter the labour market in terms of part-time employment, i.e. as an instrument for increasing employment, or making people share a scarce resource – for example, to encourage full-time employees to share their jobs with other persons. Job-sharing is a non-issue in Sweden.[43]

---

[40] See, e.g., as early a source as SOU 1946:71. *Deltidsarbete i allmän tjänst* ('Part-time Work in the Public Service') and the report from The Labour Market Committee for Women (1957; n. 10 above).

[41] See section 7.1 below.

[42] See, for example, Labour Court judgment AD 1984 No. 28 where the employer had unilaterally amended the actual working time for personnel working nights from 100% to 93%. This was held to be an unlawful termination of full-time employment in violation of the Employment Protection Act (*Lag om anställningsskydd*) 1982 and the employees were awarded general damages.

[43] Most economists, trade unions, employers and political parties in Sweden are strongly opposed to job-sharing: see A. Björklund, 'Going Different Ways: Labour Market Policy in Denmark and Sweden', in G. Esping-Andersen and M. Regini (eds.), *Why Deregulate Labour Markets?* (Oxford: Oxford University Press, 2000), pp. 148–70 at p. 154.

However, it must be mentioned that part-time work in the *civil service sector* was once legally regulated. After a survey carried out in 1946,[44] regulations were issued in the form of a Royal Circular addressed to the State agencies.[45] The aim of the Circular was to encourage them to consider more seriously whether part-time employment should be encouraged, especially in order to make it easier for women to combine work with their traditional role of mother during the period when they were also taking care of a child. Other Circulars were subsequently introduced,[46] and then a Part-time Regulation was issued in 1980.[47] It was repealed in 1991. The 1991 Regulation on Leave of Absence applicable to the central government sector states no more than that, when assessing an application for leave of absence, a State agency may take into special consideration the employee's family situation.[48] Part of this development should also be viewed through another lens. Since 1965 the State sector has been undergoing a paradigmatic shift in terms of the sources of labour law applying to civil servants. In today's Sweden, most aspects of the employment relationship applying to civil servants are subject to CA provisions. Their contract of employment is thus no longer deemed to be an offshoot of an act of State authority; it is equal to a private law contract of employment.[49]

Another aspect of part-time work *in fact* is that a plethora of options exists for a full-time employee in Sweden to take a *leave of absence* for various reasons.[50] In such cases, the legal boundaries of the individual contract of employment will not be affected or modified. Accordingly, for a period of varying duration, such an employee may in fact work fewer hours than is provided for by law or CA. This partial leave of absence may affect one working day, or continue for years. However, this is not the same as part-time employment *proper*. In cases of leave of absence the employee is entitled by law to reduce her/his full-time employment to less

---

[44] SOU 1946:71 (n. 40 above). Very few part-timers were reported as working in the central government sector at that time – only some 600 out of the total number of 176,000 government employees. It was unclear how many part-timers were employed in the local government sector. In the private sector it was estimated that only about 700 employees were part-timers.

[45] SFS 1947:542. Similar provisions were also laid down in the additional regulations applying to the general regulations related to civil servants in 1948 (SFS 1948:564 relating to SFS 1948:436).

[46] SFS 1960:275 and SFS 1970:384.   [47] SFS 1980:50.   [48] SFS 1991:1747, s. 10.

[49] See, in brief, R. Eklund, 'Deregulation of Labour Law – the Swedish Case' (1998–9) 10 *Juridisk Tidskrift* 531–51, pp. 538–9.

[50] It is not appropriate here to state all these cases. Both statutes and CAs provide for such absence.

than 100 per cent of the regular working time when, say, making use of her/his right to parental or study leave.[51] A parent is, for example, entitled to reduce working time down to ¾, ½ or ¼ of the normal working time until the youngest child is eight years of age.[52] This is by definition not part-time employment proper, since the employee is always entitled by law to resume work on a full-time basis after having given the employer due notice.

6 Current Swedish legislation on part-time work

So far, only two provisions related to part-time work have been implemented in Swedish labour law. The first refers to the option to increase the amount of part-time work (s. 25a of the Employment Protection Act 1982), and the second refers to abuses of part-time work with respect to the contractually agreed working time (s. 10 of the Working Hours Act 1982).

6.1   Employment Protection Act (Lag om anställningsskydd)

It all started with a Government Commission report from 1993.[53] The issue was stated as follows. The question was raised as to whether an employer needing to employ new manpower should first be required to ask his or her part-timers whether they wanted to increase their working time. The report concluded that, since there were already national CAs in force containing clauses concerning this issue, there was no actual need for general legislation. Employers – by means of, for example, the internal posting-up of new job opportunities at the workplace, effectively giving priority to persons already employed there part-time – were also implementing the existing clauses.

However, the same issue surfaced a few years later in the form of a Government Bill submitted to Parliament, resulting in an amendment of the Employment Protection Act.[54] Before it was submitted, the state

---

[51] The distinction between part-time proper and leave of absence was often blurred in the past: see SOU 1946:71, cited above in n. 40, p. 71. It is likewise the case in SFS 1980:50, s. 4 ('An employee may be offered part-time work by means of partial leave of absence or by means of part-time employment'). To my surprise the same confusion has returned in the context of the Swedish implementation of the Part-time Directive: see below, section 8.5.5.

[52] *Föräldraledighetslag* ('Parental Leave Act', SFS 1995:584), s. 3.

[53] SOU 1993:32. *Ny anställningsskyddslag*, pp. 531–5.

[54] Government Bill 1996/97:16, *En arbetsrätt för ökad tillväxt*.

of affairs in the labour law field was in a state of flux, since during the
1990s Sweden had had both non-socialist and socialist governments. One
proposal succeeded another. The suggestions did not contribute to stability or foreseeability in working life. After fruitless attempts to involve
the social partners in establishing a long-lasting framework, the socialist
Government, supported by the Centre Party, decided in 1996 to submit
a Bill on a moderate reform of the Employment Protection Act.[55] The
reform package included a new provision in the Act (s. 25a), with effect
as of 1 January 1997, giving a right of priority to part-time employees
with regard to an increase in individual working time. The new section
provides as follows:

> A part-time employee who has notified the employer of her or his wish
> to increase her or his working time, not exceeding full-time, has, in spite
> of what is provided for in s. 25, a right of priority to such employment. A
> condition for the right of priority to be applicable is that the employer's need
> for manpower shall be satisfied by means of the increase in the part-time
> employee's working time and that the part-time employee has qualifications
> that are adequate for the work in question.
>
> If the employer has several business units, the right of priority applies
> to the unit in which the employee is employed on a part-time basis. The
> right of priority does not apply in relation to a person who has the right to
> be transferred in accordance with s. 7, second paragraph.
>
> An employee cannot lay claim to her or his right of priority if the
> employment is in violation of s. 5, first paragraph, or s. 5a.[56]
>
> Furthermore, as a result of the amendment it is provided that, if several
> part-time employees have duly notified the employer of their interest in
> increasing their working time, a choice among the competing employees
> must be made. This should be made on the basis of seniority, with the
> person having the longest period of service being given priority (s. 26 of
> the Act).[57]

[55] The events are explained in an article of mine: Eklund, 'Deregulation' (n. 49 above),
pp. 535–8.

[56] An explanatory note relating to the references made in s. 25a of the Act is necessary.
Section 25 gives any employee who has been made redundant a preferential right, valid for
a certain period of time after the former employment ceased to have effect, to be taken back
into employment. Section 7, second paragraph, provides that the employer is required to
transfer the employee who is about to be dismissed, if it is reasonable. Sections 5 and 5a
contain restrictions on the use of fixed-term employment contracts.

[57] One of the most pervasive modern innovations in job security law is the seniority principle,
which means 'last in–first out' in redundancies. The seniority principle is, however, not
absolute. If the employee is transferred to other work tasks, s/he must have adequate
qualifications for the job, according to s. 22 of the Employment Protection Act. The

The ideological tenet inherent in s. 25a is that as a rule it supports the view that full-time employment is to be preferred; part-time employment is only a secondary solution, and even then only when there are good reasons for it, for example when the operational needs of the company's activities are such as to require it, or when the employee wishes it.[58] The provisions of s. 25a originated partly from the *gender background*. Many women employees would like increased working time in order to be able to support themselves economically. The amendment has also been placed in the context of the Swedish unemployment insurance scheme, as applied to *partially unemployed persons*. Though provisions of this kind have been in force since 1956, they have undergone changes several times. The present provisions apply to part-time workers who are unemployed for only part of the working week.[59] This group of people is not a small one, and consists mostly of women. In 1997 the partially unemployed accounted for some 17 per cent of all job-seekers registered with employment offices.[60] Against this background s. 25a of the Act may therefore be seen as a forceful weapon to increase the working time of part-time employees.[61] It is an irony of fate, however, that another Commission report from 1999 concludes that s. 25a is virtually unknown among the actors in the Swedish labour market.[62]

6.2 *Working Hours Act* (Arbetstidslag)

The second provision in Swedish labour-law with respect to part-time work is found in the Working Hours Act 1982. It relates to a part-time employee who is ordered to work more hours than previously agreed in the individual contract of employment. There is a limit on such extra work: a maximum of 200 additional hours per calendar year, provided

---

provision also applies to a fixed-term contract of employment, see Labour Court judgment AD 2000 No. 51.

[58] Government Bill 1996/97:16 (n. 54 above), p. 45.

[59] Section 40 of the Unemployment Insurance Act (*Lag om arbetslöshetsföräkring*) 1997 and s. 8 of the Unemployment Insurance Regulations (*Förordning om arbetslöshetsförsäkring*) 1997.

[60] SOU 1999:27 (n. 3 above), p. 261.

[61] The Swedish scheme is a far cry from the schemes introduced in Germany and the Netherlands, where the regulations go far beyond the absolutes of the Part-Time Directive: see A. Jacobs and M. Schmidt, 'The Right to Part-time Work. The Netherlands and Germany Compared' (2001) 17 *International Journal Of Comparative Labour Law and Industrial Relations*, pp. 371–84.

[62] SOU 1999:27 (n. 3 above), p. 301.

there exists a 'special need' for the work (s. 10 of the Act).[63] In such a case it may happen that the employer will require more work from the part-time employee on a regular basis, for reasons of convenience, the reason being that the employees are at hand and are also willing to perform more work than initially agreed. This may imply that what was once agreed as the stipulated working time is de facto set aside. The employer may then find himself to be in violation of the Swedish Employment Protection Act.

The Labour Court judgment AD 1984 No. 76 provides a pertinent illustration of this issue. In this case three dressmakers had contracts of employment stating that they had a weekly working time of either 25 or 18 hours. They had worked more hours than that on a regular basis for quite some time, but were then forced to go back to what the contracts provided. These employees filed a complaint, the essence of which was, among other things, that they were entitled to lay-off pay according to the Employment Protection Act since their working time had been reduced. The Labour Court held that uncertainty arose because the employer had made use of the employees to a much greater extent than provided for by the contract. The Court also found that this had been done on a regular basis. Furthermore, the employer had never made clear to the employees that the required additional work was of the kind set forth in s. 10 of the Working Hours Act and had hence evaded the provisions of the Employment Protection Act. Consequently, the employer in this specific case was found to have evaded the lay-off provisions of the Act and the employees were accordingly granted lay-off pay.

7   Collective agreements on part-time work

Rules relating to part-time work can be found in a few CAs. Often, a threshold number of working hours per week is laid down for the CA to be applicable. If the critical threshold number is exceeded, the CA applies. If, however, the threshold number is not attained the CA provides, in some instances, that the agreement will not apply. This issue is highly topical in the light of the EC Part-time Directive. It may imply a form of indirect discrimination against the employees who do not qualify to benefit from the scheme. Women are particularly vulnerable, since they predominate among part-time employees. A few highlights of the CAs as they stand at

---

[63] Employees cannot claim overtime pay for such work according to EC case-law: see Joined Cases C-399/92, C-409/92, C-43/93, C-50/93 and C-78/93 *Stadt Lengerich* v. *Angelika Helmig and others* [1994] ECR I-5727.

present may be pertinent at this point.[64] These CAs are found in both the public and private sectors of the Swedish labour market.

7.1 The local government sector

In the CA applying to local government at both municipality and provincial council level (called 'AB 01', General Conditions), s. 4(a) provides that permanently employed part-timers whose working time is less than 17 hours a week are dealt with in two ways. *First of all*, attempts should be made to increase the average working time to at least 17 hours per week, the reason being that various social benefits deriving from statutes and the collective agreement require a certain amount of working time in order to apply.[65] *Secondly*, s. 4(b) of the CA provides that, if the employer needs to employ new manpower, he should first determine whether any person already employed at the workplace who has notified the employer of her/his wish for increased working time can be offered such increased working time. However, this does not apply to persons whose part-time employment is connected with receiving a partial pension or early retirement. It is worth mentioning that this offer by local government employers had been in force long before a similar provision was stipulated in s. 25a of the Employment Protection Act in 1996 (see section 6.1 above).

Furthermore, the local government CA relating to additional pension benefits (PA-KL 85 and PFA 98)[66] applies only to employees whose

---

[64] A more comprehensive, but not exhaustive, survey is given in the Ministry of Industry report, Ds 2001:6. *Genomförande av deltids-och visstidsdirektiven*, pp. 36–40.

[65] Among such statutory benefits is, for example, the unemployment benefit under the Unemployment Insurance Act (s. 12), which sets the minimum working time required for the benefit to apply at 70 hours of work per month, or close to 17 hours of work per week during a six-month period falling within a framework period of 12 months. The unemployed person must moreover be prepared to work at least 17 hours per week to be able to claim the unemployment benefit according to s. 9 of the Act. The same applies with respect to becoming a member of an unemployment fund (Unemployment Funds Act (*Lag om arbetslöshetskassor*) 1997, s. 34). Thresholds of these kinds are left unaffected by the Part-time Directive.

[66] PA-KL 85 stands for 'Pensionsavtal för arbetstagare hos kommuner och landsting' ('Collective agreement on pensions for Swedish local government employees'). PFA 98 stands for 'Överenskommelse om pensions- och försäkringsavtal' ('CA on pension and insurance agreements'). It is confusing that there are two pension agreements applying to local government employees, but this is most easily explained by the fact that the two CAs reflect two different national pension systems in Sweden, whereby the old one applies to pension rights accrued under the earlier scheme, while the new one applies to future pension rights. The national pension system was changed in 1998.

employment lasts for at least three months and amounts to at least 40 per cent of a full-time post (s. 1 PA-KL 85, and s. 1, subs. 2 of PFA 98).

Similarly, a threshold of 40 per cent of a full-time post was applied in AB 98 s. 2, which meant that a great number of part-time local government employees were deprived of the benefits accorded by the same CA, such as, for example, supplementary compensation in the event of parental leave. However, the same provision was abolished in AB 01 with effect from 1 April 2001, so no 40 per cent threshold currently applies to part-timers, the reason being that the bargaining parties wanted to adjust their CA to the non-discrimination principle in the Part-time Directive.

7.2 The central government sector

The state sector's CA (called 'ALFA')[67] was designed similarly to AB 98 covering local government employment (see above). Accordingly, for the CA to apply fully with respect to employment conditions the employee had to work not less than 40 per cent of full-time, which meant a rather drastic weakening of the social benefits deriving from the CA itself, as compared with persons working more than the required minimum number of hours. However, in 2001 the social partners, recognising the need to abolish the 40 per cent threshold in the light of the Part-time Directive, amended the CA on this point and, since 1 April 2001, no threshold applies.[68]

A rather different example of a part-time regulation is found in the state sector agreement. A special provision applies to the *scheduling* of the actual working time for an employee *working* part-time.[69]

As a rule the CA assumes that part-time work is performed five days a week (horizontal part-time). Part-time work, however, can also be scheduled to be performed on only some of these days (vertical part-time). This is called 'concentrated part-time' in the CA.[70] Working 'concentrated part-time' is considered a privilege. It can be abused in the context of, for example, holidays. The stipulated vacation period could become longer

---

[67] ALFA stands for 'Allmänt löne- och förmånsavtal' ('General Agreement on Pay and Benefits').

[68] See 'Ramavtal om löner m.m. för arbetstagare hos staten' (RALS 2001) ('Framework Agreement on pay, etc., applying to state employees').

[69] A nice distinction is found here inasmuch as the CA includes in this respect employees 'working' part-time, as against 'part-time employees' proper. The inclusion of the word 'working' in the agreement is intentional.

[70] The essence of the provision goes back to a CA concluded as early as 1971, after an amendment of the Civil Service Act making it possible to conclude CAs related to the scheduling of working time: see Government Bill 1970:164.

than the equivalent period for those who are in full-time employment, which has not been regarded as proper application of the CA. Therefore, a corrective measure has been introduced stipulating that the actual working time of an employee working 'concentrated' part-time shall be deemed as if the work in question was performed five days a week. A special formula is designed for such cases. An example is appropriate. Assume that the 'concentrated part-time' employee works 20 hours per week but only on Mondays, Tuesdays and Wednesdays. The first step is to divide 20 by 5 (normal number of working days for a full-time employee) which equals 4, which is then multiplied by 3 (the number of days of the part-timer's actual working time) which equals 12. The difference between 20 and 12 is 8. The CA provides that the employee would have to work for 8 extra hours after the holidays. In such a case the employer must explicitly order the employee to do so within a short period of time. However, a common way of solving the calculation problem would be to let the vacation period also cover those days of the working week on which the part-time employee would not be working anyway. This way of calculating the vacation period does not rest on solid theoretical grounds, since it is not possible to order the employee to take vacation time when work did not have to be performed anyway.

Furthermore, central government employees, similarly to local government employees, did not accrue supplementary pension benefits under the pertinent CA concerning pensions if their employment constituted less than 40 per cent of full-time employment (PA-91, s. 2).[71] However, in December 2001 the same social partners entered into a new pension CA, providing for partial improvements for part-timers. This CA entered into force in 2003. To some extent the past threshold survives inasmuch as the qualification threshold is now set at 20 per cent of full-time; employees who do not work more than 20 per cent, as against those who do, may consequently not claim certain benefits laid down by the CA. Moreover, the CA does not apply at all to employees born in or before 1942, which means that the 40 per cent threshold will still apply to them. In another CA (called TGL-S) applying to the central government sector in the event of the employee's death,[72] similar thresholds are set up to exclude part-timers from the benefits.

---

[71] PA-91 stands for 'Pensionsplan för arbetstagare hos staten m.fl.' ('Pension plan for central government employees').

[72] TGL-S stands for 'Avtal om statens tjänstegrupplivförsäkring' ('Agreement on state employee collective insurance scheme').

7.3   The private sector

In the private sector, the Confederation of Swedish Employers (SAF) and
the Swedish Trade Union Confederation (LO) entered into a joint agreement on part-time work as early as 1980.[73] The essential stipulation of
the agreement is that the parties should take into consideration that there
are social benefits which do not apply to employees whose work does
not exceed 16 hours a week. The part-time employee should therefore
'be informed' of this fact 'whenever practicable and, if the employee so
wishes, the working time should be extended so as to make the social
benefits apply'. Part-timers should also be offered more working time if
there is a need to employ new manpower.

The leading pension agreement for white-collar workers in the private
sector (called ITP) applies, however, only to those employees who have a
regular working time of at least 8 hours a week.[74] With respect to the man-
ual workers organised in the LO there are no such threshold provisions
relating to supplementary pension benefits.

7.4   Summing-up

One is tempted to say that the problems concerning the pension regulations contained in the public sector's CAs, denying pension benefits to a
large number of employees working less than 40 per cent of a full-time
post, or close to it, are caught by the EC law on indirect discrimination
based upon gender. It is obvious that the Part-time Directive has promoted the social partners to take up negotiations in order to work out
solutions that are in compliance with the Directive, but no comprehensive solutions have yet seen the light of day, although some improvements
have been made. In view of this it is also interesting to conclude with the
fact that the former 40 per cent threshold contained in the state sector
CAs relating to general terms and conditions of employment has been
abolished as of 2001. The Swedish Labour Court has never handed down
a decision in which the various CA thresholds have been dealt with.[75]

---

[73] The same social partners made a similar recommendation on part-time work in 1974.

[74] ITP stands for 'Industrins och handelns tilläggspension för anställda' ('Supplementary
pension plan for white-collar workers in private industry and commerce'). The agreement
was amended in May 2002; the threshold was lowered from the previous figure of 16 hours
per week.

[75] See the British case, R. v. Secretary of State for Employment ex parte EOC [1994] IRLR 176.
The case concerned an unfair dismissal complaint and a claim for redundancy payment.
The employee worked less than 16 hours per week. The British statute provided that the

The Swedish Government long endorsed a CA-based solution for the implementation of the Part-time Directive.[76] In accordance with Art. 2 of the Directive, Sweden also notified the EC Commission of its intention to extend the date of implementation by another year. The Directive should accordingly have been implemented in Sweden no later than 20 January 2001. However, Sweden has delayed any action. In early 2001 a Ministry report was submitted, suggesting the implementation by statute of the non-discrimination principle with respect to both the Part-time and Fixed-term Directives,[77] which was followed by an invitation to interested parties to submit public comments. A Government Bill on the matter was finally submitted to Parliament on 20 February 2002.

8   The Government Bill on part-time work in the light of the Ministry of Industry report to implement the Part-time Directive

8.1   Introduction

The Ministry of Industry found in its report that some actions were needed in order to implement the Directive, since the social partners had not found solutions of their own to eradicate the potential discrimination ensuing from the various threshold provisions with respect to part-time work as laid down by the many CAs. It is a fact that major actors in the employer camp opted for a statute, or no statute at all, while most of the trade unions wanted to implement the Directive by means of CAs.

Both the Government Bill and the Ministry report signify a minimal approach. This is most obvious if account is taken of what it is suggested should be regulated by means of a new statute. It is held that only cl. 4(1) on non-discrimination, cl. 5(2) on refusal to transfer from part-time to full-time work or vice versa and cl. 6(5) on enforcement provisions of the Framework Agreement are mandatory upon the Member States. For

complainant needed to have worked 16 hours or more per week for two years, or five years if the employee worked between 8 and 16 hours per week. The question raised was whether the right to bring an unfair dismissal complaint as set out in the British statute is contrary to EC law because such a provision might indirectly discriminate against women. The House of Lords held that the redundancy pay provision with respect to the 16 hours per week threshold is incompatible with Art. 119 of the Treaty of Rome and EC Directive 75/117. The High Court also held that the 16 hour threshold with respect to compensation for unfair dismissal is incompatible with EC Directive 76/207.

[76] See a few articles in *Lag & Avtal* nos. 2, 9 and 10/1999; see, in particular, A. Ekström, who was State Secretary in the Ministry of Industry at the time: 'Segern måste förvaltas' (2000) 5 *Lag & Avtal* 7.

[77] Ds 2001:6 (n. 64 above).

the rest, it is argued, the Framework Agreement expresses only 'wishes and recommendations which the Member States and the social partners should strive to achieve'.[78] This is a significantly narrow approach. One of the tenets of the Part-time Directive, i.e. facilitating the development of part-time work, does not sit easily at a time when it is Swedish policy to fight involuntary part-time unemployment. The Government Bill is very clear on this point: 'The problem in Sweden is not that there are few part-time working employees. The preferred solution is not to stimulate more people to work part-time. On the contrary, the goal is to reduce involuntary part-time unemployment.'[79] Therefore, it is easy to conclude that the Part-time Directive is looked upon as a rather dubious instrument of legal intervention in Swedish working life. This is also something that was highlighted when Mona Sahlin, the responsible Minister for Labour, presented the Government Bill. She said: 'The goal of the Swedish Government is to make full-time work the main rule and part-time work an option. The new Law on part-time work must be looked upon in the context of other contributions to reduce involuntary underemployment. The idea is to find ways to reduce involuntary underemployment rather than encourage part-time work.'[80] What the Swedish Government actually did in the EC legislative process with respect to the Part-time Directive in an attempt to prevent this development is, however, written in the wind, i.e. it is impossible to know.[81]

8.2   The ILO Convention on Part-time Work

In this context it is also pertinent to bear in mind that ILO Convention No. 175 (1994) concerning part-time work, and the ensuing Recommendation No. 182, were never ratified by Sweden.[82] On the other hand, in the light

---

[78] Ibid., at p. 48.   [79] Government Bill 2001/02:97 (n. 4 above), p. 23.

[80] Ministry of Industry press release 2002-02-14.

[81] See R. Eklund, 'The Chewing-Gum Directive – Part-time Work in the European Community', in R. Eklund et al. (eds.), Festskrift till Hans Stark (Stockholm: Elander Gotab, 2001), pp. 59–78, where I probed for motives behind the Swedish stance with respect to the advent of the Directive. I found none.

[82] See Regeringens skrivelse ('The National Government's Report Series') 1995/96:158. The Government argued that Swedish CAs do not cover the entire labour market. Furthermore, the Government did not intend to assume ultimate responsibility 'to ensure that part-time workers do not, solely because they work part-time, receive a basic wage which, calculated proportionately . . . is lower than the basic wage of comparable full-time workers': cf. Art. 5 of the Convention. See, in concurring vein, Parliamentary Labour Committee Report 1996/97:AU03.

of the implementation of the EC Part-time Directive, the Government now proposes that the Convention be ratified, but there is no mention of Recommendation No. 182.[83] Although the Swedish Government is still of the view that wages should continue to be set by the social partners, the non-discrimination principle as laid down in cl. 4 of the Framework Agreement has paved the way for ratification of the Convention. It is a highly conspicuous move. Sweden, often the model of collective action, is again pressured to accept a more individualistic implementation of employees' rights as propounded by the EC regime, which has thus partly eradicated the autonomy of the social partners to design wage levels with respect to full-time or part-time employees.

8.3   The essence of the proposals to implement the Part-time Directive

The Ministry report and the Government Bill contain only a few provisions. The statute came into force on 1 July 2002.[84]

The core provision relates to the non-discrimination principle, as laid down in cl. 4 of the Framework Agreement. The Swedish solution encompasses all part-time employees. Furthermore, the transposition of the Part-time Directive into Swedish law is meant to follow the design of the other Swedish non-discrimination statutes.[85] With respect to implementation of the non-discrimination principle as applied to part-time workers, the dichotomy between direct and indirect discrimination, as developed in gender equality law, is preferred.[86] The dichotomy is not evident with respect to part-time employment.

The Ministry report gives great importance to a survey of the CAs in force that make a distinction between full-time and part-time employees, and in particular those provisions applying to different standards with respect to pensions and other major benefits.[87] It is concluded that the

---

[83] Government Bill 2001/02:97 (n. 4 above), pp. 56–8.

[84] *Swedish Official Gazette* 2002:293. The Swedish Parliament accepted the Government Bill. Nothing much was added in the Parliamentary Labour Committee Report, 2001/02:AU6.

[85] Government Bill 2001/02:97 (n. 4 above), pp. 33, 42; Ds 2001:6 (n. 64 above), p. 68.

[86] Cf. Ds 2001:6 (n. 64 above), p. 72: 'It is assumed that the non-discrimination principle in the Framework Agreement encompasses both direct and indirect discrimination.'

[87] Ibid., pp. 50–5. It is less well known to an international audience that in Sweden major employee benefits, apart from the social security provided by the State, are furnished by CAs, including severance pay or other contributions in redundancies, supplementary pensions, benefits in the event of the death of the employee and with respect to work accidents, etc. These benefits are administered through institutions set up jointly by the social partners in the Swedish labour market.

social partners have advocated different views as to whether the CAs in question are in accordance with EC law or not. The report notes: 'It is not possible to ascertain with certainty that there are always objective grounds with respect to CA-provisions making a distinction between full-time and part-time employees. This uncertainty is *per se* not satisfactory.'[88] Having considered whether Swedish law offers other means of relief to achieve a non-discriminatory standard, the Ministry report concludes that 'it is doubtful whether Swedish law can enforce the non-discrimination principle'.[89] It is, however, argued in the Government Bill that the situation is 'complicated'.[90] The Government takes the stand that the social partners will 'be given a special role in the implementation and application of the Framework Agreement'.[91] However, it concedes that 'it is not possible with certainty to preclude the possibility that discriminatory provisions may be found in CAs'.[92]

8.4 Public comments submitted by interested parties

The response of the parties concerned is diverse as regards the Ministry report. Some indicate that no legislation is needed at all, while others argue that a more detailed scheme is needed, and a third point of view is to question what practical impact the suggested statute will have.

The public comments are split with respect to the threshold provisions in many CAs concerning special benefits, in particular as applied to supplementary pensions. In quite a few CAs it is required that employees work more than 40 per cent of full-time to accrue pension benefits. Some of the parties argue that the thresholds are objective for various reasons, while others contest such a view. Quite a few of the parties concerned are also doubtful whether cl. 5(2) of the Framework Agreement is implemented in a correct manner. The Ministry report argued that cl. 5(2) is already covered by s. 7 of the Swedish Employment Protection Act, i.e. that it is not possible to dismiss an employee because s/he rejects a transfer from full-time to part-time employment, or vice versa.[93] The LO argues forcefully that a new provision, going far beyond that of s. 25a of the Employment Protection Act, is needed in order to combat involuntary

---

[88] Ibid., pp. 52–3.   [89] Ibid., p. 54.
[90] Government Bill 2001/02:97 (n. 4 above), at p. 27.
[91] With reference to the General Considerations of the Framework Agreement, point 8.
[92] Government Bill 2001/02:97 (n. 4 above), pp. 28–9.
[93] Ds 2001:6 (n. 64 above), pp. 30, 56.

part-time work,[94] maintaining that a new statute should include rules which oblige employers to organise work so as to eliminate involuntary part-time work.

The distinction made in the Ministry draft between direct and indirect discrimination is also questioned in a few comments, inasmuch as the Part-time Directive is not framed in that way. The TCO submits the view that the Ministry report is a token of a very defensive approach, holding that no political will with respect to the promotional aspects of the Part-time Directive is to be found in the report.

8.5   A closer look at the Ministry report and the Government Bill

A major discussion in the Swedish legislative history of the Part-time Directive relates to the distinction between direct and indirect discrimination as developed primarily in gender equality law. Accordingly, it is held with respect to *direct discrimination* that the employer may not treat a part-time employee unfavourably by applying or potentially applying less beneficial pay and employment conditions as compared with another employee who is in a similar situation but works full-time, unless the employer can show that the difference in treatment has no connection whatever with the fact that the employee is working part-time. Further, the ban does not apply if the application of the conditions concerned is justified on objective grounds.[95]

With respect to *indirect discrimination* it is held that the employer may not treat a part-time employee unfavourably by applying pay and employment conditions that, although they appear to be neutral, in practice will have the effect of treating part-time employees unfavourably. However, this does not apply if such application is justified and the measures are adequate and necessary to achieve the aim.

---

[94] The view propounded by the LO in May 2001 as a response to the Ministry report was only a precursor to a decision taken by the Social Democratic Party Congress in November 2001, where it was stated that 'full-time work is a right, and part-time work is an option'. In fact, the trade union representatives at the Social Democratic Party Congress asked for much more, inasmuch as they also wanted to curtail the employer prerogative to direct and allocate work at the workplace, thereby giving the trade union a say in work organisation there, which is quite a dramatic move. See M. M. Nilsson, 'Halv seger om heltid', 35 *LO-Tidningen*, 16 November 2001.

[95] In the assessment of whether objective grounds are present great weight should be accorded to what the social partners may have to say: see Ds 2001:6 (n. 64 above), p. 75 and Government Bill 2001/02:97 (n. 4 above), p. 41.

The *pro rata temporis* principle in cl. 4(2) of the Framework Agreement is not stated at all in the Swedish statute.[96]

8.5.1   Employment conditions

It follows from this brief summary that the Government Bill undoubtedly enlarges the protection of part-time employees inasmuch as the Swedish statute is also intended to apply to *pay*, while the Framework Agreement relates only to 'employment conditions' (cf. Treaty of Rome, Art. 137(6) excluding pay from Community jurisdiction). To extend the Part-time Directive in its implementation to cover pay as well will merely imply that it is intended to coincide with the formula that applies to other Swedish non-discrimination statutes; any other solution is hardly conceivable. To exclude pay from the non-discrimination principle is not realistic. It is argued that the Member States are not prevented from introducing more favourable provisions in accordance with cl. 6(1) of the Framework Agreement.[97]

8.5.2   Direct and indirect discrimination

The wording of the Swedish statute is different from that of cl. 4(1) of the Framework Agreement, which states that part-time workers 'shall not be treated in a less favourable manner than comparable full-time workers solely because they work part-time'. The Swedish design is, instead, based upon the concepts of direct and indirect discrimination with reference to gender discrimination law. This dichotomy is not uncontroversial, if the yardstick is the Part-time Directive. The Law Council[98] indicated another solution, suggesting the abandonment of the distinction between direct and indirect discrimination. The Council's main argument was that there was no different treatment based upon the person or their attributes, which was the case with discrimination bans with respect to, for example, gender, race, ethnic origin or sexual orientation. To use such a stigmatising terminology in the part-time work context where the aim was to give a certain group of employees a stronger position in labour law might water

---

[96] All that is said in the Government Bill is that it is acceptable to pay a higher pension to an employee working full-time compared with one working part-time. This statement is merely begging the question. If it were the other way round, discrimination of the full-time employee would definitely exist.

[97] Government Bill 2001/02:97 (n. 4 above), p. 37.

[98] The Law Council is a body composed of three or four high judges from the Supreme Court and the Administrative Supreme Court. The Council's main duty is to scrutinise the technical legal aspects of any important legislation before such legislation is introduced into Parliament.

down the concept of discrimination to something less than it stands for. The Council therefore preferred a less strident terminology. Nor could it find cases where indirect discrimination was present – in its scrutiny of the Government draft the Council questioned whether the provision corresponded to a real need.[99]

In spite of the Law Council's critical remarks the Government was not persuaded.[100] Certainly, it conceded that the non-discrimination principle of the Part-time Directive was of a quite different type from that found in, for example, the Swedish Equal Opportunities Act (Jämställdhetslag) where human rights aspects could be advanced. However, the Government argued that cl. 4 of the Framework Agreement speaks of the 'principle of non-discrimination'. With respect to indirect discrimination the Government did not share the view of the Law Council. It gave two examples. The first was the case where a part-timer is denied a benefit associated with the amount of work performed or a certain achievement. It is typical that someone who is working part-time may have difficulties in attaining such a benefit. Another example is where other benefits, such as a skills programme, are allocated to afternoons at a specific workplace, while in fact most part-timers work mornings.[101] At any rate, the Government concluded, it was possible to introduce more advantageous rules than those that were laid down in the Framework Agreement.

8.5.3 Refusal to accept a transfer from full-time to part-time work or vice versa

It is noteworthy that no implementing provision is suggested as regards cl. 5(2) of the Framework Agreement, to wit, that 'a worker's refusal to transfer from full-time to part-time work or vice versa should not in itself constitute a valid reason for termination of employment, without prejudice to termination in accordance with national law, collective agreements and practice, for other reasons such as may arise from the operational requirements of the establishment concerned'. It is argued in the Ministry report that no ban is necessary since it is already contrary to the

---

[99] Government Bill 2001/02:97 (n. 4 above), pp. 98, 101.   [100] Ibid., pp. 31–3.

[101] The erroneous approach of the Government reply is that it fails to take into consideration the fact that the examples given to reject the Law Council comment are also tokens of direct discrimination against part-timers. The concept of indirect discrimination in gender law presupposes a statistical assessment to find out whether there are predominantly more women than men who are negatively affected. No statistical assessment is meant to be applied with respect to part-time employees. Only a single part-timer needs to be affected to make the Directive apply.

Swedish Employment Protection act and case-law to dismiss a part-timer from her/his employment if the employer simply does not want to have part-timers on the payroll.[102] In the Government Bill a similarly opaque statement of the same kind is to be found.[103] However, the Bill concedes that there may be a genuine lack of work for part-timers or full-timers in such cases, which is in accordance with reference in the Part-time Directive to 'other reasons such as may arise from the operational requirements' as a valid reason for termination of employment.[104]

To be realistic, it should be added that an employer is almost always in a position to launch an argument in favour of a change, such as economic, technical or organisational reasons, to make an employee transfer from full-time to part-time work or vice versa. Swedish labour law does not prevent an employer, if the employee rejects such a proposal, from dismissing that employee for lack of work in the context of the employment conditions formerly offered.[105] It may in fact be less than clear what the Framework Agreement actually requires from the Member States on this specific point.[106]

8.5.4   Promotional provisions of the Framework Agreement

Clause 5(3) of the Framework Agreement is, overall, dispensed with quite rashly in the Swedish Government Bill.[107] Clause 5(3) encourages employers, 'as far as possible', to take into consideration requests by workers to transfer from, for example, full-time to part-time work, or vice versa. The Government Bill argues that the provision does not create any 'absolute

---

[102] Ds 2001:6 (n. 64 above), pp. 30, 55–6. It is an irony of fate that the case that is referred to in the report, Labour Court judgment 1984 No. 28, hardly supports this view. In the case in point the employer had unilaterally reduced the working time from 100% to 93%. The Labour Court held that this was equivalent to an unlawful termination of employment in violation of the Employment Protection Act. The Labour Court did not rule on the issue of whether the employer was lawfully entitled to dismiss the employees on the grounds of wanting to modify the contract of employment from a full-time to a part-time one. I agree with B. Nyström, *EU och arbetsrätten* (Stockholm, 2001), p. 303, when she argues that the Swedish position ought to be assessed more seriously in the light of cl. 5(2) of the Framework Agreement, if the ban is not to leak like a sieve.

[103] Government Bill 2001/02:97 (n. 4 above), p. 14.   [104] Ibid., p. 49.

[105] In Labour Court judgment 1993 No. 61 the employer was found to be lawfully entitled to modify the contracts of employment inasmuch as he no longer wanted to give the employees concerned the right to use company cars for private purposes, alleging economic reasons for the amendment of the contracts.

[106] It may be the case that the Part-time Directive is like any other 'chewing-gum' which can be drawn out in all directions until it becomes so thin that it eventually breaks: see Eklund, 'The Chewing-Gum Directive' (n. 81 above), p. 77.

[107] Government Bill 2001/02:97 (n. 4 above), p. 50.

duty laid on the employer'. The most important case in this context is probably a worker's request for a transfer from part-time to full-time work,
argues the Government, and from that point of view there are already
provisions covering the situation in s. 25a of the Employment Protection
Act.[108]

8.5.5   'Employee working part-time' defined

Lastly, the Swedish statute proposes a definition of a part-time worker.
Section 2 of the statute reads as follows: 'A part-time working employee
refers to a worker whose normal hours of work, calculated on a weekly
basis or any other period of up to one year, are less than the hours of work
of a comparable worker who is considered to work full-time in accordance
with agreement or law.'

The question as to which categories of employees working part-time
should be encompassed by the statute was not at issue. 'Casual' employees,
who may be excluded from coverage in accordance with the Framework
Agreement, are not excluded in the Swedish scheme.[109] In the legislative
history of the Act another aspect of the definition was highlighted. It
started with a query raised by the Law Council as to whether employees on leave of absence were deemed to be included by the protective
provisions of the statute. Should they be classified as employees working
part-time?[110] The Part-time Directive does seem to address this specific
issue. The Swedish Bill argues that the concept of 'employee working part-
time' is equivalent to the concept of 'part-time worker', as used in cl. 3
of the Framework Agreement.[111] The argument runs as follows. According to the Government Bill, a full-time worker who is on 100 per cent
leave of absence will retain her/his normal hours of work and is therefore not affected by the new statute. If, however, the same employee is on
only partial leave of absence s/he should be deemed an employee working
part-time and accordingly be encompassed by the statute.

How is it, though, that a worker who *normally* works full-time is all of
a sudden deemed to be a part-time worker in the sense of the Directive
if s/he is on partial leave of absence? It could be argued here that it is
not consistent to treat a full-time worker on full-time leave of absence
differently from a full-time worker on only partial leave of absence. The

---

[108] See above at section 6.1.   [109] See cl. 2(2) of the Framework Agreement.
[110] Government Bill 2001/02:97 (n. 4 above), p. 99.
[111] Ibid., p. 35. In the Swedish version of the Part-time Directive the concept of 'part-
time worker' in the Directive is transformed into 'employee working part-time', which,
however, may be something very different: see n. 51 above.

argument is not consistent in the light of the wording of s. 2 of the Swedish statute (see above).

9   Part-time work and the role of the social partners

In fact, not much is known about the attitudes of the social partners with respect to the frequency of part-time work in Sweden, apart from the fact that, in a few instances, part-time work has been subject to various stipulations by CAs. In an EC report from 1995 it is held: 'In the past, trade unions and their representatives have often been opposed to the introduction of part-time work . . . All of these representatives were male.'[112] However, this specific comment does not apply to Swedish trade unions.

Quite recently, however, the Swedish Trade Union Confederation (LO) has propounded another view. The LO has launched the idea that every worker should have a right to a full-time job, but have an option to work part-time.[113] Again, the underlying issue is so-called 'under-employment' with respect to part-time workers. From this point of view the Government Bill on the Part-time Directive[114] argues that there are very good reasons for achieving a situation where full-time work is made the main rule; it increases quality of life for employees and provides greater opportunities to make decisions about both private and working life. It also contributes, it is argued, to a better outcome – for the employer and for society as a whole. Gender aspects are also involved since women work part-time to a larger extent than men. On the other hand, the Government Bill maintains that there may be good reasons for part-time work. It is argued that a reasonable balance must be struck between, on the one hand, employee needs for good economic conditions and employment security and, on the other hand, employer needs to adapt work organisation and the workforce to externalities.

10   Part-time work and Sweden's National Action Plans in the light of EC Employment Guidelines

The topic of part-time work was not mentioned in the first 1998 Swedish National Action Plan (NAP).[115] Subsequently, however, the issue has made

---

[112] S. McRae, *Part-Time Work* (n. 22 above), p. 53.
[113] See above in n. 94; see also E. Olausson, 'LO vill minska godtycket' 5 *LO-Tidningen* 8 February 2002.
[114] Government Bill 2001/02:97, p. 23.   [115] Government Spring Bill 1997/98:150, App. 4.

(rather small) headlines in the NAPs in response to the Employment Guidelines as required by Art. 128 of the Treaty. Let me say, first of all, that it is no secret that the Swedish Government was extremely content with the fact that the Amsterdam Treaty contained provisions on employment and labour market policy.[116] A document like a NAP is scarcely a new instrument in Swedish labour market policy. For decades it has been the practice that, in the annual major Budget Bill to Parliament, the Swedish Government submits comprehensive reports on accomplishments and intentions in the labour market area. Therefore, one is tempted to say that what in fact has for decades been practice in Sweden has now become practice in all of Europe under the aegis of Art. 128 of the Treaty. Among Swedish scholars the Employment Title of the Treaty has been read as something extending the social dimension in the EU into European welfare policy where economic, employment and social policies must be co-ordinated.[117]

How are the NAPs orchestrated? Who takes the lead and which social partners, if any, participate in the deliberations? A two-level strategy – divided into consultation talks and a standing committee – was adopted in Sweden.[118] The first level implied that the State Secretary in the Ministry of Industry headed the *consultation talks* with the seven social partners, four from the employer camp and three from the employee camp, as part of the social dialogue.[119] It was the State Secretary's intent to make the tripartite consultations work openly. The consultations were held

---

[116] See the Government Bill 1997/98:58, Part 1 on approval of the Amsterdam Treaty, p. 72, where it is held: 'The outcome after negotiations within the employment field has great similarities with the proposal that Sweden presented during the deliberations. The outcome is a significant success for Sweden and other Member States that aimed to achieve Treaty amendments whose purpose was to create a better basis for the EU countries' joint efforts to fight unemployment.' See also K. Jacobsson, K. M. Johansson and M. Ekengren, *Mot en europeisk välfärdspolitik? Ny politik och nya samarbetsformer i EU* ('Towards a European Welfare Policy? New Policies and New Forms of Co-operation in the EU') (Stockholm: SNS Förlag, 2001), pp. 63–4 ('The Swedish triumph is not without substance').

[117] Jacobsson, Johansson and Ekengren (n. 16 above), pp. 23, 54.

[118] In February 2002, I interviewed former State Secretary Anna Ekström, responsible for Swedish governmental co-ordination with respect to work on the EC Employment Guidelines.

[119] The social partners include: Svenskt näringsliv (Confederation of Swedish Enterprise), Arbetsgivarverket (Agency for Government Employers), Landstingsförbundet (The Swedish Federation of County Councils), Svenska Kommunförbundet (Swedish Association of Local Authorities), LO (Swedish Trade Union Confederation), TCO (Swedish Confederation of Professional Employees) and SACO (Swedish Confederation of Professional Associations).

three times every half-year, and they were scheduled to take place when a major labour/employment issue was brought up in Brussels. Information about what happened was also released afterwards; in addition, the social partners themselves gave information about their negotiations on labour matters.[120] The second level was composed of a *standing committee* with civil servants from both the Ministries of Finance and of Industry and representatives of the seven social partners. The standing committee convened more often than consultation talks were held. The government civil servants ironed out the texts of the NAPs before the standing committee, often after a tug-of-war between the employer/employee camps. Sometimes one may find in the NAP that a text has gained the consent of the major social partners. For example, in the 2000 NAP it follows that the social partners and the Government reached consensus with respect to Guidelines 5–6, i.e. on education, skills development and life-long learning.[121] The same Ministry civil servants were also responsible for the corresponding texts in the Yearly Budget Bill and the Spring (Budget) Bill, according to the following time axis: September–Yearly Budget Bill; March–Spring (Budget) Bill; and May–NAP. Work on the NAP started in January and continued in parallel with the work on the Spring (Budget) Bill.

To what extent then is the Swedish Parliament involved? Well, not much during the run-up to the first NAP, although the State Secretary had sometimes informed the Parliamentary Committee for Labour Affairs and the standing EU Parliamentary Committee, but in a more cursory way than was the practice when the social partners were consulted. Subsequently, a timetable was followed, including provision of information to the relevant Parliamentary Committees. Every single proposal in the Spring Budget was also dealt with in Parliament. The former State Secretary added that the Guidelines and Recommendation were taken into consideration, increasingly so for the very simple reason that Sweden took part in the preparation of the Guidelines.

How, then, are the EC Employment Guidelines treated in the Budget and Spring Bills?

---

[120] The exchange of information is probably the most important contribution to the EU Employment Strategy; see Jacobsson, Johansson and Ekengren (n. 116 above), p. 159.

[121] The representatives of the public sector have so far not consented to anything; they tend to participate in the process but they are not prepared to sign any document even if consensus is reached.

The Guidelines have usually been given only cursory treatment in the Government's Spring Bill submitted to Parliament in late March every year.[122] So far, the Government has been content to state that Swedish labour market policy is well in line with the EC Employment Guidelines and that, in many areas, the Swedish policy is more ambitious than that stated in the Guidelines. In the Spring Bill of 2001 it is held, more or less as a concluding remark, that 'The co-operation between the Government and the social partners has shown that there is broad support with respect to the EC Employment Guidelines and that the ambition is to realise the goal of full employment. The Government is determined to continue its active and driving role in European co-operation.' Similar remarks are also found in the Budget Bill (Autumn 2001):

> Sweden will continue to improve the efficiency of the process and to urge that the Guidelines are designed so as to make them simple, more concrete and better suited to follow-ups. Sweden will also seek to achieve the introduction of clear and purposeful indicators with respect to the follow-up and re-reporting of the Guidelines. Furthermore, Sweden will be active in both consolidating and making the Guidelines well-anchored in the Member States and among the social partners.[123]

Let me now be a little more specific about the Swedish NAPs after 1998 with respect to part-time work. In the 1999 NAP, with reference to Guidelines 16 and 17, nothing is said other than that part-time work is quite common in Sweden. We are again reminded of the fact that more women work part-time than men (37 and 9 per cent, respectively).[124] The Government is anxious to add, however, that many part-timers are under-employed. Some 121,000 persons are registered as under-employed with the employment offices, i.e. they actually want to work more. This corresponds to 2.8 per cent of the labour force. Likewise, in the 2000 NAP, referring to Guidelines 16 and 17, the issue of under-employment is again brought up.[125] We are told that, together with the major actors of local government and a few affected trade unions, the Government has agreed to fight under-employment, particularly in the health and care

---

[122] Government Spring Bills – 1997/98:150, App. 3, p. 9; 1998/99:100, App. 2, p. 14; 1999/ 2000:100, App. 2, pp. 15–16; 2000/01:100, App. 2, p. 17; and 2001/02:100, pp. 31–2.

[123] Government Yearly Budget Bill 2001/02:1, App. 13, p. 29.

[124] Handlingsplan för sysselsättning ('National Action Plan for Employment'), May 1999, p. 30.

[125] Sveriges handlingsplan för sysselsättning ('Swedish National Action Plan for Employment'), May 2000, p. 22.

sector, where women dominate. The target is to cut the number of under-employed by 50 per cent. In the 2001 Plan, now with reference to Guideline 14, the Government concedes that the target of the previous year has not been met; yet progress has been made inasmuch as the number of under-employed was reduced by 13 per cent.[126] Nurses, in particular, benefited from this development. The Government also states that work has been resumed to implement the Part-time Directive. In the 2002 Plan nothing is said other than that the Government has submitted the Bill on Part-time Work, implementing the EC Directive. In addition, it is reported that further progress has been made up till December 2001 towards reducing the number of under-employed in the specified sectors of the labour market where women deminate, with the number of under-employed as at November 1999 now reduced by 36 per cent.[127]

The rather high number of under-employed persons was also the focus in the Budget Bill of 2001.[128] The Government states that comprehensive efforts have been made in order to reduce the number of under-employed persons, though the targets have not yet been met.[129] It is stated that 233,800 are under-employed, a much higher figure than that stated above, and that 72 per cent of them are women. Hence, the Government is of the view that training and educational programmes should be offered to targeted part-time employees. The Government also states that the Swedish National Labour Market Board will be committed to intensifying all efforts to reduce under-employment in branches other than the health and care sector, such as the retail trade and hotel and restaurant sectors. Employers must also be forced to adopt other kinds of work organisation, recruitment policies and working time planning. An appropriation of 100 million Swedish Kroner (SEK) is asked for in the Budget Bill in order to stimulate activities of the following kind: to develop competence skills among part-time under-employed persons and to disseminate information – good models – on how work organisation may be altered to satisfy part-time employees' numerous demands for full-time work. It is also indicated that a steering committee,

---

[126] Sveriges handlingsplan för sysselsättning, May 2001, pp. 22–3.
[127] Sveriges handlingsplan för sysselsättning, May 2002, pp. 56–7.
[128] Government Yearly Budget Bill 2001/02:1, App. 13, pp. 21, 34–5.
[129] In a press release of 6 December 2001, the National Labour Market Board indicated that underemployment in the health and care sector has been reduced by 36% – the target was 50% a year before – which is quite a success, it is stated. The main explanation for this development is that that there has been a demand for more labour in the health care sector.

composed of representatives from *inter alia* the National Labour Market Board, the Working Life Institute, the Workers' Environment Agency and the Equal Opportunities Ombudsman, will be appointed to initiate these activities. The work will be conducted in close co-operation with the parties concerned, focussing primarily on part-time work in local government.

The above summaries with respect to employment policies in Sweden reveal there is little deviation from the practice of past decades as regards the way in which Swedish labour market policy is worked out.[130] It is tempting to say: business as usual! Against this background it is no surprise to find that the impact of the Lisbon Declaration is hardly to be seen in Sweden. The Swedish Prime Minister, Göran Persson, was hilarious after the Lisbon summit when he exclaimed that the Lisbon process 'was a political one and not a legal one'.[131] It is no secret that Sweden favours an intergovernmental co-operation between the Member States instead of more federalism in the EU. From that viewpoint, Art. 129 of the Treaty providing that the Council shall adopt incentive measures to encourage co-operation between the Member States, but that those 'measures shall not include harmonisation of the laws and regulations of the Member States', is a perfect springboard to start out from in the light of Sweden's stand. It is also compatible with the subsidiarity principle in Art. 5 of the Treaty. One may question what the Employment Title may lead to, or whether it will merely add another to the layers of 'paperwork procedure' within the Community.[132]

11 Gender implications

Most part-time employees are women. This is basically due to the fact that women, in the late 1990s or early 2000s, take care of household chores and children more than men do.[133] In Sweden, the official reports from 1976 focussed on part-timers' employment conditions from the point of view

---

[130] See, in agreement, Jacobsson, Johansson and Ekengren (n. 116 above), pp. 159–60.

[131] Ibid., p. 9.

[132] See L. Betten, 'The Amsterdam Treaty: Some General Comments on the New Social Dimension' (2001) 13 *International Journal of Comparative Labour Law and Industrial Relations* pp. 188–92, 190.

[133] For an updated analysis regarding the division of labour between men and women, C. McGlynn, 'Reclaiming A Feminist Vision: the Reconciliation of Paid Work and Family Life in European Union Law and Policy' (2001) 7 *Columbia Journal of European Law* pp. 241–72.

of gender equality.[134] The conclusion arrived at was rather gloomy. It was found 'that part-time work as a permanent feature on the labour market does not promote gender equality'.[135] Part-time work had many negative aspects, and only exceptionally did it provide women part-timers with a lasting ability to provide for themselves.

The overall conclusions of the 1976 main report contain an ideological focal point.[136] In essence, the arguments stipulate that: women have, like men, a right to be able to provide for themselves through a job of their own. Part-time work reflects the conditions actually endemic to working life and to society at large, also indicating the workload and the division of work within families. Regular part-time jobs are seldom found in well-paid professions. It is a fact, and a sad one, that women who work part-time have little chance to be able to support themselves. Their pay is too low, not because they work fewer hours but because they work in badly paying sectors. They also miss out on social benefits that are related to either level of pay or working time. Since from the practical point of view it is almost only women who work part-time, and part-time work is most frequent in female-dominated professions, part-time work can be assumed to contribute to the preservation of differences in wages and the distribution of power between men and women in the labour market. This fact does not facilitate the task of putting an end to gender segregation in the labour market.

In this respect, the 1976 report took a decisive stand in indicating that women's situation would dramatically change if the *total working time of all employees* was reduced. It was argued that a general shortening of weekly working hours (unstated – a six-hour working day) would give all men an opportunity to work less and devote more time to the family and children, whereas women would be given a fairer chance to work full-time. Since then, it can be said that in the year 2002 the debate with respect to the reduction of total working time per individual remains a highly controversial issue in Sweden.[137] Thus, the statutory weekly working time in Sweden is the same as it was in 1972, i.e. 40 hours per week.

---

[134] SOU 1976:6, 1976:7 (n. 12 above).   [135] SOU 1976:6, p. 11.   [136] Ibid., pp. 77–87.

[137] The issue has been highlighted several times during the last few years: see, for example, SOU 1996:145, *Arbetstid – längd, förläggning och inflytande*; and, further: Ds 2000:22, *Kortare arbetstid – för och emot*; and SOU 2001:91, *Arbetstiden – lag eller avtal*. Another Parliamentary Committee was appointed in 2001. These many investigations are a reflection of the tug-of-war over who is to be the master of the regulation of working time in working life: the politicians – where opinions also are split – or the social partners. In quite a few instances, the social partners in various segments of the labour market have also shown that they are willing to shorten the regular working week, but impatient voices claim that the steps being taken are not good enough.

What has changed since 1976?
Nothing much! The situation in the early 2000s is pretty much the same as it was in the mid 1970s. The division of the Swedish labour market into gender stereotypes was analysed in 1998, in terms of both 'horizontal' and 'vertical' segregation.[138] As regards horizontal segregation it was argued that the women who entered the labour market in the 1970s were never meant to compete with men. In 1996 there was also a considerable decrease in the rate of employment, owing to the deterioration of the labour market situation in Sweden in the 1990s, which caused both men and women to suffer, with the unemployment rate consequently reaching unprecedented levels compared with the previous decades. In 1996 the proportion of women in the entire labour force was down to 70 per cent (which is as low a figure as that in the 1970s) and the proportion of men was down to 73 per cent, which is the lowest figure since the 1960s. The unemployment rate in 1998 was high for both men (8.5 per cent) and women (7.5 per cent). However, since then a dramatic improvement on the Swedish labour market has taken place. In May 2000 the unemployment rate was down to 4.1 per cent, or just about 177,000; in addition to that, some 103,000 were engaged in so-called 'labour market measures' (training, education, etc.).[139]

A good example of these stereotypes is the actual use made of the rather generous parental scheme in Sweden. Recent statistics indicate that fathers avail themselves of the parental allowance with respect to the care of the *new-born child* to only a small extent. Since the introduction of the parental insurance system in 1974 the proportional use by fathers has been increasing very slowly. In 1990, 7.1 per cent of *all* the days for which compensation is paid were granted to fathers; the figure was only marginally higher for 1998, or 10.4 per cent.[140] The figures are higher among more educated couples. The statistics with respect to *temporary care* of the child for sickness, however, are much higher. Fathers avail themselves of more than 30 per cent of *all* the days for which compensation is paid, even though the trend is slightly downward, from 34.5 per cent in 1990 to 32.3 per cent in 1998.[141]

---

[138] SOU 1998:6 (n. 30 above), pp. 76–85. The main report is based on thirteen scientific reports that contain a great deal of information on the gender aspects of the Swedish labour market. The scientific reports are only cursorily dealt with in the main report. The main report was a disappointment; no concrete proposals were put forward. The same analysis and conclusion is made in *Löneskillnader!!!* (Stockholm: SACO, 1998), p. 8.

[139] Government Bill 1999/2000:139, pp. 19, 22.

[140] Source: *Socialförsäkring 1997 och 1998. Utg. av Riksförsäkringsverket*, 1999, Table 3:1.

[141] Ibid., Table 3:3.

Why is this the case? Well, the answer is that, if one looks upon a family as 'the economic unit', the family will usually suffer economically if the husband or the male partner avails himself of the parental allowance. This is so because the husband will usually have a higher income than his wife or female partner. There are two problematic aspects of the parental scheme in Sweden. The benefits have both a 'wall' and a 'ceiling'. In calculating the parental allowance, which is equivalent to sickness benefit, no account is taken of any income beyond 7.5 'basic amounts'.[142] This means that no income beyond an annual income of SEK 284,250 will be taken into consideration when calculating the parental allowance. This is what is called the 'wall'. Furthermore, only 80 per cent of daily income is counted for the purpose of parental allowance. This is what is called the 'ceiling'. The use of 'walls' and 'ceilings' means that a parent will not be fully compensated for the loss of pay while on parental leave.

Part of the social security system is hence counterproductive from the point of view of gender equality, in spite of the fact that the Swedish parental insurance system is in other ways both generous and fair to the parents (parental allowance is given for 480 days after childbirth), as well as gender-blind inasmuch as it presupposes that the father will avail himself of half of the total amount of days available. However, in most cases the father will transfer his right to parental allowance to the mother (or vice versa, as occasionally is the case). Since 1995, however, one 'daddy-month' has been mandatory, amended in 2001 to comprise two 'daddy-months'; if the father does not avail himself of these days, they will be forfeited.[143]

Given this background it is not surprising to find supplementary schemes laid down not only by CAs but, more often, by larger companies, introducing additional parental benefits as part of a gender-aware policy. Such systems usually imply that if the parent takes leave of absence to care for the new-born child, his/her employer will give the employee a wage

---

[142] The 'basic amount' is a central concept in the Swedish social security system that is linked to the consumer index and a cornerstone of the National Insurance Act (ch. 3, s. 2). In 2002, one 'basic amount' was equivalent to SEK 37,900.

[143] The 'daddy-month' was introduced by Government Bill 1993/94:147, see National Insurance Act, ch. 4, s. 3. It was extended to two months by Government Bill 2000/01:44, in force since 1 January 2002. Technically, the legislation is gender-neutral inasmuch as it provides that two months of the entire length of parental leave may not be transferred from one partner to the other. According to ch. 4, s. 10 of the same Act, the father may also avail himself of ten additional days compensated by a parent's temporary cash benefit in order to assist the mother in connection with the birth of the child. Close to 90% of all fathers make use of all ten days; source: *Socialförsäkring 1997 och 1998* (n. 140 above), Table 3:2.

supplement.[144] Such schemes are part of a 'family-friendly workplace' policy.[145]

12 Summing-up

Sweden is remiss with respect to the implementation of the EC Part-time Directive. However, the fact that the Swedish Government has been dragging its feet is not the most crucial issue. It is the underlying reasons that are significant. The Government endeavoured for quite some time to persuade the social partners to find solutions by means of CAs regarding the Part-time Directive. In particular, efforts were made to convince the social partners to amend the numerous threshold provisions in many CAs related to part-time employees. Some progress has been achieved towards eradicating such discrimination. In the public sector a few of the former threshold provisions laid down in CAs have been abolished, giving all employees the right to claim the benefits in question. In general, a CA is preferred to any legislative solution in Sweden, but the model has come under fire with the entry of Sweden into the EU. Therefore, it was highly understandable for the Swedish Government to attempt to achieve a CA solution inasmuch as the Directive is an offshoot of the efforts to establish a labour regime among the European social partners. However, the project failed. The Swedish model did not pass muster.

The Swedish Government was accordingly forced to act on its own. The end result is extremely limited. The Government has opted for a minimalist solution, suggesting the implementation of only the mandatory provisions of the Directive, and no more. The promotional provisions of the Directive have been left untouched. The Government Bill on the implementation of the Part-time Directive provides merely cursory adherence to EC law. Underlying the whole issue is the perception that the Directive is an intrusion upon not only the freedom of contract principle, which is

---

[144] See JÄMO (Equal Opportunities Ombudsman), Rapport 2000-06-08, *Löneutfyllnad vid föräldraledighet.*

[145] Likewise, the professional employees' union in Sweden (SACO) has launched a private unemployment insurance scheme for its members in view of the fact that the state unemployment scheme offers only SEK 12,760 per month net income (which equals a monthly income of just less than SEK 16,000 before tax) in unemployment benefits. Some 90% of SACO members earn more than that. The scheme implies that 80% of the monthly income up to SEK 40,000 will be honoured. The Swedish Government is not entirely happy that a trade union has taken such an initiative, which undermines – it is argued – the legitimacy of the state unemployment insurance scheme: see Government Bill 1999/2000:139, pp. 33, 73.

deeply ingrained in Swedish labour law, but also the freedom to regulate any matter concerning working life by means of a CA. It has always been the primary instrument for regulating terms and conditions of employment in Sweden, with wide discretion enjoyed by the social partners. A legislative solution has always been only a second-stage solution. Furthermore, many of the statutory provisions of modern Swedish labour law are also optional inasmuch as they are not mandatory – if the collective bargaining parties can find another solution which is better suited to them by means of an agreement, the CA is given discretionary rights over any other statutory provision.

However, it remains to be seen if the rather narrow Swedish implementation of the Part-time Directive will survive future scrutiny by the courts.

The main aspect in the context of the Part-time Directive is, on the other hand, that the present debate on part-time work in Sweden is not related to an attempt to increase the number of part-time jobs, but rather to reduce the rather large number of under-employed persons. This is definitely an aspect that has had an impact upon the Swedish Government with respect to the Part-time Directive. Therefore, all efforts are for the moment concentrated on reducing involuntary part-time work in Sweden, with its rather high number of under-employed persons, especially in the service sector, where women working part-time are found in abundance.

10

The United Kingdom: how is EU governance transformative?

CLAIRE KILPATRICK AND MARK FREEDLAND

1 Transformation and governance

This chapter uses the example of part-time work in the UK in order to investigate the transformative nature of EU governance. In line with the other country analyses, we focus on three regulatory sources: EU gender equality law, the 1997 Part-time Work Framework Agreement and Directive (hereafter Part-time Directive) and Title VIII EC Treaty dealing with employment policy.

Given the production at EU level of these regulatory sources concerning part-time work, and the special, well-known, characteristics of the EU as a legal and political entity, rather than focussing on *whether* EU governance can be transformative, we consider how, and under what circumstances, it can transform a given policy area. Therefore, our interest does not primarily lie in measuring outcomes by, for instance, enquiring whether the lot of part-time workers in the UK has been improved as a result of EU intervention. It lies instead in analysing the distinctive spaces created by various modes of governance with regard to the regulatory and social profile of part-time work in the UK. Of course, these two issues – processes and outcomes – cannot be neatly separated since one important measure of transformative capacity is the magnitude of the change provoked, or influence brought to bear, by a given EU intervention. Notwithstanding that, it remains important to note that we are interested in outcomes from a perspective which is principally interested in the *processes* of transformation.

We are also interested in transformation in a second sense, which is how the goals, actors and tools used in governing are being transformed.

We would like to thank Lizzie Barmes and Hugh Collins for helpful suggestions on earlier drafts of this chapter.

To speak of governance rather than government is to identify this change. The shift from 'government' to 'governance' can be traced by looking at the role of government, at those participating in governance activities and at the nature of the problems to be solved today.

The change in the role of government has been described as a shift from a 'command and control' type of state towards an 'enabling' state. Government is about using the formal and constitutional powers accorded the State to define its tasks, and deploying its authority and sanctions to ensure their realisation. Governance focuses on governments using processes of steering and co-ordination to define objectives and mustering the resources of public and private actors in order to pursue them.[1] In terms of legal techniques, this might be expressed as a preference for types of legal instruction other than legally binding commands backed by sanctions for non-compliance. In terms of law-making, it might reveal itself in complex, wide-ranging consultation or deliberative mechanisms.

A different range of actors participates in new ways in governance activities. In the world of government, the national-level state aggregates preferences by providing privileged channels of access for preference-expression. In the world of governance, national-level government still has an important role to play, but other levels of government – transnational and sub-national – increasingly participate, and heterarchical rather than hierarchical relationships exist between different sites of government. In addition, non-State actors and informal channels play important roles in governance accounts.

Finally, problem-definition and problem-solution have radically altered. In adapting to this new environment the State becomes a State of governance. In some instances, a range of actors must engage in ongoing deliberative discussion and scientific research in order to define even provisionally the nature and scale of a particular problem. In other cases, resolution of particular problems, such as equal opportunities between men and women, funding old-age, or increasing the skills base, has become economically imperative rather than, as in the past, primarily socially desirable; this requires new problem-solving techniques. Because these

---

[1] B. Guy Peters and J. Pierre, 'Developments in Intergovernmental Relations' (2001) 29 *Policy and Politics* p. 131; A. Jordan, 'The European Union: an Evolving System of Multi-level Governance . . . or Government?' (2001) 29 *Policy and Politics* p. 193 at 199, discussing in particular G. Stoker, 'Governance as Theory' (1998), *International Social Science Journal* 17, p. 155; K. Jacobsson, *Innovations in EU Governance: the Case of Employment Policy Co-ordination*, SCORE (Stockholm Centre for Organisational Research) Rapportserie 2001:12 at n. 3.

new problems do not respect former demarcations, traditional justifications for action, departmental structures of State government and national boundaries need to be rethought. This encourages the decentring and restructuring of the State, and the need for ongoing learning and experimentation in order to test potential solutions to problems.[2]

This chapter therefore, by examining part-time work, explores both the transformation of governance and the ways in which EU governance can be transformative in the UK. A final distinction – between procedural and substantive governance – aims to facilitate the tracing of what is novel in contemporary UK labour law governance as well as alerting us to differentiations between levels and sites of governance. Procedural governance concerns the governance pathways by which a particular policy objective is defined, decided and pursued. It focusses on governance techniques and, though we will not explore it in detail, legitimation. Substantive governance focusses on governance objectives. It is concerned with examining the mix of policy options present in the discourse and what labour market visions underpin the various alternatives being contended for. We proceed to use these two terms to explore the regulatory terrain of part-time work in a UK–EU context. This is done by setting out a transformative check-list – that is, issues where EU law *could* play a transformative role in the UK – and then exploring more concretely how gender equality law, the Part-time Directive and Title VIII EC interacted with this check-list in practice.

2 Procedural governance

Procedural governance concerns examining, as we have said, the institutional pathway by which a particular policy objective is defined, decided and pursued. At its most basic, this could mean broadly the difference created by entrusting tasks in a particular policy field primarily to the judicial, Parliamentary or executive branches of government. Different parts of the EU and UK governance apparatus play a leading role in relation to the development of the sources relevant to part-time work. We suggest that disaggregating the state and supranational institutions by examining the changing roles they play in a specific field – here, part-time

---

[2] J. S. Mosher and D. Trubek, 'Alternative Approaches to Governance in the EU: EU Social Policy and the European Employment Strategy' (2003) 41 *Journal of Common Market Studies* p. 66; H. Collins, 'Is there a Third Way in Labour Law?' in J. Conaghan, R. M. Fischl and K. Klare (eds.), *Labour Law in an Era of Globalization: Transformative Practices and Possibilities* (Oxford: Oxford University Press, 2002), p. 449.

work – is a fruitful means of investigating shifting patterns of labour law and policy governance as well as highlighting the democratic implications of changes which occur. For instance, it makes a difference if changes in governance result in a shift of power towards executives and away from courts and legislatures.

2.1   Gender equality and the courts

At EU and UK level, the courts have played a central role in relation to the development of gender discrimination sources. These sources were either created or began to be actively used from the second half of the 1970s onwards. Hence, it is well known that although Article 141 (formerly 119) was the sole potentially 'hard' judicially enforceable obligation in the social policy chapter of the 1957 Treaty of Rome, it was not until the European Court of Justice decision in *Defrenne (No.2)* in 1976 that it began to fulfil its potential. In the UK, the Equal Pay Act 1970 and the Sex Discrimination Act (SDA) 1975 both entered into force at the end of 1975 and were rapidly the source of litigious activity, largely because the SDA had created an institution, the Equal Opportunities Commission, which could provide assistance to litigants. Litigation before the German, Dutch and UK courts, combined with use by courts in these Member States of the preliminary reference mechanism in Article 234 of the EC Treaty, created a developing jurisprudence on the concept of indirect discrimination. Much of the indirect discrimination jurisprudence generated by the ECJ concerns part-time workers. Broadly speaking, the argument was that, as most of these workers are women, norms and practices which disadvantage part-time workers have a disparate impact on women, and cannot be adequately justified by reference to state or employer needs. Hence, litigation under Article 141 (formerly 119) EC was an important means of challenging the legality of those norms and practices.

2.2   The Part-time Directive – the DTI and Parliament

The EU dimension of part-time work regulation is considered in detail elsewhere in this volume. It suffices here to point out the distinctive role of the UK in that regulatory history. Proposals from 1982 onwards at Community level to adopt directives on part-time work were blocked by successive UK Conservative governments through the exercise of a veto on social policy proposals which required, at that time, the unanimous agreement of the Council of Ministers in order to become law. This consistent resistance meant that it was only when an EU-level social policy law-making mechanism was devised from which the UK excluded itself (the Social Chapter appended to the Treaty of Maastricht) that proposals on part-time work could progress, leading to the 1997 Part-time Agreement and Directive. When the New Labour government came to power in May 1997, it signed up to the Social Chapter, which was thereafter incorporated into the main body of the Treaty by the Amsterdam Treaty. A special directive extending the Part-time Directive to the UK was passed.[3] The UK was therefore required to implement an EU directive affording protection to part-time workers. The Department of Trade and Industry (DTI), acting under legislative authority granted by Parliament in the Employment Relations Act 1999, has been at the forefront of transposition of the Part-time Directive.

Though acting as the legislature is one of the central functions of the UK Parliament, it has a range of other important tasks. One of these is the production of reports by committees specialised in different matters. This ensures that expert and concerned views are considered by MPs, and opens a process of informed dialogue between Parliament and the executive. Part-time work has recently been the subject of a significant reporting exercise by the House of Commons Select Committee on Education and Employment.[4] The Committee's work exemplifies the multi-level, polycentric nature of the part-time work discourse, as well as casting light on the stance of the New Labour government towards part-time work in the specific context of implementation of the Part-time Directive.

2.3   Title VIII EC – timing and UK responsibility

Part-time work also appears in the EU Employment Guidelines produced under Title VIII EC. These guidelines are organised around four pillars: employability; entrepreneurship; adaptability; and equal opportunities between women and men. Though the co-ordination of Member States employment policies has, since the Amsterdam Treaty, had its own Title

---

[3] Directive 98/23/EC.
[4] Second Report from the House of Commons Select Committee on Education and Employment, Session 1998–9, *Part-time Working* Volume I (23 March 1999), Volume II (Minutes of Evidence and Appendices) HC 346–1; Third Report from the House of Commons Select Committee on Education and Employment, Session 1999–2000, *The Draft Part-Time Employees (Prevention of Less Favourable Treatment) Regulations 2000* (23 March 2000). The DTI provided written responses to the Committee on each of these reports on 18 June 1999 and 25 May 2000 respectively. These will be referred to hereafter as HC 2nd/3rd Report.

in the Treaty, it began life at the Essen European Council in December 1994 where a series of employment policy priorities for the EC were agreed upon. These modest beginnings were built upon at the Cannes 1995 European Council which invited Member States to submit Multi-annual Employment Programmes on the realisation of the Essen priorities in their national policies. However, all the evidence suggests that the only impact of EU employment policy on the UK prior to the Amsterdam Treaty was to reinforce Conservative governments' views that the rest of Europe would do well to follow its example in deregulating labour markets.[5]

The election of a new government in the UK in 1997 coincided with the introduction of Title VIII EC, which requires the production of National Action Plans by the UK government on an annual basis and, since entry into force of the Treaty of Amsterdam in May 1999, permits Recommendations on the basis of any given year's National Action Plan to be addressed to the UK government by the Council acting by qualified majority vote. Responsibility for the elaboration of the National Action Plans on Employment (NAPs) in the UK is not the responsibility of the DTI which deals with employment law matters and was, as we have noted, responsible for dealing with implementation of the Part-time Directive. Originally, the NAPs were dealt with in the UK by the Treasury and the Department of Education and Employment. Following a reorganisation of government departments in June 2001, it is now the responsibility of the Treasury and the newly created Department of Work and Pensions. This Department combines the welfare and pensions responsibilities of the (abolished) Department of Social Security with the employment and disability responsibilities of the former Department of Education and Employment (renamed in the same reorganisation as the Department of Education and Skills).

Examining UK participation in this process is of great interest for a number of reasons. What is the significance of the fact that NAP

---

[5] 'It was the view of the UK [Conservative] government that it has been pursuing the objectives specified by Essen since the early 1980s and that all its current policies can be considered to be working in the agreed directions. No changes are therefore considered necessary and the implications of the UK multi-annual programme report is that the rest of Europe needs to learn from its example': J. Rubery, *1997 Report: United Kingdom*, Report to European Commission Network of Experts on 'Gender and Employment' cited in F. Bettio, E. Del Bono and M. Smith, *The Multi-Annual Employment Programmes – A Gender Perspective*, Report by the European Network of Experts on 'Gender and Employment', Equal Opportunities Unit, Directorate-General V, European Commission (1998) at p. 4.

responsibility does not lie with the government department entrusted with EU employment law matters? How can one trace the transformative capacity of Title VIII EC? This already difficult task is complicated by the fact that employment policy became an important policy field at EU level at the same time as a new government with a different outlook from its predecessors was elected in the UK. Employment policy has gone from strength to strength at EU level. In particular, the new substantive governance objective defined at the Lisbon Summit of March 2000 – 'to become the most competitive and dynamic knowledge-based economy in the world, capable of sustained economic growth and more and better jobs and greater social cohesion' – justified enriching the range of procedural governance tools. For instance, targets and intermediate targets have been set for the Member States to achieve on the employment rates of men, women and older workers, and Lisbon also resulted in the insertion of new horizontal objectives, such as life-long learning into the Employment Guidelines 2001, and quality in work in the 2002 Guidelines, to cut across all four pillars. This enriching of the co-ordination processes in the EU Employment Strategy was given recognition in Lisbon as constituting a new and distinctive type of EU governance mechanism – the open method of co-ordination (OMC).

Despite the difficulties involved in analysing EU–UK interactions concerning Title VIII EC, examination of a specific policy field, such as part-time work, at least promises to cast light on one issue. It has been suggested that the development of Title VIII EC and the OMC at EU level, on the one hand, and the ground occupied by the New Labour government on the other, share a common theme: both are instantiations of the 'third way'. It is our view that the distinction between procedural and substantive governance can fruitfully be used to probe what it is about New Labour and the European Employment Strategy which invites the 'third way' label. One possibility is that it is primarily the way of governing – the similarity of the tools and governance pathways employed to define, decide and pursue policy matters – which is the common ground. Another possibility is that it is above all the similarity of the objectives of EU and UK employment law and policy – the substantive subject-matter of governance – which is what strikes those who consider both to be illustrations of the third way. Moreover, if we find evidence of considerable differences between the UK and the EU in the important area of labour market regulation, further refinement of what is meant by 'third way' politics and policies would seem to be required.

3   Substantive governance

Substantive governance is concerned with the spectrum of different policy options present in the discourse to realise objectives, and with the labour market efficiency and equity considerations underpinning those various policy options. Substantive governance debates, like those of procedural governance, are historically entrenched and path-dependent. However, it is equally true that functional changes in production, consumption and demography act as important fresh inputs into substantive governance debates. A nice example is the argument that the regulatory institution of the contract of employment in the UK needs to be overhauled so that its terms support rather than impede changed relations of production which today require high-trust relations between employer and employee in order to create innovative products and services.[6] This is an efficiency argument although, unlike certain strains of efficiency argumentation, it is an efficiency argument which calls for specific kinds of State action. The three EU sources we are considering encompass three broad regulatory objectives: guaranteeing fundamental rights, employment protection and employment promotion. The broad outline and, often more importantly, the details of each of these can be argued about in ways which disagree on the efficiency and equity of various alternative formulations of these three objectives.[7] Hence it has been possible (though by no means easy) to obtain general agreement that gender equality is a desirable goal requiring state activity. However, there is likely to be more, and ongoing, disagreement about the type and intensity of state regulatory activity required to satisfy that objective. We will examine potential efficiency and equity arguments in relation to each of these regulatory objectives in what follows. However, one point is worth stressing from the outset. This is that the descriptor of a legal source increasingly does not serve as an accurate guide to the substantive governance objectives that underpin it. For example, one might classify our three EU regulatory sources as each corresponding to a distinct EU substantive objective. Hence gender discrimination instruments can be viewed as corresponding to the EU objective of realising the fundamental right to gender equality, the Part-time Directive

---

[6] H. Collins, 'Regulating the Employment Relation for Competitiveness' (2001) 30 *Industrial Law Journal* 17.

[7] For much fuller discussion, see H. Collins, 'Justifications and Techniques of Legal Regulation of the Employment Relation', and S. Deakin and F. Wilkinson, 'Labour Law and Economic Theory: a Reappraisal', both in H. Collins, P. Davies and R. Rideout (eds.), *Legal Regulation of the Employment Relation* (The Hague: Kluwer, 2000), pp. 3 and 29.

as pursuing an employment protection agenda, and employment policy measures as pursuing an agenda committed to job creation. Yet, what is most interesting about these various regulatory instruments is that, *to an ever-increasing degree*, they fulfil multiple and inter-linked roles. This is also true, though in a distinctive pattern, for the UK sources we will examine.

With regard to EU sources, evidence of this new tendency is abundant. One of the most interesting recent developments in EU law has been the production of new legal sources which have been created under Art. 13 of the Treaty. Article 13 is generally viewed as a new Treaty base to create fundamental rights not to be discriminated against on a range of grounds including but going beyond gender – racial or ethnic origin, religion or belief, disability, age and sexual orientation. This Treaty base was quickly used to create two new directives, one dealing with race and ethnic origin, the other a Framework Directive dealing with the remaining new grounds. These directives explicitly state, however, that they form part of an employment policy agenda to raise the employment rate and meet labour market shortages by fostering social inclusion of disadvantaged groups on the labour market.[8] Hence the Article 13 directives pursue both fundamental rights and employment policy objectives.

Similarly, the first words of the Preamble to the Framework Agreement on Part-time work make it clear that employment policy as well as employment protection objectives are being pursued.[9] The contrast with previous EU social policy directives is striking. For the first (though not the last)[10] time, employment promotion objectives became firmly ensconced within the text of a social policy measure. At the same time, Title VIII EC measures relevant to part-time work, mostly found in the pillars on adaptability and equal opportunities between women and men, are clearly not entirely divorced from employment protection and fundamental rights considerations. It could be that these new patterns of

---

[8] See Recitals (7), (8) and (25) of the Preamble to Directive 2000/78/EC and Recital (8) of the Preamble to Directive 2000/43/EC. See also S. Fredman, 'Discrimination Law in the EU: Labour Market Regulation or Fundamental Rights', in Collins, Davies and Rideout *Legal Regulation of the Employment Relation* (n. 7 above), pp. 183, 187–91.

[9] 'This Framework Agreement is a contribution to the overall European strategy on employment. Part-time work has had an important impact on employment in recent years. For this reason, the parties to this agreement have given priority attention to this form of work. It is the intention of the parties to consider the need for similar agreements relating to other forms of flexible work.'

[10] See also Council Directive 99/70/EC of 28 June 1999 concerning the framework agreement on fixed-term work concluded by ETUC, UNICE and CEEP.

intertwining substantive governance objectives within distinctive legal sources is what typifies 'third way' labour law governance. In that case, it will be of the utmost interest to compare the intertwining of EU sources very briefly indicated here with what happened in the UK.

To trace the transformative capacity of our three EU regulatory sources some information about the pre-existing and current position in the UK with regard to part-time work is required. From this brief account, we extract a check-list which will be used to trace the transformative processes of EU and UK governance in the remainder of the chapter.

4   A regulatory and social profile of part-time work in the UK

Part-time work is a significant and highly feminised form of employment in the UK. Twenty-seven per cent of the UK workforce is now employed on contracts of thirty hours or less per week, up from 18 per cent of the working population in 1990.[11] Women make up 81 per cent of part-timers and part-time work accounts for well over 40 per cent[12] of all women's jobs.[13]

These characteristics of part-time work in the UK result from a distinctive kind of gendered public policy. As Jane Lewis has convincingly demonstrated, public policy on the family in the UK, particularly following the Beveridge Report of 1942, was premised on a strong male breadwinner model.[14] As its name suggests, within this model the male partner's role was to earn sufficient for the family while the woman's role was to bear and care for children and look after the home. This public policy stance meant no development in the UK of either an active state

---

[11] Figures from Office for National Statistics, *Labour Force Survey*, Spring 2001 (London: HMSO, 2001), and N. Millward *et al., All Change at Work? British Employment Relations 1980–1998, as portrayed by the Workplace Industrial Relations Survey Series* (London: Routledge, 2000), p. 44.

[12] The UK NAP 2000 puts the figure at 44%, as does *Labour Market Trends*, 111 (March 2003) 116.

[13] These figures in fact reveal a slight move away from almost total feminisation of this employment form in the UK labour market. In 1985 women constituted 88% of part-timers; the proportion of male workers engaged in part-time work increased from 4.4% in 1985 to 7.7% a decade later. See S. Yeandle, 'Women, Men and Non-Standard Employment: Breadwinning and Caregiving in Germany, Italy and the UK', in R. Crompton (ed.), *Restructuring Gender Relations and Employment: the Decline of the Male Breadwinner* (Oxford: Oxford University Press, 1999), pp. 80, 86. The UK NAP 2000 puts the male part-time figure at 9%. Many of these men are students and older workers.

[14] See, for example, 'Gender and the Development of Welfare Regimes', (1992) *Journal of European Social Policy* 159.

childcare policy to ensure adequate provision of non-parental care or employment legislation policies aimed at making working hours compatible with childcare responsibilities.

Hence, women who had children and wanted or needed to participate in the labour market had no state or workplace support with childcare responsibilities. The solution to this problem, patched together by individual families, was a shift from a male breadwinner / female home-carer model to a male breadwinner / female part-time carer model.[15] As many employers would not allow women to convert their existing (full-time) job into a part-time position after the arrival of children, often this meant not just changing employment form but starting a new, lower-paid and lower-skilled job too. This model also meant that lone parents, an overwhelmingly female group, have been disproportionately excluded from labour market participation. The effectiveness of the male breadwinner model meant that mothers were by no means the only women who participated in the labour market on a part-time basis. It also played a role in shaping the exceptionally long, from a European perspective, full-time male working-hours in the UK.

UK labour legislative policy towards part-time workers aligned itself with this broader public policy stance. It manifested itself in two key areas: hours thresholds in relation to qualifying periods for statutory employment rights and a lower earnings limit for access to certain employment-related state payments.

An hours threshold formed part of the first modern UK employment statute, the Contracts of Employment Act 1963, its purpose being to exclude those for whom 'the employment relationship is not of substantial importance [such as] women with domestic responsibilities'.[16] It was in the Employment Protection Act of 1975 that the thresholds took the form in which they would remain for two decades. Between 1975 and 1995 UK legislation required those working between eight and sixteen hours per week to clock up five years' continuous employment in order to qualify

---

[15] B. Pfau-Effinger, 'Modernization of Family and Motherhood in Western Europe', in Crompton, *Restructuring Gender* (n. 13 above), p. 60.

[16] William Whitelaw MP, HC Debs, 5th series, Vol. 676, col. 1154, 1 May 1963: cited in S. Deakin and G. Morris, *Labour Law* (3rd edn, London: Butterworths, 2001), p. 194. The Contracts of Employment Act 1963 made access to the rights it contained subject to a qualifying weekly hours threshold of 21 hours. A week's work under a contract specifying less than 21 hours would not count as a qualifying week. The 21-hour threshold was also required for rights under the Redundancy Payments Act of 1965 and, under the Conservative Heath government, for the right not to be unfairly dismissed in the Industrial Relations Act 1971.

for a vast array of statutory rights.[17] Those working under eight hours per week were disqualified from all these statutory rights.[18] A few rights – those associated with discrimination at work – were not dependent on any qualifying period of employment.[19] It is telling that this legislative stance constituted a rather mechanical act of exclusion: while the same qualifying period (five years) was required for all rights for those working between eight and sixteen hours per week, and a blanket act of exclusion was applied to all those working under eight hours per week, the qualifying period (if any was imposed) for 'standard' employees varied enormously according to the right at issue.[20]

A similar legislative stance towards part-time workers is evident in the notion of a Lower Earnings Limit below which individuals are neither required to make National Insurance contributions (nor are their employers) nor entitled to receive benefits, of either a non-contributory nature (such as Statutory Maternity Pay and statutory sick pay)[21] or a contributory nature (such as invalidity benefit). Eleven per cent of UK employees earn below the Lower Earnings Limit.[22]

The Conservative governments in power in the UK between 1979 and 1997 retained the thresholds for the rather different reason that anything that lowered employers' labour market costs was good for the economy as it stimulated job creation. As well as retaining the thresholds, other policies pursued by Conservative governments worsened the labour market position of part-time workers.[23] Certain of these had the effect of

[17] *Inter alia*: unfair dismissal, unfair dismissal on grounds of pregnancy, a written statement of reasons for dismissal, statutory redundancy payments, time off for employees facing redundancy to seek work, 'guarantee pay', an itemised pay statement, a written statement of employment terms, maternity pay, the right to return after confinement (childbirth) and time off for trade union activities or public duties.

[18] See the useful table in E. Szyszczak, 'Employment Protection and Social Security', in R. Lewis (ed.), *Labour Law in Britain* (Oxford: Blackwell, 1986), pp. 360, 364.

[19] Rights not to be discriminated against on grounds of race or sex, and the right not to be dismissed or have action short of dismissal taken against one because of trade union membership.

[20] The most striking examples here were the rights to itemised pay statements and time off for trade union activities and public duties where no qualifying period at all was required for 'standard' employees.

[21] One of the qualifying conditions for Statutory Maternity Pay, for example, is to have earned not less than the Lower Earnings Limit in the eight weeks ending with the fifteenth week before childbirth.

[22] HC 2nd Report, para. 108.

[23] Such as rescission of the Fair Wages Resolution in 1982; compulsory competitive tendering of local government services, introduced by the Local Government Act 1988, which led to many female part-time jobs being contracted out of the public sector, frequently

making the marginal cost differential between those working over and under sixteen hours more worthy of consideration by employers considering how to structure part-time jobs.[24] As a result, the number of hours worked by part-time workers in the UK has changed over the last few decades with many more part-timers working shorter numbers of hours per week. There has also been a sharp related increase in part-timers holding multiple jobs.[25]

Employer practices, as well as collective agreements, have mirrored State policy. Part-timers have routinely been given worse terms and conditions of employment, being excluded for instance from occupational pensions or placed first in line for dismissal in redundancy situations. Adjustment of hours within the same job has not generally been permitted by employers, creating serious difficulties for workers who need to adjust their hours upwards or downwards at different periods of their working lives – as a result, for instance, of financial need or caring responsibilities.

The net result of these policies and practices is that part-timers are overwhelmingly crowded into the low-wage,[26] low-status sectors of the UK economy.[27] Archetypal UK part-timers are check-out operators employed by large supermarket chains with continuously operating stores, carers, waiters, cleaners and caterers. Many of the jobs part-timers do have been outsourced over the last decade by both public and private sector employers. As a result, *part-time workplaces* – in which only management may work full-time – are becoming increasingly common. In many of these cases, the disadvantage faced by part-timers is not that they are treated worse than full-time colleagues, but that many key benefits associated with employment are simply not offered in that particular workplace. Less than a quarter of part-timers are in occupational pension schemes, for example. Nowadays, though, this results less from unequal treatment,

---

accompanied by a worsening of terms and conditions; abolition of the Wages Council system in 1993 – this protected terms and conditions in many low-paid sectors of the UK labour market – abolition disproportionately affecting part-timers.

[24] See further S. Deakin and F. Wilkinson, *The Economics of Employment Rights* (London: Institute of Employment Rights, 1991).

[25] Deakin and Wilkinson, ibid., p. 19, note that while part-time work as a whole grew by 30% between 1979 and 1987, employment for sixteen hours or less per week increased by 66% in the same period. HC 2nd Report, para. 20, notes that almost 40% of female part-timers work less than sixteen hours per week and that multiple job-holding among female part-timers has doubled since 1984 (para. 91).

[26] The First Report of the Low Pay Commission found that part-timers were over half of low-paid workers (on the basis of hourly wages): Cm 3976 (1998) para. 3.17.

[27] Of general managers in the UK, 0.3% are part-timers; 34% of all UK part-time jobs are in sales: HC 2nd Report, para.19.

due to the impact of EU gender discrimination law, than to the fact that 54 per cent of male part-timers and 42 per cent of female part-timers work for employers who offer no such scheme. The equivalent figure for full-time workers is 25 per cent.[28]

Five specific areas of transformative potential can be extracted from this account in order to assist in the drawing of comparisons and links between different modes of EU–UK governance. The first concerns getting rid of the statutory hourly thresholds excluding part-time workers from most employment rights. A second area focusses on adjustment of the Lower Earnings Limit in the context of National Insurance contributions in order to prevent exclusion of part-timers from a range of monetary benefits linked to labour market participation. The third potential area for change involves introducing measures to ensure that part-timers are not employed on worse terms and conditions than other workers. Any such measures, to have transformative effects, would need to be sensitive to the corporate and occupational segregation of many part-time workers in the UK. A fourth possible area of change is to allow adjustment of the hours of work in a given job along a spectrum from very few hours to 'full-time' hours ('work–life balance' measures). This would be particularly important for women returning to work after absence for maternity, although this is evidently only one of many situations in which shifting work–life balance considerations might necessitate adjusting working hours and patterns. The fifth and final transformative objective one can identify is to increase the *quality* of part-time jobs in the UK. Of course, effective work–life balance measures would be an important step towards achieving that goal because creating the possibility that all jobs can be part-time would help increase the number of high-wage, high-status, part-time positions. However, this would only be one step because, as noted, outsourcing and niche contract recruitment patterns have led to pronounced corporate segregation of part-timers. Such segregation forecloses the opportunities for promotion, training and moving within the organisation (that is, quality improvement) offered within large, occupationally variegated, internal labour markets. Where the latter are in short supply, quality improvement must focus on ensuring part-time workers can acquire transferable skills. This five-point transformative

---

[28] Ibid., para. 97. On the influence of EU gender discrimination law see further below, nn. 37–8 and accompanying text. Employers have recently been placed under an obligation to provide a 'stakeholder' pension in all UK workplaces: Welfare Reform and Pensions Act 1999.

check-list: employment law thresholds, the National Insurance Lower Earnings Limit, inferior terms and conditions, work–life balance options and quality improvement will be utilised in carrying out our assessment of how, when and why EU governance has affected UK law and practice on part-time work. We turn, therefore, to investigate transformative procedural and substantive governance by examining gender discrimination sources, the Part-time Directive and Title VIII EC.

5   Gender discrimination law

Community law and UK law on gender discrimination both came to life at the same time, in the mid 1970s. However, drafting of the two UK statutes – the Equal Pay Act 1970 and the Sex Discrimination Act 1975 (SDA) – was not influenced by Community law. Both were cast in the precise and exhaustive style characteristic of UK statutes. Given that part-timers were almost exclusively women a promising argument to develop was that norms affording worse treatment to part-timers constituted indirect sex discrimination.

As a result of the Court of Justice's decisions in the *Defrenne* cases,[29] Article 119 (now 141) EC was an expression of a fundamental Community right to gender equality, was supreme and could be invoked by individuals against both the State and private employers. Chiefly as a result of a stream of preliminary references from German courts concerning part-time workers, the Court of Justice developed a robust stance on indirect discrimination. Two cases in particular stand out. In 1986 in *Bilka-Kaufhaus*,[30] concerning the exclusion of part-timers from the employer's occupational pension scheme, the Court of Justice decided that a measure which indirectly discriminated against part-timers would contravene Article 119 (now 141) EC unless the employer could objectively justify the measure. This means that the measure must correspond to a real need on the part of the undertaking, be appropriate for achieving the objectives pursued and be necessary to that end. In *Rinner-Kühn*,[31] a similar stance was taken to condemn German legislation on sick-pay which excluded part-timers, unless 'the means selected correspond to an objective necessary for its social policy and are appropriate and necessary to the attainment of that objective'. Discrimination law sources – national

---

[29] Case 43/75 [1976] ECR 455; Case 149/77 [1978] ECR 1365.
[30] Case 170/84 [1986] ECR 1607.   [31] Case 171/88 [1989] ECR 2743.

and EU – therefore afforded an opportunity to tackle the issues on our five-point transformative check-list.

5.1   The employment law thresholds

As expounded in *Bilka* and *Rinner-Kühn,* Community law provided (because of its supremacy) a unique opportunity to challenge the primary legislation in the UK which contained the hourly thresholds introduced in the Employment Protection Act 1975. The Equal Opportunities Commission, a statutory body created by the SDA 1975 to 'work towards the elimination of discrimination', took judicial review proceedings against the Secretary of State for Employment to challenge, as indirect gender discrimination contrary to Community law, the hours thresholds with regard to two statutory unfair dismissal rights and the right to statutory redundancy pay. The House of Lords in its judgment in 1994 in this case faithfully applied *Rinner-Kühn.*[32] It found that the thresholds indirectly discriminated against women and could not be objectively justified.

This case is of significance for a number of reasons. The UK government put forward employment promotion arguments to justify the thresholds objectively. It argued that the thresholds increased the number of part-time jobs available in the UK. This is clearly an attempt to argue that providing an employment law subsidy to part-time work has an employment creation effect. We have seen that this was not the original reason for the introduction of the thresholds but was rather a new gloss added by Conservative governments to justify their retention. The economic rationale for this 'job creation' argument – though this was not explicitly argued by the UK government – must be that normally part-timers are more expensive to employ than full-time workers, either because of administrative costs or productivity differences. Neither of these is convincing; indeed, the opposite is much more likely to be true with regard to productivity.[33] Therefore, neither equity nor efficiency arguments point towards retaining the hours thresholds.

Why then was the 'job creation' argument in favour of their retention found by the Divisional Court to be 'inherently logical'? This demonstrates that the question of balancing the priorities of equity and efficiency in

---

[32] [1994] IRLR 176.
[33] C. Barnard, S. Deakin and C. Kilpatrick, 'Equality, Non-discrimination and the Labour Market' (2002) 18 *International Journal of Comparative Labour Law and Industrial Relations*, p. 129.

an indirect discrimination claim is not only, or even primarily, about ensuring that equity does not prevail at the cost of efficiency gains. Indeed, it seems clear that the tougher the scrutiny of measures which disparately impact on women, the better both efficiency and equity considerations will be served in terms of assessing the necessity and appropriateness of a particular norm or practice. Rather, lax scrutiny, such as that exercised by the Divisional Court in its judgment, is indicative of judicial disagreement over who is considered best-placed to carry out that balancing of priorities; the more lax the scrutiny exercised, the more the court is indicating that the maker of the impugned norm should be allowed to balance its own priorities. It is an anti-transformative judicial stance. The House of Lords, adopting stricter scrutiny, rejected the 'job creation' argument because no evidence was put forward to back up the claim that the hours thresholds increased the number of part-time jobs in the UK economy. Lord Keith, giving the main judgment, pointed to the fact that part-time work had increased in other EU Member States where no thresholds existed.[34]

It is also worthy of note that those judges who wished to find the thresholds objectively justified rallied employment rate figures and EC law to their aid. Hence, the relatively high employment rate of women, especially on part-time contracts, in the UK was compared favourably to that in other EU Member States; the thresholds were presented as playing an important role, albeit difficult to prove, in this superior labour market performance. The 1990 EC proposals on part-time work were also deployed to argue that EC law in general could not prohibit hours thresholds as those proposals themselves contained an eight-hour threshold. Judicially enforceable discrimination rights, combined with EU judicial dialogue, can therefore provide an important channel for testing the strength of employment policy arguments relating to the effects produced by labour market legislation. However, this will only be the case when both the ECJ and national courts opt for pro-actively testing the efficiency and/or equity considerations proffered in respect of indirectly discriminatory laws.

Of equal interest is the effect of the House of Lords' judgment – a direct result of the application of Community gender equality sources – on the Conservative government in power at that time. No one would argue with the proposition that that government was distinctly unenthused by either the EU project or the prospect of extending employment protection. Yet

---

[34] Contrast with the less strict scrutiny applied by the House of Lords to the two-year qualifying threshold for unfair dismissal protection in *R. v. Secretary of State for Employment ex parte Seymour-Smith and Perez (No. 2)* [2000] IRLR 263.

the House of Lords' judgment in *ex parte EOC* led to Regulations in 1995 which went beyond what was strictly necessary to comply with the House of Lords' decision. The challenge in that case had concerned only three statutory rights while, as we have seen, the thresholds applied to most UK employment rights. Moreover, it was only the requirement of five years' continuous employment for those working between eight and sixteen hours per week which had clearly been condemned. The exclusion of those working under eight hours per week had more chance of proving itself to be objectively justified in an indirect discrimination challenge. However, the Regulations repealed the hourly thresholds throughout UK employment law with regard to both those working between eight and sixteen hours and those working under eight hours per week.[35]

A similar outcome has been achieved in litigation concerning the fate of part-timers who have been unlawfully excluded in the past from membership of occupational pension schemes.[36] The membership rights they obtained as a result of gender discrimination law were significantly reduced in value by a two-year arrears limit for equal pay claims in UK law.[37] The final outcome of a rather complex set of references to the Court of Justice[38] on this issue has once again been governmental action to remove the two-year limit from UK law.

5.2   The Lower Earnings Limit

It has also been argued before the courts that use of the Lower Earnings Limit in relation to qualification for Statutory Maternity Pay indirectly discriminates against women contrary to Article 119 (now 141) of the EC Treaty.[39] The claim failed before an Industrial Tribunal because it held that a discrimination claim, under either UK or EC law, requires a woman to compare her situation with that of a male comparator; this

---

[35] The Employment Protection (Part-time Employees) Regulations 1995 (SI 1995/31).

[36] Case C-57/93 *Vroege* [1994] ECR I-4541; Case C-128/93 *Fisscher* [1994] ECR I-4583.

[37] Section 2(5) Equal Pay Act 1970 and the analogous provisions in Reg. 5 of the Occupational Pension Schemes (Equal Treatment) Regulations 1995 and the equivalent Regulations for N. Ireland.

[38] See in particular Case C-249/96 *Magorrian* [1997] ECR I-7153 and Case C-78/98 *Preston* [2000] ECR I-2301. For a fuller discussion see C. Kilpatrick, 'Turning Remedies Around: a Sectoral Analysis of the European Court of Justice', in G. de Búrca and J. H. H. Weiler (eds.), *The European Court of Justice* (Oxford: Oxford University Press, 2001), p. 143.

[39] *Banks* v. *Tesco and Secretary of State for Social Security*, 3 June 1997, discussed in HC 2nd Report at paras. 110–11; also briefly referred to in Deakin and Morris, *Labour Law* (n. 16 above), p. 654.

was not possible here as the conditions governing eligibility for Statutory Maternity Pay involve a comparison between two groups of women.

5.3   Ensuring part-timers are not treated worse than full-timers

The multiple steps contained within the UK statutory definition of indirect discrimination (the need for an applicant to show a 'requirement or condition' with which 'a considerably smaller proportion of women than men can comply' to the applicant's 'detriment', and which is not 'justifiable' by the employer) gave the courts ample scope to reach widely divergent conclusions on whether treating part-timers worse than full-timers was indirect discrimination which could not be objectively justified. This can be demonstrated by briefly indicating three cases in which female part-timers challenged their selection for redundancy before full-time workers. In the first of these, *Clarke*,[40] disparate impact was easily established on the facts in that workplace. The Tribunal, considering justification to require the employer to show that it was right and proper in the circumstances for the company to adopt the 'part-timers first' redundancy criterion, found the employers' arguments – such as that it was the shift normally worked by part-time workers which was to be cut back on – were merely arguments of convenience and did not justify the indirect discrimination against female part-timers. This can be contrasted with the decision in *Kidd*[41] in 1985 which concerned an all-women department, made up of full- and part-time workers. Here the courts stated that no disparate impact had been established as it could not be assumed, without evidential support, that a considerably greater proportion of married women with young children (or women than men) regularly undertake a caring role. In any event, the marginal advantages obtained in getting rid of part-timers first, such as the extra laundry costs involved in employing part-timers, justified the application of this redundancy criterion. The Employment Appeal Tribunal (EAT) considered that, in the cut-throat world of modern business, 'small advantages of that kind . . . can cumulatively make a crucial difference between success or failure in attracting or maintaining orders'. In *Bhudi*[42] a part-time evening shift of female office cleaners was dismissed when management decided that it was administratively too complex and difficult to have cleaners on the premises outside

---

[40]   *Clarke* v. *Powell and Eley (IMI) Kynoch Ltd* [1982] IRLR 131.
[41]   *Kidd* v. *DRG(UK) Ltd* [1985] IRLR 190.
[42]   *Bhudi and others* v. *IMI Refiners Ltd* [1994] IRLR 204.

office hours. The full-time male cleaners who worked the day shift were not dismissed. It was argued before the EAT that the Tribunal had erred in rejecting the claim for want of a 'requirement or condition' because the ECJ equal pay case of *Enderby*[43] had found that a 'requirement or condition' was not necessary. This was rejected by the EAT on the ground that *Enderby* was an equal pay case and therefore had no bearing on cases not concerning terms and conditions of employment in the UK. Nor was it possible to reinterpret the clear wording of the SDA so as to eliminate the need to show 'a requirement or condition'. However, the Tribunal had been wrong to assume that the only possible requirement or condition could have been to work full-time and should have examined whether there was a requirement or condition to work normal hours.

The cases on part-timers and redundancy selection indicate that courts do not find it easy to ascertain indirect discrimination in situations where part-timers are disadvantaged. Two further decisions illustrate even more clearly the degree to which hard cases in this sphere make bad law.

In *Staffordshire County Council* v. *Black*[44] part-time teachers were treated worse than their full-time colleagues in relation to occupational pension credits. They were unable to show disparate impact, however, because teaching is a female-dominated profession; 90 per cent of female teachers compared with 97 per cent of male teachers (the 'pool' for comparison) could comply with the requirement to work full-time. Courts have great scope to draw pools widely or narrowly; a narrow pool in a female-dominated sector inevitably signals defeat at the disparate impact stage.

The hardest case was *Barry* v. *Midland Bank*,[45] eventually decided by the House of Lords. Ms Barry had worked full-time for eleven years for the bank until the birth of her child and had then switched to part-time work for two years. She challenged a voluntary severance scheme which gave a sum equal to the final actual salary of the employee multiplied by their years of service with the company. She argued that this ignored the fact that many women switch from full-time to part-time work and that, therefore, to calculate on the basis of the final actual salary indirectly discriminated against women. However, the proposed alternative way of creating more equity for part-timers in Ms Barry's situation – counting *hours* of service rather than *years* of service – would mean that another group of part-timers – those who had always worked part-time for the

---

[43] Case C-127/92 *Enderby* v. *Frenchay Health Authority* [1993] ECR I-5535.
[44] [1995] IRLR 234.   [45] [1999] IRLR 581.

bank – would lose out. This is because a part-timer who had worked for 10 years at 17.5 hours per week under the current system would be awarded ten years' service, but under the alternative system would only have worked the equivalent of five years. There was, therefore, clearly a need to look carefully at the disparate impact figures of 'fluctuating' and 'permanent' part-timers, as well as considering the possible purposes served by severance payments, in order to make a judgment on whether the bank's scheme could be objectively justified. However, the House of Lords never got this far, the majority deciding that there was no need to proceed to even ascertaining whether there was disparate impact, let alone objective justification. This was because, in their view, there was no difference in treatment at all. The purpose of the payment was to compensate for loss of actual income, not to remunerate for past service and, therefore, there was no relevant difference in treatment as everyone received a payment based on final salary. Placing an additional purpose test at the beginning of an indirect discrimination claim, rather than within the objective justification analysis, undermines the conceptual integrity of the structure of the indirect discrimination claim which is to challenge norms and practices which in their formulation treat everyone the same but, in their operation, disparately impact on a disadvantaged group. It is to assert on policy grounds that there is no discrimination instead of applying disparate impact analysis to find out whether there is discrimination.

It is apparent that the bits of EU indirect gender discrimination case-law considered to help part-timers, most particularly the *Bilka* objective justification test, get extremely little chance to make any showing here as claims fail before reaching that point. However, EU legislative synthesis and development of ECJ jurisprudence, in the form of Directive 97/80/EC on the burden of proof in cases of discrimination based on sex, has recently wrought some changes to the statutory definition used in employment cases brought under the SDA. A product of the Maastricht Social Chapter, though not of the social partners, it was extended to the UK by Directive 98/52/EC and implemented by secondary legislation which came into force in October 2001.[46] The Directive removes the need for a requirement or condition and places in legislative form the *Bilka* objective justification test. The UK Regulations introduce the former but not the latter change into UK law.

---

[46] The Sex Discrimination (Indirect Discrimination and Burden of Proof) Regulations SI 2001/2660; see the new definition of indirect discrimination for employment cases in section 1(2) SDA 1975.

5.4   Work–life balance options

The cases all concern women with young children, most often returning from maternity leave. They demonstrate clearly that part-time work is not a general panacea for work–life balancing. Rather, it is one possible option in a wide range of changes to working patterns which women request or resist. Hence, the women in these cases asked to be able to carry out additional responsibilities at lunchtime rather than after work, to work a three-day full-time week rather than a five-day part-time week, to retain a particular shift system which was compatible with their childcare responsibilities, and to job-share, as well as to shift from full-time to part-time work.

The courts also dealt with these cases differently from those concerning inferior treatment of part-timers. Apart from one case, notorious because it is an exceptionally bad application of the indirect discrimination formula,[47] the courts have not only easily found the existence of a requirement or condition but, more strikingly, have shown remarkable generosity and insight into the disparate impact issue. For instance, in *Carey*, the pool for comparison contained only 4 men and 292 women. Yet disparate impact could be established because none of the 4 men worked part-time and it was reasonable to suppose that many of the female health visitors would opt for half-week working if it were available to them.[48] In *London Underground* v. *Edwards (No. 2)*,[49] it was found that, of the 2,023 male train operators, 100 per cent could comply with new rostering arrangements, while 95.2 per cent of the 21 female train operators, that is all bar Ms Edwards, a single parent, could comply. Yet this was found to constitute disparate impact because it was important to look at the absolute numbers of men and women in the comparator groups and not to 'ignore the striking fact that not a single man was disadvantaged by the requirement, despite the vast preponderance of men within the group'. Moreover, courts could use their general knowledge and expertise 'to look outside the pool for comparison and take into account the national figure that 10 times as many women as men single parents have care of a child'. In other cases, the court simply decided unhesitatingly that disparate impact was established because 'despite the changes in the role of women in modern society, it is still a fact that the raising of children tends to place a greater burden upon them than it does upon men'.[50]

---

[47] *Clymo* v. *Wandsworth London Borough Council* [1989] *Industrial Cases Reports* 250.
[48] *Greater Glasgow Health Board* v. *Carey* [1987] IRLR 484.
[49] [1998] IRLR 364 (CA).   [50] *Home Office* v. *Holmes* [1984] ICR 678.

It is on the rock of justification that most of these claims perish. Where the employer is able to present reasons beyond those of mere convenience, the requirement or condition is found to be justified. The courts do not go through the three stages of the objective justification test set out in *Bilka*; they state that they are balancing the discriminatory effects on the worker with the employer's need for efficiency.

5.5 Limitations of the multi-level gender discrimination discourse

These cases illustrate perfectly the limits and boundaries imposed by UK–EU judicial dialogue on legislative definitions of discrimination: the only partial congruence of sources at national and Community level, the limited direct effect accorded to directives and the limits of indirect effect are all invoked in this case-law. Apart from those cases concerning primary legislation, the ECJ's jurisprudence was heavily mediated by the national definition and national judicial canons of statutory interpretation. Even the translation of the ECJ's definition of indirect discrimination into a directive has not had the effect of fully inserting the EU definition into UK law.

However, even leaving aside the problems of national and EU source mediation, gender discrimination suffers from a number of weaknesses with regard to tackling discrimination against part-time workers. First, the part-timer will need to find a male (invariably full-time) comparator; a task which is often difficult given occupational segregation. Secondly, occupational segregation often makes it difficult to establish disparate impact. Thirdly, even when disparate impact is established, the defence of objective justification is always available and, if satisfied, will mean that no discrimination has occurred. The differential treatment within the indirect discrimination formula accorded by the courts to work–life balance issues, on the one hand, and inferior terms and conditions on the other, demonstrates how that formula is flexible enough to adapt to varying judicial perceptions of its transformative role in different situations.

With regard to our five-point transformative check-list for part-time work in the UK, therefore, gender discrimination law allowed: one complete achievement (the thresholds); extremely limited progress on improving or maintaining the terms and conditions of part-time workers; mixed, patchy outcomes on work–life balance issues; and no progress whatsoever on either broader quality issues or the Lower Earnings Limit.

Yet court decisions on gender discrimination and part-time work have a wider social currency than their immediate outcome. In their depictions of life stories, and their efforts to grapple with complex legal tools and social problems, courts create an archive of specialised social knowledge which can be drawn upon by other actors and institutions. We shall see a number of instances where other parts of the state draw, in some way or other, on this resource.

6   Employment law measures: transposition and transformation

The Part-time Directive contains two key clauses. Clause 4 uses the technique of discrimination in order to afford worker protection to part-timers while cl. 5 contains three sub-clauses dealing with opportunities for part-time work. Its implementation therefore presented the opportunity to address a number of items on our transformative check-list: worse terms and conditions; work–life balance; and the quality of part-time jobs. Section 19 of the Employment Relations Act of 1999 – New Labour's flagship piece of labour legislation in its first term of government – gave the Secretary of State power to make regulations to ensure that part-timers are treated 'no less favourably than persons in full-time employment'. By s. 19(4) it also gave the Secretary of State wide powers to make any provision necessary or expedient to comply with obligations under the Part-time Directive. Section 20 further gave the Secretary of State power to issue codes of practice containing guidance for the purpose of eliminating discrimination against part-time workers, facilitating the development of opportunities for part-time work, facilitating the flexible organisation of working time or any other matter dealt with in the Part-time Directive.

6.1   The anti-discrimination principle: personal and comparative scope

The implementation of the Part-time Directive in the UK is an extremely interesting episode of policy-making and law-making, and one which can be seen as constituting a paradigm of the post-1997 British government's approach to the reception of EU employment law. It could even to some extent be viewed as a way of understanding the evolution of that government's stance towards employment law as a whole during its first three years in office. In this section, we seek to make good those assertions by showing how Regulations enacted to implement the Directive were framed with respect to their personal and comparative scope.

We begin by defining our terms; and in particular what we mean by 'the personal and comparative scope' of the Regulations. Personal scope and comparative scope are two distinct concepts (though, as will be seen, there may be very important connections between them). The personal scope of the Regulations refers to the category of persons to whom the Regulations apply, and more particularly to the category of persons *in favour of whom* they apply. It is obvious from the very title of the Regulations that this is a category of 'workers'; but that leaves to be explored the question of the precise definition of workers that has been chosen.

The Regulations are concerned, as their title proclaims, with 'less favourable treatment' of part-time workers. This means that, like any measure which is concerned with adverse discrimination, they address a comparison, or series of comparisons, between persons or groups of persons. We are using the term 'comparative scope' to refer to the persons or groups of persons, comparison between whom forms the subject-matter of the Regulations. Probably anybody reading the title of the Regulations, and certainly anybody with any knowledge of their background will correctly assume that the comparison in question is, basically, between part-time workers and full-time workers; but it will be explained that their comparative scope is defined much more precisely than that.

Both these issues, that of the personal scope and of the comparative scope of the Regulations, became matters of considerable sensitivity so far as the Government was concerned. The Directive itself had set out the ground-rules – though, as is typical of directives giving effect to agreements between the social partners at Community level, it had not done so with the utmost precision. There was, or at least there was perceived to be, a 'margin of appreciation' within which the Government embarked upon a difficult process of policy-making and decision-making.

So far as personal scope was concerned, the Framework Agreement on Part-time Work, which it was the task of the Directive to implement, had provided that it would apply to 'part-time workers who have an employment contract or employment relationship as defined by the law, collective agreement or practice in force in each Member State'.[51] This definition was coupled with a further provision allowing Member States, after consultation with the social partners, to exclude, 'for objective reasons' part-time workers 'who work on a casual basis'.[52] In the course of defining its comparative scope, the Agreement refers to the part-time worker to which it applies as an '*employee* whose normal hours of work . . . are less than [those] of a comparable full-time worker'[53] (emphasis added).

[51] Clause 2.1.   [52] Clause 2.2.   [53] Clause 3.1.

So far as comparative scope itself was concerned, the Agreement defines a comparable full-time worker as a full-time worker 'in the same establishment having the same type of employment contract or relationship, who is engaged in the same or a similar work/occupation, due regard being given to other considerations which may include seniority and qualification/skills'. There is a proviso that where there is no comparable full-time worker in the same establishment, 'the comparison shall be made by reference to the applicable collective agreement or . . . in accordance with national law, collective agreements or practice'.[54] It is not clear which aspects of national law, collective agreements or practice are supposed to indicate the wider comparative scope of the Agreement.

The British Government took some time to reflect on how to give effect to the Directive, for although it was enacted in 1997 and extended to the UK in 1998, it was not until January 2000 that the Department of Trade and Industry issued a consultative document about its proposals for doing so.[55] In that document, the Government located its proposals on part-time work within its general agenda of 'improving the functioning of the UK labour market whilst providing a framework of decent minimum standards for employees'.[56] An anxiety about the over-regulatory character of EU employment law was evident in the prominent re-assurance, entirely in the rhetorical tone of the Government's recent predecessors, that 'The proposals will not impose any new burdens on the vast majority of businesses. The Government has opted for a "light-touch" approach, avoiding red-tape.'[57]

At that stage, the proposed 'light-touch approach' to the issues of personal and comparative scope was a simple one; the formulas of the Agreement were closely followed in a fairly cautious way. The category of 'workers' was rendered as 'employees' working under 'contracts of employment'. The 'comparable full-time employee' was one who was engaged in the same or broadly similar work as a part-time employee, had a broadly similar level of qualification, skills and experience, and worked in the same establishment. (If there was no such employee at the same establishment, one from a different establishment could be regarded as comparable.)

This proposal appeared, in particular to the TUC and to the trade union movement, to be unduly narrow in its personal scope, because it confined

[54] Clause 3.2.
[55] *Part-Time Work Public Consultation* January 2000 DTI URN 99/1224.
[56] *Consultation* document, p. 1.   [57] Ibid.

its provisions to employees working under contracts of employment at a time when more inclusive approaches seemed to be the emerging norm for UK employment law. There were two particular manifestations of such approaches. First, all the UK legislation concerning different types of discrimination in employment – sex, race and disability – had been applied to all 'employment' contracts, so defined as to include not only contracts of employment but, in effect, all other contracts for personal work.

Secondly, the new employment legislation brought forward by the Government since its election in 1997 had generally conferred new rights not just on employees working under contracts of employment but on a broader category of 'workers', formulated with the objective of including all those working under personal work contracts save the 'genuinely self-employed' – a terminology which began to be adopted in descriptions issued by the DTI of the intended effect of the new legislation in question. The two crucial examples of this new approach were the National Minimum Wage Act 1998 and the Working Time Regulations 1998 enacted to implement the Working Time Directive.

In that legislative context, it was felt in many quarters that, even if it was technically defensible, it would be somewhat egregious to confine to 'employees' the implementation of a Directive which was nominally addressed to the larger category of 'workers'. On the other hand, the British Government was increasingly concerned not to let its 'light touch' appear to become a heavier one, especially when it concerned measures taken under the Social Chapter of the EU Treaty. In a remarkably interesting transformation, the proposals were re-worked so that their personal scope was made more inclusive, but, in a way which has perhaps not been sufficiently noted,[58] their comparative scope was made much more exclusive.

Early in May 2000, the Secretary of State for Trade and Industry, Stephen Byers, announced that the Government's response to the public consultation about its proposals was to extend the proposed legislation from employees to workers.[59] The revised draft Regulations – which constituted the text that was enacted shortly afterwards and came into force in

---

[58] The point is touched upon in A. McColgan's valuable note on the Regulations, 'Recent Legislation. Missing the Point? The Part-time Workers (Prevention of Less Favourable Treatment) Regulations 2000 (SI 2000, no. 1551)' (2000) 29 ILJ 260, p. 261.

[59] DTI News Release P/2000/305 3 May 2000, 'More people to reap the benefits of working part-time'.

July 2000[60] – duly made that change. The category of workers to which they apply is indeed the one used since 1997 to include all save the 'genuinely self-employed', that is to say the worker is defined as an 'individual who . . . works under . . . (a) a contract of employment . . . or (b) any other contract . . . whereby the individual undertakes to do or perform personally any work or services for another party to the contract whose status is not . . . that of a client or customer of any profession or business undertaking carried on by the individual'.[61] It was emphasised that this extension had been made 'in order to help thousands of extra part-timers who are some of the most vulnerable members of the workforce'.[62]

Less prominent in the news release concerned was the announcement, about which no further detail was given, that: 'However, the regulations will be introduced with a light touch by ensuring that comparison can only be made between part-time and full-time workers with the same type of contract.' This seemed to be only a slight relaxation of the foot on the accelerator of regulation. It seemed to do no more than pick up on the fact that the Directive, as we have seen, confined its comparative scope to workers with the same 'type of contract', although in the first draft of the Regulations it had not been chosen to include that restriction. The Directive had not specified what was meant by 'type of contract', and the phrase had not attracted any particular attention.

The restriction of comparison to workers with the same 'type of contract' might have remained similarly innocuous in the Regulations had they, similarly to the Directive, done no more than enact that: 'A full-time worker is a comparable full-time worker in relation to a part-time worker if . . . (a) both workers are (i) employed by the same employer under the same type of contract'.[63] In fact, however, the Regulations are a great deal more specific than the Directive about what is meant by the same type and different types of contract. The manner in which this concept is elaborated by the Regulations deserves special attention.

The relevant provision, that of Regulation 2(3), needs to be set out in full. It is that:

> the following shall be regarded as being employed under different types of contract –
>
> (a) employees employed under a contract that is neither for a fixed term nor a contract of apprenticeship;

[60] The Part-time Workers (Prevention of Less Favourable Treatment) Regulations 2000 SI 2000/1551.
[61] Reg. 1(2).   [62] DTI News Release cited in n. 59 above.   [63] Reg. 2(4).

(b) employees employed under a contract for a fixed term that is not a contract of apprenticeship;

(c) employees employed under a contract of apprenticeship;

(d) workers who are neither employees nor employed under a contract for a fixed term;

(e) workers who are not employees but are employed under a contract for a fixed term;

(f) any other description of worker that it is reasonable for the employer to treat differently from other workers on the ground that workers of that description have a different type of contract.

It is very revealing to consider how far the category of 'workers' is thereby broken down into distinct sub-categories of workers under different contract types – bearing in mind that comparison is excluded between sub-categories, so that a part-time worker in one sub-category may not compare herself or himself with someone in a different sub-category. It looks at first impression as if Regulation 2(3) has created six mutually exclusive sub-categories, (a) to (f) respectively. Actually this is a much more complex and sub-divided formulation even than that.

In order to understand these complexities, we need to consider separately the different nature of items 2(3) (a) to (e), on the one hand, and, on the other hand, item 2(3)(f) – which turns out to be the wild card in the pack. Items (a) to (e) do indeed represent five mutually exclusive sub-categories. This in itself considerably fragments the 'worker' category and considerably restricts the comparative scope of the regulations. In particular, it greatly diminishes the significance of the extension of the overall scope of the regulations from 'employees' to 'workers' by treating non-employee workers separately from employee workers. Furthermore, it introduces the potent distinction between fixed-term contracts and open-ended ones.[64]

An even more divisive provision, however, presents itself in the shape of Regulation 2(3)(f). For this is no simple sub-category; quite unlike items (a) to (e), it forms a provision enabling the employer to cite, as a restriction upon the comparative scope of the Regulations, any description of the part-time worker which differentiates that worker from the full-time worker with whom comparison is sought, as long as the description can reasonably be said to amount to a differentiation between the types of contract which the two workers have. This means that the grounds of

---

[64] Though see now, below, section 6.5.

differentiation between full- and part-time workers are not completely specified in advance; there is an open category of potentially valid differentiations.

Not only might these differentiations be numerous; it is also to be noted that they may operate cumulatively with the stated differentiation into sub-categories (a) to (e), and with each other. So, suppose that an employer can successfully argue that workers on performance-related pay have contracts of a different type from those of workers not on performance-related pay. This distinction might cut across the five sub-categories, creating ten sub-categories. A further distinction, say between workers with occupational pension schemes and those without them, might turn those ten sub-categories into twenty – and so on, exponentially.

That example might seem fanciful, but until there is a jurisprudence which gives shape to the idea of reasonable differentiations, we can by no means rule out extensive fragmentation of the area of comparison which the regulations are generally thought to have sketched out. It begins to be apparent why, in its Regulatory Impact Assessment of the re-drafted regulations, the DTI estimated that the increase in the costs of complying with the regulations, due to the extension from employees to workers, should not be more than about 5 per cent.[65] It will be extremely interesting to assess the experience of the operation of these regulations, and to learn what role is played by these formulations of their personal and comparative scope.

It is already apparent that the move from gender discrimination law to employment law did not solve, but rather presented in a new guise, the problems for part-timers in finding a suitable comparator. One might even surmise that the strong association in the UK between part-time work and gender discrimination law played some role in inspiring the move to widen the personal scope while tightening the comparative scope of the Regulations. Finally, both the EU and national-level norms on part-time work reflect the use of techniques (anti-discrimination) outside their normal employment and labour law context (the protection of rights which are regarded as fundamental in contexts other than work). Hence specific rights are swapped for comparative protections as the techniques developed to realise fundamental rights are deployed as a new kind of employment protection technique.

---

[65] See *DTI Regulatory Impact Assessment of the Part Time Workers (Prevention of Less Favourable Treatment) Regulations* (May 2000) paras. 13–19, especially para. 14.

6.2   What happened to Clause 5?

The UK Government's *Public Consultation on Part-time Work* of January 2000[66] was a strange kind of consultation document. It contained barely any discursive text at all, principally consisting of a set of draft Regulations. This approach allowed the Government not to state whether its draft Regulations adequately covered all the matters set out in the Part-time Directive. One can only deduce – from the absence of provisions in the Part-time Regulations – that the Government did not consider that cl. 5 of the Part-time Directive required transposition in the UK legal order. This would correspond with a reading of the provisions of the Part-time Directive which views cl. 4 as the hard law half of its provisions and Clause 5 as the soft law half.

However, this reading is problematic on a number of grounds. The Government's manner of consulting on the Part-time Directive eliminated its need to illustrate which bits of that Directive it considered did not require transposition, and the reasons for which that was the case. The Directive is not even mentioned in the *Public Consultation* document, save for one mention tucked inside a Summary of the Regulatory Impact Assessment on the last page. Obscuring EU law in this way was clearly not apt to encourage scrutiny of whether the draft Regulations implemented the Directive in full.

Nor can it be asserted that the Regulations constituted the first in a series of steps to implement the Part-time Directive. The deadline for transposition of the Directive in the UK (set out in Directive 98/23) was 7 April 2000. The Part-time Regulations themselves missed this deadline, let alone other possible measures. Moreover, the DTI indicates that it considers that the Part-time Regulations fully implement its obligations to transpose the Part-time Directive.[67]

Finally, cl. 5 cannot be dismissed out of hand as a purely soft law provision, containing only aspirational social protection aims and promotional employment policy goals.[68] Clause 5(2), for example, provides that refusal to transfer between full-time and part-time work and vice versa should

---

[66] N. 55 above.

[67] See www2.dti.gov.uk/er/europe/directives.htm: the DTI's implementation table of EU employment directives.

[68] See C. Barnard and B. Hepple, 'Substantive Equality' (2000) *Cambridge Law Journal*, p. 582 – 'doubtful' that the Directive is enforceable against public authorities, though they refer only to cl. 5(3)(d), on which see further below.

not be a valid reason for dismissal. No protection of this kind is provided in the Part-time Regulations. Nor can one find any governmental discussion of whether unfair dismissal law or employment contract law affords adequate protection so as to ensure, via pre-existing law, compliance with this provision. Yet this provision is as 'hard' as the anti-discrimination protection contained in cl. 4 of the Directive. It could be invoked before UK courts and be vertically directly effective in cases involving the state and its emanations.

Clause 5(3) states that 'as far as possible' employers should give consideration to:

(a) requests by workers to transfer from full-time to part-time work that becomes available in the establishment;
(b) requests by workers to transfer from part-time to full-time work or to increase their working time should the opportunity arise;
(c) the provision of timely information on the availability of part-time and full-time positions in the establishment in order to facilitate transfers from full-time to part-time or vice versa;
(d) measures to facilitate access to part-time work at all levels of the enterprise, including skilled and managerial positions, and where appropriate, to facilitate access by part-time workers to vocational training to enhance career opportunities and occupational mobility;
(e) the provision of appropriate information to existing bodies representing workers about part-time working in the enterprise.

It is not obvious that this provision requires no Member State action. It is perfectly possible to envisage a mixture of law and policy techniques being employed to realise the various parts of cl. 5(3). Employers could, for instance, be placed under a legal obligation to permit people 'as far as possible' to adjust their working hours up and downwards, and to provide accessible, timely, information on part-time and full-time opportunities in the workplace. Looking at the last sub-clause, provision of information on part-time work to workplace representatives is cheap, potentially helpful, and easily slots alongside existing information obligations on employers in UK law.

Clause 5(1) requires Member States and the social partners to review obstacles which may limit opportunities for part-time work and, where appropriate, to eliminate them. Deakin and Reed have described this clause as speaking to a demand side, deregulatory, conception of flexibility, granting employers greater autonomy to shape personnel practices to changing market conditions.[69] Though it may be read in this way in many Member States, this is not the most fitting reading of cl. 5(1) in the UK context. In the UK, it clearly points to requiring government and social partners to consider how to remove obstacles to part-time work in those sectors or levels in which part-time work is currently not acceptable. Though cl. 5(1) does not fall into the judicially enforceable rights/obligations category, this does not necessarily mean that inactivity equates to compliance.

6.3   Parliament, the DTI and implementation of the Part-time Directive

The dialogue between Parliament and the executive on the Part-time Directive did not take place primarily through Parliament's legislative powers. The powers granted in the Employment Relations Act 1999 gave the DTI a broad scope to make secondary legislation on part-time work largely free from Parliamentary legislative controls.

However, a truly fascinating example of contemporary UK governance was set in motion by the House of Commons Select Committee on Education and Employment's[70] examination of part-time work. The Committee's examination took place during the period in which the Government was required to implement the Part-time Directive. The DTI was required to provide evidence to the Committee and, even more interestingly, to provide an ongoing set of responses to recommendations and further pointed queries raised by the Committee in its Reports during the critical period of March 1999 to March 2000.

The Committee's principal (2nd) Report was published on 23 March 1999, simultaneously, or so it expected, with the DTI's consultation proposals on part-time work. In that report, the Committee's main concern was with how the DTI would define the personal and comparative scope

---

[69] S. Deakin and H. Reed, 'The Contested Meaning of Labour Market Flexibility: Economic Theory and the Discourse of European Integration', in J. Shaw (ed.), *Social Law and Policy in an Evolving European Union* (Oxford: Hart, 2000), pp. 71, 75.

[70] The Education and Employment Committee is appointed under Standing Order to examine the expenditure, administration and policy of the Department for Education and Employment and associated public bodies. It has seventeen members, it has powers to send for persons, papers and records, to issue reports, to appoint specialist advisers, to appoint two sub-committees, and to communicate or meet with other committees appointed under the same Standing Order for the purposes of deliberating, taking evidence or considering draft reports.

of the anti-discrimination principle. It urged the DTI to ensure that all workers (not just 'employees') were covered, to allow broad spatial comparisons so that part-time workers could compare themselves with those working in the same establishment or service, and to maximise the comparative scope of the anti-discrimination protection by permitting the use of a hypothetical full-time comparator. This reflected the Committee's recognition that one of the great weaknesses of gender equality instruments with regard to part-time work is that many part-timers work in feminised, part-time only, workplaces. It further recommended that the DTI should introduce a right for women to be allowed to return to work on a part-time basis after maternity leave unless the employer could show that this would be to the detriment of the business.

The Government had two stock replies to the matters raised in the Committee's 2nd Report in its response to the Committee on 18 June 1999. Issues concerning the personal and comparative scope of the anti-discrimination principle were matters for consultation; all other issues would be dealt with in the Code of Practice on part-time work which the DTI was going to produce.

Events had taken a rather different course by the time the Committee issued its 3rd Report of 23 March 2000. This report was sharply critical of the DTI's approach to implementing the Part-time Directive, and, prior to issuing this report, the Committee called the Minister before it to account for the DTI's handling of the matter. The Committee had three key points of criticism, all of which are highly relevant to our discussion. The first concerned the time-table for consultation and implementation of the Regulations. The consultation paper, expected in the first half of 1999, then promised in the second half of 1999, was not published, as we have seen, until January 2000. At that point, the three-month consultation period promised was curtailed to two months. Implementation of the Regulations, despite the curtailed public consultation period, did not occur before the transposition deadline (7 April 2000) and was now planned for (and did occur in) July 2000. The justification proffered by the DTI to the Committee for the delay, and subsequent curtailment, of the public consultation period, was that it had decided to engage in a period of private consultation first with the CBI, the TUC and the Equal Opportunities Commission; this had proved so fruitful that a long public consultation period was not then felt to be necessary. The Committee was unimpressed with the DTI's justifications: 'We are not persuaded that the Government's reasons for delaying the publication of the consultation paper were sound . . . Although we recognise the value of private and

informal consultation while draft statutory instruments are being prepared, we do not believe that it should be treated as a substitute for an
open public consultation exercise' (Para. 5).

The Committee was also unimpressed that the DTI had chosen to
restrict the anti-discrimination protection to 'employees' and suggested
that this could breach the Part-time Directive. It reiterated its concerns
about the comparative scope of the Regulations.

The real weight of the Committee's disapproval, however, was reserved
for the DTI's *volte-face* on its plans, repeatedly referred to by the DTI in
its response to the Committee's 2nd Report, and explicitly provided for in
s. 20 of the Employment Relations Act 1999, to produce a Code of Practice.

What the Government had intended to place in the Code of Practice
is revealed in the Committee's 3rd Report. It was intended to encourage
employers to consider increasing part-time and flexible working at senior
levels and to make it easier for all workers to change their hours of work
by setting out criteria for employers to consider. It would also include
ways in which public sector employers could help part-time workers, in
particular, by identifying obstacles which might limit opportunities for
part-time work, and taking steps to eliminate them where appropriate.
From this, we can see that the role of the Code of Practice was to place in a
legal form some parts of cl. 5(2) and (3) of the Directive. A Code of Practice
issued by the Secretary of State is as close to hard law as soft law can get in
the UK. Although failure by an individual to observe any part of a Code
of Practice will not render that person liable to any proceedings, Codes
of Practice set out desirable behaviour; their provisions are admissible in
evidence and must be taken account of where relevant by Employment
Tribunals in cases before them. Their importance as a source of law is
increased by the fact that a draft Code must be approved by both Houses
of Parliament before becoming a Code.

What the Government in effect did was to downgrade its soft law commitment to cl. 5. The Minister dismissed Codes of Practice before the
Committee as 'big, dense slabs of print which lead to a confrontational
situation in workplaces'.[71] The Committee, given that the Code of Practice had been abandoned, asked the Government for a fresh response on
how it intended to implement cl. 5 – in particular, the two 'hardest' commitments in that clause: cl. 5(2) which states that a worker's refusal to
transfer between full- and part-time work should not in itself constitute
a valid reason for termination of employment, and cl. 5(3) in so far as it

---

[71] HC 3rd Report, para. 19.

states that employers should consider requests from workers to transfer between full- and part-time work.

The Government's response to the Committee's 3rd Report was to reply, in May 2000, that: 'The whole of Clause 5 (including 5(2) and 5(3)) will be implemented through a Programme of Information, including guidance, which will be available on the DTI's part-time work web-site.' Three observations can be offered on this governance episode. The first is that the long consultation period on the Part-time Regulations with apparent extensive recourse to informal channels, might be seen as exemplifying new 'third way' patterns of procedural governance. However, before this claim can be made, it would be necessary to consider whether private and public consultation fulfil the same roles, or have the same value, in 'good' procedural governance. A particular concern is how one can ascertain in a private consultation process whether the Government gave equal consultation opportunities to employers and unions.

The second observation concerns how cl. 5 was dealt with. This illustrates well how the simple distinction between hard and soft law does not do justice to the much more varied repertoire of legal techniques available to Government. A Code of Practice and a Programme of Information are both 'soft law', but the downgrading from the former to the latter in the Government's response to cl. 5 is highly significant. This also shows that a move from hard to soft and even softer law may on occasion represent 'smart' procedural governance, in the sense of seeking new, and more effective, ways of achieving substantive objectives. It may also, though, more banally indicate a desire by government not to pursue a particular objective at a particular juncture – here to increase the protection and opportunities afforded to part-time workers.

The third issue is how the changing legal architecture of EU social policy instruments affects implementation processes at national level. The mixed nature, and softer edges of cl. 5, partly a result of its genesis in an Agreement by the social partners, made the task of ascertaining the meaning of compliance more complex. Neither the Committee nor the Government seems to have considered that some parts of cl. 5 might require the creation of legally enforceable rights. Hence, the changing nature of Title XI EC measures creates greater margins of manoeuvre for national executives.

6.4   On-going part-time work governance

This law-making process and its outcomes in the Part-time Regulations 2000 are interesting because they show just how reluctant the DTI was to embrace the Directive's provisions. The result is that the Part-time Regulations, at very best, may assist in the achievement of exceptionally modest progress with regard only to the third item on our transformative check-list – amelioration of the inferior terms and conditions of part-time work.

There are a number of possible explanations for the muted and diluted reception of the Part-time Directive. One is that New Labour shares the same broad vision of the labour market as its Conservative predecessors: that ensuring that the State and employers incur minimal costs is the best recipe for a competitive, employment-creating, economy. On the basis of the Part-time Regulations taken alone, we would be driven to conclude that New Labour provided no concrete evidence whatsoever that it wished to embrace a vision of labour market equity and efficiency different from its predecessors. The many opportunities offered by the Part-time Directive to do just that were all firmly spurned.

Perhaps, however, it is the case that New Labour does embrace some distinctive efficiency and equity considerations from its Conservative predecessors but that its approach to procedural governance prevented these making their presence felt in the Part-time Regulations. A second possibility points more to multi-level governance as an explanatory variable; the UK Government had its own agenda on part-time work and the Part-time Directive did not fit well with that domestic agenda. A third possibility is that New Labour does embrace different efficiency and equity considerations from its recent predecessors but has greater difficulty, possibly for path-dependent historical reasons, in taking them into account in employment protection law than in other governmental activities (such as social welfare law and policy, tax law, employment promotion). These possibilities are not mutually exclusive as general approaches to procedural and multi-level governance will be adapted to specific substantive governance situations.

Nor do we need idly to speculate on these possibilities. We look first at subsequent initiatives taken by New Labour with regard to part-time work to investigate, in particular, the procedural and multi-level governance hypotheses with regard to Title XI EC measures. To test the employment law versus other kinds of governmental activity explanation, a broader range of social and employment laws and policies must be examined. One useful way of doing that is to look at the UK Government's participation in Title VIII EC. This examination also serves the function of testing multi-level governance in the context of Title VIII EC.

6.5   The Part-Time (Prevention of Less Favourable Treatment) Regulations 2000 (Amendment) Regulations 2002

Knock-on effects for the Part-time Regulations 2000 arose from implementation of the second EU social partners' agreement on atypical work, that concerning fixed-term work, which had also been attached to a Directive (1999/70/EC). As in the case of part-time work, implementation was accompanied by debate as to whether the appropriate personal scope of the Fixed-term Regulations was the narrow category of 'employee' or the broader category of 'worker'. On this second occasion, the Government did not alter its decision to apply the anti-discrimination principle between work under fixed-term and that under permanent contracts only to those working under contracts of employment rather than to the broader category of 'worker'. However, even this narrow formulation of what the Fixed-term Directive required clearly necessitated changes to the complex set of options concerning comparative scope in Regulation 2(3) of the Part-time Regulations. As noted earlier, several different kinds of slicing of the comparators available to a part-time worker result from Regulation 2(3). One significant manifestation of this was that a part-timer who otherwise worked under the same type of contract (of employment, apprenticeship, as a worker) as her full-time comparator was prohibited from comparing herself to that full-time comparator if one of them worked under a fixed-term contract and the other under a permanent contract.

The 2002 Amendment Regulations, which came into force on 30 June 2002, remove the distinction between fixed-term and permanent contracts for the purpose of determining whether the part-timer works under the same type of contract as her comparator. This, however, still leaves the distinctions between contracts of employment, apprenticeship and workers in place, as well as the wild-card provision, which, as we saw, permits the employer to introduce any other valid differentiation, which will then have the effect of slicing through, and in this way multiplying, the enumerated distinctions.[72]

---

[72] The new Regulation (3) reads as follows: 'the following shall be regarded as being employed under different types of contract –

(a) employees employed under a contract that is not a contract of apprenticeship;
(b) employees employed under a contract of apprenticeship;
(c) workers who are not employees;
(d) any other description of workers that it is reasonable for the employer to treat differently from other workers on the ground that workers of that description have a different type of contract'.

6.6   Policy autonomy and ownership: UK work–life
balance initiatives

The Government's determination to deny any normative weight to cl. 5 of the Part-time Directive has been clearly demonstrated. By December 2000, the DTI had placed Guidance on its web site relating to part-time work.[73] The first part of this document is entitled 'Compliance Guidance' and deals with the non-discrimination principle. The last four pages, entitled 'Best Practice Guidance', raise the issues in cl. 5. The part of greatest interest is the guidance for dealing with workers wishing to increase or decrease their hours (relating to cl. 5(3)(a) and cl. 5(3)(b) of the Part-time Directive). Workers are advised to present a good argument for their change in hours. Employers should have a procedure for considering their request and workers should be prepared to accept a refusal if there are good reasons for it.[74]

However, most interestingly, despite their relevance in terms of both subject-matter and timing, the Part-time Directive and its UK transposition *neither prevented nor influenced* parallel, and much more high-profile, debates on how to achieve work–life balance for parents of young and disabled children and work–life balance for the UK workforce in general.

While the House of Commons' Committee was berating the DTI for sweeping cl. 5 of the Part-time Directive under the carpet, on 9 March 2000 Prime Minister Blair launched the Work–Life Balance campaign. The launch was accompanied by distribution of over 20,000 copies of a document entitled *Changing Patterns in a Changing World* which contained nine statements such as 'employers should consider doing more to help their employees achieve a better work–life balance', to which respondents could indicate their response along a spectrum from strongly agree to strongly disagree. Backed up by a series of large conferences across the United Kingdom, the campaign 'is about helping the workplace culture to catch up with the changes in the workforce and the way we do business'.[75] This initiative, equipped with its own impressive web site[76] and accompanying documentation, espouses a voluntary approach to work–life balance issues. However, this is backed by Work–Life Balance Challenge Funds,

---

[73] *The Law and Best Practice: a detailed guide for employers and part-timers* (13 pages) available at www2.dti.gov.uk/er/pt-detail.htm.

[74] Ibid. at pp. 11–12.

[75] *Changing Patterns in a Changing World: Feedback*, July 2000, Department for Education and the Environment (20 pages). Responsibility for the Work–Life Balance Campaign initially lay with the DFEE but subsequently passed to the DTI.

[76] www.dti.gov.uk/work-lifebalance.

which provide £10.5 million over three years (2000–3) in consultancy support to employers who want help in introducing working patterns which support workers in achieving work–life balance goals. This funding is released in tranches for which employers can bid; the results are widely disseminated. There is no mention of the EU Part-time Directive, the UK Part-time Regulations or the EU Employment Guidelines in the voluminous Work–Life Balance campaign literature. The emphasis is on how work–life balance measures create a win-win situation for employers, workers and the broader community, as workers are more loyal, motivated and productive when they are given the opportunity to engage in other desired, and socially desirable, activities such as voluntary work, sports and caring activities.

While a voluntary approach, backed up by *dominium* measures to encourage employer interest and an extensive publicity campaign,[77] was considered adequate for workers in general, in June 2000 the Government opened a separate process of review and consultation on working parents. A Ministerial Review Group on Work and Parents, headed by the Secretary of State for Trade and Industry, sought: 'To examine how the economy is changing, particularly in relation to working patterns, what the needs of the modern economy will be and to identify how competitiveness and productivity in this context can be enhanced through giving families reasonable choices to help them balance the needs of their children and work.'[78] This resulted in publication of a substantial Green Paper entitled *Work and Parents: Competitiveness and Choice* on 7 December 2000 which sought views on a number of practical measures to help working parents. The substantive governance objectives of this consultation were made very explicit. It was overwhelmingly concerned with increasing the employment rate of young mothers in order to plug skills and participation gaps in the economy as well as with preventing loss of human capital and recruitment costs through staff turnover (when mothers do not return to work after maternity leave). A further consideration, involving fathers as well, was to increase the productivity of working parents by reducing stress and absenteeism through the provision of flexible working. A final objective, resulting from an increased employment rate, was a reduction in child poverty.

---

[77] See, for example, the 4-page supplement on work–life balance in the *Observer* newspaper of 3 March 2002, produced by the *Observer* in association with the DTI.

[78] *Work and Parents: Competitiveness and Choice* (DTI, December 2000, 66 pages), para. 1.13.

Therefore, employment policy objectives were paramount in the Green Paper. Fundamental rights played two supporting roles. The Green Paper noted that mothers may obtain rights to reduced hours by using indirect gender discrimination arguments but that this route had the disadvantage of 'a lack of clarity for employers and employees about their respective rights and responsibilities'.[79] Much less visible was the role such measures might play in reducing inequalities between women and men. Employment protection arguments were absent.

The Green Paper then considered how these objectives might be realised. It weighed up the relative merits of proceeding by best practice or by legislation. In relation to the former it noted, 'in implementing the European Directive on equal treatment for part-time workers, for example, the Government decided to eliminate any obstacles to part-time working through developing best practice advice'.[80] However, with regard to reduced hours in this context:

> Best practice is unlikely to permeate the whole economy and frequently does not reach the lowest paid. Statutory options may therefore need to be considered to provide minimum standards but these must be developed with care and properly designed for small business (para. 1.18). Clear legislation on the existence of a right to work reduced hours, which sets out the rights of both employers and employees, might also be easier for employers than the current legal uncertainty. (para. 6.28)

Three legislative rights to reduced hours were canvassed in the Green Paper: an unrestricted right for mothers to work reduced hours during the non-compulsory part of maternity leave, a right for fathers to work reduced hours during maternity leave with an exemption for small employers, and a right for parents to work reduced hours after maternity leave with an exemption for small employers and a harm test for all other employers.

Consultation on the Green Paper closed on 7 March 2001. The reduced hours proposals proved to be the most controversial. Parent-workers wanted legislation but wanted such legislation to provide a palette of flexible working options and not simply a right to work reduced hours. Employers were opposed to legislation, stated that a harm test was too difficult to meet, and pointed out the difficulties for small businesses. It is also noteworthy that the Government did not refer to a difference of position between management and labour, or even between employers

[79] Ibid., para. 4.14.   [80] Ibid., para. 6.13.

and workers. Instead, the two sides consist of employers, and parents and parents' organisations.

Faced with these polarised positions, as well as disagreement on the techniques proposed in the Green Paper, the Government adapted its procedural governance stance and the regulatory technique to realise its substantive governance objectives. It decided that there would be legislation, but not a right to work reduced hours. Instead the new remit was: 'To design a light touch legislative approach to giving parents of young children a right to make a request to work flexible hours and to have this request considered seriously by management, [taking] fully into account the particular needs of small employers in designing such a solution, including whether they would be subject to special conditions.' To thrash out the all-important details of this duty to consider flexible working requests – who would qualify and under what circumstances employers could refuse a request – the Government set up a Work and Parents Taskforce on 28 June 2001. It was required to report on its remit to Government by November 2001.[81] The Taskforce had ten members. Employers had five representatives: two from small businesses, one from large employers from both the private and public sector and one from the CBI. On the other side, there were two TUC representatives, an EOC representative and the Chief Executive of Parents at Work, a campaigning charity. The tenth member, who chaired the Taskforce, was Professor Sir George Bain, an academic with an industrial relations background who also chairs the Low Pay Commission. The Government described this as the Taskforce 'being composed of equal numbers of business and family organisations'. The reason for adopting the procedural governance technique of setting up a Taskforce was to develop policy and legislation 'in a sensitive area involving a number of stakeholders' and the Government responded to its report by congratulating the Taskforce's members on having 'worked hard to develop a cautious compromise which goes with the grain of good practice'.[82]

The Government immediately accepted the Work and Parents Taskforce legislative proposals and, having drafted them in legislative form, introduced them into the Employment Bill 2002 in January 2002. Employees who are parents of children under six or disabled children

[81] *About Time: Flexible Working*, Work and Parents Taskforce Report, 20 November 2001 (66 pages).
[82] *Government Response to the Recommendations from the Work and Parents Taskforce*, DTI, November 2001 (30 pages), paras. 7 and 8.

will have a right to request in writing a different working pattern, to be specified in the request. The employer is required to consider this request by having a meeting with the employee and giving written reasons for accepting or refusing the request. The legislation sets out reasons for refusing a request, such as the burden of additional costs or detrimental impact on quality or performance. Following an internal appeal, and recourse to alternative dispute resolution mechanisms, the employee may make a complaint to an Employment Tribunal that the employer has failed to comply with the procedural steps in the duty to consider (the meeting, written reasons, an appeal) or that the facts adduced by the employer to reject an application were incorrect. In other words, tribunals cannot test the necessity or proportionality of the business reasons adduced by the employer. Unlike indirect gender discrimination legislation, there is no need for the employer to demonstrate that it did not accept a request because to do so would cause harm to the business.

This is not the place to provide a detailed analysis of the discussions in the Work and Parents Taskforce. However, a few points are worth noting. The Taskforce's substantive governance objectives were slightly different from those of the Green Paper. Its report stressed, as did the Green Paper, the benefits for employers as a result of reduced recruitment costs linked to lower staff turnover as well as improved staff morale. However, unlike the Green Paper, some place was given to employment protection, so that easing pressure on parents was viewed as an end in itself rather than simply a means of increasing productivity. Moreover, a new substantive governance objective emerged which might be termed intergenerational investment. From this perspective, parents are to be assisted because they create children who will in the future supply the funds to support all those no longer in work as well as train and educate their children to be useful workers and citizens as adults.[83]

A second point worth noting is that once again sources stemming from UK implementation of the Part-time Directive were not mentioned. This is despite the strong similarities between the right to request and duty to consider flexible working and the Guidance relating to the Part-time Directive. There was also no discussion of how these proposals match the EU Employment Guidelines. Gender equality sources were considered, though largely to note that the tougher test of objective justification of an employer's reasons to reject a request for flexible work under gender discrimination sources could not be ousted to make way for the new

---

[83] Paras. 1, 2 and 6.25 of the Taskforce Report.

light-touch duty to consider because of the supremacy of EU law.[84] It is noteworthy that no discussion occurred of the actual application of the objective justification test in work–life balance gender discrimination cases. As we have seen, had this exercise been undertaken, it would have placed in a different light fears that a harm test would place an undue burden on employers.[85]

6.7   Conclusions on flexible working

Overall the process leading to the duty to consider flexible working illustrates a step-by-step governance approach. This was for both substantive and procedural governance reasons. What it was desirable to legislate for was not clear. Hence the legislative technique of providing a standardised, legislatively defined, flexible working option – reduced hours – was replaced by the more sophisticated technique of allowing parents to define for themselves the working pattern they needed. The Part-time Directive, with its pre-defined categories of 'full'- and 'part'-time work, did not sit entirely comfortably with the legislative technique which was finally chosen. However, this parent-sensitive sophistication was accompanied by the need not to antagonise employers. In order to obtain employer acceptance, a toothless right for a narrowly defined group was introduced, which could subsequently be built upon when it had settled in and cultural attitudes had had time to adjust. Hence the Taskforce recommended, and the Government agreed, that the legislation should be reviewed three years after its introduction.

What does this tell us about multi-level governance? On the issue of flexible work, the UK Government wished publicly to own and control its own agenda. It did not want it to seem as though it was introducing flexible work measures in order to comply with EU instructions of any kind. It could have used either Title XI (the Part-time Directive) or Title VIII (the many relevant EU Employment Guidelines on this issue) of the ECT to justify, or bolster, its work–life and working parents' initiatives. It chose not to do so, and pushed the Part-time Directive as far out of the limelight as it could. This is related to, though not determined by, the fact that new substantive governance imperatives in relation to working parents required a marked departure from previous UK regulatory practice. This, in turn, was seen to necessitate special procedural techniques, requiring slow consensus-building, widespread consultation, and mechanisms

---

[84] Appendix 3, Taskforce Report.   [85] Above, section 5.3.

requiring compromise between conflicting interests. The transposition date of the Part-time Directive did not fit well with this procedural governance stance either.

7 Title VIII EC and part-time work in the UK

In this section, we contend that the Government's approach to employment matters is underpinned by a strongly held belief that the workplace is a threshold which it will be extremely reluctant to cross in order to realise its objectives. It is most likely to consider crossing that threshold in a decisive manner where not to do so would prevent it from addressing social exclusion (in the sense of people being excluded from labour market access). This contention explains much about the management of the employment policy process in the UK, and its transformative capacity, which it would otherwise be difficult to explain. It also sheds light on the role of employment law in realising the substantive governance objectives of the current government: because employment law often involves new workplace standards being set through regulatory intervention inside firms it will not be favoured by New Labour. A further effect of this belief is that it limits in crucial respects the capacity of the UK Government to realise certain of its substantive governance objectives and, it will be suggested, in the near future this tension could provide an increasingly clear test of the pressures which the Luxembourg process can exert on UK policy choices. It is this belief which primarily explains (rather than it being explained by) the answers to questions concerning procedural and substantive governance issues under Title VIII EC in the UK context.

Procedural governance issues concerning Title VIII EC in the UK require a response to two questions. The first is: *who* is responsible for Title VIII EC? In the UK, the Treasury has been firmly at the helm of Title VIII from the outset,[86] and remains there. One can search for a long time and scant reward at the DTI and the Department of Work and Pensions[87] (the co-author with the Treasury of the UK NAPs) for information on the Luxembourg process and the Lisbon objective. At the Treasury, there are richer pickings. Most important are the references to the Lisbon objective

---

[86] For instance, the Treasury produced a UK National Action Plan on Employment (28 pages) *prior* to the Luxembourg Summit. The pre-Luxembourg NAP was launched by the Chancellor on 13 October 1997.

[87] However, the Department of Work and Pensions is still in a transitional phase of putting itself together which may partly explain this.

in the 2002 Budget[88] and an extremely interesting White Paper from the Treasury in February 2002, designed to inform the Barcelona Spring Summit, which contains an extensive discussion of the Luxembourg process from the Treasury's perspective.[89] The second question concerns: *how* does New Labour propose to realise its substantive governance objectives and *how* does it engage in multi-level dialogue concerning its choices via its NAPs or other means.

Substantive governance is concerned with *what* employment policies and goals the UK Government seeks to realise. We propose briefly to examine these and to use them to explore procedural governance issues more closely, most particularly in relation to our transformative checklist for part-time work. The New Labour government has two headline employment policy objectives.

The first is to increase the number of jobs as well as the employment rate, and to reduce unemployment, for both efficiency and equity reasons, the latter because 'the best safeguard against social exclusion is a job'.[90] The efficiency reasons are multiple. People in jobs cost the state less in benefits and give money to the state as tax-payers. Demographic shifts – the increase in the number of older people and the decreasing birth-rate – have shrunk the proportion of the population in work and will place ever greater pressure on pension systems. Keeping older workers in the labour market is one important way of addressing this problem. Skills and participation gaps in the UK labour market can be addressed by ensuring that workers – especially those with needed skills – do not exit the labour market for reasons, such as caring responsibilities, which can be dealt with through alternative arrangements. This objective can be summarised as 'more jobs, more people in jobs'.

The second is to reduce the UK's serious skills and productivity gaps with its EU neighbours and the USA. The UK has an acute skills problem which is outlined well in the 2002 Treasury White Paper. Skills are divided into the categories of low, intermediate and high. The UK percentages on low, intermediate and high skills are 56.9, 27.7 and 15.4. This can be contrasted with Germany where the corresponding figures are 20, 65 and 15 and the USA where they are 53.7, 18.6 and 27.7.[91] A fifth of adults in the

---

[88] UK Budget 2002, *Economic and Fiscal Strategy Report* paras 3.11 and 3.12 available at www.hm.treasury.gov.uk/Budget.
[89] *Realising Europe's Potential: Economic Reform in Europe*, Cm 5318, February 2002 (121 pages), hereafter referred to as 'Treasury WP'.
[90] Ibid., para 7.7.   [91] Ibid., Table 7.2.

UK lack functional literacy.[92] It is evident that countries such as the UK and the USA, in which there is a heavy reliance on the market to supply skills, have a large percentage of people with low skills and few people with intermediate skills. However, such countries may have a respectable number of people with high skills, market provision potentially working better in this case.

The skills gap in turn plays a significant role in creating the productivity gap. While other factors, such as investment in physical capital, are also extremely important, human, physical and financial capital factors are related. Hence a skilled workforce will be the driver for the introduction and effective exploitation of better physical capital investment which will, in turn, increase productivity. One study has concluded, for example, that Britain's productivity gap with Germany is eliminated when skills differences are taken into account.[93] This can be summarised as the objective of creating 'better jobs', or increasing the quality of the UK's human capital base in order to maintain competitiveness in the knowledge economy.

There can be no doubt that the desire to create more and better jobs, for similar reasons, also underpins the Luxembourg process. We suggest that the real value of the NAPs, however, and the annual re-elaboration of the Employment Guidelines, is that significant differences between the national and supranational visions gradually become apparent. This is because, as we stated earlier, agreement on headline substantive governance objectives does not entail agreement on their more concrete specification. Moreover, the different procedural governance set-ups at EU level and in the UK can have a profound effect on how headline substantive governance issues get translated into more concrete proposals. The question then arises of how these differences are dealt with within the Luxembourg process: can co-ordination ever deliver integration and, if so, through what processes will that integrative transformation occur?

7.1 More jobs, more people in jobs

7.1.1 More jobs

The UK Government is clear on what is preventing job growth in the EU: 'Barriers to cross-border trade and integration in key areas of the Single Market, combined with overly restrictive labour market institutions and

---

[92] Ibid., para. 7.35.   [93] Ibid., para. 7.30.

product market regulation, all help explain why unemployment (and particularly long term unemployment) remains unsatisfactorily high within the EU.'[94] In respect of labour market regulation, the UK differentiates itself from its fellow Member States. It considers the UK, by and large, to have the right amount and kind of labour regulation. According to its NAPs, UK employment contract law aims to facilitate rather than prescribe. This individual contract-based system has allowed a highly diverse and adaptable range of working practices to develop in the UK.[95] The elements lacking to ensure that this system is underpinned by 'decent minimum standards of fairness' have been supplied by New Labour through the National Minimum Wage and the trade union recognition rights and family-friendly rights in the Employment Relations Act of 1999. Hence, while the UK states in its NAPs that it has considered whether it is necessary, under the adaptability pillar, to introduce more adaptable contracts, it does not consider it necessary to make changes to UK law in that regard.

Other EU Member States, by contrast, would, in its view, be well advised to make such changes. This push is reflected in the Treasury White Paper, in the Prime Minister's pronouncements in the run-up to the Barcelona Summit of March 2002, and in the conclusions of the ECOFIN (Economics and Finance) Council immediately prior to the Barcelona Summit. There is a marked contrast between the conclusions of the ECOFIN Council and those of the Employment and Social Policy Council, possibly reflecting the differentiated views of labour markets emanating from economic and labour ministries. The ECOFIN conclusions are focussed on labour market reform by, for example, asking Member States to assess 'the costs attached to the formulation and termination of employment contracts, with a view to strik[ing] a better balance between flexibility and social protection'.[96] The Employment and Social Policy Council, by contrast, is focussed primarily on pushing ahead with increasing job quality.[97] In the Barcelona Conclusions, the 'more jobs' lobbying wins the day. While quality in work is mentioned, it is given much less prominence than it had been given at the Lisbon and Stockholm Summits. Instead, Member States

---

[94] Ibid., para 1.17.
[95] For example see Department for Education and Employment, UK NAP 2000, p. 22, though each year's NAP contains similar pronouncements.
[96] Report from the Economic and Financial Affairs Council to the European Council (5 March 2002), para. 39.
[97] Report from the Employment and Social Policy Council to the European Council (7 March 2002), para. 5.

are invited as a priority 'to review employment contract regulations, and where appropriate costs, with a view to promoting more jobs'.[98] The UK Government's view that it has the right amount of labour regulation is, of course, a strangely unsubstantiated proposition as well as a movable feast. It does not say what it is about the current bundle of UK laws which makes it the right combination, though, given the ad hoc way in which labour legislation has been built up in the UK, as elsewhere, it is highly likely that some parts could be profitably removed or replaced, and new parts added. The lack of a coherent rationale explaining why the UK has the 'right amount' of labour law means that such discussions cannot sensibly be entered into. Moreover, this approach means that what constitutes the 'right amount' has to keep changing – in particular, because of the need to implement EU law such as the Working-Time Directive, and the Part-time and Fixed-term Directives.

There are two UK methods of dealing with this. One is simply to expand in the NAPs what constitutes the right amount. Hence, while in 1999 the UK already had what it needed, in the year 2000 its NAP informs us that legislation will ensure that 'part-time employees (by definition mostly women) are not treated less favourably than comparable full-timers'. A similar stance has been taken with the new information and consultation directive. In general, however, the UK Treasury line is that national labour law can discourage the creation of entry-level jobs and protect insiders.[99]

The second, and closely related, line of argument is to argue that there is no further need for EU legislation in this area. This is one of the key thrusts of the Treasury's White Paper. Past EU legal intervention is criticised as having been ad hoc.[100] The legislative method is contrasted unfavourably with the open method of co-ordination in the Luxembourg process which permits a variety of approaches appropriate to the diversity of labour markets in the EU. The White Paper comments that: 'There is now a considerable body of legislation in place at EU level which safeguards employee rights . . . the challenge now for the EU is to implement existing legislation in a better and more effective fashion, making full use of peer review and the exchange of best practice.'[101] Two observations are worth making on this statement. The first is that, taking the Part-time Directive as an example, our detailed examination of its implementation in the UK puts paid to the notion that the UK Government has any serious intention

---

[98] Presidency Conclusions, Barcelona European Council, 15 and 16 March 2003 Bull. EU 3-2002, pp. 1–56.
[99] Treasury WP, paras 7.23 and 7.24.   [100] Ibid., para. 7.53.   [101] Ibid., para 5.78.

of implementing existing legislation 'in a better and more effective fashion'. Any residual doubts on that score can be banished by examining the discussion of labour legislation in the UK NAPs. These discussions are uniformly bland and uninterrogative. A typical example of how searching the analysis of legal efficacy is can be taken from the 1998 NAP: 'The UK supports the Parental Leave Directive, the Part-time Work Directive and the Working-Time Directive which will lead to a welcome improvement in family-friendly policies and flexible working. For example, the Part-time Work Directive will promote flexibility across Europe and improve the quality of part-time jobs.'[102] The second observation is that this contrasts with the dominant EU policy discourse. The UK Government's preference effectively to stop using Title XI EC for new employment law measures can be contrasted with the use of procedural governance tools proposed by the Nice Social Agenda: 'In the implementation of the social agenda all existing Community instruments bar none must be used: the open method of co-ordination, legislation, the social dialogue, the Structural Funds, the support programmes, the integrated policy approach, analysis and research.'[103]

7.1.2   More people in jobs

Four primary means of having more people in jobs can be discerned in current UK and EU employment policy discourse. The first is pursuit of active labour market policies for those who are not employed, with a special focus on groups vulnerable to labour market exclusion, such as ethnic minorities or the disabled. A second is ensuring that work pays by removing the twin traps of unemployment and poverty. A third is making sure that mothers' labour market participation is not prevented by an absence of arrangements permitting work and care obligations to co-exist. A fourth is to make sure that people do not exit the labour market earlier than necessary either because of early retirement or some sort of incapacity.

One of the main procedural governance developments of Title VIII EC has been the setting of targets to measure Member State progress in getting more people in jobs. Hence, Lisbon and Stockholm set an overall employment rate target (70 per cent by 2010), a female employment rate target (60 per cent by 2010) and an older worker (55–64) target (50 per cent

---

[102] Department for Education and Employment, UK NAP 1998, p. 22.
[103] Nice Social Agenda 7–9 December 2000 (OJ 2001/C 157/02) para. 28.

by 2010). The UK already meets all these targets, largely because of its significant part-time work population.

The NAPs suggest that this area – getting more people into jobs – is the primary focus of the UK Government's attention. The Jobseekers Allowance (JSA) and the New Deals for Young People, Lone Parents and other groups identified as vulnerable constitute the UK's active labour market policy.[104] Ongoing development of an extensive system of tax credits for low-income workers, especially parents, and the introduction of a National Minimum Wage, aim to ensure that work pays. The introduction of the National Minimum Wage illustrates the exceptional goals which will push New Labour into decisive standard-setting action of a traditional employment protection kind: it was a critical plank of an agenda to address poverty and social exclusion. To ensure that women do not exit labour markets, the main policy is the National Childcare Strategy which, through public–private partnerships at local level, is expanding, from an extremely low base, the availability of nursery and out-of-school care. The point about these initiatives is that the Government takes them very seriously – it sets targets, it measures progress, it adds new resources for expansion and improvement. The UK Government is engaged in an active process of policy implementation and monitoring and it has prevailed on its EU partners to be equally engaged via the Luxembourg process, and other economic reform activities, to meet the Lisbon objective. Hence the Treasury White Paper proclaims: 'Successful reform requires not only debate and agreement on processes and benchmarks, but also – and essentially – action. The challenge for the EU is to demonstrate both macro-ambition and micro-imagination; to combine breadth of vision with concrete steps. Over the coming months and years, Europe's governments must demonstrate that they can deliver.'[105] But – and this is critical – bar the one-off exception of the National Minimum Wage none

---

[104] This provides a good example of a sharp disagreement between the EU and the UK. Recommendations under Title VIII EC have admonished the UK for not pursuing active labour market policy. The UK has not altered its position but has forcefully argued (in its NAPs and in the 2002 White Paper) not only that the JSA and New Deals do constitute active (rather than passive) labour market policies but that research shows that, of the various active labour market options available, those chosen by the UK Government (support and assistance in job search) are the most effective. See most recently the 2002 NAP at pp. 10–11.

[105] Treasury WP, para. 2.53. See also the Barcelona Presidency Conclusions (n. 98 above), para. 49 – 'The European Council urges the Council and Commission to streamline the relevant processes: the focus must be on action for implementation, rather than on the annual elaboration of guidelines' – and the five-year review of the EES, discussed below.

of this action involves requiring firms to change their behaviour. To be sure, we have seen that the UK Government has now legislated to place a duty on employers to consider requests by parents for flexible working. Yet this was an exceptional foray inside the firm mandated by an accumulation of reasons for intervention. Such a duty forms a key plank of the pressing need to have 'more people in jobs' and complements, in particular, the National Childcare Strategy. It also fits comfortably with an agenda to offset the demographic shift by providing conditions which encourage raising the birth-rate. Finally, work–life balance measures of this type can increase the quality of women's jobs, hence addressing both quality and equality concerns. Yet, despite all these good reasons for decisive legal intervention, its possible detrimental effect on firms was addressed *inter alia* by making the legal intervention so light as to threaten its very efficacy. Hence, where legal intervention in firms is concerned, 'more jobs' considerations (understood as not overburdening firms) undercut – in ways which do not occur with other non-firm-intrusive policy measures – rigorous attempts to ensure the efficacy of a given intervention. Indeed the UK government expressed its concern that employers may be put off offering part-time work to women and older workers if this form of work is over-regulated: 'It is essential that regulation of such work does not close off employment opportunities for these individuals.'[106]

This can be further illustrated by looking at the policy objective of ensuring people do not exit labour markets too early because of age or incapacity. This is clearly something the UK Government is worried about. It is also an issue which the Employment Guidelines have increasingly focussed on in recent years.[107] Obvious policy measures to address these concerns are rights not to be discriminated against on grounds of age or disability, and a right for workers to work part-time or to adapt their working pattern in some other way in order to facilitate their continued participation in the labour market.

These proposed measures, however, all entail legal interventions into firms' behaviour. This example provides a neat illustration of the conjunction of New Labour's 'right amount' vision of UK labour law and how it deals with new EU employment law interventions.

UK law already outlaws disability discrimination and therefore this can be used, along with other tools, to reduce labour market exit through

---

[106] Treasury WP, para. 7.59.
[107] See, in particular, Guideline 3 of the Employment Guidelines 2001 under the employability pillar on 'Developing a Policy for Active Ageing'.

incapacity. UK law does not, however, outlaw age discrimination. Nor does it provide any right for older workers to request part-time work or any other flexible working pattern. Hence, in line with its 'right amount' vision, in its reply to the new Employment Guideline on active ageing introduced in 2001, the UK stated that its action consisted of piloting approaches and developing guidance for employers on the benefits of replacing compulsory retirement on grounds of age with more flexible phased retirement, encouraging more opportunities for employees to move from full-time to part-time work, and the production of a Code of Practice on Age Diversity. Less than a year later, in the 2002 White Paper, its policy on active ageing still consisted of encouragement of flexible work organisation to suit different lifestyles but had altered to include measures to combat discrimination, especially when recruiting or restructuring, in view of the need to implement the age provisions of Directive 2000/78/EC.[108]

7.2 Better jobs

The UK Government's reluctance to engage in firm-level intervention clearly has an impact on attainment of the objective 'more jobs, more people in jobs'. However, at the same time, there can be little doubt that such measures could make only a small contribution to achieving this objective. Widespread access to good quality and affordable childcare, for instance, will make a more substantial contribution to permitting women to balance work and care commitments than would flexible working rights.

By contrast, a reluctance to engage in firm-level intervention creates greater obstacles to achieving the employment policy objective of creating 'better jobs' in the UK. Yet this objective is particularly pressing in the UK labour market context. As the UK part-time work populace exemplifies, too many people in the country are stuck in low-wage, low-skill positions with little chance of improving their position. The Government is clearly and rightly very concerned about the UK's skills and productivity gaps. Furthermore, as a substantive governance objective of the EU, 'better jobs' has become very prominent in recent years. This prominence has been accompanied by significant enrichment of the procedural governance tools to achieve the 'better jobs' objective.

Attaining 'better jobs' encompasses two distinct, though overlapping, objectives. One is to increase the *quality of work* by augmenting the skills

[108] Treasury WP, para. 7.50.

levels of the working population, the other is to provide *quality in work*. The most important overlap between the two is that both focus on improving skills, training and career development. The distinction between them, however, is that the former focusses more on non-firm policies for attaining this goal, while the latter focusses more on the role of the firm itself. It also does not focus solely on this goal. Instead, the quality in work objective is premised on the argument that a secure, protected, worker is a more productive worker. That is, it argues that the objective of employment protection is compatible with, and indeed forms an important part of, achieving competitiveness. In line with what we have argued so far, it should come as no surprise that the UK Government is comfortable with measures to improve quality of work but faces immense difficulties in addressing the quality in work agenda.

Indeed, with regard to quality of work, the UK Government's NAPs and the Treasury White Paper set out an extensive array of initiatives: increased spending on primary and secondary education, expansion of places in higher education, policies to equip adults with basic skills through a 'Skills for Life' initiative, and so on.[109]

Quality in work was placed very firmly in a central position in EU employment policy discourse by the Nice Social Agenda. This stated that the Luxembourg process should focus more on attaining quality in work 'and its importance for growth as a significant attractive factor and as an incentive to work'. A Commission Communication on the content of quality in work[110] was built upon by the Employment Committee which has provided ten dimensions of quality in work.[111] These are used to define the notion in the new Horizontal Objective on quality in work which is inserted into the Employment Guidelines 2002. This states:

> With a view to raising employment rates, promoting social cohesion and social progress, enhancing competitiveness, productivity and the functioning of the labour market, Member States will endeavour to ensure that policies across the four pillars contribute to maintaining and improving quality in work. Such actions should take into account both job characteristics (such as intrinsic job quality, skills, lifelong learning and career development) and the wider labour market context encompassing gender equality, health and safety at work, flexibility and security, inclusion and

---

[109] Ibid., para. 7.40.
[110] *Employment and Social Policies: a Framework for Investing in Quality* COM (2001) 313, 20.6.2001.
[111] Report by the Employment Committee (23 November 2001), *Indicators of Quality in Work* (Luxembourg: OOPEC, 2001).

access to the labour market, work organisation and work–life balance, social dialogue and worker involvement, diversity and non-discrimination and overall work performance and productivity.[112]

The quality objective is also used increasingly from 2000 onwards in the Guidelines under the four pillars, so that the 2002 Employment Guidelines are packed full of quality objectives. Hence the active ageing guideline under the employability pillar has been redrafted to add that 'the promotion of quality in work should also be considered as an important factor in maintaining older workers in the workforce'. A new guideline in the entrepreneurship pillar identifies the knowledge-based service sector as providing considerable potential for jobs and for increasing quality in work and calls on Member States 'to exploit fully the employment potential of the full range of the services sector to create more and better jobs'. The adaptability pillar now requires the modernising of work organisation to 'contribute to improvements in quality in work' and under the equal opportunities pillar, since 2001, the gender mainstreaming guideline states that flexible forms of work organisation for women must be 'without loss of job quality'.

Moreover, the Employment Committee did not merely identify the ten dimensions of quality in work used in the 2002 Employment Guidelines Horizontal Objective. It also developed a set of indicators to be used to measure Member State progress in achieving these goals. Most interesting for our purposes are the indicators to measure flexibility and security. The Employment Committee proposes measuring the number of employees working voluntarily and involuntarily on part-time and fixed-term contracts and states that this should be accompanied by information on the extent to which these workers enjoy entitlements to social protection and legal rights equivalent and commensurate to those of full-time and permanent workers.

A final source of pressure on the UK's non-firm based employment policy can be found in a Recommendation addressed to the UK which it responded to in its 2002 NAP. This states that the UK should 'reinforce current efforts to encourage and develop work-based training to address increasing workforce skill gaps and low levels of basic skills'.

---

[112] The ten are organised as follows by the Employment Committee: (1) intrinsic job quality; (2) skills, lifelong learning and career development; (3) gender equality; (4) health and safety; (5) flexibility and security; (6) inclusion and access to labour markets; (7) work organisation and work–life balance; (8) social dialogue and worker involvement; (9) diversity and non-discrimination; (10) overall work performance.

It is evident that the substantive governance objective of 'better jobs' is more difficult to achieve without significant firm-level intervention touching on core issues relating to the efficiency and equity of the exercise of managerial power in UK workplaces.

The UK's 2002 NAP was, therefore, required to address the quality in work Horizontal Objective. Its response was essentially to argue that 'more jobs' is a more important objective than 'better jobs':

> Much of our focus in this overview, and throughout the Plan, is on getting people into work in the first place. We have stressed at EU level that it is essential that attempts to improve quality of employment do not jeopardise the creation of jobs and the promotion of social inclusion. The basic prerequisite for quality in work is work itself – there is no quality for those without a job; therefore meeting the Lisbon targets must be the first priority.[113]

However, given that the UK has already met the Lisbon targets, unlike many other Member States, might it not be argued that while other Member States' priority is 'more jobs', the UK's priority is clearly that of focussing on the 'better jobs' agenda? The 2002 NAP made it clear that the information on how the UK performs against the quality indicators was in the process of being produced. This very interesting procedural governance innovation provides the exciting possibility of testing whether employment law initiatives actually achieve their substantive governance objectives. It is evident that the area of quality in work provides the greatest potential test of whether Title VIII EC can be transformative in the UK. Can it nudge the UK into changing its mind on the value of employment law in increasing competitiveness? Or is it more plausible – and the Treasury White Paper and the Barcelona Summit provide support for this hypothesis – that the UK will instead succeed in transforming Title VIII EC?

Informed bets must take into account the five-year review of the EES[114] which was considered by the Brussels Spring Summit of March 2003. Subsequent Employment Guidelines, including those for 2003 which were delayed until April to allow completion of the review, will take their direction from it. The Brussels Summit endorses more streamlined, simplified and results-oriented Employment Guidelines. To push this forward, the

---

[113] UK NAP 2002, p. 3.
[114] See the Communication from the Commission to the Council, the European Parliament, the Economic and Social Committee and the Committee of the Regions: *The Future of the European Employment Strategy (EES) 'A Strategy for Full Employment and Better Jobs for All'*, COM (2003) 6 final, Brussels 14.1.2003.

European Council has asked for a European Employment Taskforce to be set up, to report by the 2004 Spring Summit. It is to carry out an in-depth examination of key employment-related policy challenges and to identify practical reform measures that can have the most direct and immediate impact on the ability of Member States to implement the revised EES and to achieve its objectives and targets.[115] Three overarching objectives will henceforth inform the EES: full employment by increasing employment rates; quality and productivity at work; social cohesion and an inclusive labour market – objectives which are interrelated and mutually supportive. On the whole, at Brussels a more balanced approach was adopted in relation to more jobs and better jobs than at Barcelona. Hence, the Brussels European Council does state that 'there is an urgent need to step up the momentum of reform of national labour markets by identifying measures which can rapidly have a positive effect on employment levels and growth'.[116] It also, however, 'urges a review of ongoing efforts to improve the quality of work and welcomed the Commission's intention to prepare a report on quality at work by end 2003. The European Council urges agreement by December 2003 on temporary agency work.'[117]

8   Conclusions

This chapter has noted and explored the implications of the fact that different branches or parts of government have taken a leading role in relation to each of our three sources. The courts at UK and EU level have been key players in putting the flesh on the bones of gender discrimination legislation. A rich and complex mix of those mandated to be law-makers in the UK and EU developed various kinds of employment law intervention. Executives led the way in developing employment policy and its EU co-ordination.

It is evident that all of these institutional actors have been engaged in a process of re-imagining, each in its own way, labour law governance. For the UK actors, an important component in this process has been EU law and policy. This is because EU sources have to be dealt with in some way or other. We have also seen, though, the influence that UK policy can exert on EU developments.

Perhaps what is most intriguing about UK and EU judicial developments in the context of part-time work is that one can see that the courts have their own views about the broader substantive governance

[115] Brussels Presidency Conclusions, para. 44.   [116] Ibid., para. 41.   [117] Ibid., para. 47.

objectives to be pursued, and these become expressed, in the examples here, within the structure of indirect discrimination claims. Hence the macro-economic and social benefits of female labour market participation seem to be more visible to the courts in relation to work–life balance issues than with regard to inferior treatment of part-timers, and this is reflected in how they carry out disparate impact analysis. At the same time, when considering justification, the courts, especially the UK courts, tend to be very deferential to the short-term cost considerations of businesses rather than considering the long-term competitive advantage which may derive from stricter scrutiny of employers' decisions concerning part-time work.

We hope that the examination of how New Labour has dealt with the Part-time Work Directive and regulatory initiatives concerning work–life balance has illustrated the extensive changes in how, compared with previous administrations, the executive conceives of both procedural and substantive labour governance. The executive obtained a Parliamentary mandate in the Employment Relations Act 1999 to use the Part-time Directive broadly. The point of proceeding in this fashion is to give it the opportunity to engage in extensive compliance with EU instructions should it so desire, and the time to consider whether it wishes actually to do so. New Labour is more likely to decide to use that mandate when it considers that it is necessary to combat social exclusion or, in the translation of social exclusion with regard to firm behaviour, to act against extreme forms of workplace exploitation. New Labour then chose not to use that mandate in relation to the Part-time Directive, and deflected pressure to make the Part-time Work Regulations more effective by playing with the personal and comparative scope of the Regulations. The role of the House of Commons Committee reveals perhaps that traditional government arrangements also contained dialogue mechanisms and that these 'old' government mechanisms may have a renewed importance in questioning the legitimacy of new, executive-dominated, governance arrangements.

In any event, it is clear that horizontal dissonance exists between these sites of government. Courts, executives and Parliaments do not sing from the same songbook on part-time work or any other issue. While distinctive inputs and stances may positively contribute to good governance, it is worth considering whether one governance task is to create better communication or co-ordination mechanisms between these different parts of government.

This chapter has also argued that the example of part-time work provides clear evidence of vertical dissonance between levels of government.

We have noted a similar focus on headline 'third way' substantive governance objectives at EU and UK levels: to make the economy competitive and, by combating social exclusion, to ensure that its citizens contribute to the fullest possible degree to this goal while enjoying its fruits.[118] However, we have suggested that it is also significant that the sharing of similar headline substantive governance goals translates neither into similar substantive proposals nor into congruent procedural governance practices. This is because each polity – UK and EU – is constituted differently. The Part-time Directive exemplifies this. The EU has re-imagined labour governance to align it with a competitiveness agenda by combining employment policy with employment protection and/or fundamental rights objectives, and by changing the nature of employment protection norms from specific standards to comparative protections. In other words, as the Part-time Directive illustrates, EU policy discourse retains a role for law and holds onto, though modifies, employment protection as a substantive objective. In the UK, as transposition of the Part-time Directive illustrates, the competitiveness / social exclusion realignment means that there is a hefty presumption against the need for new employment protection measures outside those essential to provide minimum standards to prevent social exclusion and workplace exploitation. Measures which look like employment protection measures, such as the right to request flexible working, are wholly underpinned by other, largely employment policy related, objectives. Even then, these employment protection-like measures have changed their nature so that they differ in important ways from old-style employment protection measures. This is because the use of law to create judicially enforceable obligations, backed up by sanctions, is viewed as a regulatory technique to be resorted to only in the most exceptional of circumstances. However, vertical dissonance should not just be seen as a price to be reluctantly paid for the current structure of the EU. It can also be viewed more positively as an essential condition for creating governance spaces for necessary ongoing debate, dissent and experimentation on the future of labour law in Europe.

---

[118] See further Collins, 'Is there a Third Way?' in Conaghan, Fischl and Klare, *Labour Law in an Era* (n. 2 above).

INDEX